THE STUDY OF RELIGION IN SWEDEN

Also Available from Bloomsbury

The Bloomsbury Handbook of Religion and Heritage in Contemporary Europe, edited by Todd Weir and Lieke Wijnia
The Study of Religions in Ireland, edited by Brendan McNamara and Hazel O' Brien
Young Muslims and Christians in a Secular Europe, Daan Beekers

THE STUDY OF RELIGION IN SWEDEN

Past, Present and Future

Edited by
Henrik Bogdan and Göran Larsson

BLOOMSBURY ACADEMIC
LONDON • NEW YORK • OXFORD • NEW DELHI • SYDNEY

BLOOMSBURY ACADEMIC
Bloomsbury Publishing Plc, 50 Bedford Square, London, WC1B 3DP, UK
Bloomsbury Publishing Inc, 1359 Broadway, New York, NY 10018, USA
Bloomsbury Publishing Ireland, 29 Earlsfort Terrace, Dublin 2, D02 AY28, Ireland

BLOOMSBURY, BLOOMSBURY ACADEMIC and the Diana logo are trademarks of
Bloomsbury Publishing Plc

First published in Great Britain 2024
This paperback edition published 2025

Copyright © Henrik Bogdan, Göran Larsson and contributors, 2024

Henrik Bogdan and Göran Larsson have asserted their right under the Copyright,
Designs and Patents Act, 1988, to be identified as Editors of this work.

Cover image © Zoonar GmbH / Alamy Stock Photo

All rights reserved. No part of this publication may be: i) reproduced or transmitted
in any form, electronic or mechanical, including photocopying, recording or by means
of any information storage or retrieval system without prior permission in writing from
the publishers; or ii) used or reproduced in any way for the training, development or
operation of artificial intelligence (AI) technologies, including generative AI technologies.
The rights holders expressly reserve this publication from the text and data mining
exception as per Article 4(3) of the Digital Single Market Directive (EU) 2019/790.

Bloomsbury Publishing Plc does not have any control over, or responsibility for, any
third-party websites referred to or in this book. All internet addresses given in this
book were correct at the time of going to press. The author and publisher regret any
inconvenience caused if addresses have changed or sites have ceased to exist,
but can accept no responsibility for any such changes.

A catalogue record for this book is available from the British Library.

A catalog record for this book is available from the Library of Congress.

ISBN: HB: 978-1-3504-1328-3
PB: 978-1-3504-1332-0
ePDF: 978-1-3504-1329-0
eBook: 978-1-3504-1330-6

Typeset by Newgen KnowledgeWorks Pvt. Ltd., Chennai, India

For product safety related questions contact productsafety@bloomsbury.com.

To find out more about our authors and books visit www.bloomsbury.com
and sign up for our newsletters.

CONTENTS

List of Contributors — ix

INTRODUCING THE STUDY OF RELIGION IN SWEDEN — 1
   Göran Larsson and Henrik Bogdan

Part I
HISTORICAL APPROACHES

Chapter 1
ANCIENT NEAR EASTERN RELIGIONS — 21
   Therese Rodin and Heike Peter

Chapter 2
OLD NORSE RELIGION — 37
   Olof Sundqvist

Chapter 3
INDIGENOUS RELIGIONS — 55
   Daniel Andersson and Bodil Liljefors Persson

Chapter 4
JUDAISM — 68
   Svante Lundgren and Martin Lund

Chapter 5
ISLAM — 83
   Göran Larsson, Susanne Olsson and Simon Sorgenfrei

Chapter 6
INDIAN RELIGIONS — 95
   Kristina Myrvold, Katarina Plank and Ferdinando Sardella

Chapter 7
WESTERN ESOTERICISM — 113
   Henrik Bogdan

Chapter 8
NEW RELIGIOUS MOVEMENTS AND NEW AGE SPIRITUALITY   129
Peter Åkerbäck and Sanja Nilsson

Part II
SOCIAL SCIENTIFIC APPROACHES

Chapter 9
PSYCHOLOGY OF RELIGION   143
Göran Ståhle and Tomas Lindgren

Chapter 10
SOCIOLOGY OF RELIGION   159
Mia Lövheim and Magdalena Nordin

Chapter 11
THE COGNITIVE SCIENCE OF RELIGION   177
Jonas Svensson and Egil Asprem

Chapter 12
RELIGIOUS EDUCATION   189
Christina Osbeck and Olof Franck

Part III
THEMES IN THE STUDY OF RELIGION IN SWEDEN

Chapter 13
COMPARATIVE STUDIES   205
Stefan Arvidsson and Peter Jackson Rova

Chapter 14
RITUAL STUDIES   217
Anne-Christine Hornborg

Chapter 15
LIVED RELIGION   229
Daniel Enstedt, Jessica Moberg and Katarina Plank

Chapter 16
GENDER STUDIES   242
Manon Hedenborg White

Chapter 17
VIOLENCE 257
    Tomas Lindgren, Göran Larsson and Isak Svensson

AFTERWORD: REFLECTIONS ON THE STUDY OF RELIGION IN
SWEDEN THROUGH THE LENS OF IAHR AND EASR 268
    Jenny Berglund and Tim Jensen

Index of Names 275

CONTRIBUTORS

Peter Åkerbäck has a PhD in History of Religions, and works in the Department of Sociology at Stockholm University. His research interests are new religious movements and current spiritual movements. He is currently doing research on the neo tantra milieu, Plymouth Brethren and the Unification Church. Recent publications include *New Religiosity in Contemporary Sweden* (2015) with Liselotte Frisk and *Children in Minority Religions* (2018) with Liselotte Frisk and Sanja Nilsson.

Daniel Andersson is Associate Professor in Religious Studies at the University of Gothenburg. His research interests include Judaism and the multireligious landscape in Sweden and religious conceptualizations of indigenous peoples. His latest monographs are *Indianska religioner. Från vandringar till imperiebyggande* (Indian Religions. From Wanderings to Imperial Constructions, 2015) and *Ursprungsfolkens religioner. Land, minne, kultur* (Religions of Indigenous Peoples. Land, Memory, Culture, 2019).

Stefan Arvidsson is Professor in the History of Religions at Linnæus University, focusing on the cultural history of modern ideologies. His publications in English includes *Aryan Idols: Indo-European Mythology as Ideology and Science* (2006), *The Style and Mythology of Socialism: Socialist Idealism 1871–1914* (2017), *Socialist Imaginations: Utopias, Myths, and the Masses* (2019, editor together with Jakub Beneš and Anja Kirsch) and *Religion and Politics under Capitalism: A Humanistic Approach to the Terminology* (2019).

Egil Asprem is Professor of the History of Religions at Stockholm University, Sweden. His research interests include the history of esotericism and ritual magic, new religious movements and theory and method in the study of religion and esotericism. He is the author of *The Problem of Disenchantment: Scientific Naturalism and Esoteric Discourse, 1900–1939* (2014/2018) and *Arguing with Angels: Enochian Magic and Modern Occulture* (2012), and co-editor of *The Brill Handbook of Conspiracy Theory and Contemporary Religion* (2018) and *New Approaches to the Study of Esotericism* (2021). He is currently editor-in-chief of *Aries: Journal for the Study of Western Esotericism*.

Jenny Berglund is Professor in Religion Education at Stockholm University. She is the general secretary of the European Association for the Study of Religions (EASR). Her research focuses on religious education in Europe, specifically Islamic education. One of her publications is *European Perspectives on Islamic Education and Public Schooling* (2018).

Henrik Bogdan is Professor of Religious Studies at the University of Gothenburg. His main areas of research include esotericism, new religious movements and Freemasonry. He is the author of *Western Esotericism and Rituals of Initiation* (2007), editor of *Brother Curwen, Brother Crowley* (2010) and co-editor of *Aleister Crowley and Western Esotericism* (2012), *Occultism in a Global Perspective* (2013), *Sexuality and New Religious Movements* (2014), *Handbook of Freemasonry* (2014) and *Western Esotericism in Scandinavia* (2016), among others. Bogdan is the editor of the Oxford Studies in Western Esotericism book series, the Palgrave Studies in New Religions and Alternative Spiritualities book series and secretary of the European Society for the Study of Western Esotericism (ESSWE).

Daniel Enstedt is Associate Professor of Religious Studies in the Department of Literature, History of Ideas, and Religion at the University of Gothenburg, Sweden. His current areas of scholarship are contemporary religion in Western Europe, examining lived religion and social mobility among migrants in Sweden, spiritual health practices in Zhineng Qigong and religion and spiritualities in healthcare encounters.

Olof Franck is Professor in Subject Matter Education, specializing in social studies subjects, and Associate Professor in Philosophy of Religion in the Department of Pedagogical, Curricular and Professional Studies at the University of Gothenburg. His publications have their focus in Ethics Education (EE), Religious Education (RE), Philosophy of Religion and ESD. Franck is leading an explorative workshop on powerful knowledge in social studies subjects, funded by the Swedish Research Council (SRC). He has, in recent years, been engaged in two research projects on conceptions of ethical competence in EE and RE, funded by SRC and the Swedish Institute for Educational Research, respectively.

Manon Hedenborg White is Associate Professor in History of Religions at Malmö University, Sweden. Her research interests focus on modern (Western) esotericism, new religious movements and contemporary spirituality, as well as issues of gender, sexuality and authority in religions. Her notable publications include *The Eloquent Blood: The Goddess Babalon and the Construction of Femininities in Western Esotericism* (2020) and *Esotericism and Deviance* (with Tim Rudbøg, 2023).

Anne-Christine Hornborg is Professor Emerita in History of Religions at Lund University, Sweden. *A Landscape of Left-Overs* (2001) is grounded on extensive field work among the Canadian Mi'kmaq. She has also been field working in Tonga, the Peruvian Andes and the Amazon. In focus is indigenous cosmologies, animism, the phenomenology of landscape, the anthropologist in field and ecology and religion. Another focus is rituals as in *Ritualer. Teorier och tillämpning* (Rituals. Theories and Application, 2005) and *Den rituella människan – flervetenskapliga perspektiv* (The Ritual Human – Multidisciplinary Perspectives, 2010). Her discussions on ritualization, ritual practices, neo-spiritual therapy and coaching in late modern Sweden have attracted attention in a wider public.

Peter Jackson Rova is a professor in the History of Religions at Stockholm University, Sweden. He specializes in Germanic, Greek and Indo-Iranian religions with an additional broad interest in the theory, method and conceptual underpinnings of religious studies. Among his recent publications are the co-edited volumes *Philosophy and the End of Sacrifice: Disengaging Ritual in Ancient India, Greece and Beyond* (with Anna-Pya Sjödin, 2016) and *Transforming Warriors: The Ritual Organization of Military Force* (with Peter Haldén, 2016), as well as the monograph *Devotion and Artifice: Themes of Suspension in the History of Religions* (2023).

Tim Jensen is Adjunct Professor in the Study of Religions at the University of Southern Denmark and Honorary Professor at Leibniz University. Jensen is currently (2015–) serving as President of the International Association for the History of Religions (IAHR), served (2000–4) as the first General Secretary of the European Association for the Study of Religions (EASR), and then (2005–15) as IAHR General Secretary. His research interests include study-of-religion linked and based methodology and religion education, representations of religion/s in public, including legal and human rights discourses, and religion in the Homeric epics.

Göran Larsson is Professor of Religious Studies in the Department of Literature, History of Ideas, and Religion at the University of Gothenburg. Larsson's main research is on Islam and Muslims in Europe in past and present times, but he has also published on religion and the media, global conflicts, violent extremism and security studies. Since January 2023, he is also guest professor at the Police Academy at Borås University. His latest publication is the edited volume, *The Legacy, Life and Work of Geo Widengren and the Study of the History of Religions after World War II* (2022).

Bodil Liljefors Persson is Professor, History of Religions, Malmö University. Her research focus on the Maya religion in both the precolonial time and the present. She also conducts research in religion education, sexuality and relations education and citizenship education. Among her latest publications are *Maya Religion and History*, edited by Christophe Helmke, Harri Kettunen and Bodil Liljefors Persson (2023); and *Religion och samhällsförändring – Aktuella perspektiv på religionsvetenskaplig forskning* (Religion and Social Change – Current Perspectives on Research in Religious Studies), edited by Dennis Augustsson, Charlotta Carlström, Emma Hall and Bodil Liljefors Persson (2023).

Tomas Lindgren is a professor at Umeå University in the Department of Historical, Philosophical and Religious Studies. His research interests focus on social and cultural psychology of religion, evolutionary psychology, religion and politics, Indonesian Islam and anomalous experiences. He has published on radicalism, radicalization, fundamentalism, religious conflicts, Islamic nonviolence, spirituality and religious experiences. His most recent book is *Fundamentalism och helig terror* (Fundamentalism and Holy Terror, 2023).

Martin Lund has a PhD in Jewish studies from Lund University (2013) and is currently Assistant Professor in Religious Studies at Malmö University. His research interests include formations of Jewishness in popular culture, category formation in religious studies and racial formation. He has published widely on these and other topics, including the monograph *Re-Constructing the Man of Steel: Superman 1938–1941, Jewish American History, and the Invention of the Jewish-Comics Connection* (2016).

Svante Lundgren is Associate Professor of Jewish Studies and is presently working at Lund University. His research interests focus on modern Jewish history, Jewish-Christian relations and on Christian communities in and from the Middle East, especially Assyrians and Armenians. He is the co-editor of *Nordisk judaistik/ Scandinavian Jewish Studies*.

Mia Lövheim is Professor in Sociology of Religion in the Faculty of Theology at Uppsala University, and leader for the theme 'Democracy, Communication and Media' at the Centre for Multidisciplinary Research on Religion and Society (CRS). Her research focuses on representations of religion in Swedish and Nordic daily press, public service media and social media in the context of social and political change. She is the editor of *Media, Religion and Gender: Key Issues and New Challenges* (2013) and *A Constructive Critique of Religion: Encounters between Christianity, Islam, and Non-religion in Secular Societies* (with Mikael Stenmark, 2020).

Jessica Moberg is an associate professor at the University of Gothenburg, specializing in contemporary religion, including Pentecostal Christianity and non-Christian spiritualities. Her research focuses on the practical aspects of religion, particularly ritual, embodied practices, and the materiality of religion. In her 2013 dissertation, she explored the cultivation of embodied and material piety in Stockholm's Pentecostal landscape. She has also studied the connection between popular culture and spiritualism, analysing reality TV shows featuring spiritualist mediums. Moberg draws on theories of religion and popular culture, ritual studies, embodied learning and the habitus to inform her analysis.

Kristina Myrvold is Visiting Professor in History of Religions at the Centre for Theology and Religious Studies, Lund University. Her research interests focus on South Asian religions, especially Sikh religious practices, scriptures and migration in the past and the present. Myrvold has published numerous journal articles and book chapters on the Sikhs in Europe and India, and she is the editor of more than ten edited volumes. Her current research focuses on print histories and politics of religious Sikh texts in colonial Punjab. Myrvold is also one of the editors of *Brill's Encyclopedia of Sikhism*.

Sanja Nilsson is Assistant Professor in Religious Studies and Sociology at Dalarna University, Sweden. Her research interests include childhood studies, studies in new religions and alternative spirituality, minority studies and the sociology of deviance. She is co-author of the book *Children in Minority Religions: Growing Up in Controversial Religious Groups* (2018). Her most recent book is *Living in and Leaving Swedish Knutby Filadelfia Congregation* (2023).

Magdalena Nordin is Associate Professor in Sociology of Religion at the Department of Literature, History of Ideas, and Religion at the University of Gothenburg. Her research focus has been about religion and migration, focusing on change of religiosity among migrants, religious plurality and public institutions (such as the healthcare sector and educational institutions), interfaith dialogue and change, continuity and reinterpretation of religious practices. Among her recent publications, we find *Migration and Religion*, IMISCOE Short Readers (2023); *Migration, religion och integration* (Migration, Religion, and Integration, 2023); *Sociologiska perspektiv på religion i Sverige* (Sociological Perspectives on Religion in Sweden, 2022).

Susanne Olsson is Professor in the History of Religions at Stockholm University, Sweden. Her research interests are in Islamic studies where she has conducted research on political reinterpretations of Islam, with a special focus on fundamentalism and traditionalism. Her most recent book is *Contemporary Puritan Salafism: A Swedish Case Study* (2019).

Christina Osbeck is Professor in Subject Matter Education, specializing in social studies in the Department of Pedagogical, Curricular and Professional Studies at the University of Gothenburg. In her research, she is especially focused on religious education, ethics education and existential questions of young people, their life interpretations and life views –how they are negotiated in school and classroom practice – among others. She is one of the authors of *Didactic Classroom Studies – a Potential Research Direction* (2018).

Heike Peter is Assistant Professor in History of Religions at Halmstad University, Sweden. Her research interest focus on ancient religions, historical anthropology, discourse analysis and praxis theory, specializing in Ancient Near Eastern religions and religions in the Roman provinces; she has also been engaged within the field of Religion Education.

Katarina Plank is Associate Professor in Religious Studies at Karlstad University. Her ethnographic research focuses on lived religious perspectives of migrants and of contemporary spirituality in Sweden. She has a special research interest in Buddhism, meditation and materiality. She is the principal investigator for the research project *The New Faces of the Folk Church*, and she is also involved in the research project *Religion in times of Crises – Religious Responses to Covid-19*. Together with Enstedt, she is researching everyday religion, social mobility and integration among different migrant groups of Christian, Muslim and Buddhist traditions.

Therese Rodin is Assistant Professor in Religious Studies at Dalarna University. Her research interests cover themes like goddesses, women, power relations and literacy in the Ancient Near East. She is particularly interested in highlighting the lack, as well as inclusion, of females in the scholarly text production.

Ferdinando Sardella is Associate Professor at the Department of Ethnology, History of Religions and Gender Studies at Stockholm University. He is the co-director of the project 'Bengal Vaishnavism in the Modern Period' at the Oxford Centre for Hindu Studies, where he is a research fellow. His research interests focus on South Asian studies, Bengal studies, yoga, new religious movements and modern Hinduism. He is the author of the monograph *Modern Hindu Personalism: The History, Life and Thought of Bhaktisiddhānta Sarasvatī* (2013) and has co-edited the *Handbook of Hinduism in Europe* (with Knut A. Jacobsen, 2020).

Simon Sorgenfrei is Professor of the Study of Religions and Director of the Institute for the Study of Multireligiosity and Secularity (IMS) at Södertörn University. His research primarily concerns different aspects of Islam, as well as subjects relating to religion and migration. Among his most recent publications are *'De kommer att vara annorlunda svenskar'. Berättelsen om Sveriges första muslimer* ('They Will Be Different Swedes'. The Story about Sweden's First Muslims, 2022), *Näktergalen. Erik Johan Stagnelius* (The Nightingale. Erik Johan Stagnelius, 2023) and *Religion, migration och polisiärt arbete* (Religion, Migration, and Police Work, edited with Göran Larsson and Tanja Viklund, 2023).

Göran Ståhle is Associate Professor in the Study of Religions at Södertörn University, Sweden. His research interests include Indic religions, psychology of religion and religion and health. He has published on Hindu rituals, the globalization of Ayurveda, contemporary spirituality and migration.

Olof Sundqvist is Professor of History of Religions in the Department of Ethnology, History of Religions and Gender Studies at Stockholm University. He is a specialist on Old Norse religion and has written the books *Freyr's Offspring: Rulers and Religion in Ancient Svea Society* (2002), *Oden och Mithraskulten* (Odin and the Mithras Cult, with Anders Kaliff, 2004), *Kultledare i fornskandinavisk religion* (Cultic Leaders in Old Norse Religion, 2007) and *An Arena for Higher Powers: Ceremonial Buildings and Religious Strategies for Rulership in Late Iron Age Scandinavia* (2016).

Isak Svensson is Dag Hammarskjöld Professor at Uppsala University in the Department of Peace and Conflict Research. His research interests are religion and conflict, international mediation and civil resistance. His most recent books include *Religion, Conflict, and Global Society: A Festschrift Celebrating Mark Juergensmeyer* (co-edited with Mona Kanwal Sheikh, 2021), *Confronting the Caliphate: Civil Resistance in Jihadist Proto-States* (2022) and *Conflict Mediation in the Arab World* (co-edited with Ibrahim Fraihat, 2023).

Jonas Svensson is a professor in the Study of Religions at Linnaeus University. His current research interest revolves around integrating the cognitive science of religion into Islamic studies and digitally augmented Islamic studies. He has published on, for example, gender and Islam, Islamic bioethics, Islamic education in East Africa, Qur'an as an artefact, Qur'an desecration and Salafism. His most recent book is *Människans Muhammed* (Mind and Muhammad, 2015), and he has been a co-editor of the volumes *Building Blocks of Religion* (2020) and *Doing Digital Humanities* (2020).

INTRODUCING THE STUDY OF RELIGION IN SWEDEN

Göran Larsson and Henrik Bogdan

The aim of this volume, *The Study of Religion in Sweden: Past, Present and Future*, is to cast light on both the history and the current state of the non-confessional study of religion in Sweden. What is the legacy and what is the future of the study of religion in Sweden? The different chapters collected in this volume are a reminder and display of the great diversity that exists within the field of Religious Studies, and with this introduction, we want to provide an overview of the history of the field in Sweden. Besides presenting how the discipline has developed over time, we also discuss how Swedish scholars have been connected to international research trends and networks.

It should be stated at the outset that this volume does not cover the history of the academic study of Christianity (e.g. systematic theology, church history, the Old and New Testaments, etc.), for the simple reason that religious studies in Sweden, as in many other countries, to a large extent developed as a separate and distinct field of research from the study of Christianity or theology. While the distinction between theology and religious studies in many ways is artificial and arbitrary, it is a distinction that has been upheld from both disciplines – both in theory and in practice – and which we therefore have chosen to follow in this collection. Furthermore, it needs to be acknowledged that for a long time, religious studies, like most other forms of higher education in Sweden, excluded women scholars. This exclusion is evident in the history of religious studies, which until the 1960s almost exclusively consisted of men – a fact which is reflected in the overview of the history of religious studies which follows in this introduction.

Situating the Study of Religion in Sweden

The foundation, development and growth of the study of religion in Sweden mirror the historical, cultural and sociopolitical processes that have influenced religion in Sweden and thus Sweden's transformation from a predominantly Lutheran country to a diverse and pluralistic religious landscape. Sweden's religious history is anchored in Lutheranism, which became the state religion during the Reformation era, with the Church of Sweden founded in the sixteenth century (although it was only in the second half of the nineteenth century that the church adopted the name 'Church of Sweden', Sw. *Svenska kyrkan*). For centuries, Lutheranism was deeply ingrained in Swedish society, with the Church of Sweden playing a central role in the country's religious and social fabric. It was only in 1860 that it became legal to leave the Church of Sweden and to convert to another confession or religion, provided that one became a member of another officially recognized religious denomination. By the end of the nineteenth century, the question of religious liberty was fiercely debated in the Swedish press, and influential intellectuals like August Strindberg (1849–1912) and Ellen Key (1849–1926) were highly critical of the hegemony of the Swedish State Church. In 1907, the socialist agitator Kata Dalström (1858–1923) – often referred to as 'the mother of the Swedish socialist working-class movement' – famously declared that she was a Buddhist, thus not only challenging the limits of religious freedom at the time but also indicating that the religious landscape was changing. In their critique of Evangelical Lutheranism and the Church of Sweden, intellectuals often turned to non-Christian religious traditions as expressed in the literature of the emerging field of comparative religion, and in particular the works of Max Müller (1823–1900), of which the first Swedish translation appeared in 1868.[1] The interest in non-Christian religions and literature of the then-nascent field of *Religionswissenschaft* was, thus, at the turn of the century, in many ways entangled with progressive politics, religious liberty and the critique of the hegemony of the Church of Sweden. It is against this backdrop that one needs to understand the birth of the non-confessional study of religion in Sweden and the work of early pioneers such as Nathan Söderblom (1866–1931) and Tor Andræ (1885–1947).

However, the twentieth century witnessed a gradual decline in religious observance and affiliation, partly due to secularization trends and changing societal attitudes as well as a growing criticism of the theology of the Church of Sweden (not least from the Uppsala philosopher Ingemar Hedenius (1908–1982); on him, see Nordin (2004)). Influenced by increasing industrialization, urbanization and scientific advancements, Swedish society underwent a process of secularization, challenging the traditional dominance of the Church of Sweden. This shift led to a decline in religious observance, reduced influence of the Church of Sweden and a growing acceptance of secular values. In terms of freedom of religion, the law from 1860 stipulating that one could only leave the Church of Sweden on the condition that one became a member of another recognized denomination was finally abolished in 1951 (Enkvist 2013). It now became legal to leave the Church without joining another denomination or providing any reason for the decision.

Sweden's secularization is also reflected in the separation of church and state. The disestablishment of the State Church of Sweden in 2000 marked a significant turning point in the country's religious history. This separation reinforced the idea that religion is a personal matter rather than a state-endorsed institution, further promoting secular values and pluralism. However, although the Church of Sweden's influence has diminished, it continues to play a vital role in the country's religious landscape.² The church has adapted to changing societal norms and has made efforts to become more inclusive and progressive. It has embraced gender equality by ordaining female priests and has advocated for LGBTQ+ rights. Moreover, Sweden's commitment to religious freedom and tolerance played a significant role in fostering religious pluralism. Immigration from various parts of the world further contributed to the religious mosaic in Sweden. Consequently, a multitude of religious traditions, including Islam, Buddhism, Hinduism, Sikhism and others, are now represented and practiced in the country (Willander 2019).

While Sweden has become more secular and diverse, religion continues to shape the collective identity of its citizens. Many Swedes may identify as culturally Lutheran, even if they do not actively participate in religious practices. National holidays such as Christmas and Easter retain their significance, albeit with a more secular and commercialized focus. Additionally, many individuals engage in alternative spiritual practices, emphasizing mindfulness, nature worship or so-called New Age beliefs, which reflect a growing trend towards personalized spirituality.

In sum, Sweden's religious landscape has undergone significant transformations, from a predominantly Lutheran nation to a diverse and pluralistic society. The forces of secularization, religious pluralism and changing societal values have shaped this development. While the Church of Sweden maintains its role, other religious traditions have gained prominence. Sweden's journey towards secularization has been characterized by a progressive shift away from traditional religious norms and a focus on individual autonomy and freedom. Factors such as changing societal attitudes, multiculturalism and the separation of church and state have contributed to Sweden's status as one of the most secularized countries in the world (Andersson and Sander 2005: 25–33; Willander 2019), although it can be questioned to what extent Sweden is actually secularized (Thurfjell 2019, 2020). While secularization has brought about positive changes in terms of social policies and inclusivity, it also poses challenges and sparks important debates about the role of religion in society and, consequently, the study of religion in Sweden.

The Early History

Leaving aside the long history of the study of theology or religion as a confessional subject at Uppsala (Bergman 1976; Bexell 2021) and Lund universities (Österlin 2001), the academic, non-confessional study of religion in Sweden is approximately 120 years old.³ Nathan Söderblom, Professor at Uppsala University, is considered the founding father of the History of Religions in Sweden. However, it should be stressed that Söderbloms's chair was in Theological Propaedeutics and Theological Encyclopaedia, not in History of Religions. Söderblom had studied Iranian languages and religions at the Sorbonne University in Paris, and in 1901, he defended his thesis, *La Vie Future d'après à la lumière des croyances parallèles dans les autres religions. Étude d'eschatologie comparée*, before he became professor at Uppsala University. In 1912, Söderblom was also awarded with a professorship at the University of Leipzig, Germany (Hultgård 2002: 137). Besides his many publications in several languages, Söderblom also contributed to the important German reference work, *Die Religion in Geschichte und Gegenwart* (Stausberg 2007: 309); in 1908, he published a three-volume compendium of translations of ancient and oriental texts for the study of religions (in Swedish: *Främmande religionsurkunder i urval och öfversättning*). This publication was inspired by the Sacred Books of the East series that had been started by the Oxford professor and pioneer for the History of Religions, Max Müller (Bergman 1976: 8).

With Söderblom, the study of non-Christian religions became the hallmark of the History of Religions as an independent but integrated discipline within the study of Theology, Church History and Biblical Studies. Like most international scholars at this time, Swedish historians of religions primarily worked with philological and comparative methods. During Söderblom's stint at Leipzig University, his absence in Uppsala was filled by Edgar Reuterskiöld (1872–1932), who worked as a full-time professor between 1916 and 1928. Besides his interest in the so-called sacramental meals, Reuterskiöld had an interest in the religions of the indigenous Sami-population in Sweden (Bergman 1976: 10).

After Reuterskiöld, the position in Uppsala was filled by Tor Andræ, who became the chair of History of Religions in 1929 (Bergman 1976: 11–14; Widengren 1947a). As demonstrated in Chapter 5 in this volume, Andræ had a special interest in the study of the early history of the prophet Muhammad, Islamic historiography and Islamic mysticism; prior to his professorship in Uppsala, he was working as a full-time professor at Stockholm College (*Stockholm högskola* in Swedish, later renamed Stockholm University; on this period in Andræ's life, see Widengren 1947a).

In addition to their academic interest in the History of Religions, Söderblom and Andræ were also devout Christians, and both terminated their academic careers for positions as bishops in the service of the Church of Sweden (Söderblom was appointed archbishop in 1914; Andræ became bishop for the Linköping diocese in 1936). As pointed out by Hedin (1997) and Hjärpe (2022), Söderblom's and Andræ's personal faith and connection to the majority Church made them somewhat biased, not least when it came to value judgements about non-Christian religion. According to Professor Anders Hultgård, this bias was not strange since the overarching aim of the science of religion(s) at the time was to promote 'a better understanding of Christianity and demonstrating its superiority' (Hultgård 2002: 134).

Like many of his contemporary scholars, Söderblom was influenced by Romanticism, Liberal Protestantism and especially the ideas of German theologians like Friedrich Schleiermacher (1768–1834) and Adolf von Harnack (1851–1930) (Hultgård 2002). At a time when belief in Christianity was put to question by scientific discoveries and novel lines of reasoning (i.e. the Enlightenment, but also the discoveries of Charles Darwin, 1809–1882), many theologians as well as Historians of Religions were looking for other ways of legitimating a belief in something supernatural. Instead of rationalism and reason, emotions, feelings, 'nature' and the 'holy' were emphasized (Kippenberg 2002). For Söderblom, the origin of religion(s) as well as the so-called prophetic and revealed religions were at the forefront (Bergman 1976: 5). Besides Schleiermacher, Söderblom was influenced by the German scholar Rudolph Otto (1869-1937) and his emphasis on the holy and the 'numinous' (Stausberg 2007: 302; e.g. Alles 2017). While Schleiermacher and Otto were translated into Swedish, the works of scholars like Émile Durkheim (1858-1917), Henri Hubert (1872-1927) and Marcel Mauss (1872-1950) seem to have been of less importance for scholars of religions in the first half of the twentieth century in Sweden. As late as 1947, Geo Widengren (1907-1996), whom we shall return to soon, discarded the importance and validity of Durkheim's theory on the nexus between religion and society (Widengren 1947b).

Even though scholars like Söderblom and Andræ stressed that the History of Religions was not a subordinated discipline, the connection with theology and confessional claims remained until the 1940s in Sweden. One example of this affinity is illustrated by the conflict that erupted when Torgny Segerstedt (1876-1945) defended his doctoral thesis, *Till frågan om polyteismens uppkomst. En religionshistorisk undersökning*, at Uppsala University in 1903. While the thesis was well received by the examining committee, it failed as it did not defend the Lutheran belief system. Without going into any details (on this conflict, see Stohlander Axelsson 2001a, 2001b), in 1903, Segerstedt was quickly offered a position at Lund University as docent, and in 1913, he was awarded a professorship at the Faculty of Philosophy at Stockholm College. This position was facilitated by a personal donation, and it is the first professorship in the History of Religions outside a theological faculty (Arbman 1949; Bergman 1976: 7; Stohlander Axelsson 2001b: 66-7).

With some minor exceptions, the development at Lund University mirrors the situation in Uppsala. In 1913, the Danish scholar Edvard Lehmann (1862-1930) left his position in Berlin and became the first Professor in Theological Propaedeutics and Theological Encyclopaedia at Lund University.[4] Lehmann was a specialist in ancient Iranian religions and a firm believer in the comparative method and evolutionistic theories, that is, that Christianity was the most advanced and developed form of religion (on Lehmann, see Reenberg Sand and Podemann Sørensen 2001). On these two points, he resembles Nathan Söderblom. Lehmann served as a professor in Lund between 1913 and 1927 and was followed by Efraim Briem (1890-1946). Briem was a comparativist with a special interest in Near Eastern religions, spiritism, mysticism and psychology of religion. In 1933, it was decided that the professorship in Theological Propaedeutics and Theological Encyclopaedia should be changed to a professorship in History of Religions and Psychology of Religion. Briem served as a professor between 1928 and 1946 (Olsson 2001: 78).

After Andræ left his position at Stockholm College, Ernst Arbman (1891-1959) became Professor of General History of Religions in 1937. His academic background was Uppsala, and Arbman was a specialist in Indian religions; he served as a professor in Stockholm between 1937 and 1958 (Bergman 1976: 14). Arbman was later replaced by Åke Hultkrantz (1920-2006), who served as professor at the Department of Comparative Religion at Stockholm University from 1958 until his retirement in 1986. Compared to his predecessors in both Uppsala and Lund, Hultkrantz emphasized field studies and ethnographical and anthropological methods. Among his many publications (altogether 471 texts in different languages), he became famous in Sweden and internationally especially for his studies of North American and circumpolar religions among indigenous populations (Drobin 2008).

The Study of Religion after the Second World War

Although professorships in subjects that would eventually become the first chairs in the History of Religions were established in Uppsala (1901), Lund (1913) and Stockholm (1913), most Swedish scholars and students still had to turn to international textbooks if they wanted to learn how to pursue comparative religious studies as an academic discipline. We know, for instance, that Pierre-Daniel Chatepie de la Saussaye's (1848–1920) *Lehrbuch der Religionsgeschichte* (2 vols, 1887–9) was used at Uppsala University till the 1940s (Widengren 1947a: 160–1; on the importance of this textbook, see Stausberg 2007: 309–10). In 1912, Söderblom also published a 'thorough revision and enlargement' of the renowned Leiden Professor C. P. Tiele's (1830–1902) *Kompendium der Religionsgeschicthe* (Bergman 1976: 9). However, the dependence on international textbooks partly changed when the young Professor Geo Widengren published the first edition of his textbook, *Religionens värld*, in 1945. This book was later published in several editions and translated into German (1969), Spanish (1976) and Italian (1984). The importance of this publication is, for instance, noted by the student Hultkrantz, who was to replace Arbman as Professor in the History of Religions at Stockholm University in 1958 (Hultkrantz 1986a: 10; see also Drobin 2006).

Like his predecessors, Widengren was a comparativist who stressed the importance of philological knowledge as the basis for the History of Religions as an independent academic discipline (on Widengren, see Larsson 2022a, 2023). When he was awarded the professorship in Uppsala in 1940, the title of the chair was changed to History of Religions and Religious Psychology. In his research, Widengren placed emphasis on a comparative and typological phenomenology, but he was also influenced by the German *Religionsgeschichtliche Schule* (Rudolph 2005; Thomassen 2022) and the British myth-and-ritual school (Harrelson 2005). Detecting recurring patterns in religions, cultures and languages became a hallmark for Widengren. Following in the footsteps of Söderblom and Andræ, Widengren was an internationalist, and among his many achievements, he is one of the founding fathers of both the International Association for the Study of the History of Religions (today abbreviated as IAHR) and its journal, *Numen* (Casadio 2016; Jensen and Fujiwara 2022). His academic networks include contacts with leading Historians of Religions, such as Mircea Eliade (1907–1986), George Dumézil (1898–1986; between 1931 and 1933, Dumézil was active at Uppsala University as a lecturer in the French language) and Gerardus van der Leeuw (1890–1950), to name a few.

From the biography on his teacher, friend and later supervisor Andræ, we learn that Widengren was immersed in the latest theories, methods and research questions during his first studies at Stockholm College and later at Uppsala University. We also know that he participated in several of the so-called Olaus Petri lectures that had started in Uppsala in 1917. Among international guests, Widengren listened, for example, to lectures given by the Italian Professor Raffaele Pettazzoni (1883–1959) and Professor Wilhelm Schmidt (1868–1954); both had a great influence on Widengren and especially on his studies of so-called High Gods and Sacred Kings (i.e. Larsson 2022a). Besides Pettazzoni and Schmidt, Professors Ignaz Goldziher (1850–1921), Franz Cumont (1868–1947), Adolf Deißmann (1866–1937) and Antoine Meillet (1866–1936) were also invited to give Olaus Petri lectures (Bergman 1976: 8). Some of these lectures were also translated and published in Swedish.

Without going into any details, Widengren's list of publications includes more than two hundred books, articles, essays and reviews in Swedish, German, English, Italian and Spanish (Casadio and Larsson 2022), and he was closely connected with many of the most important scholars of his time. Furthermore, one of the most distinguishing characters of Widengren was his strong emphasis on the non-confessional approach towards the study of religion. Compared to his predecessors, Söderblom and Andræ, Widengren never showed any interest in defending Christianity or any other religion for that matter. With this attitude, one can argue that Widengren liberated the History of Religions from its Christian legacy and made it into an independent discipline within the study of religions. In line with the German *Religionsgeschichtliche Schule*, Widengren viewed Christianity as one religious tradition among many religions, and to understand this tradition(s), it is necessary to place Christian thoughts in a larger Near Eastern tradition(s).

In 1959, the Faculty of Arts (Humanities) decided to establish a chair in the History of Religions at Uppsala University. The position was awarded to Carl-Martin Edsman (1911–2010) who had worked as a so-called preceptor lecturer in the History of Religions at the Faculty of Arts since 1949. Edsman had a broad interest in Near Eastern traditions, folk religiosity in the Nordic countries and Christianity. Instead of strengthening the study of religions at Uppsala University, this new position caused a split between the Faculty of Theology and the Faculty of Arts. The conflict was also personal for Widengren and Edsman (on this conflict, see Edsman 1949, 2001 and Bexell 2021).

While most scholars at Uppsala University were interested in comparative studies and phenomenological approaches, Lund University partly took a different route. With Erland Ehnmark (1903–1966; professor from 1949 to 1966), History of Religions became a subject that paid close attention to psychological aspects and the so-called limits of the history of religions (i.e. what we can know about religions) – according to Tord Olsson, who later became Professor in the History of Religions (Olsson 2001: 78–9). Ehnmark was also a advocate of animism as the oldest form of religions, a theory that was discarded by Widengren at Uppsala (Larsson 2019). But like Widengren, Ehnmark was a scholar who emphasized philology and the need to make comparisons between different religious traditions. Enhmark's thesis, *The Idea of God in Homer* (1935), is also a reminder that he was a classist, and from this point of view, he was close to Professor Martin

P:son Nilsson (1874–1967) who also had a great influence on the study of both the Classics and the History of Religions. Unfortunately, Widengren and Nilsson rarely shared the same interpretations, and they seem to have developed a strong dislike for each other. Although we should refrain from over-emphasizing this conflict, the division and hostility that had started between Uppsala and Lund with the conflict over Segerstedt's thesis continued also after the Second World War (cf. Schalk, no year).

Contemporary Perspectives: From 1968 to the Present

Between 1969 and 1983, Sven S. Hartman (1917–1988) was Professor in the History of Religions at Lund University.[5] Like many of his Swedish predecessors, Hartman had an interest in Oriental and Iranian religions, and he had obtained his formal training at Uppsala University under the guidance of Widengren, Professor H. S. Nyberg (1889–1974) and Professor Stig Wikander (1908–1983; on Wikander and the study of religions, see Arvidsson 2006). Hartman's most important work is his thesis, *Gayômart: Étude sur le syncretisme dans l'ancient Iran* (1953). According to Olsson, Hartman was a structuralist who was inspired by the French social-anthropologist, Claude Lévi-Strauss (1908–2009), and he had also participated in the seminars that George Dumézil held in Paris. Another novelty with Hartman was that he was not only interested in the textual sources but also paid attention to the oral traditions of the Parsis in Bombay. In his final and unpublished work on the Avesta and Zoroastrianism, he even relied on audio and film recordings of the rituals of the Parsis, and this indicates, at least according to Olsson, that the study of religions in Lund took a different turn from Uppsala. While Uppsala primarily focused on texts – with some minor exceptions (i.e. Johannes Kolmodin, 1884–1933, who used oral sources, like songs, proverbs, etc., for studying Ethiopic languages, cultures and customs (Kahle 2006)) – Lund (like Stockholm University under the guidance of Professor Hultkrantz) opened the subject matter for field studies. Unfortunately, Hartman died before he had the opportunity to finalize his last magnum opus that was partly based on field recordings (Olsson 2001: 79).

In Lund in 1979/1980, the title of the professorship was changed to History of Religions and Religious Phenomenology. The possibility to use field material as a source for the History of Religions introduced by Hartman was also continued and developed by Associate Professor Olof Pettersson (1920–1986), who was a specialist on African, Sami and North Siberian religions (Hultkrantz 1986b). Compared to the classical studies that had focused on dogmatics, Pettersson stressed that scholars of religions should focus more on how religions function and their role in the society. With this emphasis in mind, it is quite surprising to learn that Petterson bragged that he had never set his foot on African soil (Olsson 2001: 80). Among his students, we find a young scholar, Tord Olsson (1942–2013), who later became professor in 1984 at the very same department in Lund (Olsson 2001: 80–1). Professor Olsson is a rare example of a historian of religions who combined philological studies with field work with a special emphasis on rituals in East and West Africa. The methodology of Olsson is described in the following way:

> The method involves, among other things, getting the tradition bearers to interpret their oral texts themselves and to investigate how religious terms and expressions are used in different types of speech situations. (Olsson 2001: 81; our translation)

As already noted, the changes within the academia are also reflected in the larger society. For instance, in 1969, the Swedish school subject *Kristendomskunskap* ('Knowledge about Christianity') was replaced with *Religionskunskap* ('Knowledge about Religions'), which indicates a broader and more neutral approach to religion (on this development, see Chapter 12 in this volume). In 1971, the Swedish Higher Education Authority (*Universitetskanslerämbetet*) divided the academic study of religion and theology into five sub-disciplines (Biblical Studies, History of Religion, Church History, Systematic Theology and Sociology/Psychology of Religions), which had a massive impact on how religion as a subject was and still is being taught at Swedish universities (on this reform, see *Utredningen angående den religionsvenskapliga utbildningens mål och metoder* (1971)).

The mid-1980s and early 1990s marked a new phase in the history and development of the study of religion in Sweden. During this period, the study of religion went through a process of increased specialization, resulting in new disciplines and fields of research. This development – which is covered in detail in the various chapters of this volume – to a certain extent reflects new trends on the international scene as well as the division of the study of religions as an academic discipline. Most notably, the growing criticism levelled against phenomenology and the comparative study of religion during the 1980s as epitomized by Mircea Eliade and the Chicago School led to a gradual fragmentation of the field and reluctance in making global or universal claims about religion. Instead, the study of religion was increasingly divided into sub-disciplines, covering specific areas, approaches and theoretical perspectives. To a large extent, this situation still characterizes the study of religion in Sweden today, as will be discussed in this volume.

Institutional Developments, Textbooks and Journals

If we focus on institutional developments, it should be highlighted that new departments for the academic study had emerged with time. For instance, in 1973–4, it became possible to study religions at the University of Gothenburg (Berntson and Bogdan 2002), and in the 1990s several so-called regional colleges (Högskolor) were created in Sweden that often included departments or sections for the study of religion (i.e. Falun; Gävle, Malmö, Södertörn) (see, for instance, Stausberg 2008: 314). Another development was the rise of the Swedish journal *Svensk religionshistorisk årsskrift* (1985–2007). This journal was published by the Swedish Association for the Study of the History of Religions (SSRF), that is, the organization that today represents Sweden in the IAHR. There have also been attempts to publish journals on specific topics: for instance, *Chakra* (published between 2004 and 2005), *Tidskrift för Mellanösternstudier* (published between 1994 and 2004) and the e-journals *Religion* (published between 2018 and 2021), *Religion och livsfrågor* (published in print during 1977–2019 and restricted to only e-publications since 2019) and the annual yearbook for religious education teachers, *Föreningen lärare i religionskunskap årsbok* (started in 1968, at present an e-publication) and *Aura: tidskrift för akademiska studier av nyreligiostitet* (published in print between 2009 and 2018). Other important journals for the study of religion in Sweden are, for instance, *Svensk teologisk kvartalskrift* (started in 1925) and *Nordic Journal of Religion and Society* and *Temenos: Nordic Journal for the Study of Religion*. Besides academic journals, there are numerous journals published by religious communities in Sweden, but so far, they have received little systematic attention (one exception is Jonas Otterbeck's thesis on the Muslim journal, *Salaam*: Otterbeck 2000). However, with the rapid development of social media, most journals today have been replaced by online bulletins, Facebook pages and e-newsletters.

Since many textbooks and introductions to the study of religion have been published in Sweden, there is no room to go into any details, but some books have had a more general outlook and therefore deserve some attention (on the importance of textbooks, see Stausberg 2009). We have already mentioned Geo Widengren's textbook, *Religionens värld*, but we also would like to draw attention to Helmer Ringgren and Folke V. Ström's book, *Religionerna i historia och nutid* (first published in 1957, also published in an American edition in 1967; Stausberg 2009: 263), Hultkrantz's *Metodvägar inom den jämförande religionsforskningen* (1973) and the Nordic textbook *Religionshistoria. Ritualer, mytologi, ikonografi* (Jensen, Rothstein and Podemann Sørensen 1996). More recent examples are, for instance, Daniel Andersson and Åke Sander's edited volume *Det mångreligiösa Sverige* (first published in 2005) that focuses on globalization, migration processes and the Swedish religious landscape; Egil Asprem and Olof Sundqvist's edited volume *Religionshistoria. En introduction till teori och metod* (2021) that emphasizes theoretical and methodological questions for the study of religions; and Katarina Plank and Daniel Enstedt's edited volume, *Levd religion. Det heliga i vardagen* (2018). For sociology of religion, one should mention Göran Gustafsson's *Tro, samfund och samhälle. Sociologiska perspektiv* (first published in 1991) and Mia Lövheim and Magdalena Nordin's edited volume, *Sociologiska perspektiv på religion i Sverige* (first published in 2015); for the study of psychology of religion, Hjalmar Sundén's *Religionspsykologi. Problem och metoder* (first edition in 1974) or Antoon Geels and Ove Wikström's *Den religiösa människan* (first edition in 1985) should be mentioned. While the earlier textbooks mainly focus on historical periods and classical texts, the latter focus on theory, method and social aspects for the study of religions. Most of the above-named introductions or surveys to the history of religions were intended for the public or for university students, and they were therefore written in Swedish. However, one early example that shows that Swedish scholars contributed to the history of religions as a discipline is the two-volume set, *Historia Religionum: Handbook for the History of Religions*, that Widengren and the Dutch scholar Claas Jouco Bleeker (1898–1983) edited between 1969 and 1971.

Future Challenges and Possibilities

As noted in several chapters in this volume, the study of religion boomed in the 1970s, and the number of departments and chairs have grown 'on an unprecedented scale' both in Sweden and elsewhere (Stausberg 2008: 305). The History of Religions as well as the more general study of religion(s) as a discipline has not only been consolidated and institutionalized over time, but new methods and theories for how to approach the subject matter that we call 'religion' have also grown rapidly since the 1970s. For example, designated chairs in the study of psychology of religion and sociology of religion were established in Uppsala and Lund from the late 1960s and mid-1970s (for more details, see Chapters 9 and 10 in this volume).

Whereas Nordic and Swedish scholars had been leading figures in the early institutionalization of the study of religions in Europe, the 1960s and 1970s marked a change. New players emerged and the competition from international scholars became increasingly prominent (Stausberg 2008). These processes concurred with drastic changes in the Swedish university system. From the late 1960s and the early 1970s, humanistic and classical studies (not least the study of languages) were downplayed in favour of social sciences, and higher education became more often viewed as instrumental for social engineering (i.e. the education of civil servants and as a tool for combatting unemployment). Without downplaying our predecessors, these processes had an impact on the study of religion in Sweden. While the founding fathers of the History of Religions had been comparativists who based their investigations on philological methods and tried to establish general theories, most scholars from the 1970s onwards became specialists within various sub-disciplines in the study of religion, and today, there is a much stronger emphasis on contemporary time periods. With the growing impact of globalization processes, for example, migration and faster ways of communication, the focus of the discipline has changed from history to more current affairs. These developments have provided opportunities for greater specialization, but the competition within and between each sub-discipline is hard, and at present, it is increasingly difficult to be a so-called all-round historian of religions, not least when it comes to philological competences (Stausberg 2008).

However, there are signs of change, and several Swedish scholars have yet again shown a strong interest in international cooperations like the IAHR and EASR (e.g. Jenny Berglund has been serving as the general secretary for the EASR since 2020), and many serve as editors or members of editorial boards of prestigious book series and journals (e.g. Henrik Bogdan is the editor of the two book series 'Oxford Studies in Western Esotericism' and 'Palgrave Studies in New Religions and Alternative Spiritualities'). There are also several examples of Swedish scholars who have contributed to international encyclopaedias, handbooks and reference books for the study of religions over the last two decades (e.g. Bogdan 2016a, 2016b; Larsson 2016a, 2016b, 2022c). Furthermore, in 2009, Södertörn University arranged the first EASR conference in Stockholm (the first after the IAHR meeting in Stockholm in 1970), and in 2024, the University of Gothenburg will arrange the second EASR conference in Sweden. Even though this is not the first time Sweden has been the host for international conferences in the study of religions or adjacent subjects (i.e. Stockholm-Kristiania, 1889; Lund, 1913; and Stockholm, 1970; on these meetings, see, for instance, Nylander 1890), the development over the last decades illustrates that Swedish research on the study of religions is fruitful, competitive and vibrant.

However, before presenting an outline of this volume, we would like to take the opportunity to address some questions that might merit future research as well as encourage cooperation between Swedish and international scholars within the study of religions. For example, as far as we know, there are few systematic reception studies that address if, how and when Swedish scholars picked up or rejected theories, explanations or proposals that had been formulated by international scholars. We believe that this is an important topic that merits study in the future, and to map out research networks among scholars of religions would be a research project that could engage scholars from several academic milieus. This lacuna is, however, not unique for Sweden, on the contrary. International networks and connections between scholars are an understudied topic. For us, this is surprising since the establishment of the discipline is very much a study of groups of scholars that come together and unite under one theoretical, methodological or geographical area of research. Or to put it in the words of Hofstee:

> The history of the science of religion is to a considerable extent the history of groups. What I refer to is groups of friends, discussion partners, close-knit circles that in some respects seem to have the characteristics of social movements. (Hofstee 2000: 176)

The observations made by Hofstee is primarily based on Dutch material, but we believe that there are good reasons to argue that similar patterns (i.e. group constellations) are also found in Sweden and elsewhere (i.e. Larsson 2022b).

Without tapping into the somewhat tiresome discussion if religious studies is a broad field or a specific discipline,[6] we can argue with strong confidence, not least based on the different chapters included in this volume, that the study of religion in Sweden is vibrant and meets the criteria for being a proper scientific field. To quote Stausberg, it is correct to talk about a 'professionalization, specialization, and diversification', and that there is a 'canon of academic scientific disciplines operating with a specific set of legitimate methods' in the study of religions in Sweden (2007: 303).

An Outline of the Volume

The Study of Religion in Sweden: Past, Present and Future provides a comprehensive exploration of the field of religious studies in Sweden. The book is divided into three main parts, each focusing on different aspects of the study of religion in Sweden.

Part I: Historical Approaches

This section delves into the study of specific religious traditions in Sweden. It includes chapters dedicated to Ancient Near Eastern religions, Old Norse religion, Indigenous religions, Judaism, Islam, Indian religions, Western esotericism and New Religious Movements and New Age Spirituality. Each chapter is written by experts in the respective fields, providing in-depth insights into the historical and contemporary study of these religious traditions in Sweden.

Part II: Social Scientific Approaches

This section critically examines four sub-disciplines that have emerged as significant components of the study of religion in Sweden. The chapters in this section explore psychology of religion, sociology of religion, cognitive studies of religion and religious education. The authors provide an analysis of the theories, methods and approaches used in these sub-disciplines and highlight their contributions to the broader field of religious studies.

Part III: Themes in the Study of Religion in Sweden

The third part of the book focuses on central questions and themes that have attracted Swedish scholars in the study of religion. These chapters explore various topics such as comparative studies, ritual studies, lived religion, gender studies, and violence. The authors offer nuanced perspectives and examine the interplay between religion and these themes within the Swedish context.

The concluding chapter by Jenny Berglund and Tim Jensen offers reflections on the study of religion in Sweden, highlighting emerging trends, potential areas of exploration and the evolving nature of religious phenomena.

It is our aim that *The Study of Religion in Sweden: Past, Present and Future* will serve as a comprehensive resource for scholars, students and anyone interested in understanding the multifaceted aspects of religious studies in Sweden. The diverse range of topics covered, combined with the expertise of the contributing authors, provides a thorough examination of the field and its implications for the past, present and future of the study of religion in Sweden.

Notes

1 Works by Max Müller translated into Swedish include *Mytologi och religion, eller om den grekiska mytologiens ursprung och betydelse* (Stockholm: H. Pettersson, 1868), *Inledning till den jemförande religionsvetenskapen* (Stockholm: Seligmann, 1874), *Religionens ursprung och utveckling med särskild hänsyn till Indiens religioner*

(Stockholm: Looström, 1880), *Naturlig religion i utdrag* (Helsingfors: n.p., 1897) and *Bönen i olika religioner: en inblick i jämförande religionsforskning* (Stockholm: Skoglund, 1897).

2 In 2000, at the time of the separation of the Church of Sweden from the state, 83 per cent of the Swedish population were members of the Church. Twenty years later, in 2020, 55 per cent remained members of the Church of Sweden.

3 With this demarcation, we are aware of the complexity of defining when a comparative study of religions emerged in Europe as a distinct field of research. However, this volume and the present introduction does not deal with the pre-history of the History of Religions in Europe. Some of the 'old roots of the discipline' are addressed in Larsson and Sorgenfrei (2019), but this pre-history is also left out of this book while 'the study of religion(s) practiced by these learned scholars [i.e. those comparativists that date to the pre-nineteenth centuries] is confessional, often polemical, almost always explicitly religiously motivated, and deeply immersed in religious world-views and frames of reference', in the words of Stausberg (2008: 298).

4 As pointed out by Stohlander Axelsson (2001b: 65) the liberal theologian and later Professor Pehr Eklund (1846–1911) had already, prior to the appointment of Lehmann, lectured on the subject that today we would call History of Religions.

5 Before this position in Lund, Hartman, like many other Swedes, was awarded a position as professor at the Åbo Akademi, the Swedish university in Åbo/Turko, Finland, in 1956 (Bergman 1976: 20; Stausberg 2008: 307). Even though the connection between Sweden (especially Uppsala University) and Åbo/Turko was and still is strong, there is no systematic study of the relationship between the study of religion in Sweden and Finland. The academic, intellectual and institutional connections between Finland and Sweden remain to be studied in the future.

6 On this debate, see Stausberg (2007: 303), especially footnote 21.

References

Alles, G. (2017), 'Rudolf Otto and the Idea of the Holy', in R. King (ed.), *Religion, Theory, Critique: Classic and Contemporary Approaches and Methodologies*, 213–19, New York: Columbia University Press.

Andersson, D., and Å. Sander, eds (2005), *Det mångreligiösa Sverige. Ett landskap I förändring*, Lund: Studentlitteratur.

Arbman, E. (1949), 'Religionshistoria', in *Stockholms högskola under Sven Tunbergs rektorat*, 115–25, Stockholm: P. A. Norstedt & Söners förlag.

Arvidsson, S. (2006), *Aryan Idols: Indo-European Mythology as Ideology and Science*, Chicago: University of Chicago Press.

Asprem, E., and O. Sundqvist, eds (2021), *Religionshistoria. Enntroductionn till teori och metod*, Lund: Studentlitteratur.

Bergman, J. (1976), 'The History of Religions', in H. Ringgren (ed.), *Uppsala University 500 Years: Faculty of Theology at Uppsala University*, 3–23, Uppsala: Acta Universitatis Upsaliensis.

Berntson, M., and H. Bogdan (2002), *Religionsvetenskap i Göteborg – 25 år*, Gothenburg: Skrifter utgivna vid Institutionen för religionsvetenskap, Göteborgs universitet.

Bexell, O. (2021), *Teologiska fakulteten vid Uppsala universitet 1916–2000. Historiska studier*, Uppsala: Acta Universitatis Upsaliensis.

Bogdan, H. (2016a), 'Initiations and Transitions', in M. Stausberg and S. Engler (eds), *The Oxford Handbook of the Study of Religion*, 582–95, Oxford: Oxford University Press.

Bogdan, H. (2016b), 'Western Esotericism and New Religious Movements', in J. R. Lewis and I. B. Tøllefsen (eds), *The Oxford Handbook of New Religious Movements*, vol. II, 455–68, New York: Oxford University Press.

Casadio, G. (2016), 'NVMEN, Brill and the IAHR in Their Early Years: Glimpses at Three Parallel Stories from an Italian Stance', in T. Jensen and A. W. Geertz (eds), *NVMEN, the Academic Study of Religion, and the IAHR*, 303–48, Leiden: Brill.

Casadio, G., and G. Larsson (2022), 'Geo Widengren's Bibliography', in G. Larsson (ed.), *The Legacy, Life and Work of Geo Widengren and the Study of the History of Religions after World War II*, 386–403, Leiden: Brill.

Drobin, U. (2006), 'Åke Hultkrantz', *Dagens Nyheter*, 10 November. Retrieved from https://www.dn.se/arkiv/familj/ake-hultkrantz/ (accessed 21 November 2020).

Drobin, U. (2008), 'Obituary Åke Hultkrantz (1920–2006)', *Numen* 55 (1): 99–100.

Edsman, C.-M. (1949), *Res aut Verba. Erinringar med anledning av sakkunnigutlåtandena rörande preceptorsbefattningen i religionshistoria vid Uppsala universitet*, Lund: AB. Ph. Lindstedst Univ. Bokhandel.

Edsman, C.-M. (2001), 'Ein halbes Jahrhundert Uppsala-Schule', in M. Stausberg (ed.), *Kontinuität und Brüche in der Religionsgeschichte. Festschrift für Anders Hultgård zu seinem 65. Geburtstag am 23.12.2001*, 194–209, Berlin: Walter de Gruyter.

Enkvist, V. (2013), *Religionsfrihetens rättsliga ramar*, Uppsala: Iustus förlag.

Geels, A., and O. Wikström (1985), *Den religiösa människan. Psykologiska perspektiv. En introduktion till religionspsykologin*, Löberöd: Plus ultra.

Gustafsson, G. (1991), *Tro, samfund och samhälle. Sociologiska perspektiv*, Örebro: Libris

Harrelson, W. (2005), 'Myth and Ritual School', in Lindsay Jones (ed.), *Encyclopedia of Religion*, vol. 9, 6380–3, New York: Thomson Gale.

Hartman, S. (1953), *Gayômart: Étude sur le syncrétisme dans l'ancient Iran*, Uppsala: Almqvist & Wiksell.

Hedin, C. (1997), 'Nathan Söderbloms uppfattningar om islam. Exempel på svensk orientalism', *Tidskrift för Mellanösternstudier* 1: 32–62.

Hjärpe, J. (2022), 'Tor Andæ and Geo Widengren: Perspectives and Purposes of the Study of the History of Religions', in G. Larsson (ed.), *The Legacy, Life and Work of Geo Widengren and the Study of the History of Religions after World War II*, 238–48, Leiden: Brill.

Hofstee, W. (2000), 'Phenomenology of Religion versus Anthropology of Religion? The "Groningen School" 1920–1990', in S. Hjelde (ed.), *Man, Meaning and Mystery: 100 Years of History of Religions in Norway. The Heritage of W. Brede Kristensen*, 173–90, Leiden: Brill.

Hultgård, A. (2002), 'Integrating History of Religions into the Theological Curriculum: Nathan Söderblom and the Emerging Science of Religion', in C. R. Bråkenhielm and G. Winqvist Hollman (eds), *The Relevance of Theology: Nathan Söderblom and the Development of an Academic Discipline*, 133–41, Uppsala: Acta Universitatis Upsaliensis.

Hultkrantz, Å. (1973), *Metodvägar inom den jämförande religionsforskningen*, Stockholm: Esselte studium.

Hultkrantz, Å. (1986a), 'Religionshistoriens vägar under efterkrigstiden. Några personliga erinringar', *Svensk religionshistorisk årsskrift* 2: 7–19.
Hultkrantz, Åke (1986b), 'Olof Pettersson (1920–1986)', *Temenos* 22: 146–8.
Jensen, T., and S. Fujiwara (2022), 'Professor Geo Widengren, IAHR Vice-Preseident 1950–1960, IAHR President 1960–1970, IAHR Honorary Life Member 1996', in G. Larsson (ed.), *The Legacy, Life and Work of Geo Widengren and the Study of the History of Religions after World War II*, 50–70, Leiden: Brill.
Jensen, T., M. Rothstein and J. Podemann Sørensen, eds (1996), *Religionshistoria. Ritualer, mytologi, ikonografi*, Nora: Nya Doxa.
Kahle, S. (2006), 'Johannes Kolmodin: His Youth, Political Thinking, and Life with the Turks Reflected in His Letters to His Parents', in E. Özdalga (ed.), *The Last Dragoman: The Swedish Orientalist Johannes Kolmodin as Scholar, Activist and Diplomat*, 7–70, London: I. B. Tauris.
Kippenberg, H. (2002), *Discovering Religious History in the Modern Age*, Princeton: Princeton University Press.
Larsson, G. (2016a), 'Demography', in R. A. i Segal and K. von Stuckrad (eds), *Vocabulary for the Study of Religion*, 396–401, Leiden: Brill.
Larsson, G. (2016b), 'Power', in R. A. Segal and K. von Stuckrad (eds), *Vocabulary for the Study of Religion*, 103–9, Leiden: Brill.
Larsson, G. (2019), 'It's Not *mana*, It's High Gods! Another Conceptual History or Another Explanation, but a Similar Problem', *Method and Theory in the Study of Religion* 31 (4/5): 447–56.
Larsson, G., ed. (2022a), *The Legacy, Life and Work of Geo Widengren and the Study of the History of Religions after World War II*, Leiden: Brill.
Larsson, G. (2022b), 'Pondering the Legacy of Geo Widengren: Isolated Genius, or Uncritical Supporter of a Band of Brothers?', *Method & Theory in the Study of Religion*, 35 (4): 281–92.
Larsson, G. (2022c), 'Internet', in G. Krämer (ed.), *Encyclopaedia of Islam, TREE*, 51–6, Leiden: Brill.
Larsson, G. (2023), *En stridbar professor i en föränderlig tid*, Stockholm: Langenskiöld.
Larsson, G., and S. Sorgenfrei (2019), *Religion*, Stockholm: Liber.
Lövheim, M., and M. Nordin, eds (2022/2015), *Sociologiska perspektiv på religion i Sverige*, Malmö: Gleerups Utbildning.
Nordin, S. (2004), *Ingemar Hedenius. En filosof och hans tid*, Stockholm: Natur & Kultur.
Nylander, K., ed. (1890), *Orientalistkongressen i Stockholm-Kristiania. Några skildringar från Utlandet*, Upsala: Almqvist & Wiksell.
Olsson, T. (2001), 'Religionshistoria', in B. Olsson, G. Bexell and G. Gustafsson (eds), *Theologicum i Lund. Undervisning och forskning i tusen år*, 76–83, Lund: Arcus.
Österlin, L. (2001), 'Teologi i Lund före 1900', in B. Olsson, G. Bexell and G. Gustafsson (eds), *Theologicum i Lund. Undervisning och forskning i tusen ar*, 11–37, Lund: Arcus.
Otterbeck, J. (2000), *Islam på svenska. Tidskriften Salaam och islams globalisering*, Stockholm: Almqvist & Wiksell International.
Plank, K., and D. Enstedt, eds (2018), *Levd religion. Det heliga i vardagen*, Lund: Nordic Academic Press.
Reenberg Sand, E., and J. Podemann Sørensen, eds (2001), *Edvard Lehmann og religionshistorien. Et symposium ved fagets 100-års jubilæum in Danmark*, København: Institut for Religionshistoire, Københavns Universitet.
Ringgren, H., and Å. V. Ström (1957), *Religionerna i historia och nutid*, Stockholm: Diakonistyrelsen.

Rudolph, K. (2005), 'Religionsgeschichtliche Schule', in L. Jones (ed.), *Encyclopedia of Religion*, vol. 11, 7706–9, New York: Thomson Gale.
Schalk, P. (n.d.), 'Historik', *Swedish Society of Research in the History of Religions*. Retrieved from https://svenskreligionshistoria.wordpress.com/om/ (accessed 11 March 2023).
Stausberg, M. (2007), 'The Study of Religion(s) in Western Europe (I): Prehistory and History until World War II', *Religion* 37 (4): 294–318.
Stausberg, M. (2008), 'The Study of Religion(s) in Western Europe (II): Institutional Developments after World War II', *Religion* 38 (4): 305–18.
Stausberg, M. (2009), 'The Study of Religion(s) in Western Europe (III): Institutional Developments after World War II', *Religion* 39 (3): 261–82.
Stohlander Axelsson, E. (2001a), *Ett brännglas för tidens strålar. Striden om Torgny Segerstedts docentur 1903*, Lund: Arcus.
Stohlander Axelsson, E. (2001b), 'Kring den religionshistoriska professuren i Lund', in E. Reenberg Sand and J. Podemann Sørensen (eds), *Edvard Lehmann og religionshistorien. Et symposium ved fagets 100-års jubilæum in Danmark*, 65–8, København: Institut for Religionshistoire, Københavns Universitet.
Sundén, H. (1974), *Religionspsykologi: problem och metoder*, Stockholm: Proprius.
Thomassen, E. (2022), 'Widengren, Gnosticism, and the Religionsgeschichtliche Schule', in G. Larsson (ed.), *The Legacy, Life and Work of Geo Widengren and the Study of the History of Religions after World War II*, 275–90, Leiden: Brill.
Thurfjell, D. (2019), *Det gudlösa folket. De postkristna svenskarna och religionen*, Stockholm: Norstedts.
Thurfjell, D. (2020), *Granskogsfolk. Hur naturen blev svenskarnas religion*, Stockholm: Norstedts.
Utredningen angående den religionsvetenskapliga utbildningens mål och metoder Religionsvetenskaplig utbildning: betänkande (1971), Stockholm: Utbildningsförlag.
Widengren, G. (1947a), *Tor Andræ*, Uppsala: J. A. Lindblads förlag.
Widengren, G. (1947b), 'Kring begreppet helighet. En orientering i religionshistorisk metod', *Tiden* 5 (39): 282–8.
Widengren, G., and C. J. Bleeker, eds (1969–71), *Historia Religionum: Handbook for the History of Religions*, 2 vols, Leiden: Brill.
Willander, E. (2019), *Sveriges religiösa landskap. Samhörighet, tillhörighet och mångfald under 2000-talet*, Stockholm: SST.

Part I

HISTORICAL APPROACHES

Chapter 1

ANCIENT NEAR EASTERN RELIGIONS

Therese Rodin and Heike Peter

This chapter will examine the research being carried out in Sweden from 1900 until the present, in the field of Ancient Religions, a sub-discipline within the History of Religions. One important way that we have limited this study is that we have focused on scholars working within the field of the History of Religions and largely set aside the contributions made by scholars from subjects such as Egyptology, Old Testament Studies and Classical Studies.

Uppsala and the Study of Iranian Religions

The History of Religions as a research area was established in Sweden at Uppsala University in 1878. However, it began to take off as an independent subject when in 1901 Nathan Söderblom was appointed professor of what was then called 'Theological Prenotions and Theological Encyclopaedia' (Bergman 1976: 3–5). The study of ancient religions in Sweden has developed into two subfields: Ancient Near Eastern religions – represented by ancient Iranian, Mesopotamian and Egyptian religions – and Greek and Roman religions. This chapter reflects this basic division, beginning with an account of the scholarship into Ancient Near Eastern religions and concluding with a survey of the work into Greek and Roman religions. Its aim is to identify the central actors and trends in each research area and discuss the impact and significance their contributions have had to the History of Religions, both in Sweden and abroad.

According to Jan Bergman, Söderblom came to write his doctorate in theology on Iranian religion[1] due to 'circumstances of a partly accidental nature', reading Viktor Rydberg's (1828–1895) studies in comparative German mythology, Friedrich Nietzsche's (1844–1900) *Also sprach Zarathustra* as well as an article by James Moulton (1863–1917) (Bergman 1976: 5–6), a philologist and specialist in Iranian religion. Söderblom defended his thesis successfully at the Sorbonne in 1901, and, as was mentioned, he was appointed Professor in the History of Religions at Uppsala University that same year (Brodd 2005: 374). His thesis is a comparison of the belief in a life after death in the Avestan texts with the same belief in several other religions. Although the phenomenological and comparative approach in Söderblom's doctoral thesis is considered today to be a conventional way of working within the tradition of the History of Religions, at the time it was highly innovative, since it treated these religions in a more or less equal and neutral way.

During Söderblom's time as professor, the Theological Faculty at Uppsala was quite conservative, with its dominance of biblical exegetes who saw Christianity as the true religion and showed little interest in new methods like the historico-critical approach to the Bible (Bergman 1976: 6). However, Söderblom had returned to Sweden from the Sorbonne with a more open attitude towards other religions than Christianity. Even though Söderblom's writing, in Bergman's words, still showed 'a strain of Christian apologetics', he equally had 'an absolute confidence in science' (1976: 6–7). Among other things, Söderblom contributed to the establishment of the Olaus Petri Foundation,[2] which enabled the invitation of distinguished scholars to Uppsala to participate in the so-called Olaus Petri Lectures. Söderblom himself was invited to both Berlin and Leipzig to help found the subject of the History of Religions. He accepted the invitation to Leipzig in 1912 (Bergman 1976: 8), where he held the professor's chair in the History of Religions for two years (Brodd 2005: 374).

Another scholar who became central for the development of the History of Religions in Uppsala was H. S. Nyberg (1889–1974). He was Professor in Semitic Languages but also had a wider interest in the history and religion of the cultures he studied (e.g. Larsson 2018: 184–5). As a young student, he had read a printed copy of Söderblom's inaugural professorial lecture from 1901. It dealt with the introduction of the study of non-Christian religions at Uppsala University. Nyberg later described the bare holding of the text as 'an electric shock', and in the words of his daughter, Sigrid Kahle (1928–2013), this incident 'became decisive for his life' (Kahle 1991: 51, translated from Swedish). Besides Semitic languages, Nyberg also specialized in Iranian languages. According to Geo Widengren, 'the pioneering work of H.S. Nyberg in Uppsala' was the reason for the establishment of a school of Iranian studies within the field of the History of Religions in Uppsala (Widengren, in Hultgård 2022: 75, translated from German).

Widengren himself has been called 'one of the most famous historians of religions of the twentieth century' (Ciurtin 2005: 9732). He was awarded his doctoral degree at the University of Uppsala in 1936 with a thesis where he compared Akkadian and Hebrew psalms of lamentations. According to Göran Eidevall, Professor of Old Testament Studies at Uppsala, his thesis was 'a truly pioneering study' for the time (2022: 40–1). Four years later, Widengren was appointed professor at the same university. With Widengren, the non-denominational perspective on religions initiated by Söderblom took a further step. In Michael Stausberg's words, 'liberating the history of religions from Christian "valuations" – a de-Christianization of the discipline – was one of Widengren's main programmatic aims' (2022: 5). Widengren also contributed substantially to the research in Iranian religion. According to Eugen Ciurtin, Widengren's book *Hochgottglaube im Alten Iran* (1939) has been one of the most important contributions from the 'Swedish school' of studies into Iranian religion (2005: 9732). Widengren was one of the founders of the International Association for the History of Religions (IAHR), as well as of the association's journal *Nvmen* (Larsson 2022: 4, 12). Göran Larsson writes that 'Widengren was important in making progress with the study of the History of Religions as an academic field both in Sweden and internationally' (2022: 4). Nevertheless, Larsson acknowledges that there are very few reviews of Widengren's publications in prestigious scholarly journals (2022: 25-6).

Another Swedish scholar who wrote about Iranian religion was Stig Wikander (1908-1983), who, like Widengren, studied Avestan under Nyberg. Wikander wrote his doctoral thesis about ancient Iranian male war associations (1938). He published two additional books, also about Iranian religion. His books, according to Mihaela Timuş, 'made him known as an eminent Iranist, although he was a controversial representative of the Uppsalian school' (2005: 9735). The controversial part of his thesis was that he applied the Nazi historian Otto Höfler's theory to his material and collaborated closely with him. Furthermore, he even considered publishing his thesis with the Nazi SS-Ahnenerbe publishing house (Arvidsson 2002). There has been a recent revival of the theory of an Iranian male war association (*Männerbund*), which is, for example, reflected in Touraj Daryaee's article 'The Iranian Männerbund Revisited' (2018). Daryaee writes that Wikander's thesis is still probably the most important publication on the topic (2018: 38).

Sven S. Hartman (1917-1988) was a student of Widengren, and he successfully defended his doctoral thesis in 1953 on the subject of Gayōmart, 'the first man' in Iranian literature. He later became Professor in the History of Religions, first at the university in Turku (1965-9) and then in Lund (1969-83). He remained as professor in Lund until his retirement (Bergman 1988: 107; Olsson 1989: 33-4). Hartman's research does not seem to have had a significant influence on the scholarship of Iranian religion or on the History of Religions, neither in Sweden nor internationally.

The latest scholar in Sweden to specialize, at least partially, in Iranian religion is Anders Hultgård,[3] whose doctoral thesis deals with messianic conceptions in Judaism (1971). Hultgård had an international career including visiting professorships abroad. He got a permanent position as Professor in the History of Religions in Uppsala from 1995 (Stausberg 2001: VII), where he stayed until his retirement in 2001. Within the field of Iranian religion, Hultgård specialized in comparisons with ancient Judaism (e.g. 1979, 1982, 1988, 2000). He has written extensively on these themes, and six of his publications are included in the bibliography of the *Wiley Blackwell Companion to Zoroastrianism* (Stausberg and Vevaina 2015). This suggests that his research is still relevant in the field.

The Study of Mesopotamian and Egyptian Religions

Within the study of ancient Mesopotamian religions in Sweden, four scholars are of interest.[4] The first is Efraim Briem (1890-1946). He obtained his doctorate at Lund University in 1918 with a dissertation in Swedish about Sumerian and Babylonian goddesses related to motherhood and fertility. Ten years later, he became a professor at the same university (*Nordisk familjebok* 3 1951: 822). In his overview of Swedish Assyriologists, Jakob Andersson mentions Briem. He writes about Briem's thesis that 'the work is representative of the level of research at that time, and does not come across as a piece of research any less informed than works produced in continental Europe at the time'. Andersson continues that 'had it been written in English, Briem would no doubt have been far more well-known' (2019: 12). Despite writing in Swedish, Briem's work did not have a substantial impact on his Swedish colleagues either, even though several of them worked with cuneiform sources.[5]

Helmer Ringgren (1917–2012) studied the Old Testament and its religious context in the Ancient Near East. His doctoral thesis dealt with the argument that, in the Ancient Near East, 'Word' and 'Wisdom' became hypostatized deities from great gods (1947). His thesis was based on sources in several different languages, among them Akkadian and a little Sumerian. There are a few reviews of Ringgren's thesis. Robert Pfeiffer's has a generally positive tone (1947: 478), while Johannes van der Ploeg questions Ringgren's theory of hypostatization (1948). During the rest of his career, Ringgren continued to study and teach in the fields of both Old Testament Studies and the History of Religions, holding alternating positions in both fields as (associate) professor. His last position was as Professor of Old Testament Studies at Uppsala University (Hidal 2012: 255). Ringgren was a diligent writer, and as Sten Hidal writes, 'a surprisingly large amount of Ringgren's production was student literature' (2012: 255–6, translated from Swedish). His book *Främre Orientens religioner i gammal tid* (1967) is now a classic. It has been translated into English (*Religions of the Ancient Near East* ([1973]1976)) and German (*Die Religionen des alten Orients* (1979)) and was published as a Swedish audiobook in 2003.[6] All of these editions and translations show that his books were quite popular and that he spent much of his time disseminating his research to students as well as a wider audience. This is probably Ringgren's greatest contribution to the study of ancient Mesopotamian religion, which he treated alongside other Ancient Near Eastern religions.

The two other scholars of interest within the field of ancient Mesopotamian religions in Sweden are the authors of this chapter, Heike Peter and Therese Rodin. Peter's doctoral thesis explores how contemporary Hittitologists write about and explain Hittite rituals, showing that they explicitly or implicitly have an evolutionistic approach. Her thesis suggests new methods from Historical Anthropology, applying these on three rituals (2004). A review of Peter's thesis is written by Hittitologist Theo van den Hout. He agrees with her criticism that Hittitologists are not up to date regarding their application of theories of religion, although he points out that Peter could have been more up to date in her use of new transliterations of Hittite texts (2007). Regarding contemporary impact, we have found references to Peter as support for the discussion in Anna Törngren's doctoral thesis in the History of Religions from 2008.

Rodin's thesis is an analysis of the two myths where the Sumerian mother goddess features as one of the central actors (2014). There are several references to Rodin's thesis, primarily in Assyriological publications.⁷ This suggests that her thesis has had an impact on the contemporary research in the field of Assyriology. There are two positive reviews of Rodin's thesis by scholars in the History of Religions (Näsström 2014; Sedláček 2015).

Jan Bergman (1933–1999) introduced Egyptian religion as a new subfield in the History of Religions in Sweden with his thesis about Isis (1968). Widengren was one of his supervisors, as was Torgny Säve-Söderbergh (1914–1998), renowned Professor of Egyptology at Uppsala University.⁸ Bergman succeeded Widengren as professor in 1975 (Bergman 1976: 20-1). Bergman's thesis was mostly well received, although some contemporary reviewers expressed a few criticisms (see Cefarelli 1975 and Smith 1971). R. E. Witt, himself an Isis specialist, was probably the most positive in his assessment (see Witt 1972). Witt writes that Bergman's thesis is 'a key work in a field of increasing interest for students of Hellenistic and Graeco-Roman religion'. He also praises Bergman's extensive bibliography (Witt 1972: 222). On the negative side, Witt points out that Bergman's use of certain sources could have been done with more caution (Witt 1972: 222-3). Several contemporary publications contain references to Bergman's work (e.g. Quack 2002: 99; Billing 2002, 2013; Meyer-Dietrich 2001, 2006, 2018).

In 2001, Erika Meyer-Dietrich, a student of Bergman, presented her doctoral thesis, which is an interpretation of a coffin from the Middle Kingdom. Reviews of her thesis have been very positive. The Egyptologist Louise Gestermann states that Meyer-Dietrich's 'ecology of religion' model is highly innovative (2003). Håkan Rydving, a scholar of the History of Religions, also praises her work (2004). Meyer-Dietrich's second book, written about another coffin from the Middle Kingdom (2006), has also been well received, and through it she received the title of Associate Professor at Uppsala University. The Egyptologist Rune Nyord writes about this book that it is 'an inspiring and important contribution to our understanding of funerary religion in the Middle Kingdom' (2008: 368). Meyer-Dietrich has gone on to publish two books about sound in ancient Egyptian culture (2011, 2018). She has also co-edited a book called *The Pyramids: Between Life and Death; Proceedings of the Workshop Held at Uppsala University, May 31st to June 1st., 2012* (Hein, Billing and Meyer-Dietrich 2016). Meyer-Dietrich has clearly been an active scholar, and her work has been well received in the scholarly community.

A third Swedish scholar in the field of Egyptian religion is Nils Billing, who received his ThD in the History of Religions in 2013 with a thesis where he interpreted the architecture of a pyramid through ritual theory. Billing already had a PhD in Egyptology from 2002, with a thesis about the goddess Nut. Today he works as an Assistant Professor in the History of Religions at Uppsala University. He has written several popular books about Egyptian religion (2009, 2016, 2023) and contributed to a book about Antiquity (2017). Furthermore, he is a co-editor of the above-mentioned book about the pyramids (Hein, Billing and Meyer-Dietrich 2016). Meyer-Dietrich refers to Billing in several of her publications (e.g. 2006, 2018).

The Study of Greek and Roman Religions

Turning to the study of Greek and Roman religions in Sweden since 1900, we present the scholars in chronological order. Although several dissertations on Greek and Roman religion were completed in Sweden before this date, most of them were conducted at the departments of Classical Archaeology and Ancient History at Uppsala or Lund. According to the Swedish national library catalogue since 1900, about one hundred dissertations by Swedish scholars have been produced on topics relating to Greek religion and about fifty-three on Roman religion (catalogue –1957 and libris.kb.se 03-09-23). When the History of Religions was starting to grow as a separate discipline, in the decades after 1900, both Torgny Segerstedt and Efraim Briem published texts on Greek and Roman religions (Segerstedt 1905; Briem 1928), but it was Erland Ehnmark (1903–1966) who wrote the first dissertation on Greek religion from the perspective of the History of Religions in Sweden. He defended his thesis in 1935 at Uppsala University and then moved to Lund where he was inaugurated as Professor of History and the Psychology of Religion in 1949 (Ehnmark 1950).

Ehnmark had studied classical languages, history and philosophy, and he had been quite close to M. P. Nilsson (1874–1967) (Bengtsson 1967; Pettersson 1967; Schalk 1987), one of the most famous Swedish scholars on Greek religion (cf. Gjerstad 1968). Ehnmark's thesis examines the ideas of God in the Homeric epics (1935) and combines philological methods with theories from Comparative Religion. Even though a common understanding at the time, Ehnmark denied that a pre-animistic theory of religion and an impersonal power could be verified in Greek literature. Another example of the new understandings he constructed was his proposition that the anthropomorphism of the gods was a result of the mythical style of the texts. Religion was clearly treated as a human reaction (Ehnmark 1939: 210–11; cf. Pettersson 1967: 180). Besides Greek religion, Ehnmark published on theories of comparative religion in general (1949, 1956), wrote for students on world religions (1955, 1960, 1966) and for a broader audience (Ehnmark and Öjvind 1962). He returned to Greek authors regularly (e.g. Ehnmark 1939, 1946, 1957, 1960, 1965), and 'from these he developed his life-long interest in the religious ideas of the Greeks', as Olof Pettersson expressed it in an obituary of him (1967: 179). Ehnmark was entrusted with the revision of Nilsson's *Geschichte der griechischen Religion* (Bengtsson 1967), a great honour which may account for his wider international impact.

Alongside Ehnmark, Carl-Martin Edsman (1911–2010) is an important figure within the Swedish study of Greek and Roman religions. Like Söderblom, he studied at the Sorbonne in Paris, and, back in Sweden, he defended his second thesis (the first was in the field of theology) in 1949 on the purifying role of fire in diverse myths. He applied a phenomenological approach to the question of whether a fire ritual could be the basis for myths of immortality. He concluded that a ritual basis for the myths could not be verified in most cases (Rose 1950: 160). Edsman was appointed as professor in Lund and later in Uppsala (Bexell 2014). He published on a range of religions and in a variety of languages for both students (e.g. 1957, 1971, 1973) and for the general public (e.g. 1950, 1953, 1968). His work, with its distinctive 'folkloristic' emphasis, has been translated into French, German, English and Swedish. That he was entrusted with the prestigious task of concluding a revision of Karl Kerényi's (1897–1973) classical work on Greek and Roman religion from 1969 was an indicator of the esteem with which he was held within his scholarly discipline.

After the generation of Ehnmark and Edsman, Britt-Mari Näsström was the first Swedish scholar working within this field. She defended her dissertation in 1986 at the University of Gothenburg where she subsequently also became professor. Her thesis examines the emperor Julian's discourse on the mother of the gods, and in 1990, it was published in a second edition. Her second book, on the self-castration of Attis in a poem of Catullus (1989a), shows Näsström's continued interest in the study of gender questions in Antiquity. It treats this act of self-castration relative to the spheres of man, woman and the androgyne, and was reviewed in the recognized journal *The Classical Review* (Dowden 1991). Näsström started her scholarly career in the study of Roman religion (1986), then deepened her study of Antiquity with a consideration of Greek religion (1992) and since then has branched out into a consideration of Old Norse religion (1994).

In all of her publications, Näsström has maintained her interest in goddesses. They have formed a trail in her research on ancient Mediterranean and Old Norse religion. Kybele, Aphrodite and Nerthus are just some examples of the goddesses she has returned to in her monographs (Näsström 1989b, 1997, 1998, 2009, 2019). She describes the development, contexts and importance of these godly figures for their adherents. Understandings of goddesses was also a central feature of her work together with international researchers (Billington and Green 1996). Besides her study of deities, Näsström has also investigated myths and rituals in the Mediterranean world and the northern hemisphere (e.g. Näsström 1989a, 1997). Like Ehnmark and Edsman, Näsström has written for diverse audiences. Her books for university students on Mediterranean and Roman religions have been published in several editions (2003, 2005). As an author, she is widely read in Scandinavia, especially on Roman and Old Norse religions.

Since Näsström, there have not been more than four theses about Greek or Roman religion within the subject, namely Gabriella Gustafsson (now Gabriella Beer) (Gustafsson 1999), Per Lerjeryd (2000), Anna Törngren (2008) and Paulina Partanen (2016). Beer, now Assistant Professor in the History of Religions at Uppsala University, investigated in her doctoral thesis rituals of *evocatio* in Republican Rome (Gustafsson 1999). She observed the complex relationship between historiography and myth in the narratives of the ritual and highlighted their un-fixedness, against a quite common prejudice about Roman religion. After completing her thesis, Beer continued to publish on aspects of Roman religion (e.g. Gustafsson 2002, 2016). In all her writings, she demonstrates an interest in the theory of religion which shows, for example, in the way she treats terms and concepts such as 'divination' or 'eschatology' (e.g. 2016, 2024). Beer has been, and continues to be, involved in several international philological projects, working together with Jörg Rüpke from Erfurt University, one of the most prominent recent scholars on Roman religion (cf. Gustafsson 2015b). She has also written for international encyclopaedias (2015a).

Lerjeryd's thesis critically engages with Mithraism over a long-term perspective. He shows that, because of a lack of sources, there has been the construction of a meta-text on Mithraism as a monolithic religion, but he stresses its diversity instead (2000). He seems not to have published any additional writings within this field. The same is true for Törngren, a former student of Ehnmark, who maintained her interest in Greek religion, sparked while a student, to write a doctoral thesis about the central concept of *psychê* in Homer (2008). Like Peter, she sought to apply a perspective of Historical Anthropology. Her theoretical interest is also exposed in other works, where she has written on Marxism and religion (1968, 1969). Partanen has also adopted a theoretical approach to the Homeric Odyssey in her thesis where she deconstructs the space of the female immortal threat (2016). She uses gender theory inspired by Judith Butler and Jack Halberstam to question sexuality as the dominant focus in the reading of these adventures. Partanen states that the female immortal can operate both as the mortal female and the mortal male and can, by so doing, exceed the status of the male gender.

Scholarly work in Sweden on Greek and Roman religions within the field of Indo-European studies is worthy of separate mention. One of the most important scholars in this field is Peter Jackson Rova. Jackson Rova has been a productive author, writing especially about myths within the Indo-European context both for his doctoral thesis and in subsequent publications. In his thesis, he uses not only Greek and Roman sources but also those from other Indo-European traditions (Jackson 1999a). Within the field of Roman and Greek religions, he has published philological articles and monographs on subjects such as ritual speech, eschatological themes and sacrifices (2005, 2006, 2014). In general, Jackson Rova tends to raise theoretical questions regarding the role of language such as in oral and written traditions and the rhetorical and economic dimensions of rites and myths (e.g. 1999b, 2005). Like Beer, he is involved in European research projects together with scholars from different disciplines and has published in international encyclopaedias (e.g. Jackson 2011, 2014, 2020–5).

In the later part of the twentieth and early twenty-first century, there have been several theses written on Gnostic religions (Vramming 1983; Hagman 1994; Peste 2002; Magnusson 2006) that have drawn on the History of Religions approach rather than theological questions. The lack of space does not allow us to explore this area of research. However, it is interesting that all of these authors worked explicitly with methods and theories from the History of Religions, not theology *per se*. Jörgen Magnusson, for example, argued for a perspective taken from the Sociology of Religions and treated the gnostic movement within its Hellenistic contexts, as did Jonathan Peste (Magnusson 2006, 2019; Peste 2002).

Conclusions

This chapter has shown that individuals as well as scholarly traditions have been essential in the development of the study of Ancient Religions in Sweden. Söderblom introduced the study of Iranian religion into Swedish universities and Nyberg played an important role in the continuation of that research, as did Widengren. Ehnmark and Edsman undertook a similar role in the promotion of the study of Greek and Roman religions in Sweden. Every scholar discussed here has contributed to the development of the History of Religions in Sweden in one way or another. Some have also been part of the formation of their field of research on an international level. Some of the themes that Swedish scholars have consistently focused on are philology, 'de-Christianization', internationalization, international collaboration and popularization.

Unfortunately, the amount of research on religions of Antiquity within the subject of History of Religions in Sweden is quite low in comparison with other areas. Except for the study of Old Norse religion, History of Religions in this country is primarily concerned with world religions or new religious movements. Work on cuneiform, hieroglyphs and other classical sources on ancient religions are being published in the fields of archaeology and philology. It is difficult to become an expert in two subjects, and the time-consuming effort to read and understand ancient texts does not seem to fit with actual academic praxis.

One final point that comes to the fore when studying these pioneers is that during the first hundred years, almost all of them were men. It was not until 1986 that Näsström became the first woman in Sweden to be awarded a PhD in the field of Ancient Religions, and it was only in 2001 that Meyer-Dietrich became the first Swedish woman with a PhD in the subfield of Ancient Near Eastern religions. Why has this been the case? The absence of women from the historical origins of the field of Ancient Religions in Sweden and their subsequent entrance into that field would be an interesting theme for future research.[9]

Notes

1 Regarding the choice of the term 'Iranian religion' and not Zoroastrianism, see Anders Hultgård (2022: 76) as well as Albert de Jong (2022: 110, 112–13).
2 The foundation was named after Olaus Petri (1493–1552), the man who implemented the Protestant reformation of the Swedish Church.
3 In 1994, a doctoral thesis was produced by Lennart Olsson titled *De avestiska gatha'erna: Inledande studie* (The Avestan Gathas: Introductory Study), but as far as we are aware, he has not published anything in the field since then.
4 Torgny K. Segerstedt had studied Akkadian and used it in his thesis (1903), but he did not continue these studies. The same applies to Widengren (1936).
5 Both Widengren (1936) and Ringgren (1947) used cuneiform sources in their doctoral theses, but neither of them referred to Briem.
6 A further example is the book *Religionerna i historia och nutid* (The Religions in History and the Present) that was written together with Åke V. Ström ([1957] 1993). It was translated into Polish in 1975, with a new edition in 1990, and was turned into a Swedish audiobook in 2004.
7 Such as the book *Mythische Sphärenwechsel*, edited by Annette Zgoll and Christian Zgoll (2020) and *Lieber Mensch als Göttin!*, a doctoral thesis by Dorothee Keßeler (2020). In both cases, Rodin is used to support the argument. In the article

'Engendered Cosmic Spaces in ancient Mesopotamia' by Lorenzo Verderame (2022), her work is only mentioned as a reference.
8   For the contributions of Säve-Söderbergh, see, for example, *Ägypten und Nubien* (1941), *Temples and Tombs of Ancient Nubia* (1987) and *Uppdrag Nubien* (1996).
9   Ingvild Gilhus has only recently emphasized the need for research about the emergence and impact of women in these scholarly environments (2022: 1–2, 7–8).

References

Andersson, J. (2019), 'Do Not Study Assyrian! A Survey of Swedish Assyriological and Ancient Near Eastern Researchers ca. 1760–2000', in M. Karlsson (ed.), *The Rod and Measuring Rope: Festschrift for Olof Pedersén*, 162–83, Wiesbaden: Harrassowitz Verlag.

Arvidsson, S. (2002), 'Stig Wikander och forskningen om ariska mannaförbund', *CHAOS* 38: 55–68.

Beer, G. (2024), 'Evocatio', in D. K. Falk and R. A. Werline (eds), *Prayer in the Ancient World (1)*, Leiden: Brill Academic.

Bengtsson, H. (1967), 'Vorwort des Herausgebers zur dritten Auflage', in M. P. Nilsson (ed.), *Geschichte der griechischen Religion: Erster Band*, Handbuch der Altertumswissenschaften, München: Beck.

Bergman, J. (1968), *Ich bin Isis: Studien zum memphitischen Hintergrund der griechischen Isisaretalogien*, Uppsala: Uppsala University.

Bergman, J. (1976), 'The History of Religions', in H. Ringgren (ed.), *Uppsala University 500 Years 1, Faculty of Theology at Uppsala University*, 3–23, Uppsala: Acta Universitatis Upsaliensis.

Bergman, J. (1988), 'In Memoriam: Sven S. Hartman 22.6.1017 – 1.4.1988', *Svensk religionshistorisk årsskrift* 3: 104–7.

Bexell, O. (2014), 'Prokanslerämbetets avveckling och frågan om Nathan Söderbloms utnämning 1914', in P. Ström (ed.), *Nya professorer: Installation 2014*, 7–41, Uppsala: Acta Universitatis Upsaliensis.

Billing, N. (2002), *Nut: The Goddess of Life in Text and Iconography*, Uppsala: Uppsala University.

Billing, N. (2009), *Egyptens pyramider: Evighetens arkitektur i forntid och nutid*, Stockholm: Carlsson.

Billing, N. (2013), *The Performative Structure: Ritualizing the Pyramid of Pepy I*, Uppsala: Uppsala University.

Billing, N. (2016), *De dödas bok: den fornegyptiska dödsboken i översättning och kommentar*, Stockholm: Carlsson.

Billing, N. (2023), *Unis pyramid – Död och förvandling i en fornegyptisk kungagrav*, Stockholm: Carlsson.

Billing, N., S. Carlsson, R. Hedlund, A. Klynne, M. Lindblom and H. Montgomery (2017), *Antiken: Från faraonernas Egypten till romarrikets fall*, Stockholm: Natur & Kultur.

Billington, S., and M. Green, eds (1996), *The Concept of the Goddess*, London: Routledge.

Briem, E. (1918), *Studier över moder- och fruktbarhetsgudinnorna i den sumerisk-babyloniska religionen*, Lund: Lund University.

Briem, E. (1928), *Zur Frage nach dem Ursprung der hellenistischen Mysterien*, Lunds universitets årsskrift, Första avdelningen, 25: 5, Lund: Lund University.

Brodd, S.-E. (2005), 'Nathan Söderblom – religionshistoriker, ärkebiskop och internationell ekumenisk kyrkoledare', in I. Brohed (ed.), *Sveriges kyrkohistoria: religionsfrihetens och ekumenikens tid*, 374–80, Malmö: Verbum.

Cefarelli, N. (1975), 'Reviewed Work(s): *Ich bin Isis: Studien zum memphitischen Hintergrund der griechischen Isisaretalogien* by Jan Bergman', *Journal of Near Eastern Studies* 34 (4): 285–8.

Ciurtin, E. (2005), 'Widengren, Geo', in L. Jones (ed.), *Encyclopedia of Religion*, 2nd edn, 9732–4, Detroit: Macmillan Reference.

Daryaee, T. (2018), 'The Iranian *Männerbund* Revisited', *Iran and the Caucasus* 22: 38–49.

de Jong, A. (2022), 'The Eclipse of Geo Widengren in the Study of Iranian Religions', in G. Larsson (ed.), *The Legacy, Life and Work of Geo Widengren and the Study of the History of Religions after World War II*, 89–124, Leiden: Brill.

Dowden, K. (1991), 'Reviewed Work: Britt-Mari Näsström: The Abhorrence of Love: Studies in Rituals and Mystic Aspects in Catullus' Poem of Attis, Uppsala', *The Classical Review, New Series* 41: 501–2.

Edsman, C.-M. (1949), *Ignis Divinus: Le feu comme moyen de rajeunissement et d'immortalité: contes, légendes, mythes et rites*, Lund: Gleerup.

Edsman, C.-M. (1950), *Nödelden: Gammal västgötamagi i religionshistorisk belysning*, Uppsala: Uppsala universitet.

Edsman, C.-M. (1953), *Studier i jägarens förkristna religion: Finska björnjaktsriter. Tillika ett bidrag till frågan om kyrkan och folklig tro och sed. Särtryck ur kyrkohistorisk Årsskrift*, Uppsala: Svenska kyrkohistoriska föreningen.

Edsman, C.-M. (1957), *Religionshistoriska urkunder*, Stockholm: Svenska Bokförlaget.

Edsman, C.-M. (1968), *Myt, saga, legend*, Stockholm: Sveriges radios förlag.

Edsman, C.-M. (1971), *Asiens huvudreligioner av idag*, Stockholm: Almkvist & Wiksell.

Edsman, C.-M. (1973), *Antik och modern Sibylla*, Uppsala: Almkvist & Wiksell.

Ehnmark, E. (1935), *The idea of God in Homer*, Uppsala: Uppsala University.

Ehnmark, E. (1939), *Anthropomorphism and miracle*, Uppsala: Lundequistiska bokh.

Ehnmark, E. (1946), 'Fjalar och Oidipus', *Ord och Bild* 55: 15–22.

Ehnmark, E. (1949), *Religionsproblemet hos Nathan Söderblom*, Lund: Gleerup.

Ehnmark, E. (1950), *Religionshistoriens gräns: Installationsföreläsning i Lund den 22. oktober*, Lund: Gleerup.

Ehnmark, E. (1955), *Världsreligionerna*, Stockholm: Folkbildningsserien.

Ehnmark, E. (1956), 'Religion and Magic. Frazer, Söderblom, and Hägerström', *Ethnos* 21: 1–10.

Ehnmark, E. (1957), 'Transmigration in Plato', *Harvard Theological Review* 50 (1): 1–20.

Ehnmark, E. (1960), *Etiska idéer i främmande religioner*, Geijersamfundets akademiska kurser, Stockholm: Bonnier.

Ehnmark, E. (1965), *Processen mot Sokrates och andra studier*, Lund: Gleerup.

Ehnmark, E. (1966), *Levande religioner: Naturfolken, Indien, islam*, Stockholm: Liber.

Ehnmark, E., and J. Öjvind (1962), *Världens bästa sagor i urval*, Stockholm: Natur och kultur.

Eidevall, G. (2022), 'Hebrew Laments in the Light of Mesopotamian Material', in G. Larsson (ed.), *The Legacy, Life and Work of Geo Widengren and the Study of the History of Religions after World War II*, 36–49, Leiden: Brill.

Gestermann, L. (2003), 'Meyer-Dietrich, Erika – Nechet und Nil. Ein ägyptischer Frauensarg des Mittleren Reiches aus religionsökologischer Sicht (Acta Universitatis Upsaliensis, Historia Religionum 18). Uppsala, 2001', *Bibliotheca Orientalis* 60: 594–602.

Gilhus, I. S. (2022), 'Learning from the Past', *Method & Theory in the Study of Religion* 35 (4): 1–13, doi.org/10.1163/15700682-bja10092.

Gjerstad, E. (1968), *Martin P. Nilsson in Memoriam: A Complete Bibliography by Erik J. Knudtzon and Christian Callmer*, Lund: Gleerup.

Gustafsson, G. (1999), *Evocatio deorum: Historical and Mythical Interpretations of Ritualised Conquests in the Expansion of Ancient Rome*, Uppsala: Uppsala University.

Gustafsson, G. (2002), 'Självoffer och syndabockar: rituella, komparativa och mytiska aspekter av devotio-motivet i romersk krigföring', *Svensk religionshistorisk årsskrift* 10: 139–70.

Gustafsson, G. (2015a), 'Evocatio', in E. Orlin (ed.), *The Routledge Encyclopedia of Ancient Mediterranean Religions*, 325, London: Routledge.

Gustafsson, G. (2015b), 'Verbs, Nouns, Temporality and Typology: Narrations of Ritualized Warfare in Roman Antiquity', in B.-C. Otto, S. Rau and J. Rüpke (eds), *History and Religion: Narrating a Religious Past*, 355–70, Berlin: Walter de Gruyter.

Gustafsson, G. (2016), ' "Whoever Is Not with Me Is against Me": Accounts of Rituals Securing the Loyalty of Individual Gods in Republican Rome', in M. Tilly, M. Morgenstern and V. H. Drecoll (eds), *L'adversaire de Dieu/Der Widersacher Gottes: 6. Symposium Strasbourg*, Tübingen, Uppsala 27.-29. Juni 2013, 219–30, Tübingen: Mohr Siebeck.

Hagman, Y. (1994), *Katarerna: Enhet och mångfald inom den kataro-bogomiliska rörelsen*, Ulricehamn: Esclarmonde.

Hartman, S. S. (1953), *Gayōmart: étude sur le syncrétisme dans l'ancien Iran*, Uppsala: Uppsala University.

Hein, I., N. Billing and E. Meyer-Dietrich (2016), *The Pyramids: Between Life and Death; Proceedings of the Workshop Held at Uppsala University, May 31st to June 1st., 2012*, Uppsala: Uppsala University.

Hidal, S. (2012), 'Helmer Ringgren in Memoriam', *Svensk exegetisk årsbok* 77: 255–8.

Hultgård, A. (1971), *Croyances messianiques des Test: XII Patr. Critique textuelle et commentaire des passages messianiques*, Uppsala: Uppsala University.

Hultgård, A. (1979), 'Man as Symbol of God', *Scripta Instituti Donneriani Aboensis*, 10: 110–16.

Hultgård, A. (1982), 'Ecstasy and Vision', *Scripta Instituti Donneriani Aboensis* 11: 218–25.

Hultgård, A. (1988), 'Prêtres juifs et mages zoroastriens. Influences religieuses à l'époque hellénistique', *Revue d'histoire et de philosophie religieuses* 68 (4): 415–28.

Hultgård, A. (2000), 'La chute de Satan. L'arrière-plan iranien d'un logion de Jésus (Luc 10, 18)', *Revue d'histoire et de philosophie religieuses* 80 (1): 69–77.

Hultgård, A. (2022), 'Geo Widengren and the Study of Iranian Religion', in G. Larsson (ed.), *The Legacy, Life and Work of Geo Widengren and the Study of the History of Religions after World War II*, 73–88, Leiden: Brill.

Jackson, P. (1999a), *The Extended Voice: Instances of Myth in the Indo-European Corpus*, Uppsala: Uppsala University.

Jackson, P. (1999b), 'Den viskande Hermes: tankar kring skriftbegreppets religionshistoriska implikationer', *Svensk religionshistorisk årsskrift* 8: 217–41.

Jackson, P. (2005), 'Retracing the Path: Gesture, Memory, and the Exegesis of Tradition', *History of Religions* 45 (1): 1–28.

Jackson, P. (2006), *The Transformations of Helen: Indo-European Myth and the Roots of the Trojan Cycle*, Münchener Studien zur Sprachwissenschaft, Beiheft 23, Dettelbach: Röll.

Jackson, P. (2011), 'Rekonstruktion gemeinsamer Elemente des indogermanischen Sprachgebietes', *Münchener Studien zur Sprachwissenschaft* 65: 123–39.

Jackson, P. (2014), 'A Song Worth Fifty Cows: Graeco-Indo-Iranian Variations on the Etiology of Sacrifice', *Münchener Studien zur Sprachwissenschaft* 68: 101–18.
Jackson Rova, P. (2020–5), *Language and Myths of Prehistory*, project financed by Riksbankens jubileumsfond, https://lamp-project.se (accessed 15 March 2023).
Kahle, S. (1991), *H.S. Nyberg: en vetenskapsmans biografi*, Stockholm: Norstedts.
Keßeler, D. (2020), *Lieber Mensch als Göttin!*, Berlin: Freie Universität Berlin.
Larsson. G. (2018), 'H. S. Nyberg's Encounter with Egypt and the Mu'tazilī School of Thought', *Philological Encounters* 3: 167–92.
Larsson, G. (2022), 'Pondering the Legacy of Geo Widengren: Isolated Genius, or Uncritical Supporter of a Band of Brothers?', *Method & Theory in the Study of Religion* 35 (4): 1–12, doi.org/10.1163/15700682-bja10093.
Lerjeryd, P. (2000), *Mithraismens miljöer: Text, tecken och tolkningsproblem från antikens Rom till nutida religionshistoria*, Stockholm: Stockholms universitet.
Magnusson, J. (2006), *Rethinking the Gospel of Truth: A Study of Its Eastern Valentinian Setting*, Uppsala: Uppsala University.
Magnusson, J. (2019), 'Leaving Religion in Antiquity', in D. Enstedt, G. Larsson and T. T. Mantsinen (eds), *Handbook of Leaving Religions*, 43–54, Leiden: Brill Academic.
Meyer-Dietrich, E. (2001), *Nechet und Nil: Ein ägyptischer Frauensarg des Mittleren Reiches aus religionsökologischer Sicht*, Uppsala: Uppsala University.
Meyer-Dietrich, E. (2006), *Senebi und Selbst: Personenkonstituenten zur rituelle Widergeburt in einem Frauensarg des Mittleren Reiches*, Fribourg: Academic Press.
Meyer-Dietrich, E. (2018), *Auditive Räume des alten Ägypten: die Umgestaltung einer Hörkultur in der Amarnazeit*, Leiden: Brill.
Meyer-Dietrich, E., ed. (2011), *Laut und Leise: der Gebrauch von Stimme und Klang in historischen Kulturen*, Bielefeld: transcript Verlag.
Näsström, B.-M. (1986), *'O Mother of the Gods and Men': Some Aspects of the Religious Thoughts in Emperor Julian's Discourse on the Mother of the Gods*, Göteborg: Göteborgs universitet.
Näsström, B.-M. (1989a), *The Abhorrence of Love: Studies in Rituals and Mystic Aspects in Catullus' Poem of Attis*, Uppsala: Uppsala University.
Näsström, B.-M. (1989b), 'Gudinnans ankomst: introduktionen av Kybeles kult i Grekland och Rom', *CHAOS* 12: 3–16.
Näsström, B.-M. (1990), *'O Mother of the Gods and Men': Some Aspects of the Religious Thoughts in Emperor Julian's Discourse on the Mother of the Gods*, Lund: Plus Ultra.
Näsström, B.-M. (1992), 'Pharmakoi: det antika Greklands syndabockar', *Medusa* 13: 12–17.
Näsström, B.-M. (1994), 'Gudinnans förvandling: från Freyja till Jungfru Maria vid religionsskiftet i Norden', in J. P. Schjødt and U. Drobin (eds), *Myte og ritual i det forkristne Norden*, 95–112, Odense: Odense universitetsforlag.
Näsström, B.-M. (1997), 'Den jordiska och den himmelska Afrodite', *Medusa* 18: 26–34.
Näsström, B.-M. (1998), 'Cybele and Aphrodite: Two Aspects of the Great Goddess', in L. Larsson Lovén and A. Strömberg (eds), *Aspects of Women in Antiquity, Nordic Symposium on Women in Antiquity*, 29–43, Jonsered: Åström.
Näsström, B.-M. (2003), *Forntida religioner*, Lund: Studentlitteratur.
Näsström, B.-M. (2005), *Romersk religion*, Lund: Studentlitteratur.
Näsström, B.-M. (2009), *Nordiska gudinnor: nytolkningar av den förkristna mytologin*, Stockholm: Bonnier.

Näsström, B.-M. (2014), 'Therese Rodin. The World of the Sumerian Mother Goddess. An Interpretation of Her Myths. 2014. Avhandling. Acta Universalis [sic] Upsaliensis 35', *CHAOS* 62: 249–50.
Näsström, B.-M. (2019), 'Gudinnan Kybele i Rom: en receptionshistoria i tre akter', *CHAOS* 71: 109–120.
Nordisk familjebok, encyklopedi och konversationslexikon, 3 (1951), 'Briem', 822, Malmö: Förlagshuset Norden AB.
Nyord, R. (2008), 'Reviewed Work(s): Senebi und Selbst – Personenkonstituenten zur rituellen Wiedergeburt in einem Frauensarg des Mittleren Reiches (Orbis Biblicus et Orientalis 216) by Erika Meyer-Dietrich', *Wiener Zeitschrift für die Kunde des Morgenlandes* 98: 364–77.
Olsson, L. (1994), *De avestiska gatha'erna: Inledande studie*, Lund: Stockholm University.
Olsson, T. (1989), 'Sven S. Hartman *22/6 1917 †1/4 1988: Minnesord av Tord Olsson', in Kungl. Humanistiska vetenskapssamfundet i Lund, *Årsberättelse*, 32–7, Lund: Kungl. Humanistiska vetenskapssamfundet i Lund.
Partanen, P. (2016), *Navigating Female Power: (De-)Constructing the Space of the Immortal Threat in Homer's Odyssey*, Uppsala: Teologiska institutionen.
Peste, J. (2002), *The Poimandres Group in Corpus Hermeticum: Myth, Mysticism, and Gnosis in Late Antiquity*, Göteborg: Göteborgs universitet.
Peter, H. (2004), *Götter auf Erden: Hethitische Rituale aus Sicht historischer Religionsanthropologie*, Lund: Lund University.
Pettersson, O. (1967), 'Obituaries: Erland Ehnmark, 1903–1966', *Temenos* 2: 178–82.
Pfeiffer, R. (1947), 'Reviewed Work(s): *Word and Wisdom: Studies in the Hypostatization of Divine Qualities and Functions in the Ancient Near East* by Helmar [sic] Ringgren', *Journal of Biblical Literature* 66 (4): 477–8.
Quack, J. F. (2002), 'Königsweihe, Priesterweihe, Isisweihe', in J. Assmann (ed.), *Ägyptische Mysterien?*, 95–108, München: Fink.
Ringgren, H. (1947), *Word and Wisdom: Studies in the Hypostatization of Divine Qualities and Functions in the Ancient Near East*, Uppsala: Uppsala University.
Ringgren, H. (1967), *Främre Orientens religioner i gammal tid*, Stockholm: Svenska bokförl.
Ringgren, H. ([1973] 1976), *Religions of the Ancient Near East*, trans. J. Sturdy, London: SPCK.
Ringgren, H. (1979), *Die Religionen des Alten Orients*, trans. Helmhart Kanus-Credé, Göttingen: Vandenhoeck & Ruprecht.
Ringgren, H. (2003), *Främre Orientens religioner i gammal tid*, Enskede: TPB. (audiobook)
Ringgren, H., and Å. V. Ström ([1957] 1993), *Religionerna i historia och nutid*, 9th edn, Malmö: Gleerup.
Ringgren, H., and Å. V. Ström ([1975] 1990), *Religie w przeszłości i dobie współczesnej*, trans. B. Kupis, Warsaw: Krajowa Agencja Wydawnicza.
Ringgren, H., and Å. V. Ström (2004), *Religionerna i historia och nutid*, Enskede: TPB. (audiobook)
Rodin, T. (2014), *The World of the Sumerian Mother Goddess: An Interpretation of Her Myths*, Acta Universitatis Upsaliensis, Historia Religionum 35, Uppsala: Uppsala University.
Rose, H. J. (1950), 'Reviewed Work: Carl-Martin Edsman: Ignis Divinus: le feu comme moyen de rajeunissement et d'immortalié: contes legends mythes et rites, Lund: Gleerup', *The Classical Review* 64: 160–1.

Rydving, H. (2004), 'Erika Meyer-Dietrich, *Nechet und Nil. Ein ägyptischer Frauensarg des Mittleren Reiches aus religionsökologischer Sicht* (Acta Universitatis Upsaliensis. Historia Religionum 18). Uppsala University Library, Uppsala 2001. 328 s.', *CHAOS* 41: 164–6.

Säve-Söderbergh, T. (1941), *Ägypten und Nubien: ein Beitrag zur Geschichte altägyptischer Aussenpolitik*, Lund: H. Olsson.

Säve-Söderbergh, T., ed. (1987), *Temples and tombs of Ancient Nubia: The International Rescue Campaign at Abu Simbel, Philae and Other Sites*, London: Thames & Hudson.

Säve-Söderbergh, T. (1996), *Uppdrag Nubien: hur världen räddade ett lands kulturminnen*, Stockholm: Atlantis.

Schalk, P. (1987), 'Religionshistoria', in Y. Wessman (ed.), *Vetenskap idag*, Lund: Doxa.

Sedláček, T. (2015), 'Therese Rodin, The World of the Sumerian Mother Goddess: An Interpretation of Her Myths, (Historia Religionum 35), Uppsala: Acta Universitatis Upsaliensis 2014, 350 s.', *Religio* 23 (1): 116–20.

Segerstedt, T. (1903), *Till frågan om polyteismens uppkomst: En religionshistorisk undersökning*, Uppsala: Stockholm University.

Segerstedt, T. (1905), *Ekguden i Dodona*, Lunds universitets årsskrift, Lund: Lund University.

Smith, J. Z. (1971), 'Reviewed Work(s): *Ich bin Isis: Studien zum memphitischen Hintergrund der griechischen Isisaretalogien* by Jan Bergman: *Sylloge inscriptionum religionis Isiacae et Sarapiacae* by Ladislaus Vidmann: *Aramaic Ritual Texts from Persepolis* by Raymond A. Bowman', *History of Religions* 11 (2): 236–49.

Söderblom, N. (1901), *La vie future d'après le mazdéisme à la lumière des croyances parallèles dans les autres religions: Étude d'eschatologie comparée*, Paris: Ernest Leroux.

Stausberg, M. (2001), 'Vorwort', in M. Stausberg, O. Sundqvist and A. van Nahl (eds), *Kontinuitäten und Brüche in der Religionsgeschichte: Festschrift für Anders Hultgård zu seinem 65. Geburtstag am 23.12.2001*, VII–X, Berlin: de Gruyter.

Stausberg, M. (2022), 'Taking Stock of the Academic Work of Geo Widengren: Some Observations on a Forgotten Classic and an "All-Round Historian of Religion"', *Method & Theory in the Study of Religion* 35 (4): 1–13. doi.org/10.1163/15700682-bja10091.

Stausberg, M., and Y. S.-D. Vevaina, eds (2015), *Wiley Blackwell Companion to Zoroastrianism*, Chichester: John Wiley & Sons.

Timuș, M. (2005), 'Wikander, Stig', in L. Jones (ed.), *Encyclopedia of Religion*, 2nd edn, 9734–7, Detroit: Macmillan Reference.

Törngren, A. (1968), *Tradition och revolution: Huvuddrag i det europeiska tänkandet*, Staffanstorp: Cavefors.

Törngren, A. (1969), *Opium för folket: Till kritiken av religionshistorien*, Lund: Cavefors.

Törngren, A. (2008), *Psychê själens antropologi i det antika Grekland*, Lunds Studies in History of Religions 24, Lund: Lund University.

Törngren, A., R. Ambjörnsson and A. Elzinga (1969), *Opium för folket: Till kritiken av religionshistorien*, Lund: Cavefors.

van den Hout, T. (2007), 'Reviewed Work(s): *Götter auf Erden: Hethitische Rituale aus Sicht historischer Religionsanthropologie* by Heike Peter', *History of Religions* 47 (1): 104–7.

van der Ploeg, J. (1948), 'Reviewed Work(s): *Word and Wisdom. Studies in the Hypostatization of Divine Qualities and Functions in the Ancient Near East* by Helmer Ringgren', *Revue Biblique* 55 (1): 110–13.

Verderame, L. (2022), 'Engendered Cosmic Regions in Ancient Mesopotamian Mythologies', in K. De Graef, A. Garcia-Ventura, A. Goddeeris and B. A. Nakhai (eds),

The Mummy Under the Bed: Essays on Gender and Methodology in the Ancient Near East, Cutting-Edge Researches in Cuneiform Studies 1, 157–72, Münster: Zaphon.

Vramming, Y. (1983), *Anathema: en vändpunkt i den manikeisk-kristna troskonfrontationen*, Lund: Lund University.

Widengren, G. (1936), *The Accadian and Hebrew Psalms of Lamentation as Religious Documents: A Comparative Study*, Uppsala: Uppsala University.

Widengren, Geo (1939), *Hochgottglaube im alten Iran: Eine religionsphänomenologische Untersuchung*, Uppsala: Lundequistska bokh.

Wikander, S. (1938), *Der arische Männerbund: Studien zur indo-iranischen Sprach- und Religionsgeschichte*, Uppsala, Lund: Håkan Ohlssons Buchdruckerei.

Witt, R. E. (1972), 'Reviewed Work(s): *Ich bin Isis: Studien zum memphitischen Hintergrund der griechischen Isisaretalogien* by J. Bergman', *The Journal of Hellenistic Studies* 92: 222–3.

Zgoll, A., and C. Zgoll (2020), *Mythische Sphärenwechsel: Methodisch neue Zugänge zu antiken Mythen in Orient und Okzident*, Berlin: De Gruyter.

Chapter 2

OLD NORSE RELIGION

Olof Sundqvist

The concept *Old Norse* is a philological term which has been given as a general meaning of early Scandinavia, referring to a geographic area, including Denmark, Sweden, Norway and Iceland. It should be noticed, however, that this linguistic category does not coincide with the geographic boundaries of the Nordic countries, but rather to that part of the Nordic area whose population spoke Old Norse languages (Nordberg 2012: 122–3). Actually, these languages sprung from a proto-Nordic language, which around AD 600–800 was divided into a West Nordic language, called *Old Norse*, and East Nordic languages, called *Old Danish* and *Old Swedish* (Wessén [1965]1975: 29–102). Most scholars use the term *Old Norse* today as a linguistic concept for all the Germanic languages spoken in early Scandinavia. The concept *Old Norse* has also developed into a religious category. In the present survey, the term *Old Norse religion* refers to the religion, which was used by the people who spoke Old Norse languages during the Late Iron Age in Scandinavia and the early Middle Ages (*c.* 550–1100).[1] In what follows, the Swedish research on this religion is surveyed.

Brief Historical Overview (1500–1900)

Early Histography

During the Vasa era, in the mid-sixteenth century, Humanist achievements, including questions related to the cultural and religious heritage, were essential for the Swedish state formation. There was a competition between Sweden and Denmark, with war not only on the battlefield but also on the cultural field. In the latter case, the intention was to create a national history which also aimed at legitimizing political ambitions of the nation (cf. Malm 2018a: 188). An ancient glorious history and old monuments became important ideological arguments in this discourse. Two important agents to these nationalistic aspirations were the brothers Johannes Magnus (1488–1544) and Olaus Magnus (1490–1557). Both were in long-term exile in Rome away from King Gustav Vasa Eriksson (r. 1523–60).

Johannes Magnus's main work *Historia de omnibvs Gothorvm Sveonvmqve regibvs* (1554) had an anti-Danish tendency. It aimed at showing that the Goths actually had their origin in Sweden, where one of Noah's sons called Magog had settled after the Flood. His sons were the eponymous Suenno, Ubbo and Siggo, who lived in Suenia, Uppsala and Sigtuna. By means of relating the national origins to Noah's descendants, Johannes achieved an authoritative historical past for Sweden in his chronicle. Although the pre-Christian religion of the Goths included human sacrifices and certain delusions regarding the gods, Johannes framed these customs in a sympathetic way (Malm 2018a: 191). He also described the temple of Uppsala as the centre of the Nordic countries, where the three gods Óðinn, Þórr and Fricco-Frigga were worshipped. Olaus Magnus's *Historia de gentibus septentrionalibus* ([1555]1982) was more influential than his brother's work. It covered various themes concerning the old customs of the Nordic peoples, including religious practices. Olaus repeated Johannes's information about the Uppsala temple, but he developed this description with more details (Book 3, chapter 6). He also described the three major gods, Óðinn, Þórr and Frigga (Venus) (Book 3, chapter 3).

From Latin Texts to Old Norse Sources

The scholars of the sixteenth century were more or less restricted to the Latin sources. During the seventeenth century, medieval parchments written in Old Norse were collected by antiquarians on Iceland. In 1643, an old parchment, later called *Codex Regius* (GkS 2365 4to) (*c.* 1270), came into the hands of the Icelandic bishop Brynjólfur Sveinsson (1605–1675). It included the Eddic poems and was called the *Sæmundar Edda* (*Edda Sæmundi multiscii*), since it was believed to have been written by a predecessor of Snorri Sturluson (1179–1241), Sæmundr Sigfússon (1056–1133). Brynjólfur had previously owned a parchment, today called *Codex Upsaliensis* (DG 11 4to) (*c.* 1300–25). It begins with the following sentence: 'This book is called Edda. Snorri Sturluson has compiled it in the manner in which it is arranged here' (Heimir Pálsson 2012: 6–7). Brynjólfur donated this codex in 1639 to the Danish collector Stephanus Johannis Stephanius. His widow sold it in 1651, together with some other manuscripts, to Magnus Gabriel De la Gardie in Sweden. He donated it in 1669, together with other manuscripts (totally sixty-five books), including the Silver Bible (Codex Argenteus), to Uppsala University Library, where it is stored today (Grape 1962: 9–23).

Some Old Norse texts were also printed during the seventeenth century. Parts of the Poetic Edda (*Vǫluspá* and *Hávamál*) together with Snorri's *Edda* were published by Peder Resen (1625–1688) in his *Edda Islandorum* 1665. *Gautreks saga* was edited by antiquarians Olaus Verelius (1618–1682) and Johannes Schefferus (1621–1679) and printed in Uppsala 1664. A passage in it was essential for the widespread notion that old and sick people in ancient times throw themselves down from a high cliff called *ætternisstapi* (family cliff), in Swedish *ättestupa* (Malm 2018a: 204–6).

In Denmark and Sweden, runic inscriptions were studied and documented. A pioneer in this field was the Dane Ole Worm (1588–1654), who published a book called *Literatura runica* (1636) and later the more impressive work *Danicorum monumentorum libri sex* (1643), where the runes were related to old religious customs. In Sweden, the runes were also a topic of interest for antiquarians. Johannes Bureus (1568–1652) printed an ABC-book in 1611 using runes instead of Latin characters, while his major work on runes *Monumenta Sveo-Gothica* was published in 1624, with illustrations of a number of Swedish runestones and comments on their religious contexts (on Bureus's world view, see e.g. Jackson Rova forthcoming).

Rudbeck, Old Uppsala and the Swedish Empire

Olaus Verelius was also involved in an infected dispute with Johannes Schefferus concerning the location of the pre-Christian temple called Ubsola (Uppsala), described by Adam of Bremen in his *Gesta Hammaburgensis Ecclesiae Pontificum* (c. 1075). Schefferus had argued that it originally was located in present-day Uppsala, at Domberget (Herrens berg), where the archbishop cathedral is erected. Together with Olaus Rudbeck (1630–1702), Verelius opposed this theory. They argued that the tower of Old Uppsala church included remains of the old pagan sanctuary, which was still visible (see Alkarp 2009). In his *Atlantica* (1679–1702), Rudbeck stated further that Sweden was the legendary island of Atlantis described by Plato in his *Critias*. The Poseidon temple mentioned there, as well as Adam of Bremen's temple, referred both to the pre-Christian sanctuary located in Old Uppsala. With an euhemerized method, he explained that the pagan deities worshipped in that temple actually were ancient kings, who, due to their actions and merits, had been so famous that they came to be understood as gods by the ancient Swedes (cf. Malm 2018a: 211). Rudbeck's grandiose and imaginative interpretations of Old Uppsala gained an important ideological significance during the era of Swedish empire.

The Reception in the Eras of Enlightenment and Romanticism

The Enlightenment led to a crisis of authority regarding religious belief systems. Deism was the form of religious belief which was most congenial with Enlightenment philosophers. Another important movement in the contemporary thinking was towards rationalism in terms of the so-called universal 'natural religion' (Clunies Ross 2018a: 250). Scholars now stated that the Old Norse religion was not just a barbaric superstition but a Germanic-Scandinavian version of this universal religion (Lönnroth 2018: 280). In the Swedish context, historian Olof von Dalin (1708–1763) applied some Enlightenment ideas to Old Norse religion and mythology in his *Svea rikes historia* (1747–62). With support from Old Norse texts, he also attacked Rudbeck's far-reaching ideas about the glorious history of the Swedes. At the same time, he praised the Old Norse religion and believed that it was as enlightened as that one formed by the ancient Egyptians, Chaldeans and Persians (Lönnroth 2018: 276). During the Enlightenment and Romanticism periods in Sweden, not so much the histography as cultural, artistic and aesthetic interpretations of Old Norse religion were developed, perhaps most purely in the movement called Gothicism. Inspired by the natural philosophy of Schelling, Swedish Romantic poets, such as Per Daniel Amadeus Atterbom (1790–1855), Pehr Henrik Ling (1776–1839), Erik Gustaf Geijer (1783–1847), Essias Tegnér (1782–1846) and Carl Johan Love Almqvist (1793–1866), interpreted the Old Norse religion and mythology in poetic expressions (Malm 2018b; Skånby forthcoming). Gothicist interpretation of Old Norse mythology had a great impact also on painting and sculpture in Sweden (Grandien 2018).

Comparative Religion

During the nineteenth century, there was a general need among antiquarians for reliable text editions, not least of the Old Norse mythological texts. Text-critical editions were thus published, as well as grammars and dictionaries. The Dane Rasmus Kristian Rask (1787–1832) as well as the Germans Franz Bopp (1791–1867) and Jacob Grimm (1785–1863) were all instrumental in this process (Clunies Ross 2018b: 581–9). The development of the Old Norse philology coincided with the scholarly paradigm, often called comparative philology, where, for instance, the Indo-European languages were compared. This paradigm also came to influence the comparative study of ancient religions (Nordberg 2013: 109–98). Friedrich Max Müller (1823–1900) laid the grounds for the study of comparative religion, by comparing the myths from all Indo-European people in his *Comparative Mythology* (1854). Max Müller considered that Johann Wolfgang von Goethe's (1749–1832) 'dictum' about language also applied to religion: 'He who knows one, knows none.'[2] Max Müller's research is usually designated 'the nature mythology school'. The name of the Vedic sky god, for example, was *Dyaus* (*pitr*), '(father) Heaven'. This name was historically and linguistically related to other Indo-European sky gods, such as, for example, the Greek *Zeus*, the Roman *Jupiter* (**Djous pater*) and Old Norse *Týr* (**Tīwaz*). These gods all seemed to derive from an older Indo-European god **Dyeus*, whose name was identical to the noun **dyeus*, which means both 'god (in general)' and '(the shining day's) sky'. According to Max Müller, such connections showed that the sky god was a personification of the daytime sky, which in turn originally constituted a poetic representation of 'the Eternal' manifested in the heavenly light. In the Swedish context, Viktor Rydberg (1828–1895) published his *Undersökningar i germanisk mythologi* (1886–9), where he maintained the comparative approach of Max Müller. By means of this method, he stated, it is possible 'to distinguish between older and younger elements of Teutonic mythology, and to secure a basis for studying its development through centuries which have left us no literary monuments' (Rydberg 1889: 21).

This type of comparative research reached its peak later through the works of the French historian of religions and mythologist Georges Dumézil's structuralist and comparative studies of traditions from the Indo-European language area. Dumézil (1898–1986) argued that Old Norse myths and especially the world of gods that it presents were taxonomically structured in the same way as the pantheon of other Indo-European mythological systems, including Indo-Iranian, Greek, Roman,

Baltic, Slavic and the Celtic traditions. This common Indo-European ideology was composed of three fundamental principles: (1) the maintenance of cosmic and juridical order, (2) the exercise of physical prowess and (3) the promotion of physical well-being. The Æsir gods Óðinn and Týr were related to the first function, Þórr to the second, while the Vanir deities (Njǫrðr, Freyr and Freyja) were connected to the third function. Dumézil had many connections to Sweden. He taught French at Uppsala University between 1931 and 1933. He became a friend to the famous Iranist H. S. Nyberg (1889–1974) and his students Stig Wikander (1908–1983) and Geo Widengren (1907–1996), who both became professors at Uppsala University. Via them, he became acquainted with the Austrian Germanist and folklorist Otto Höfler (1901–1987), who also was a guest lecturer at Uppsala University. Widengren dedicated the second edition of his *Religionens värld* (1953) to Dumézil, and he also wrote a friendly foreword to the Swedish translation of Dumézil's *Les dieux des Germains* (1959), *De nordiska gudarna* (1962) (Arvidsson 2006; Larsson 2022). Dumézil in turn exerted a great influence on the Swedish historian of religions Åke V. Ström (1909–1994) (Uppsala University and University of Lund) (see further below).

Key Issues and Scholars in the Twentieth-Century Research

From an Interdisciplinary Approach to a Disciplinary Division

During the first half of the twentieth century, the study of Old Norse religion was a multidisciplinary field. Researchers from different disciplines, such as archaeology, folkloristics, place-name research and the history of religions, were able to approach one and the same problem area in the study of Old Norse religion with different methods, because the borders between these academic fields were still diffuse. Actually, they were merely aspects of a grand cultural historical discipline (cf. Nordberg 2013: 203–389). However, between the 1930s and 1950s, the interest in pre-Christian religion within place-name research and folkloristics fell, and soon archaeology came to follow, which contributed to a fragmentation of the research field. The reasons for this development are not easy to explain; however, the increasing institutionalization of European universities could be one cause. This development probably created academic boundaries between the scientific disciplines, which also led to a specialization of research interests within the individual discipline and certain territorial claims in relation to other research fields. In Sweden, folklorist Carl Wilhelm von Sydow (1878–1952) (University of Lund) and his disciples strongly stated that it was not possible to study Old Norse religion from the perspective of folkloristics, while the Professor in Nordic Languages and Place-name Research Jöran Sahlgren (1884–1971) (University of Lund and Uppsala University) and his followers stated the same about place-names. Names should not be used as sources when studying Old Norse religion, since interpretations of them were regarded as a risky business. Valid interpretations could only be carried out by a few trained linguist-specialists. Using place-names in the study of religion was, in general, considered as dangerous (Swedish *farligt*) by Sahlgren (Hellberg 1986: 42–4; see below). Also, many archaeologists, belonging to the research paradigm called 'Processual Archaeology' – which had a positivist character and advocated an increased use of natural science methods and theories within the field – lost their interest in the history of religions during the 1960s. Previously, during the first half of the century, a number of archaeologists at Uppsala University, such as Oscar Almgren (1869–1945), Birger Nerman (1888–1971), Sune Lindquist (1887–1976) and folklorist Hilding Celander (1876–1965) (University of Gothenburg) contributed to the field of Old Norse mythology and religion with important ideas. In the period from the 1960s to the 1980s, it was basically only philologists and historians of literature and religion who devoted themselves to Norse religion, and, for natural reasons, mythology was at the centre of this research, because the myth-traditions were the best-preserved sources. These scholars thus became more isolated in this field of research, and the study of ancient Scandinavian religion became almost identical with the study of Old Norse mythology for some decades.

Source Criticism, Philology and Comparative Approaches

A radical change in the study of Old Norse religion appeared during the late nineteenth century when several scholars argued that Christian elements could be discerned in, for instance, the myth of Óðinn's hanging on the tree in *Hávamál* (stanzas 138–41). The one who most thoroughly discussed this theme was the Norwegian Sophus Bugge (1833–1907), who used a philological approach to the study of Old Norse mythology. Bugge (1881-9) applied a radical source criticism and claimed that earlier researchers increasingly wanted to see a Germanic-Nordic background in the Eddic poems. In fact, these texts were influenced by Christian or Graeco-Roman traditions. Bugge's view that traditions on Old Norse religion carried Christian elements became a leitmotif in, for instance, Walter Baetke's (1884–1978), Lars Lönnroth's (1935–) (University of Gothenburg), Olaf Olsen's (1928–2015) and Klaus Düwel's (1935–2020) studies.[3]

Eventually, source criticism and philology combined with comparative approaches developed to standard methods in the Swedish research on Old Norse religion. The internationally recognized philologist Dag Strömbäck (1900–1978) came to develop these approaches to their perfection. He received his doctorate in Nordic languages at Uppsala University on the highly influential thesis *Sejd* (1935). With a philological approach, he argued that *seiðr* was a form of ritual, which in the mythology was especially related to the ambiguous god Óðinn. He arranged his analysis according to the different textual genres, resulting in a division of 'white' divination *seiðr* and 'black' devastating *seiðr*. In the last part of the thesis, he also touched upon Old Norse soul conceptions and a discussion of changing shapes (Old Norse *at skipta hǫmum, at hamskiptaz*) (Swedish *hamnskifte*). This book had a great impact also on the international research on Old Norse religion and it is, even today, the major study of *seiðr*. In 1948, Strömbäck advanced to Professor of Nordic and Comparative Folklore Research, especially folklore, at Uppsala University, where he also stayed until 1967. A prominent disciple to Strömbäck was philologist Bo Almqvist (1931–2013), who studied Old Norse *níð* (libel) poetry (Almqvist 1965, 1974).

During the middle of the twentieth century, researchers focused mainly on the Old Norse gods and mythology. For example, historian of religions Åke Ohlmarks (1911–84) defended his thesis *Heimdalls Horn und Odins Auge* at the University of Lund in 1937, where he argued that Heimdallr was a sun god. A few years later, Birger Pering (1894–1963) defended his dissertation *Heimdall* (1941) also at the University of Lund. He stated that a *kenning* of Heilmdallr, *vǫrðr goða*, should not be interpreted in line with Snorri, as 'guardian of gods' but as 'Wicht der Götter', referring to a being called *vätte* (Swedish *hustomte*). The historian of religions and bishop, Helge Ljungberg (1904–83) (Uppsala University), wrote a book on Þórr, published in 1947, which was inspired by the Indo-European comparative approaches. His dissertation on the conversion of Scandinavia is regarded as a classical work (Ljungberg 1938).

One of the Swedish historians of Old Norse religion who stands out during the mid-twentieth century is Folke Ström (1907–1996) (Stockholms högskola and University of Gothenburg). He defended his thesis *On the Sacral Origin of the Germanic Death Penalties* in Stockholm (1942). Over several decades, he published a series of important works on Old Norse religion and mythology (see e.g. Ström 1947, 1948, 1974, 1985). With support of the comparative category the sacral kingship, for instance, he studied the pre-Christian rulers in Scandinavia using a philological approach combined with comparative methods (Ström 1954, 1968, 1981, 1983).[4]

Åke V. Ström together with Haralds Biezais (1909–1995) published the internally recognized handbook *Germanische und Baltische Religion* in the series 'Die Religionen der Menschheit' (volume 19.1) in 1975. Based on Dumézil's three-function structuralist model, Ström arranged the materials related to Germanic religion. Ström gave a lot of space to the rule of the gods and myths, while cult, society and social conditions were given a much more modest space. Like other historians of religion of his time who were studying Germanic religion, Ström essentially analysed and interpreted written sources by means of source criticism. During the decades that followed, some distinguished historians of religion and literature made several important critical contributions to this field, for instance, Ulf Drobin (1935–2023) (Stockholm University), Lars Lönnroth (1935–) (University of Gothenburg), Anders Hultgård (1936–) (Uppsala University) and Britt-Mari Näsström (1942–) (University of Gothenburg).[5]

The Revival of Interdisciplinary Methods

One can undoubtedly speak of an 'interdisciplinary turn' in the study of Old Norse religion during the last few decades (Sävborg 2022; Sundqvist 2015a, 2021b;). In an article published twenty years ago, Anders Hultgård (2003b) argued that there was a clear tendency in the most recent research on Old Norse religion to bring archaeological material into the investigations. Previously, the historians of religions studying Old Norse religion essentially analysed and interpreted written sources based on accepted philological and source-critical methods. During 1950–80, there were few historians of religion who worked more explicitly with archaeological sources in reconstructions of the Old Norse religion. Archaeologists also did not use the archaeological materials to study religion during this period. Previously explanatory models based on religion as a culture-creating force were common in archaeology, but after the 1950s, these were completely overshadowed by economic, functional and social interpretations in the New Archaeology (Engdahl and Kaliff 1996: 5). Development over the last decades, however, has taken a dramatic turn, and there is a renewed interest among archaeologists to address questions about rituals, symbols and world views. Several archaeologists at Uppsala University and Stockholm University have also made important contributions to the history of religion, such as, for example, Anne-Sofie Gräslund (1940–), Bo Gräslund (1934–), Frands Herschend (1948–), Anders Andrén (1952–), Torun Zachrisson (1960–), Anders Kaliff (1963–) and Neil Price (1965–). A similar development as that of archaeology can be noted in the onomastic research on place-names. In a classic article from 1986, the skilful place-name researcher Lars Hellberg (1914–2006) (Uppsala University) contradicted Sahlgren's veritable campaign against all research on sacral place-names. Hellberg's important article came to break the resistance that Sahlgren built up with his criticism of this research field. Several prominent place-name researchers, such as Lennart Elmevik (1936–) and Thorsten Andersson (1929–2018), both at Uppsala University, also followed Hellberg's path by publishing articles related to theophoric and cultic place-names and thus legitimated this 'new-old research field'. Over the last decades as well, Stefan Brink (1952–) and Per Vikstrand (1963–) have contributed with ground-breaking results to the field of Old Norse religion, by means of investigating place-names. Both defended their doctoral theses at Uppsala University. In addition, there has been an increasing usage of the methods of folklore in the study of Old Norse mythology and religion during the last decades. This turn to folkloristics is manifested in the volume from the Helsinki Conference of 2017, *Folklore and Old Norse Religion* (Frog & Ahola 2022).

As a rule today, historians of religion have Old Norse and Latin texts as their starting points for their studies. But in addition to them, other types of sources are increasingly included in the analyses. The interest in the fields of archaeology and place-names among historians of religions, and vice versa, can be explained in several ways, which also includes certain new aims in the scholarly investigations of Old Norse religion as well as in the history of religions in general:

1. One explanation can be linked to recent discussions about the concept of religion and the way researchers often perceive and apply this concept today. In one preceding dominant research tradition, as represented by Mircea Eliade, for instance, religious expressions were described as ahistorical and apolitical phenomena. The 'sacred was conceived as *sui generis*, absolutely unique, separate, and thereby its own cause' (McCutcheon 1997: 52; cf.

Lincoln 2018: 18–24). Today, many historians of religions regard religion as an integral part of culture and society. They argue that religion is influenced by, for example, social, political, cultural and gender relations (see e.g. Lincoln 2018: 14–24). Therefore, the expressions of religion in comparative research cannot be studied isolated from further cultural-historical contexts. To access these further contexts, the historians of religions need the archaeological sources, and the analyses that archaeologists have made of them, where both culture and society are taken into consideration.[6]

2. In recent studies, the issue of variation in Norse religion has also been addressed, which has probably also opened the door for archaeology and place-name research.[7] The ancient written sources, which are often the core of historical studies, are primarily relevant for Western-Nordic conditions. They thus have a limited value when questions about regional variations of religion are discussed. The archaeological material and the place-names, on the other hand, have key roles in such discussions, as they have a more even distribution across the Nordic region. The texts were also composed during the High Middles Ages, that is, long after the demise of the Old Norse religion (see further below).

3. In addition to spatial aspects of religion, archaeological sources can also inform us about variation over time and social differences in religious expressions. The written sources do not give many clues to religious changes in the time before Christianization in the tenth and eleventh centuries, for instance. Moreover, these texts are often occupied with the religion of the elite, at least when it comes to cultic matters. By means of archaeological finds, scholars may establish chronological layers and developments and changes of religion, as well as, to a certain degree, cultic expressions not only of the elite but also of the common people. With the support of archaeological material and analyses, they can also access the so-called household religion, women's religiosity and the lived religion. The written sources are often preoccupied with the official religion and men's practices and conceptions of the world.[8]

4. It is a well-known fact that mostly mythical traditions about the Old Norse gods were preserved by the medieval author whilst information about ritual activities performed by the ancient Scandinavians is not well documented (Clunies Ross 2002). With the support of archaeological findings, researchers today can, to some extent, reconstruct the burial practice, ritual sites, cult buildings and cultic paraphernalia. Based on archaeological finds, they can also study pre-Christian religious iconography such as rock carvings, Gotlandic picture stones, statuettes, gold bracteates and gold foi figures, as well as runic inscriptions.[9]

5. In addition to this, the issue of the interreligious and intercultural context of the Old Norse religion have been addressed in recent studies. How was this religion influenced by Greeks, Romans and Celtic-speaking groups? Did the Germanic-speaking northerners have an intercultural and religious exchange with the Sami, Finns or Baltic people? How did Christianity affect Germanic religion, especially during its final phase? In order to answer these questions that often appear in recent research on Old Norse and Germanic religion,

one must apply an interdisciplinary approach, where historical-philological methods are combined with archaeological and onomastic approaches.[10]
6. In recent research, the archaeological sources have also been appreciated, since they can be highly assessed in a source-critical sense (see e.g. Hultgård 2003b; Sundqvist 2016: 21–6). The archaeological finds can be regarded as 'direct sources', since they were created by people who themselves were part of the respective prehistoric society and culture. These materials thus inform us about the Late Iron Age culture and religion in a direct way, from an 'insider's' perspective, and have not been distorted by tradition and ideology as in the medieval written sources. However, source criticism and other disciplines besides archaeology, such as anthropology, onomastics, philology and history of religions, must help to interpret and give meaning to them. Postholes, for instance, are mute and must be interpreted by the archaeologist. Identifying a ceremonial building is thus an interpretation argued for with all kinds of source-critical considerations that are engaged 'along the road' of research, integrating information from different disciplines.

In order for the present presentation not to become biased and unbalanced, it must also be pointed out that there are still historians of religion who work mainly with written sources. Peter Jackson Rova (1972–) (Stockholm University) has for several decades written many internationally important works in which the Old Norse religion is illuminated in the light of comparative Indo-European languages (Jackson (Rova) 2012, 2014a,b,c, 2015). Sebastian Cöllen (1982–) defended his thesis at Uppsala University on the god Heimdallr, *Der rätselhafte Gott* (2011; revised 2015), where the narrative and mythical material are in focus. The runic inscription (the text) on the Rök stone (*c.* 800) has recently also received a noteworthy reinterpretation where the distinguished runologist Henrik Williams (1958–) (Uppsala University) together with sociolinguist Per Holmberg (1964–) (University of Gothenburg), Bo Gräslund (Uppsala University) and historian of religions Olof Sundqvist (1959–) (Stockholm University) collaborated (Holmberg et al. 2021). Frederik Wallenstein's (1979–) dissertation *Muntlighet och minne* (2023) (Stockholm University) is also mainly based on analyses of the written sources.

Impact and International Significance

The significance of Swedish scholars working with Old Norse religion and international impact have for a long time been strong by means of several important contributions made by Dag Strömbäck, Folke Ström, Åke V. Ström, Lars Lönnroth, Ulf Drobin, Britt-Mari Näsström and Anders Hultgård. The recent interdisciplinary turn where historians of religions working with archaeologists and place-name researchers have specifically been significant in Uppsala, Stockholm and Lund. Prominent in this interdisciplinary collaboration are the historians of religions Anders Hultgård, Olof Sundqvist, Catharina Raudvere (1960–) (University of Lund and University of Copenhagen) and Andreas Nordberg (1972–) (Stockholm

University), who all have contributed to the research on an international level. Jackson Rova and Hultgård have also written several internationally acknowledged works where the Old Norse religion is placed in an Indo-European context. In recent years, a new generation of historians of religions with connections to Stockholm University has also defended doctoral theses on Old Norse religion, for example, Tommy Kuusela (1980–), Klas Wikström af Edholm (1988–) and Frederik Wallenstein. In addition, international conferences have recently been organized and held in Sweden, such as *Old Norse Religion in Long-Term Perspective* in Lund in 2004 (see Raudvere, Andrén and Jennbert 2006) and *Saga Conference* in Uppsala in 2009, as well as *Mythology Conference* in Stockholm in 2015 and in Uppsala 2018 (see Sundqvist 2015a and 2021b).

Notes

1. There was probably a continuum concerning the religious tradition that extends beyond these time boundaries.
2. In the posthumously published work *Maximen und Reflexionen* (1833), Goethe wrote the famous phrase: 'Wer fremde Sprachen nicht kennt, weiss nichts von seiner eigenen.'
3. See, for example, Baetke (1964), Lönnroth (1963–4), Olsen (1966) and Düwel (1985), respectively.
4. On Ström's research, see Nordberg and Sundqvist (2019).
5. See, for example, Drobin (1968, 1991a,b), Lönnroth (1963–4, 1986) Hultgård (1984, 1993, 1997, 2003a, 2017, 2022a,b), Näsström (1991, 1995, 1996a,b, 2001, 2006) and Sundqvist (2020b), respectively.
6. See, for example, Adetorps (2008), Bertell (2003), Blomkvist (2002), Habbe (2005), Hultgård (2017, 2022a,b), Hultkrantz (1989), Jackson (Rova) (2014a,b,c), Kaliff and Sundqvist (2004), Kuusela (2017), Näsström (2006), Nordberg ([2003] 2004, 2006, 2008, 2013, 2018, 2020, 2022), Olsson (2016, 2019), Raudvere (1993, 2003), Sundqvist (2002, 2007, 2016, 2017) and Wikström af Edholm (2020).
7. See, for example, Nordberg (2012), Sundqvist (2012, 2016) and Sundqvist and Vikstrand (2014).
8. See, for example, Blomkvist (2002), Hultgård (1992), Näsström (1996a,b, 2006), Nordberg ([2003] 2004, 2006, 2013, 2022), Raudvere (1993, 2003) and Sundqvist (2002, 2020a, 2021a).
9. See Adetorps (2008), Görman (1987), Hultgård (1984, 1992, 1998, 2017), Hultkrantz (1989), Jackson (Rova) (2014a), Kaliff and Sundqvist (2004), Sundqvist (2015b), Sundqvist and Hultgård (2004) and Wikström af Edholm (2020).
10. See, for example, Adetorp (2008), Bertell (2003), Drobin and Keinänen (2001), Görman (1987), Hultgård (2017), Kaliff and Sundqvist (2004), Rydving (2020) and Sundqvist (2021a).

References

Adam of Bremen (1917), *Magistri Adam Bremensis Gesta Hammaburgensis Ecclesiae Pontificum*, ed. Bernhard Schmeidler, Scriptores rerum germanicarum in usum scholarum, Ex Monumentis Germaniae Historicis, Editio Tertia, Hanover: Hahnsche Buchhandlung.

Adetorp, J. (2008), *De guldglänsande ryttarna. C-brakteaternas ikonografi i ny belysning*, Lund: Centrum för teologi och religionsvetenskap, Lunds universitet.

Almqvist, B. (1965), *Norrön Niddiktning. Traditionshistoriska studier i versmagi. 1. Nid mot furstar*, Nordiska texter och undersökningar 21, Stockholm: Almqvist & Wiksell.

Almqvist, B. (1974), *Norrön Niddiktning. 2:1-2. Nid mot missionärer*, Nordiska texter och undersökningar 23, Stockholm: Almqvist & Wiksell.

Alkarp, M. (2009), *Det Gamla Uppsala: Berättelser & metamorfoser*, Occasional Papers in Archaeology 49, Uppsala: Uppsala University.

Arvidsson, S. (2006), *Aryan Idols Indo-European Mythology as Ideology and Science*, Chicago: University of Chicago Press.

Baetke, W. (1964), *Yngvi und die Ynglinger. Eine quellenkritische Untersuchung über das nordische 'Sakralkönigtum'*, Sitzungsberichte der sächsischen Akademie der Wissenschaften zu Leipzig. Philologisch-historische Klasse. Band 109, Heft 3, Berlin: Akademie-Verlag.

Bertell, M. (2003), *Tor och den nordiska åskan. Föreställningar kring världsaxeln*, Stockholm: Stockholm University.

Blomkvist, T. (2002), *Från ritualiserad tradition till institutionaliserad religion: Strategier för maktlegitimering på Gotland under järnålder och medeltid*, Uppsala: Uppsala University.

Bugge, S. (1881-9), *Studier over de nordiske Gude- og Heltesagans Oprindelse*, Oslo: Cammermeyer.

Clunies Ross, M. (2002), 'Närvaron och frånvaron av ritual I norröna medeltida texter', in Kristina Jennbert, Anders Andrén and Catharina Raudvere (eds), *Plats och praxis: Studier av nordisk förkristen ritual*, 13-30, Vägar till Midgård, 2, Lund: Nordic Academic Press.

Clunies Ross, M. (2018a), 'Myth and Religion in the Enlightenment and Pre-Romantic Period', in M. Clunies Ross (ed.), *The Pre-Christian Religions of the North: Research and Reception, Volume 1. From the Middle Ages to c. 1830*, 249-53, Turnhout: Brepols.

Clunies Ross, M. (2018b), 'Enabling Philology: Essential Preconditions for a Scholarly Reception of the Pre-Christian Religions of the North', in M. Clunies Ross (ed.), *The Pre-Christian Religions of the North. Research and Reception, Volume 1. From the Middle Ages to c. 1830*, 581-9, Turnhout: Brepols.

Cöllen, S. (2011), *Der Rätselhafte Gott: Heimdallr im Licht altnordischer Vorstellungen von Ahnen und Ordnung*, Uppsala: Uppsala University.

Cöllen, S. (2015), *Heimdallr - der rätselhafte Gott: eine philologische und religionsgeschichtliche Untersuchung*, Ergänzungsbände zum Reallexikon der Germanischen Altertumskunde 94, Berlin: de Gruyter.

Drobin, U. (1968), 'Myth and Epical Motifs in the Loki-Research', *Temenos* 3: 19-39.

Drobin, U. (1991a), 'Indoeuropeerna i myt och forskning', in *Nordisk hedendom. Et symposium*, 65-86, Odense: Odense universitetsforlag.

Drobin, U. (1991b), 'Mjödet och offersymboliken i fornnordisk religion', in L. Bäckman, U. Drobin, A. Hultkrantz and P.-A. Berglie (eds), *Studier i religionshistoria tillägnade Åke Hultkrantz professor emeritus den 1 juli 1986*, 97-141, Löberöd: Plus Ultra.

Drobin, U., and M.-L. Keinänen (2001), 'Frey, Veralden olmai och Sampo', in M. Stausberg, O. Sundqvist and A. van Nahl (eds), *Kontinuitäten und Brüche in der Religionsgeschichte: Festschrift für Anders Hultgård zu seinem 65. Geburtstag am 23.12.2001*, 136-69, Berlin: de Gruyter.

Düwel, K. (1985), *Das Opferfest von Lade: Quellenkritische Untersuchungen zur Germanischen Religionsgeschichte, Wiener Arbeiten zur germanischen Altertumskunde und Philologie 27*, Wien: Verlag Karl M. Halosar.
Dumézil, G. (1959), *Les dieux des Germains: essai sur la formation de la religion scandinave, Mythes et religions 38*, Paris: Presses Universitaires de France.
Dumézil, G. (1962), *De nordiska gudarna: en undersökning av den skandinaviska religionen*, original title *Les dieux des Germains*, trans. Å. Ohlmarks, Stockholm: Aldus/Bonniers.
Engdahl, K., and A. Kaliff, eds (1996), *Religion från stenålder till medeltid*, Riksantikvarieämbetet. Arkeologiska undersökningar, Skrifter nr 19, 25–57, Linköping: Riksantikvarieämbetet.
Frog and J. Ahola, eds (2022), *Folk Lore and Old Norse Mythology*, FF Communications 323, 133–59, Helsinki: The Kalevala Society.
Goethe, Johann Wolfgang von ([1833] 1988), *Goethes Werke in zwölf Bänden, Bd 7: Wilhelm Meisters Wanderjahre; Maximen und Reflexionen*, Berlin: Aufbau-Verlag.
Görman, M. (1987), *Nordiskt och keltiskt: Sydskandinavisk religion under yngre bronsålder och keltisk järnålder*, Lund: Wallin & Dalholm.
Grandien, B. (2018), 'Painting and Sculpture in Sweden', in M. Clunies Ross (ed.), *The Pre-Christian Religions of the North. Research and Reception, Volume 1. From the Middle Ages to c. 1830*, 469–502, Turnhout: Brepols.
Grape, A., ed. (1962), Snorri Sturluson, *Edda, Uppsala-handskriften DG 11*, Stockholm: Generalstabens Litografiska Anstalt.
Habbe, P. (2005), *Att se och tänka med ritual: Kontrakterande ritualer i de isländska släktsagorna, Vägar till Midgård 7*, Lund: Nordic Academic Press.
Hellberg, L. (1986), 'Hedendomens spår i uppländska ortnamn', in K. I. Sandred (ed.), *Ortnamnssällskapets i Uppsala Årsskrift 1986*, 40–71, Lund: Bloms tryckeri.
Holmberg, P., B. Gräslund, O. Sundqvist and H. Williams (2021), 'The Rök Runestone and the End of the World', *Futhark: International Journal of Runic Studies* 9–10 (2018–19): 7–38.
Hultgård, A. (1984), 'De äldsta runinskrifterna och Nordens förkristna religion', *Religion och Bibel* 41 (1982): 57–73.
Hultgård, A. (1992), 'Religiös förändring, kontinuitet och ackulturation/synkretism ivikingatidens och medeltidens skandinaviska religion', in B. Nilsson (ed.), *Kontinuitet i kult och tro från vikingatid till medeltid*, Projektet Sveriges Kristnande. Publikationer. 1, 49–103, Uppsala: Lunne böcker.
Hultgård, A. (1993), 'Altskandinavische Opferrituale und das Problem der Quellen', in T. Ahlbäck (ed.), *The Problem of Ritual*, Scripta Instituti Donneriani Aboensis XV, 221–59, Stockholm: Almqvist & Wiksell.
Hultgård, A. (1997), 'Från ögonvittnesskildring till retorik: Adam av Bremens notiser om Uppsalakulten i religionshistorisk belysning', in A. Hultgård (ed.), *Uppsalakulten och Adam av Bremen*, 9–50, Nora: Nya Doxa.
Hultgård, A. (1998). 'Runeninschriften und Runendenkmäler als Quellen der Religionsgeschichte', in K. Düwel (ed.), *Runeninschriften als Quellen interdisziplinärer Forschung. Abhandlungen des Vierten Internationalen Symposiums über Runen und Runeninschriften in Göttingen vom 4.–9. August 1995*, 715–37, Ergänzungsbände zum Reallexikon der Germanischen Altertumskunde 15, Berlin–New York: de Gruyter.
Hultgård, A. (2003a), 'Ár-"Gutes Jahr unt Ernteglück"—ein Motivkomplex in der altnordischen Literatur und sein religionsgeschichtlicher Hintergrunt', in Wilhelm Hiezmann and Astrid van Nahl (eds), *Runica—Germanica—Mediaevalia*, 282–308,

Ergänzungsbände zum Reallexikon der Germanischen Altertumskunde, Band 37, Berlin/New York: de Gruyter.

Hultgård, A. (2003b), 'Akademien granskar (Anders Hultgård)', in *Saga och Sed. Kungl. Gustav Adolfs Akademiens Årsbok 2003*, 143–9, Lund: Kungl. Gustav Adolfs Akademiens.

Hultgård, A. (2017), *Midgård brinner. Ragnarök i religionshistorisk belysning*, Acta Academiae Regiae Gustavi Adolphi 146, Uppsala: Kungl. Gustav Adolfs Akademien för svensk folkkultur.

Hultgård, A. (2022a), *The End of the World in Scandinavian Mythology: A Comparative Perspective on Ragnarök*, original title Midgård brinner. Ragnarök i religionshistorisk belysning, New York: Oxford University Press.

Hultgård, A. (2022b), 'Offerkult och prästerskap i Europas och Västasiens gamla religioner', in S. Karlin Björk and O. Sundqvist (eds), *Kultledare i fornnordisk religion: ett symposium*, 111–24, Acta Academiae regiae Gustavi Adolphi. 164, Uppsala: Kungl. Gustav Adolfs Akademien för svensk folkkultur.

Hultkrantz, Å. (1989), 'Hällristningsreligion', in S. Jansson, E. B. Lundberg and U. Bertilsson (eds), *Hällristningar och hällmålningar i Sverige*, 43–58, Uddevalla: Forum.

Jackson (Rova), P. (2012), 'The Merits and Limits of Comparative Philology. Old Norse Religious Vocabulary in a Long-Term Perspective', in C. Raudvere and J. P. Schjødt (eds), *More than Mythology. Narratives, Ritual Practices and Regional Distribution in pre-Christian Scandinavian Religions*, 47–64, Lund: Nordic Academic Press.

Jackson (Rova), P. (2014a), *Det öppna och det slutna. Religionshistoriska essäer*, Stockholm: Molin & Sorgenfrei.

Jackson (Rova), P. (2014b), 'Alhs och gudhūs. Kultplatsbeteckningar och översättningsanomalier i den gotiska bibeln', in E. Nyman, J. Magnusson and E. Strzelecka (eds), *Den heliga platsen. Handlingar från symposiet Den heliga platsen Härnösand 15–18 september 2011*, 39–47, Sundsvall: Mittuniversitetet.

Jackson (Rova), P. (2014c), 'Themes of Commensality in Indo-European Lore: Greek ξένος and Proto-Germanic *etuna-', in H. Craig Melchert, E. Rieken and T. Steer (eds), *Munus amicitiae: Norbert Oettinger a collegis et amicis dicatum*, Ann Arbor: Beech Stave Press.

Jackson (Rova), P. (2015), 'Den ditematiska namntypens mening och ursprung', *Studia Anthroponymica Scandinavica* 33.

Jackson Rova, P. (forthcoming), 'Bureus och trollen: En antikvarisk komplikation', *Saga och sed. Kungl. Gustav Adolfs Akademiens Årsbok 2023*.

Kaliff, A., and O. Sundqvist (2004), *Oden och Mithraskulten: Religiös ackulturation under romersk järnålder och folkvandringstid*, Occasional Papers in Archaeology 35, Uppsala: Uppsala University.

Kuusela, T. (2017), *'Hallen var lyst i helig frid': krig och fred mellan gudar och jättar i en fornnordisk hallmiljö*, Stockholm: Stockholm University.

Larsson, G., ed. (2022), *The Legacy, Life and Work of Geo Widengren and the Study of the History of Religions After World War II*, Numen Book Series 174, Leiden: Brill.

Lincoln, B. (2018), *Apples and Oranges: Explorations In, On and With Comparison*, Chicago: University of Chicago Press.

Ljungberg, H. (1938), *Den nordiska religionen och kristendomen: Studier över det nordiska religionsskiftet under vikingatiden*, Nordiska texter och undersökningar 11, Stockholm: Hugo Gebers.

Ljungberg, H. (1947), *Tor: undersökningar i indoeuropeisk och nordisk religionshistoria. 1 Den nordiske åskguden och besläktade indoeuropeiska gudar: den nordiske åskguden i bild och myt*, Uppsala: Lundequistska bokhandeln.
Lönnroth, L. (1963–4), 'Kroppen som själens spegel – Ett motiv i de isländska sagorna', in *Lychnos. Lärdomshistoriska samfundets årsbok 1963–64*, 24–61, Uppsala: Lärdomshistoriska samfundet.
Lönnroth, L. (1986), 'Dómaldi's Death and the Myth of Sacral Kingship', in J. Lindow, L. Lönnroth and G. Wolfgang Weber (eds), *Structure and Meaning in Old Norse Literature: New Approaches to Textual Analysis and Literary Criticism*, The Viking Collection 3, 73–93, Odense: Odense University Press.
Lönnroth, L. (2018), 'Dalin, Ramsay and the Enlightened Reaction to Rudbeckianism', in M. Clunies Ross (ed.), *The Pre-Christian Religions of the North: Research and Reception, Volume 1. From the Middle Ages to c. 1830*, 273–80, Turnhout: Brepols.
McCutcheon, R. T. (1997), *Manufacturing Religion: The Discourse on Sui Generis Religion and the Politics of Nostalgica*, Oxford: Oxford University Press.
Magnus, Johannes (1554), *Historia de omnibvs Gothorvm Sveonvmqve regibvs qui vnquam ab initio nationis extitere, eorúmque memorabilibus bellis late varieqve per orbem gestis, opera Olai Magni Gothi fratris eiusdem autoris ac etiam archiepiscopi Vpsalensis in lucem ędita: Cvm gratia et privilegio Ivlii III*, Pont: Romae, quartohttps://litteraturban ken.se/f%C3%B6rfattare/JohannesMagnus/titlar/Historia/faksimil.
Magnus, Olaus ([1555]1982), in R. Geete, G. Thörnell, C. Cavalin, O. Almgren, I. Collijn, G. Collin, A. nilsson and R. Sernander (eds and trans.), *Historia om de nordiska folken*, orig. title Historia de gentibus septentrionalibus, Stockholm: Gidlund.
Malm, M. (2018a), 'The Humanist Reception in Scandinavia', in M. Clunies Ross (ed.), *The Pre-Christian Religions of the North. Research and Reception, Volume 1. From the Middle Ages to c. 1830*, 187–218, Turnhout: Brepols.
Malm, M. (2018b), 'Swedish Romanticism and Gothicism: Aesthetic Synergies', in M. Clunies Ross (ed.), *The Pre-Christian Religions of the North. Research and Reception, Volume 1. From the Middle Ages to c. 1830*, 351–6, Turnhout: Brepols.
Max Müller, F. (1854), *Comparative Mythology*, reprinted in *Chips from a German Workshop*, vol. II, New York: Scribner, Armstrong, and Co (1876).
Näsström, B.-M. (1991), 'Freyjas funktioner. En spegling av den ideala kvinnan', in *Nordisk hedendom. Et symposium*, 261–72, Odense: Odense universitetsforlag.
Näsström, B.-M. (1995), *Freyja—the Great Goddess of the North*, Lund Studies in History of Religions 5, Department of History of Religions, Lund: University of Lund.
Näsström, B.-M. (1996a), 'Offerlunden under Frösö kyrka', in S. Brink (ed.), *Jämtlands kristnande*, Projektet Sveriges kristnande. Publikationer 4, 65–85, Uppsala: Lunne Böcker.
Näsström, B.-M. (1996b), 'Torgerd Holgabrud och Pytonsanden', *Religion och Bibel. Nathan Söderblom-Sällskapets Årsbok* 1996 (55): 104–15.
Näsström, B.-M. (2001), *Blot: Tro og offer i det førkristne Norden*, Oslo: Pax.
Näsström, B.-M. (2006), *Bärsärkarna. Vikingatidens elitsoldater*, Stockholm: Nordstedt.
Nordberg, A. ([2003] 2004), *Krigarna i Odins sal: Dödsföreställningar och krigarkult i fornnordisk religion*, Stockholm: Stockholm University.
Nordberg, A. (2006), *Jul, disting och förkyrklig tideräkning: Kalendrar och kalendariska riter i det förkristna Norden*, Acta Academiae regiae Gustavi Adolphi 91, Uppsala: Kungl. Gustav Adolfs Akademien för svensk folkkultur.
Nordberg, A. (2012), 'Continuity, Change and Regional Variation in Old Norse Religion', in C. Raudvere and J. P. Schjødt (eds), *More than Mythology: Narratives, Ritual*

Practices and Regional Distribution in pre-Christian Scandinavian Religion, 119–51, Lund: Nordic Academic Press.

Nordberg, A. (2013), *Fornnordisk religionsforskning mellan teori och empiri. Kulten av anfäder, solen och vegetationsandar i idehistorisk belysning*, Acta Academiae Regiae Gustavi Adolphi, 126, Uppsala: Kungl. Gustav Adolfs Akademien för svensk folkkultur.

Nordberg, A. (2014), 'Kultplatser och tolkningsperspektiv i fornnordisk religionsforskning' in E. Nyman et al. (eds), *Den heliga platsen. Handlingar från symposiet Den heliga platsen Härnösand 15–18 september 2011*, 11–22, Sundsvall: Mittuniversitetet.

Nordberg, A. (2018), 'Old Customs – The Vernacular Word siðr and Its Cognates in the Study of (Lived) Religion in Viking and Medieval Scandinavia', *Temenos* 54 (2): 125–47.

Nordberg, A. (2020), 'Ritual Time and Time Reckoning', in J. P. Schjødt, J. Lindow and A. Andrén (eds), *The Pre-Christian Religions of the North. History and Structures*, vol. II, 725-38, Turnhout: Brepols.

Nordberg, A. (2022), 'Some Thoughts on the Category of Religion in Research of Viking Age Scandinavia', in D. Sävborg (ed.), *Crossing Disciplinary Boundaries in Studies of the Viking Age*, 253-76, The North Atlantic World, 4, Turnhout: Brepols.

Nordberg, A., and O. Sundqvist, eds (2019), *Religionshistorikern Folke Ström: föredrag från ett symposium i Uppsala den 8 november 2017*, Acta Academiae Regiae Gustavi Adolphi, 157, Uppsala: Kungl. Gustav Adolfs Akademien för svensk folkkultur.

Ohlmarks, Å. (1937), *Heimdalls Horn und Odins Auge: Studien zur nordischen und vergleichenden Religionsgeschichte*, vol. 1: Heimdall und das Horn, Lund: Gleerup.

Olsen, O. (1966), *Hørg, hov og kirke: Historiske og arkæologiske vikingetidsstudier*, København: Det Kongelige nordiske Oldskriftselskab.

Olsson, S. (2016), *Gísl: givande och tagande av gisslan som rituell handling i fredsprocesser under vikingatiden*, Bergen: University of Bergen.

Olsson, S. (2019), *The Hostages of the Northmen: From the Viking Age to the Middle Ages*, Stockholm Studies in Comparative Religion 41, Stockholm: Stockholm University Press.

Pálsson, H., ed. (2012), Snorri Sturluson, *The Uppsala Edda, DG 11 4to*, Viking Society Northern Research, London: University College London.

Pering, B. (1941), *Heimdall: Religionsgeschichtliche Untersuchungen zum Värständnis der altnordischen Götterwelt*, Lund: Gleerup.

Raudvere, C. (1993), *Föreställningar om maran i nordisk folktro*, Lund Studies in History of Religions 1, Lund: Religionshistoriska avdelningen, Lunds universitet.

Raudvere, C. (2003), *Kunskap och insikt i norrön tradition: Mytologi, ritualer och Trolldomsanklagelser*, Vägar till Midgård 3, Lund: Nordic Academic Press.

Raudvere, C., A. Andrén, K. Jennbert, eds (2006), *Old Norse Religion in Long-Term Perspectives: Origins, Changes, and Interactions: An International Conference in Lund, Sweden, June 3–7, 2004*, Vägar till Midgård 8, Lund: Nordic Academic Press.

Rydberg, V. (1886-9), *Undersökningar i germansk mytologi*, vols I–II, Stockholm: Bonniers.

Rydberg, V. (1889), *Teutonic Mythology: Gods and Goddesses of the Northland*, original title *Undersökningar i germansk mytologi*, R. B. Anderson (trans.), London: Sonnenschein.

Rydving, H. (2020), 'The Christianization of the Sámi', in Jens Peter Schjødt, John Lindow and Anders Andrén (eds), *The Pre-Christian Religions of the North. History and Structures, Volume 4: The Christianization Process, Bibliography, and Index*, 1745–1761, Turnhout: Brepols.

Sävborg, D., ed. (2022), *Crossing Disciplinary Boundaries in Studies of the Viking Age*, The North Atlantic World, 4, Turnhout: Brepols.
Skånby, S. T. G. (forthcoming), 'Att remytologisera sin samtid: Pehr Henrik Lings (1776–1839) användning av den fornnordiska mytologin', Forthcoming.
Ström, Å. V. (1975), 'Germanische Religion', in Å. V. Ström and H. Biezais, *Germanische und Baltische Religion*, Die Religionen der Menschheit, vol. 19.1, 15–306, Stuttgart: Kohlhammer, cop.
Ström, F. (1942), *On the Sacral Origin of the Germanic Death Penalties*, Lund: H. Ohlsson.
Ström, F. (1947), *Den döendes makt och Oden i trädet*, Göteborgs högskolas årsskrift 53:1, Göteborg: Elander.
Ström, F. (1948), *Den egna kraftens män: En studie i forntida irreligiositet*, Göteborgs högskolas årsskrift 54:2, Göteborg: Elander.
Ström, F. (1954), *Diser, Nornor, Valkyrjor. Fruktbarhetskult och sakralt kungadöme i Norden*, KVHAAH. Filologisk-Filosofiska Serien, 1, Stockholm: Almqvist & Wiksell.
Ström, F. (1968), 'Kung Domalde i Svitjod och "kungalyckan"', in *Saga och Sed. Kungl. Gustav Adolfs Akademiens Årsbok 1967*, 52–66, Lund: Kungl. Gustav Adolfs Akademien.
Ström, F. (1974), *Níð, Ergi and Old Norse Moral Attitudes*, Viking Society for Northern Research, London: University College London.
Ström, F. (1981), 'Poetry as an Instrument of Propaganda. Jarl Hákon and his Poets' in U. Dronke, G. Helgadóttir, G. Wolfgang Weber and H. Bekker-Nielsen (eds), *Specvlvm norroenvm. Norse Studies in Memory of Gabriel Turville-Petre*, 440–58, Odense: Odense University Press.
Ström, F. (1983), 'Hieros gamos-motivet i Hallfreðr Óttarssons Hákonardrápa och den nordnorska jarlavärdigheten', *Arkiv för Nordisk Filologi* 98: 67–79.
Ström, F. ([1961] 1985), *Nordisk hedendom: Tro och sed i förkristen tid*, 3rd edn, Göteborg: Scandinavian University Books.
Strömbäck, D. (1935), *Sejd. Textstudier i nordisk religionshistoria*, Nordiska texter och undersökningar 5, Stockholm: Geber.
Sundqvist, Olof (2002), *Freyr's Offspring: Rulers and Religion in Ancient Svea Society*, Acta Universitatis Upsaliensis, Historia Religionum 21, Uppsala: Uppsala University.
Sundqvist, O. (2007), Kultledare i fornskandinavisk religion, *Occasional Papers in Archaeology 41*. Uppsala: Uppsala University.
Sundqvist, O. (2012), 'Religious Ruler Ideology in pre-Christian Scandinavia: A Contextual Perspective', in C. Raudvere and J. P. Schjødt (eds), *More than Mythology: Narratives, Ritual Practices and Regional Distribution in pre-Christian Scandinavian Religion*, 225–62, Lund: Nordic Academic Press.
Sundqvist, O. (2015a), 'Akademien granskar … Bruket av arkeologiska källor i nyare svensk religionshistorisk forskning om fornskandinavisk religion', in *Saga och Sed. Kungl. Gustav Adolfs Akademiens Årsbok 2015*, 182–90, Lund: Kungl. Gustav Adolfs Akademien.
Sundqvist, O. (2015b), 'Contributions of the Oldest Runic Inscriptions to the Reconstruction of Ancient Scandinavian Religion: Some Methodological Reflections with References to an Example of the Phenomenological Category of "Ritual Specialists"', in Oliver Grimm and Alexandra Pesch (eds), *Archäologie und Runen.: Fallstudien zu Inschriften im älteren Futhark*, 121–43, Kiel: Wachholtz Verlag.
Sundqvist, O. (2016), *An Arena for Higher Powers: Ceremonial Buildings and Religious Strategies for Rulership in Late Iron Age Scandinavia*, Numen Book Series 150, Leiden: Brill.

Sundqvist, O. (2017), 'The Temple, the Tree, and the Well: A Topos or Cosmic Symbolism at Cultic Sites', in P. Hermann, S. A. Mitchell, J. P. Schjødt and A. J. Rose (eds), *Old Norse Mythology: Comparative Perspectives*, Publications of the Milman Parry Collection of Oral Literature 3, 163–90, Boston: Harvard University Press.

Sundqvist, O. (2020a), 'Cultic Leaders and Religious Specialists', in Jens Peter Schjødt, John Lindow and Anders Andrén (eds), *The Pre-Christian Religions of the North. History and Structures. Volume 2, Social, Geographical, and Historical Contexts, and Communication between Worlds*, 739-79, Turhout: Brepols.

Sundqvist, O. (2020b), 'Freyr', in Anders Andrén, John Lindow and Jens Peter Schjødt (eds), *Pre-Christian Religions of the North. History and Structures, Vol. 3, Conceptual Frameworks: The Cosmos and Collective Supernatural Beings*, 1195-245, Turnhout: Brepols.

Sundqvist, O. (2021a), 'The Role of Rulers in the Winding Up of the Old Norse Religion', *Numen* 68: 272-97.

Sundqvist, O. (2021b), 'A "Turn to Interdisciplinary Methods" in the Study of Mythology and Old Norse Religion', in Frog and J. Ahola (eds), *Folk Lore and Old Norse Mythology*, FF Communications 323, 133-59, Helsinki: The Kalevala Society.

Sundqvist, O., and A. Hultgård (2004), 'The Lycophoric Names of the 6th to 7th Century Blekinge Rune Stones and the Problem of Their Ideological Background', in A. van Nahl, L. Elmevik and S. Brink (eds), *Namenwelten. Orts- und Personennamen in historischer Sicht*, Ergänzungsbände zum Reallexikon der Germanischen Altertumskunde 44, 583-602, Berlin: de Gruyter.

Sundqvist, O., and P. Vikstrand (2014), 'Disevid och Distingen – par av östnordisk diskult?', in Eva Nyman, J. Magnusson and E. Strzelecka (eds), *Den heliga platsen. Handlingar från symposiet Den heliga platsen Härnösand 15–18 september 2011*, 153-78, Sundsvall: Mittuniversitetet.

Von Dalin, Olof (1747), *Svea Rikes Historia*, Förste Delen. Stockholm: Lars Salvius, https://litteraturbanken.se/f%C3%B6rfattare/DalinOvon/titlar/SveaRikesHistoria1/sida/VII/faksimil.

Wallenstein, Frederik (2023), *Muntlighet och minne: Sagatraditionen, kulturhistorien och det kulturella minnets blinda fläck*, Stockholm: Stockholm University.

Wessén, E. ([1965] 1975), *De nordiska språken*, Stockholm: AWE/Gebers.

Widengren, G. (1953), *Religionens värld: Religionsfenomenologiska studier och översikter*, Stockholm: Svenska Kyrkan Diakonistyrelses Bokförlag.

Wikström af Edholm, K. (2020), *Människooffer i myt och minne En studie av offerpraktiker i fornnordisk religion utifrån källtexter och arkeologiskt material*, Åbo: Åbo Akademi.

Chapter 3

INDIGENOUS RELIGIONS

Daniel Andersson and Bodil Liljefors Persson

For the last two hundred years or so, the European and North American study of religion focused mainly on scriptures and edicts, as well as architecture in temples, pyramids, churches and synagogues. The so-called indigenous peoples belonging to 'oral cultures' were for various reasons deprived of their own stories and their own skills, and the anthropologist, the ethnographer and the historian were often – even if the work they conducted was well crafted – perceived as one of many colonial figures with unclear aims and poor insight. Why should someone foreign write about indigenous people at all? Why, when and for whom is such research relevant? To whom is the researcher responsible? Analyses could be brilliant but were not infrequently half-hearted and/or created confusion (Rydving 1993: 4).

The following text aims to give a short but hopefully comprehensive account of how Swedish researchers have approached the field of global Indigenous religions.

It has to be noted that such a research overview on 'religious' action also must include works on colonial history, mission history and observations that can be linked under the term 'postcolonial theories'. It is impossible to provide a complete overview of this global and not infrequently politicized theme and adjacent theoretical perspectives. Also, it must be mentioned that the religions of indigenous peoples include Christianity, Islam, Hinduism and Buddhism. The absolute majority of the Sami population today is Christian.

When looking into the cultures of indigenous peoples from an academic point of view, t a few tendencies appear. There is often a somewhat imagined link between origins, nature and religion. There is also a tendency to write about the clear impact that colonialism and the Christian mission had in the past. The third topic, the exploitation of natural resources in areas where indigenous people are situated, has also been heavily researched.

In 1975, the International Workgroup for Indigenous Affairs (IWGIA) was founded. Subsequently, the following definition was born:

> Indigenous people are those who consider themselves to belong to a people that has a historical continuity with pre-colonial times, and who consider themselves different from the surrounding society. They belong to a non-dominant sector

of society and strive to preserve their cultural heritage in accordance with their own social structures and patterns.

In Sweden, there were, above all, two larger organizations, Svenska Amerikanistsällskapet (SAMS, the Swedish American Society), where, among others, Åke Hultkrantz was chairman for several years; and Svenska Samfundet för Religionshistorisk Forskning (SSRF, the Swedish Society for Religious History Research), which for many years brought together researchers in the loosely joined field of Indigenous religions.

Today, the United Nations (UN) and the UN Educational, Scientific and Cultural Organization (UNESCO) classify between 380 and 500 million people as indigenous peoples, Aboriginals, First Nations, People of the land and so on. They live in roughly ninety countries and make up more than 6 per cent of the world's population. Many of them live in poverty and have a low average life expectancy. Child mortality is high and illiteracy is widespread. As a rule, they belong to the informal sector.

In the discussion regarding the religions of indigenous peoples, it is urgent to emphasize that this text is precisely about the religions of different indigenous peoples around the world, which in addition are characterized by diversity within the respective tradition. In the past, it was common to use the concept of Nature religions or Non-scripture religions, as well as Primitive religions. Nowadays, these designations are not used. 'Nature religions' was defined based on the idea that the peoples were considered to live more in close harmony with nature than other religious groups. The term 'Primitive religions' was applied because it was thought to refer to that which was original and thus of older chronology, partly because it was associated with the simple way of living. The term 'Non-scripture religions' included, for example, the false notion that there were no written sources or sacred texts among these traditions.

Today, these explanations and concepts are no longer suitable and valid. Indigenous peoples do not only live in the countryside and thus 'closer to nature', but they are also unaffected by the surrounding world. These religions are also no less complex than, for example, the monotheistic religions which, according to the paradigm of evolution, were considered to constitute the highest form of development of religion, which meant that the so-called animistic religions were considered to be of lower rank.

Many researchers, however, are and were aware of this complicated world of religions and spiritualities and had no obvious problems in performing research on both scripture religions and indigenous cultures. One example is Martin P. Nilsson (1874–1967), who was Professor in *Antikens kultur och samhällsliv* (Ancient Culture and Social Life) at Lund University between 1909 and 1939. His dissertation on the Attic festivities of Dionysos was defended in 1900 at Lund University (Nilsson 1900). In the years following his doctoral studies, he devoted himself not only to Greek religion but also to Indigenous religions. In 1911, he published *Primitiv religion* (Primitive Religion). The same year, a German edition of this book was published in Tübingen (Nilsson 1911). Nilsson is an early example of a scholar with broad knowledge in languages and foreign cultures and who – from a comparative perspective – tried to harmonize Western research results on monotheistic, ancient polytheistic and contemporary Indigenous religions.

With influences from postcolonial theory-building, it became obvious that it was more correct to broaden the field on polytheism and indigenous cultures and thus apply names and concepts that the ethnic groups use about themselves, for example, Sami, Maori, Maya and Mi'kmaq. Sometimes it is fair to add a further specification if it is a larger group that speaks different languages, such as Yucatec Maya, Aboriginals in Australia or Swedish Sami. It is nowadays common to employ the term 'indigenous' in English, *indígenas* in Spanish or *ursprungsfolk* in Swedish.

Limitations and Boundaries

When regarding Swedish scholars doing research in this broad field, we have tried to limit the following account to academic PhDs. We have as well listed the scholars according to the region where they did most of their important works. The scholar Hultkrantz (1920–2006), for example, conducted research on Sami as well as North American indigenous groups. He will therefore be included in both the European and American scenes.

The aim of this chapter has been to cover the research area; hopefully, the result is a reasonable representative selection of scholars.

The account is also based on a somewhat arbitrary division into regions, where we start with Europe – due to the simple fact that this is about Swedish research, and we have one of the oldest indigenous populations in Scandinavia. Then follows in alphabetical order research on Indigenous religions in Africa, America, Asia and Australia/Oceania.

Europe

In Europe, we have few indigenous groups left. The most researched are the Sami and we concentrate on them. As in the case of all indigenous cultures, it is difficult – from both an etic as well as an emic perspective – to differ between culture, religion and spirituality.

The most important source material regarding the Sami originates from the sixteenth, seventeenth and eighteenth centuries and consists mostly of the accounts from Swedish and Danish-Norwegian priests. Since then, there have been numerous books written on the subject.

An early description and research overview is *De nordiska lapparnas religion* (The Religion of the Nordic Lapps) from 1912, by the bishop and Professor in Theology and Historian of Religions Edgar Reuterskiöld (1872–1932), a man with broad interests and deep skills in languages.

Rafael Karsten (1879–1956) was a Finnish-Swedish philosopher, sociologist and anthropologist, and became Associate Professor of Comparative Religious

Studies at the University of Helsinki in 1907. He is most renowned for his field works among South American indigenous peoples, visits that resulted in a series of articles, pamphlets and books. Among his works, we find *The Civilization of the South American Indians*, from 1926. In 1952, he published a careful and well-spread study called *Samefolkets religion* (The Religion of the Sami People).

Carl-Martin Edsman (1911–2010) was a Swedish priest and Professor of History of Religions at Uppsala University. He studied at the Sorbonne in the years 1938–9 and was appointed professor at Lund University during 1946–9, where he wrote his thesis (Edsman 1949). In 1959, he became Professor in the History of Religions in Uppsala. His production includes theories from theology, psychology and sociology. Like other scholars in the field of Sami religion, he – among other things – wrote on bear ceremonies among the Sami and Finns (Edsman 1994). There is a wealth of material on this particular ritual from the seventeenth century to the present day.

Probably the most influential scholar of Scandinavian Sami research is Louise Bäckman (1926–2021). She grew up in the Vapsten Sami village, Västerbotten, and went to both residential school and nomadic school, events that shaped her future interests in noaidi, shamans and bear-mythologies. She received her PhD in 1975 with a thesis in the History of Religions on Sami spiritual forces, *Sájva. Föreställningar om hjälp- och skyddsväsen i heliga fjäll bland samerna* (Sájva. Beliefs about Protection Spirits in Sacred Mountains Among the Sami).

Subsequently she was appointed Professor of History of Religions at Stockholm University. Among her other prominent works are *Studie i de förkristna samernas föreställningar om dödsriket med tonvikten lagd på de skandinaviska samerna* (Study in the Pre-Christian Sami Beliefs about the Underworld with Emphasis on the Scandinavian Sami, published in 1964), and various works with Hultkrantz (Bäckman and Hultkrantz 1978, 1985).

The Swedish-Sami linguist and Professor of Sami Languages Israel Ruong (1903–1986) presented in *Samerna i historien och nutiden* (The Sami in History and the Present, published in 1982) a structured overview of Sami history. Ruong has written numerus books, both in Sami and Swedish.

The ethnographer and comparative scientist on religions, Hultkrantz, wrote extensively on Sami culture and circumpolar religions as well as Old Norse religion. His written corpus includes the publication of some four hundred papers and approximately twenty-five books. He edited numerous works and was a source of inspiration for many writers with similar interests. He carried out fieldwork among the Sami in 1944 and 1946 and later among North American indigenous populations.

A successor to both Bäckman and Hultkrantz is Håkan Rydving, whose thesis *The End of Drum-Time* (1993) set the course for his subsequent research on Sami Religion, source criticism, religious change and continuity and language variation in the Circumpolar area. He has also broadened the perspective by publishing in Spanish on the subject of Sami culture (Rydving 2012).

Historian Daniel Lindmark's thesis *En lappdrängs omvändelse* (A Lappish Peasant's Conversion, 2006) deals with various court cases from the end of the seventeenth century. Lindmark shows not only how the Swedish authorities acted to force the Sami to abandon their religion but also how the arguments for Swedish settlement in Lappland were formulated.

Finally, we have to add that the Sami population has been depicted by a number of other scholars and writers – Ebba Olofsson (1998), Christer Persson, Karin Granqvist, Peter Johansson, Carl-Gösta Ojala, Anna-Lill Ledman, Åsa Virdi Kroik, Lotta Umma, Olle Sundström, Lilian Ryd (Ryd 2013, 2015) and the recent Birgitta Simma, whose book *Samiskt kyrkoliv* (Sami Churchlife, 2022) contributes to the overall picture of contemporary Sami indigenous culture; the absolute majority of the Sami are Christians.

Africa

In Sweden, there is a long academic tradition of performing research in various African countries. The oldest studies are related to missionary work, and later we find detailed explorations of religions, more specifically on mythology and rituals such as rites of passage, medical healing rituals and rituals connected to sorcery. Also, we have several accounts of the everyday life among the various ethnic groups.

Research at Lund University continued after the already mentioned Martin P. Nilsson with – among others – Erland Ehnmark (1903–1966), who published in the fields of world religions as well as Indigenous religions (Ehnmark 1966).

Olof Pettersson (1920–1986), also at Lund University, focused on African religions. His dissertation *Chiefs and Gods: Religious and Social Elements in the South Eastern Bantu Kingship* (1953) focused on the historical and religious context of the Bantu chief. He also discussed if influences of Christian and Muslim ideas of God were reflected in the indigenous African religions, a question that many scholars had dealt with (Pettersson 1966). The tradition of research on African religions continued with Professor Tord Olsson (1942–2013), who defended his doctoral thesis, *Lévi-Strauss och totemismens teoretiker* (Lévi-Strauss and the Theorists of Totemism, published in 1972). This work was a highly theoretical contribution to the studies in History of Religions. He has published studies on Iranian culture as well as on Islamic Sufi orders and is well-known for his fieldwork in both Kenya, among the Maasai, and Mali and Gambia, among the Bambara. We might say that he went from having a more theoretical and textual-based focus in his earlier research to the study of rituals and of how people actually live and practise their faith, what we maybe today would label 'everyday' or 'lived' religion. Among the publications, we find orally transmitted stories about mythological themes and rituals from the Maasai and ritual practices in Gwanyebugu in Mali (Olsson 2000). During his years, the discipline of History of Religions at Lund University was developed to encompass more anthropologically oriented studies.

One of the more important researchers on African religions, and especially on Zulu religion, is Axel-Ivar Berglund (1929–2015). He was born in South Africa to missionary parents, became a missionary himself, learned Zulu and Swati and worked with the Evangelical Lutheran Church in Southern Africa and with the South African Council of Churches. He was later connected to Nordiska Afrikainstitutet at Uppsala University. His reworked thesis *Zulu Thought-Pattern and Symbolism (årtal?)* was praised by Victor Turner, who, on the cover of the book, stated, 'One of the most important statements of the "inside view" of an African religious system ever made ... unique in its richness and depth' (Berglund 1975).

Roland Hallgren, Professor Emeritus in Religious Studies at Linnaeus University in Kalmar/Växjö, carried out fieldwork in Nigeria among the Yoruba in the 1980s. His thesis, *The Good Things in Life: A Study of the Traditional Religious Culture of the Yoruba People*, was defended in 1988. Later, he continued to work on myths and rituals within this culture (Hallgren 1995).

Historian of Religions Inger Callewaert conducted fieldwork in the Balanta area in Guinea-Bissau. Her doctoral thesis (Callewaert 2000) focuses on the rise and development of the prophetic movement Kiyang-yang in Guinea-Bissau.

David Westerlund, Professor of History of Religions at Södertörn University in the Department of Gender, Culture and History, wrote his thesis on society and religion in Tanzania. It was called *Ujamaa na dini: A Study of Some Aspects of Society and Religion in Tanzania, 1961–1977* and was published in 1980. In his teaching and research, he has focused on indigenous African religions, Islam and Christianity. The African research was primarily conducted in Tanzania, Nigeria and South Africa. He has – among other works – published *Afrikanska religioner* (African Religions, 2011), an introductory book to the field.

North America

When it comes to the North American continent, the research material is basically insurmountable – and has been so for a long time. Thus, here follows a tentative and concise research overview that cannot in any way pretend to be complete.

The ethnographer and historian of religions Hultkrantz became an early expert on North American indigenous groups and conducted field research among the Shoshoni Indians of Wyoming in the United States in 1948 and 1955–8. Among these groups, he identified three coherent systems of religious elements. The systems were related to the hunter's vision quest, the Sun dance and the myth-telling. His thesis from 1953 is called *Conceptions of the Soul among North American Indians*. His writings on North America, ancient Nordic religions and Shamanism were influential, and he was an inspiration for a whole generation of scholars. His *De amerikanska indianernas religioner* (The Religions of the American Indians, 1967), was widely used at introductory courses in History of Religions in Sweden. In the years 1958–86, he was Professor of History of Religions at Stockholm University and Head of the Department of Religious History.

Sociologist and Anthropologist Christer Lindberg, Professor Emeritus at the Department of Social Anthropology at Lund University and associate professor of Comparative Religion at the Turku University, did in his thesis *Erland Nordenskiöld – en antropologisk biografi* (Erland Nordenskiöld – an Anthropological Biography,

1995), depicts the life of Erland Nordenskiöld, who became known for his popular books on indigenous cultures and who exposed the abuses that occurred against the indigenous populations in America at the time.

Anne-Christine Hornborg is Professor Emerita in the History of Religions. Her dissertation *A Landscape of Left-Overs: Changing Conceptions of Place and Environment among Mi'kmaq Indians of Eastern Canada* (2001)was built on historical source research and fieldwork (in 1992–3, 1996 and 2000) among the Mi'kmaq. Hornborg also conducted fieldwork in the Tonga Islands in 1998 and 2001, and in Peru in 2004. Apart from her field studies, her focus has been on cosmologies, animism, perceptions of nature, ecology and religion. She works within the field of Ritual Studies with a special focus on themes like new ritual practices and neo-spiritual 'therapy'.

Mikael Kurkialas thesis *Building the Nation Back Up* (1997) was based on lengthy periods of fieldwork between 1991 and 1997 in the Pine Ridge Reservation in South Dakota, home to the Oglala Lakota people. Here he examined how an ethnic identity is negotiated between the demands of the majority society, the dictates of tradition, the expectations of kinship and the notions of belonging and exclusion. Kurkiala is Associate Professor in Cultural Anthropology.

Mesoamerica and the Caribbean

As in the North American case, the source and research material regarding Mesoamerica and South America is insurmountable. Here follows a tentative and short research overview.

Jan Lundius defended his dissertation *The Great Power of God in San Juan Valley: Syncretism and Messianism in the Dominican Republic* on syncretism and messianism in the Dominican Republic (Lundius 1995). He has since continued his research and published on cofradias among the Maya in Guatemala, but mostly focuses on Dios Olivorio and the Palma Sola movement among peasants in the Dominican Republic.

In 2000, Bodil Liljefors Persson, Professor in History of Religions, defended her thesis, *The Legacy of the Jaguar Prophet: An Exploration of Maya Religion and Historiography*, at Lund University. It focused on the early colonial sources called the Books of Chilam Balam. Since then, she has regularly conducted fieldwork on the Yucatán peninsula. Main themes in her research are linked to mythology, beliefs, rituals and shamanism, as well as on contemporary spirituality, wellness, ecology and sustainability. Her published works include the anthology *Ecology, Power and Religion in Maya Landscapes* (Isendahl & Liljefors Persson 2011) and *Maya Religion and History* (Liljefors Persson, Kettunen & Helmke 2023). For several years, Liljefors Persson has been the secretary of WAYEB, the European Association of Mayanists (www.wayeb.org).

Daniel Andersson's thesis *The Virgin and the Dead: The Virgin of Guadalupe and the Day of the Dead in the Construction of Mexican Identities* (2001) is an interview and observation study from Central Mexico dealing with religious and spiritual issues among the so-called neo-Aztecs. *Indianska religioner* (Indian Religions), from 2015, depicts the Mesoamerican cultures before the time of conquest and concentrates on themes such as migrations, empire building and rituals concerning time and death. Andersson has then continued with describing and analysing indigenous cultures and religions in both Europe, Asia and Australia (Andersson 2019).

Magnus Lundberg, Professor in Church and Mission Studies, has dealt with the Catholic Church in colonial Latin America. In 2002, he obtained a PhD in Theology in Missionary Studies with Ecumenics at Lund University. He has, since his thesis, *Unification and Conflict: The Church Politics of Alonso de Montúfar OP, Archbishop of Mexico, 1554–1572* (2002), worked with the research project 'Religion in the Borderland: Resistance, Adaptation and Dialogue in Colonial Mexico' (2006–9), which aimed at studying the relationship between parish priests and Native American parishioners in Central Mexico. In a later monograph (2011), he analyses the interaction between the indigenous parishioners and the secular priests working in the parishes.

Stefan Permanto defended his anthropological thesis *The Elders and the Hills: Animism and Cosmological Re-Creation among the Q'eqchi' Maya in Chisec, Guatemala* at the University of Gothenburg in 2015. This is a study of ritual practices among the Maya group q'eqchi' in Guatemala. He has since continued his research and published around the religion of the q'eqchi'.

South America

Erland Nordenskiöld (1877–1932) is known for his many expeditions to South America. He was a zoologist who later became one of the most famous ethnographers in the history of Swedish Americanists. Unlike other contemporary researchers, he described the indigenous people he met all around South America in positive words and combined ethnographic research with an activist defence for the people he studied and lived among during his fieldworks. He researched in the Gran Chaco area as well as in Colombia and among the Cuna people in Panama, and he published his widely known book *Ett Indianlif i Gran Chaco* (Indian Life 1910), followed by *Indianer och hvita i nordöstra Bolivia* (Indians and White in Northeastern Bolivia) in 1911 and *De sydamerikanska indianernas kulturhistoria* (The Cultural History of the South American Indians) in 1912. Nordenskiöld also built up and was curator at the Ethnographic Museum in Gothenburg as well as being appointed Professor in Ethnography at the University of Gothenburg.

Another well-known researcher is Henry Wassén (1908–1996), who was one of Nordenskiöld's students. He mainly studied the indigenous people Chocó and Cuna of Colombia and Panamá and published on cultural history and shamanism and the use of various drugs also among Central American indigenous peoples (see Wassén 1965).

Kaj Århem, now Professor Emeritus in Cultural Anthropology and Ethnology affiliated to Uppsala University, has conducted fieldwork among the Makuna in

Amazonas, the Maasai in Tanzania and the Khmer people in Cambodia (Århem and Sprenger 2016). Århem has published extensively on the Makuna and their sociopolitical organization and religion, as can be seen in his dissertation *Makuna Social Organization: A Study in Descent, Alliance and the Formation of Corporate Groups in the North-Western Amazon*, defended at University of Gothenburg (1981).

Alf Hornborg, now Professor Emeritus in Human Ecology at Lund University, did his research on socio-ecological systems not only in the Western Amazonas but also among the Mik'maq in Nova Scotia. Following his dissertation *Dualism and Hierarchy in Lowland South America: Trajectories of Indigenous Social Organization* (1986), he has published extensively (i.e. Hornborg 1998) on sociopolitical, cultural and ecological issues among indigenous people in the Americas as well as in Oceania.

Anthropologist Dan Rosengren received his doctorate at the University of Gothenburg in 1987 on the thesis *In the Eyes of the Beholder: Leadership and the Social Construction of Power and Dominance among the Matsigenka of the Peruvian Amazon*. He has also worked in Angola as a socio-economic advisor at the Ministry of Fisheries' department. He has written extensively on various adjacent topics and became appointed docent in 2005 and has been a member of the international board of IWGIA.

Finally, Jan-Åke Alvarsson is, since 2009, Professor of Cultural Anthropology at the Department of Cultural Anthropology and Ethnology at Uppsala University. He is Director of the Institute for Pentecostal Studies, Uppsala, since 2007. He has returned not only to the themes of his thesis *The Mataco of the Gran Chaco: An Ethnographic Account of Change and Continuity in Mataco Socio-Economic Organization* (1988) in various publications but also to the interplay between myth, nature and shamanism in Native American religions.

Asia

Concerning the whole of Asia – from the Middle East to Thailand and Japan – it is, of course, impossible to give a fair overview of the research conducted on indigenous groups. But it can be said that there are fewer works conducted by Swedish scholars focusing on religions in this region than there are on America and Africa. We also do not have a clear distinction between precolonial and postcolonial times in Asia, and, therefore, the concepts of 'traditional', 'original' and 'indigenous' become imprecise. Much research has been conducted on, for example, Indian and Chinese rural life, but that falls outside the scope of this text.

Here follows a short description of some of the research done on Asian Indigenous religions.

Beginning with the multifaceted scene of Japan, we have Katarina Sjöberg, who, in her ethnographic thesis *The Return of Ainu: Cultural Mobilization and the Practice of Ethnicity in Japan* (1993), deals with the phenomenon called Fourth World Populations and the Ainu population, a people found mainly on the island of Hokkaido. Sjöberg has since then continued to write about the Ainu from an anthropological and historical perspective.

The thesis by historian of religions Pavel Wolf, *Seger åt gudarna. Rituell besatthet hos ladakhier* (Victory for the Gods. Ritual Obsession among the Ladakhis) was defended at Stockholm University in 1994 and deals with shamanistic rituals in Ladakh, Northern India.

Social anthropologist Bengt G. Karlsson has worked at and been a visiting researcher at several universities in Sweden and abroad. Since his thesis *Contested Belonging: An Indigenous People's Struggle for Forest and Identity in Sub-Himalayan Bengal* (1997), he has published numerous articles and other texts on indigeneity in India, indigenous governance and state ethnicity (Karlsson 2016).

Oceania, Australia

When it comes to Australia and the entire vast Pacific region, we have selected a handful of researchers that we believe cover the field reasonably well. Here, too, we are limited to the textual scope of the chapter, and we easily realize that a more comprehensive research overview would have been beneficial. It must be said, however, that compared to America and Africa, this area is not as thoroughly researched.

In her thesis *'Who Are You to Tell Us Our History': Culture and Religion in Hawaiians' Encounter with the American Mission* which was defended in 2007 at Lund University, Historian of Religions Kristina Hellner Taylor focuses on Hawaiian history with particular emphasis on the encounters between traditional Indigenous religion, identity negotiations and the Christian mission.

In 1998, Monica Engelhart defended her thesis in History of Religions, *Extending the Tracks: A Cross-Reductionistic Approach to Australian Aboriginal Male Initiation Rites*. Here, she focuses on the culture of the indigenous people from early colonial time and from various regions in Australia, with special focus on male initiation rites and how they are performed.

In 2001, Social Anthropologist Ulf Johansson Dahre defended his thesis, *Det förgångna är framtiden. Ursprungsfolk och självbestämmande i Hawai'i* (The Past Is the Future: Indigenous Peoples and Self-Determination in Hawai'i).

Dahre has since then continued his research and published on indigenous people on a more general level, focusing on political questions and human rights issues.

Conclusions

A large part of the research on indigenous groups in Swedish universities is less regional than thematically oriented and aims to see similarities and differences in, among other issues, minority policy or contemporary migrations and the rights of indigenous peoples. Many works have points of intersection that transcend the purely regional.

In an attempt to summarize this somewhat fragmented research discourse, we can note a few things. First, Swedish researchers have been very active in exploring, analysing and debating indigenous peoples, their history, their languages and their current rights. Second, there has been a tendency over the long term in Stockholm to focus on North America and the Swedish Sami populations, while in Lund there has also been a focus on Africa and the Americas. In Gothenburg, Central and South America has been the main research area. In general, it can be said that Swedish scholars have conducted more research in America than in Asia and Oceania. It can also be stated that the Sami culture quite early was researched and discussed, often carefully depicted – not seldom by Sami academics – and with quite a lot of empathy; it is not a forgotten group we are dealing with here. Third, it might be said that within the disciplines of History of Religions and Anthropology, the research has been carried out as solitarian projects. This may also be related to the phenomenological direction in the study of comparative religion and anthropology of religions in the early twentieth century.

References

Alvarsson, J.-Å. (1988), *The Mataco of the Gran Chaco: An Ethnographic Account of Change and Continuity in Mataco Socio-Economic Organization*, Uppsala Studies in Cultural Anthropology No. 11, Uppsala: Almqvist & Wiksell International.

Andersson, D. (2001), *The Virgin and the Dead: The Virgin of Guadalupe and the Day of the Dead in the Construction of Mexican Identities*, Göteborg: Göteborgs universitet.

Andersson, D. (2015), *Indianska religioner. Från vandringar till imperiebyggande*, Stockholm: Dialogos.

Andersson, D. (2019), *Ursprungsfolkens religioner*, Lund: Studentlitteratur.

Århem, K. (1981), *Makuna Social Organization: A Study in Descent, Alliance and the Formation of Corporate Groups in the North-Western Amazon*, Uppsala: Acta Universitatis Upsaliensis.

Århem, K., and G. Sprenger, eds (2016), *Animism in Southeast Asia*, New York: Routledge.

Berglund, Axel-Ivar (1975), *Zulu Thought-Pattern and Symbolism*, Uppsala: Studia missionalia Upsaliensia.

Bäckman, L. (1964), *Studie i de förkristna samernas föreställningar om dödsriket med tonvikten lagd på de skandinaviska samerna*, Stockholm: Stockholms universitet.

Bäckman, L. (1975), *Sájva. Föreställningar om hjälp- och skyddsväsen i heliga fjäll bland samerna*, Stockholm: Stockholms universitet.

Bäckman, L., and Å. Hultkrantz (1978), *Studies in Lapp Shamanism*, Stockholm: University of Stockholm.

Bäckman, L., and Å. Hultkrantz (1985), *Saami Pre-Christian Religion. Studies on the Oldest Traces of Religion Among the Saamis*, Stockholm: Almqvist & Wiksell.

Callewaert, I. (2000), *The Birth of Religion Among the Balanta of Guinea-Bissau*, Lund: Lunds universitet.

Dahre Johansson, U. (2001), *Det förgångna är framtiden. Ursprungsfolk och självbestämmande i Hawai'i*, Lund Monographs in Social Anthropology, Lund: Lunds universitet.

Edsman, C.-M. (1949), *Ignis Divinus: Le feu comme moyen de rajeunissement et d'immortalité: contes légendes mythes et rites*, Lund: Gleerup.
Edsman, C.-M. (1994), *Jägaren och makterna. Samiska och finska björnceremonier*, Uppsala: Dialekt- och folkminnesarkivet.
Ehnmark, E. (1966), *Levande religioner: Naturfolken, Indien, islam*, Stockholm: Liber.
Engelhart, M. (1998), *Extending the Tracks: A Cross-Reductionistic Approach to Australian Aboriginal Male Initiation Rites*, Stockholm: Almkvist & Wiksell International.
Hallgren, R. (1988), *The Good Things in Life: A Study of the Traditional Religious Culture of the Yoruba People*, Lund: Lund Studies in African and Asian Religions.
Hallgren, R. (1995), *The Vital Force: a Study of Àṣẹ In the Traditional and Neo-Traditional Culture of the Yoruba People*, Stockholm: Almqvist & Wiksell International.
Hellner Taylor, K. (2007), *'Who Are You to Tell Us Our History': Culture and Religion in Hawaiians' Encounter with the American Mission*, Lund: Lunds universitet.
Hornborg, A., and M. Kurkiala, eds (1998), *Voices of the Land: Identity and Ecology in the Margins*, Lund: Lund university Press.
Hornborg, A. (1986), *Dualism and Hierarchy in Lowland South America: Trajectories of Indigenous Social Organization*, Uppsala: Uppsala Studies in Cultural Anthropology.
Hornborg, A.-C. (2001), *A Landscape of Left-Overs: Changing Conceptions of Place and Environment among Mi'kmaq Indians of Eastern Canada*, Lund: Lunds universitet.
Hultkrantz, Å. (1953), *Conceptions of the Soul among North American Indians: A Study in Religious Ethnology*, Stockholm: Etnografiska Museet.
Hultkrantz, Å. (1967), *De amerikanska indianernas religioner*, Stockholm: Bonniers.
Isendahl, C., and B. Liljefors Persson, eds (2011), *Ecology, Power and Religion in Maya Landscapes*, Acta Mesoamericana, Vol X, Schwaben: Verlag Anton Saurwein.
Karlsson, B. G. (1997), *Contested Belonging: An Indigenous People's Struggle for Forest and Identity in Sub-Himalayan Bengal*, Lund: sociologiska institutionen, Lunds universitet.
Karlsson, B. G. (2016), 'Jorden vi ägde: Resursanvändning, genus och privatisering av mark i nordöstra Indien', in *Kungl. Vitterhets Historie och Antikvitets Akademiens årsbok*, 77–95, Stockholm: Kungl. Vitterhets Historie och Antikvitets Akademien.
Karsten, R. (1926), *The Civilization of the South American Indians: With Special Reference to Magic and Religion*, London: Kegan Paul, Trench, Trubner.
Karsten, R. (1952), *Samefolkets religion. De nordiska lapparnas hedniska tro och kult i religionshistorisk belysning*, Stockholm, Hugo Gebers förlag.
Kurkiala, M. (1997), *Building the Nation Back Up: The Politics of Identity on the Pine Ridge Indian Reservation*, Uppsala: Acta Universitatis Upsaliensis, Uppsala Studies in Cultural Anthropology.
Liljefors Persson, B. (2000), *The Legacy of the Jaguar Prophet: An Exploration of Yucatec Maya Religion and Historiography*, Lund: Lunds universitet.
Liljefors Persson, B., Kettunen, H., Helmke, C. (eds.) (2023) *Maya Religion and History*, Acta MesoAmericana 31, Anton Saurwein, Munich.
Lindberg, C. (1995), *Erland Nordenskiöld – en antropologisk biografi*, Lund: Lunds universitet.
Lindmark, D. (2006), *En lappdrängs omvändelse. Svenskar i möte med samer och deras religion på 1600- och 1700-talen*, Umeå: Umeå Universitet.
Lundberg, M. (2002), *Unification and Conflict: The Church Politics of Alonso de Montúfar OP, Archbishop of Mexico, 1554–1572*, Lund: Lunds universitet.
Lundberg, M. (2011), *Church Life between the Metropolitan and the Local: Parishes, Parishioners and Parish Priests in Seventeenth-Century Mexico*, Orlando: Iberoamericana Vervuert.

Lundius, J. (1995), *The Great Power of God in San Juan Valley: Syncretism and Messianism in the Dominican Republic*, Stockholm: Almqvist & Wiksell International.
Nilsson, M. P. (1900), *Studia de Dionysiis atticis*, Lund: Lunds universitet.
Nilsson, M. P. (1911), *Primitiv religion*, Stockholm: Hugo Gebers förlag.
Nordenskiöld, E. (1910), *Indianlif i El Gran Chaco*, Stockholm: Bonnier.
Nordenskiöld, E. (1911), *Indianer och hvita i nordöstra Bolivia*, Stockholm: Bonnier.
Nordenskiöld, E. (1912), *De sydamerikanska indianernas kulturhistoria*, Stockholm: Bonnier.
Olofsson, E., ed. (1998), *Trolldomsprocesser, myter, helande och modern samisk identitet*, Lund: IWGIA.
Olsson, T. (1972), *Lévi-Strauss och totemismens teoretiker*, Lund: Lunds universitet.
Olsson, T. (2000), 'De rituella fälten i Gwanyebugu', in *Svensk religionshistorisk årsskrift*, Stockholm: Tibatr.
Permanto, S. (2015), *The Elders and the Hills: Animism and Cosmological Re-Creation among the Q'eqchi' Masya in Chisec, Guatemala*, Göteborg: University of Gothenburg.
Pettersson, O. (1953), *Chiefs and Gods: Religious and Social Elements in the South Eastern Bantu Kingship*, Lund: Gleerup.
Pettersson, O. (1966), *Afrikas religioner*, Stockholm: Svenska Bokförlaget (Bonnier).
Reuterskiöld, E. (1912), *De nordiska lapparnas religion*, Stockholm: Norstedts.
Rosengren, D. (1987), *In the Eyes of the Beholder: Leadership and the Social Construction of Power and Dominance among the Matsigenka of the Peruvian Amazon*, Göteborg: Göteborgs universitet.
Ruong, I. (1982), *Samerna i historien och i nutiden*, Stockholm: Bonniers.
Ryd, L. (2013), *Renskötarkvinnor och livet i de sista rajderna*, Skellefteå: Ord&visor.
Ryd, L. (2015), *Urfödan. Om självhushållets mat hos folk i Lappland*. Borås: Ord&visor.
Rydving, H. (1993), *The End of Drum-Time: Religious Change among the Lule Saami, 1670s–1740s*, Uppsala: Uppsala University.
Rydving, H. (2012), *Perspectivas del norte: cinco textos sobre la lengua y la cultura de los samis*, Serie Antropológica 21, México D F: Universidad Nacional Autónoma de México.
Simma, B. (2022), *Samiskt kyrkoliv. Historia, kultur, teologi*, Luleå: Argument.
Sjöberg, K. (1993), *The Return of Ainu. Cultural Mobilization and the Practice of Ethnicity in Japan*, N.p.: Harwood Academic.
Wassén, H. S. (1965), *The Use of Some Specific Kinds of South American Indian Snuff and Related Paraphernalia*, Göteborg; Enografiska muséet.
Westerlund, D. (1980), *Ujamaa na dini: A Study of Some Aspects of Society and Religion in Tanzania, 1961–1977*, Stockholm: Almqvist & Wiksell International.
Westerlund, D. (2011), *Afrikanska religioner*, Stockholm: Dialogos förlag.
Wolf, P. (1994), *Seger åt gudarna. Rituell besatthet hos ladakhier*, Stockholm: Stockholms universitet.

Chapter 4

JUDAISM

Svante Lundgren and Martin Lund

Any attempt to encapsulate the history of an academic field and to sketch key issues in its present within a single chapter is a daunting task. It always carries the risk of projecting contemporary perspectives and definitions back onto past understandings and endeavours. For example, Jews and Judaism were discussed in Swedish academia long before the idea of a *Wissenschaft des Judentums* was articulated in the nineteenth century (Wiese 1999). Like elsewhere, scholars in Sweden have studied Judaism with the aim of understanding Jewish religion, culture and history for centuries, but perhaps more commonly from a more clearly Christian, and sometimes Christianizing, perspective than from an academic one. In the latter case, the study of Judaism does not fit with contemporary understandings of Jewish Studies, as a teaching subject and a research area that investigates 'Jewish experience in its widest sense' – whether that entails a focus on religion, history, philosophy, culture, languages, literatures or any other of a host of foci – from a non-doctrinal, non-parochial and non-denominational perspective (Jick et al. 2007: 316). Nevertheless, they mark the foundations of the study of Judaism in Sweden and so cannot be ignored.

Similarly, as suggested by the description of Jewish Studies quoted above, the area today is so broad-based and interdisciplinary that any attempt to chart it in its entirety would be futile. Only a century, or even a half-century, ago, there were few institutions of higher education in Sweden, and only a small number of scholars whose work touched on what could be described as either study of Judaism or Jewish studies; today, there are too many departments with too many scholars to ever think it possible to account for everyone whose work could fit the description. This is true not least because religious studies, and the many subfields and areas that comprise the discipline, is in a comparatively privileged position in Sweden. Owing both to the country's long history with a state church and the existence of religion education as a mandatory subject through much of primary and secondary schooling, religious studies is part of most university and university colleges' curricula. Because of this, some measure of Jewish studies is also taught at most departments that offer religious studies education, even though not everyone who teaches about Judaism focuses their research efforts on that subject and vice versa.

It is under these conditions that the following survey is offered. The chapter makes no claim to comprehensiveness but rather attempts to capture some of the major beats in the long history of academic study of Judaism in Sweden and some of the strongest tendencies within the area of study at present, as described by Swedish Jewish Studies scholars themselves.

Historical Overview

There has never been a big Jewish community in Sweden. At the time of writing, it is estimated that around twenty thousand people in Sweden identify as Jewish. The Jewish presence in the country is young. Jewish visitors had come before, sometimes for shorter stays in the country, but a settled Jewish community has only been present since 1775, when Sweden's King Gustav III invited a group of German Jews to settle in Stockholm. The Jewish community has subsequently grown, particularly through different waves of immigration, for example, by Russian Jews in the early twentieth century, by Holocaust survivors after the Second World War and by Jews from Poland in the late 1960s (Carlsson 2021).

The study of Judaism in Sweden long predates the country's Jewish communities. Sweden's first university was established in Uppsala in 1477. Research about Judaism has been carried out at its Faculty of Theology almost ever since, at first mainly in the field of what was until recently called Old Testament Studies. The study of Hebrew was part of general university education until the beginning of the nineteenth century, and it was common to see Hebrew quotes in dissertations. Some dissertations were even written in Hebrew, for example, the dissertation of theologian Jordan Edenius, who was rector of Uppsala University in 1663 (Harviainen 1995). Gösta Lindeskog, a theologian and New Testament scholar, earned his doctorate from Uppsala University in 1938 with a dissertation about 'the Jesus question' in modern Judaism, a topic he also discussed in other academic and popular works. The Centre for Multi-Ethnic Research was established at the Department of History at Uppsala University in the 1980s. In 2010, it was renamed the Hugo Valentin Centre after the Swedish-Jewish historian Hugo Valentin, who wrote one of the most comprehensive, and still the most influential, histories of Jewish communities in Sweden. The centre has two main areas of research: cultural and social phenomena and processes of change related to ethnicity, and Holocaust and genocide studies (Hugo Valentine Centre n.d.). Uppsala University's multidisciplinary Forum for Jewish Studies has since 2013 worked with a mission 'to support research and education in Jewish studies broadly, e.g., Jewish history, Judaism, Jewish culture, Hebrew language, and the Jewish minority in Sweden', currently under the leadership of New Testament scholar Cecilia Wassén and historian Lars M. Andersson (Forum for Jewish Studies n.d.).

Lund University, located in the small southern city from which it gets its name, has had a Faculty of Theology since its founding in 1666. As in Uppsala, Hebrew was included in the curriculum, here in the field of Old Testament Studies. The first chair in Jewish Studies in Swedish academic history was established there in 1987. Its first holder, from 1989, was Karl-Erich Grözinger, a Jewish Studies scholar from Germany whose interests included music and song in early Jewish theology and histories of Jewish thought. Grözinger was succeeded in 1993 by Hanne Trautner-Kromann from Denmark, whose research interests included Jewish reactions to Christian pressures and persecution as expressed in medieval Jewish polemics and Jewish-Christian relations (Johnson 1990; Trautner-Kromann 2001). The chair was left empty upon Trautner-Kromann's retirement in 2011. The current head of Jewish Studies at Lund University is Karin Hedner Zetterholm, whose interests include rabbinical Judaism and its influences on modern Judaism as well as its developments in relation to early Jesus-oriented movements.

Today, Jewish Studies is organizationally situated at Lund University's multidisciplinary Centre for Theology and Religious Studies (CTR). Four doctoral degrees in Jewish Studies were awarded in the years between the subject's establishment as an independent research subject and Trautner-Kromann's retirement: Eva-Maria Jansson (*The Message of Mitzvah: The Mezuzah in Rabbinic Literature*, 1999), Zetterholm (*Portrait of a Villain: Laban the Aramean in Rabbinic Literature*, 2002); Johan Åberg (*Det föreställda ghettot. Ultraortodox gränsdragning och identitetskonstruktion i* The Jewish Observer *1983–2002* (The Imagined Ghetto. Ultraorthodox Boundary Demarcation and Identity-Construction in *The Jewish Observer* 1983–2000) (2003); and Martin Lund (*Rethinking the Jewish–Comics Connection*, 2013). It was not possible to get a doctoral degree in Jewish Studies from Lund University for a period following Trautner-Kromann's retirement, but graduate students could study the subject as a History of Religions specialization. As of this writing, Jewish Studies has been reinstated as a research discipline and new PhD students are once again accepted. Dissertations in other subjects such as Biblical Studies and Global Christianity have also touched upon Jewish subjects, for example, New Testament scholar Jennifer Nyström's *Reading Romans, Constructing Paul(s): A Conversation Between Messianic Jews in Jerusalem and Paul within Judaism Scholars* (2021),[1] as have a variety of publications by faculty at CTR and at other departments and centres at Lund. Two theologians from Lund University with a substantial research output on Judaism are the Old Testament scholar Bo Johnson (e.g. 2020) and the New Testament scholar Jesper Svartvik (e.g. 2011). Since 2008, Lund University's Centre for Languages and Literature has also been home to a program in Yiddish, one of Sweden's officially recognized minority languages. Headed since its inception by Yiddishist Jan Schwarz, the program teaches Yiddish language, cultures and literatures, and Schwarz has actively researched these topics, with a long-standing interest in the works of Isaac Bashevis Singer and post-Holocaust Yiddish cultures (e.g. 2015).[2] Both Lund and Uppsala continue teaching courses in classical Hebrew although in a more specialized way than in previous centuries, with Uppsala offering a variety of courses that include biblical literatures as well as Hebrew literatures up to and including the present, while Lund offers a similarly wide array of courses as well as courses in modern Hebrew.

A Society for Jewish Studies was established in 1973 as a national, Swedish association. It organized a Nordic conference in 1975, after which the society was expanded into a Nordic association that also included members from Denmark, Norway and Finland. The first issue of the scholarly journal *Nordisk judaistik – Scandinavian Jewish Studies* was also published that year. It normally published two issues a year between 1975 and 1993 but reduced its frequency to an annual schedule from 1994 until 2005. After a hiatus of a few years, a final issue was published in 2008. It was revived in 2016 as a multidisciplinary, online-only journal with the aim of 'promoting Jewish studies in Scandinavia by publishing scholarly articles, surveys and documents, by reviewing recent literature, and compiling bibliographies' (Nordisk judaistik n.d.). The revived journal was edited by Ruth Illman (Finland) and Zetterholm (Lund University), who has since been replaced by another Lund University scholar, Svante Lundgren. The Society for Jewish Studies also organized several Nordic conferences: 1975 in Stockholm, 1981 in Copenhagen, 1985 in Turku/Åbo, 1990 in Trondheim, 1993 in Lund, 1996 in Aarhus and 2000 in Järvenpää.[3] The Society has been largely inactive in the twenty-first century, but an attempt to form a new Nordic Network for Jewish Studies is underway as of the early 2020s, spearheaded by Katharina Keim and Zetterholm and based at the Centre for Theology and Religious Studies at Lund University.

Several projects related to the Holocaust were initiated under the prime ministership of Göran Persson (1996–2006). In 2000, the Swedish state allocated money to enable the founding of an educational institute in Stockholm named Paideia – The European Institute for Jewish Studies in Sweden, 'with the mandate to nurture the renewal of European Jewish culture, to support cross-cultural dialogue, and to promote a positive paradigm of a minority culture within European societies' (Paideia n.d.). To that end, Paideia offers a one-year program with a focus on Jewish textual sources, a project incubator to support the development of new initiatives for European Jewish life and other ideas-centred or public programs. Over the years, several well-known international scholars have taught at Paideia, and hundreds of students from more than forty countries have studied at the institute. The state also established the Living History Forum in 2003. The Forum works with Holocaust education and remembrance, with the broader aim of promoting democracy and equality and spreading knowledge about the Holocaust, but it also publishes reports about antisemitism and other forms of racism (Forum för levande historia n.d.). The Segerstedt Institute at the University of Gothenburg, which was established in 2015 as a national resource centre for knowledge about violent ideologies, includes scholars who do research about antisemitism (The Segerstedt Institute n.d.).

Key Issues

Because of its interdisciplinarity and its diffusion into so many different religious studies and teacher training programs, Jewish Studies is difficult to chart on a national level in Sweden. However, the Lund-based Nordic Network for Jewish Studies solicited information from scholars who view themselves as doing work in the area. In addition to active scholars at Lund University in the south and Uppsala University in the north, respondents from the University of Gothenburg, Malmö University, Paideia, the Institute for Holocaust Research in Sweden (IHRS), Södertörn University in the Stockholm area and Umeå University help paint a broader – but far from complete – picture of the field and its key issues today. It is possible to map out some general common threads and key issues in Jewish studies research in Sweden from these self-reports.

The topic that perhaps stands out most among self-reports of Swedish Jewish Studies scholars is Holocaust research. Much of this research focuses on understandings and experiences of the Holocaust in Sweden and is not limited to scholars who identify with Jewish Studies. Early examples include Hans Lindberg's 1973 doctoral dissertation *Svensk flyktingpolitik under internationellt tryck 1936–1941* (Swedish Refugee Policy under International Pressure 1936–1941) and Steven Koblik's *The Stones Cry Out: Sweden's Response to the Persecution of Jews 1933–1945* (1988). A small trickle of research publications followed in the intervening years (e.g. Levine 1996; Lomfors 1996), but it was with the turn of the millennium that the topic really became a major area of interest (see Åmark 2021). Scholars have focused on Sweden's official policy during the Holocaust (e.g. Andersson and Tydén 2007; Koblik 1988), media reportage during the Holocaust (e.g. Svanberg and Tydén 1997) and other topics. Among scholars who identify their work as being within the orbit of Jewish Studies, research interests range from studying the experiences of Jewish refugees and exiles from Nazi-occupied territories and the reception of Jewish refugees before and during the war and of Holocaust survivors after the war (e.g. Thor Tureby 2005, 2012; see also Andersson and Kvist Geverts 2008; Kvist Geverts 2008; Rudberg 2017) to problematizing archival practices in relation to Holocaust collections (Thor Tureby and Wagrell 2020). Some scholars also focus specifically on the teaching of Holocaust-related subjects in Swedish schools and the use of study trips in teaching (e.g. Flennegård 2022; Flennegård and Mattson 2023). While much Holocaust research is focused on Swedish contexts, scholars in Sweden have also studied topics such as Holocaust denial (Karlsson 2015), European historical cultures of the Holocaust in contemporary Europe (Karlsson 2008; Karlsson and Zander 2003, 2004, 2006) and questions about Holocaust witness and memory in a time when the last survivors will soon be gone (Katz Thor 2018). Holocaust research is also done at several departments of history and at the recently established IHRS in Stockholm, funded by a private foundation (IHRS n.d.).

Another common topic of interest is Jewish–non-Jewish relationships of various kinds. Research is evenly distributed between historical studies and more present-focused ones. Some scholars study or work to promote dialogue. After the Second World War, for example, the Church of Sweden established the Swedish Theological Institute in Jerusalem with an orientation towards Jewish-Christian relations (Bengtsson 2015). Although the institute is owned and operated by the Church of Sweden, it has hosted numerous university students and scholars who have done research about Jewish-Christian relations and other issues connected to Judaism. In later years, the institute has broadened its focus to also cover Islam and Palestinian Christianity. One of its directors, Göran Larsson, has published extensively about Jewish faith and praxis (e.g. Larsson 2017), and he has been a central figure in Jewish-Christian dialogue, both in Sweden and in Israel. A person with an international impact in this field was the New Testament scholar Krister Stendahl, who was professor and dean at the Divinity School at Harvard University before becoming the bishop of Stockholm. In the 1960s, he was instrumental in the paradigm shift in research about the apostle Paul and became, with his interest in the Jewish background of the New Testament, an influential actor in Jewish-Christian dialogue. He is also famous for his three rules of religious understanding, basic guidelines about how to approach another religion (Fredriksen and Svartvik 2018). Others focus on tensions and challenges, as, for example, Magdalena Dziaczkowska, whose work has addressed Jewish responses to the challenges of 'multicultural contemporaneity' and US American responses to the Second Vatican Council (2020; Dziaczkowska and Messina 2020). Yet others are more interested in the role of inter-group relations in the development of Judaism and in present-day comparative work. Keim, for example, has studied Jewish-Christian-Muslim relations in early Islamic history while Lena Roos has studied Jewish and Christian eschatology in the twenty-first century (2021) as well as relations between Jews and Christians, and Jews and Muslims in the Middle Ages (2002, 2003, 2006). Simon Sorgenfrei's *'De kommer att vara annorlunda svenskar': Berättelsen om Sveriges första muslimer* ('They Will Be Different Swedes': The Story of Sweden's First Muslims) (2022) discusses Muslim-Jewish relations in twentieth-century Sweden.

Swedish Jewish history is another key issue. The paradigmatic work in this category is, and is likely to remain, Valentin's history of Sweden's Jewish communities, *Judarnas historia i Sverige* (Jewish History in Sweden) (1924). It would take nearly another century before another similarly ambitious attempt to write a synthesis of Jewish history in Sweden was undertaken, by Carl Henrik Carlsson in his *Judarnas historia i Sverige* (Jewish History in Sweden) (2021), which fills the gap well. Many scholars who focus on Jews and Judaism in Sweden discuss the histories and present shapes of antisemitism in the country. Research about antisemitism has focused on hostility towards Jews in Sweden, both historically (e.g. Lundqvist 2021; Tydén 1986) and in the present (e.g. Bachner 2004; Bachner and Bevelander 2021; Wigerfelt and Wigerfelt 2016), and has covered both political (e.g. Blomqvist 2013) and cultural spheres such as stereotyped images in mass media (Andersson 2000), in public discourse about belonging and modernity (Rosengren 2007) or belonging and antisemitism (Christensen 2021), and in schools (Katzin 2021). Evin Ismail studied antisemitism in the Muslim Brotherhood and the Islamic State (2022). The Swedish Committee Against Antisemitism, an educational and advocacy organization, actively opposes antisemitism and promotes research about it (SKMA n.d.).

Others focus on topics related to Jewish emancipation in Sweden (e.g. Carlesson Magalhães 2020). Since many of Sweden's Jewish citizens and inhabitants have come as immigrants or refugees, some researchers have focused on topics related to migration and integration (e.g. Carlsson 2011; Ilicki 1988) or with a focus on specific contexts of migration, such as Södertörn PhD student Martin Englund's research about Jewish refugees from the antisemitic campaign in Poland between 1967 and 1972. Malin Thor Tureby has studied the Hehalutz in interwar Sweden (2005), for example, while Pia Lundqvist has studied Jewish immigrants in nineteenth-century Gothenburg with a focus on international trade contacts and the textile trade (e.g. Brismark and Lundqvist 2015).

Most readers will likely have noticed that what many view as the classical preoccupations of religious studies have been absent from this survey of key issues. This is because a relatively small number of self-reported Jewish Studies scholars are engaged in such scholarship. Nevertheless, as seen above, there has been a strong tradition of textual scholarship in Sweden which is being continued today, particularly in scholarship on Rabbinical and Classical Judaism. One of the most prominent figures in this type of scholarship is Karin Hedner Zetterholm, whose work on Jewish scriptural interpretation discusses ancient and modern contexts (2012) and cross-cultural analysis of ancient milieus (Zetterholm et al. 2022). Another prominent figure is New Testament scholar Magnus Zetterholm, whose work has involved a sustained focus on, among other things, the importance of reading Paul in relation to Jewish history and interpretive traditions (e.g. 2009; see also Nanos and Zetterholm 2015). Studies that further suggest the diversity of approaches to the topic include Erik Alvstad's work on conceptions and practices related to dreams in early Rabbinic Judaism (2010), Thomas Karlsson's research on Kabbalah and Gothicist esotericism (2010), and Kamilla Skarström Hinojosa's work on Serek ha-Yahad, one of the so-called Dead Sea Scrolls (2016). Karin Almbladh from Uppsala University has published studies about both the Hebrew Bible and rabbinic literature (e.g. Almbladh 1986; Ha-Kohen 1981). Several scholars are also focused on modern Jewish thought, from Ulrika Björk's work on Hannah Arendt's philosophy (e.g. 2018, 2021), to PhD student Nicholas Lawrence's ongoing work on the relationship between Salomon Maimon's *Lebensgeschichte* and his transcendental philosophy, and on to Alana Vincent's work on memorialization and theology, Jewish approaches to social justice and Jewish thought, utopia and revolution (2013, 2017; Namli, Svenungsson and Vincent 2014).

Historically, the study of Judaism has often been engaged with questions of language, and, as has been suggested here, Sweden is no exception. As noted at the outset of this chapter, Hebrew has been part of Swedish academia since the founding of the country's first universities. While it is a far more specialized subject in the twenty-first century than it was in centuries past, it is nevertheless thriving. In addition to the study of Classical and Rabbinic Judaism already discussed, scholars in Sweden focus their efforts on everything from linguistic and philological studies of ancient Israeli texts (e.g. Wikander 2014) to critical discourse analyses of interpretations and depictions of the 'Hebrew Bible' in Swedish daily newspapers (Liljefors 2022), showing that the subject remains both lively and diverse in approaches as well as areas of focus. Schwarz's work has already been mentioned, but he is far from alone in studying Yiddish language and literatures. Tal Davidovich and Torkel Lindquist, for example, have discussed the importance of the Yiddish language (2006), while Håkan Blomqvist has studied 'socialism in Yiddish' in Sweden via the history of the Bund Labor Organization (2022). While Yiddish is a far smaller subject than Hebrew, it is nevertheless beginning to grow into a variegated and active research area in Sweden.

Finally, there are several smaller strands of research that seem to be growing in importance. Several scholars study questions of cultural heritage, with many focusing on Jewish identity in Sweden and elsewhere. Lars Dencik, who was Professor of Social Psychology at Roskilde University (Denmark), has written extensively on Jewish identity in the contemporary world. Based on a comprehensive questionnaire study among Jewish residents in all Nordic countries, he coined the expression 'smorgasbord'-Judaism, as most Jews in these countries (as in many other countries) tend to pick and choose freely which Jewish traditions to follow and not (Dencik 2011, 2014). He has also done important research on antisemitism (Dencik 2020).

In line with growing interest in urban humanities more broadly, several scholars also report interest in urban Jewish history. Maja Hultman's doctoral dissertation focused on the role of Jewish–non-Jewish relations, intracommunal hierarchies and urban topography in the construction of Jewish religious diversity in Stockholm between 1870 and 1939,[4] while Daniel Leviathan's doctoral research focuses on Swedish synagogues and funeral chapels. Martin Lund has also incorporated urban cultural formation in his work on Jewish American comics production (e.g., 2016). As is the case more generally in Jewish Studies, scholars in Sweden are also showing a growing interest in various literatures and popular cultures. Elizabeth Kella has written about journalist and author Margit Silberstein's autobiography, focusing on her experiences as the child of Holocaust survivors (2023), Alvstad has studied Jewish American cartoonist Eli Valley's work (2013), and Åberg has written about Jewish humor and Jewish identity (2005).

One final topic that warrants mention here is scholarship about the ongoing conflict in Israel–Palestine. The conflict has been extensively studied in the field of peace and conflict studies by figures like Helena Lindholm Schulz and Michael Schulz (1995), Isabell Schierenbeck (2006) and Anders Persson (2020), but while there is much writing and discussion of the topic, we will limit ourselves here to work that fits the description of Jewish Studies above, that is, work that focuses on 'Jewish experience in its widest sense'.[5] Karin Aggestam has often focused on peace-building efforts and their gaps (e.g. 1999; Aggestam and Strömbom 2013; Aggestam, Strömbom and Persson 2014), sometimes in collaboration with Lisa Strömbom, who has also focused on such topics as urban planning policy in Jerusalem and other facets of placemaking in contested areas (e. g. Strömbom 2010; Strömbom and Mannergren Selimovic 2015). The impact of the conflict on perceptions of Jews in other places have also been the focus of research, in relation to, for example, the United States (Christensen and Enlund 2021) and in Sweden (Katzin 2021).

Conclusions

There is no denying that Jewish Studies in Sweden is a relatively small subject area, especially in comparison with many of the more nationally prominent subfield of Religious Studies and History of Religions. It is also arguably scattered, marked as it is by a strong multidisciplinarity, but likely also because it is spread out over several disciplines and departments across the country. Nevertheless, it is undeniably a vibrant and active area of study with many strong focus areas and significant discussions. Any judgement of the area's international impact should be tempered by the observation that much of the research is focused on the histories of Jewish communities in Sweden and on the impact, experience and memory of the Holocaust in the country, and published in Swedish. This means that its strongest impact is limited to a fairly small intellectual context.

With that said, it should also be noted that many of the scholars cited above have made a mark on the field in international circles and many are involved in international networks and collaborations. A primary example of this activity can be seen in the transnational, Nordic efforts of scholarly networks and the editors of and contributors to *Nordisk judaistik* across their decades of work. Many Jewish Studies scholars and scholars of Judaism also publish internationally, and work by scholars in Sweden often appears in journals and on the lists of publishers in other countries. It is, therefore, possible to speak of different levels of impact: on the one hand, scholars in the country engage in an active and ongoing local – national and regional – scholarly conversation with long roots and many branches; on the other hand, Swedish scholars contribute internationally to an extent that is arguably larger than their numbers would suggest.

It is impossible to say what the future will hold for Jewish Studies and the study of Judaism in Sweden in years to come, but one thing seems certain: whatever new key issues may appear, and whatever new directions researchers branch out into, its diversity will remain a central feature and a core strength. There are, of course, weaknesses associated with a scattered research area, not least the potential that we speak past each other or miss important findings in the fog of multidisciplinarity. It is not likely that these weaknesses will ever be overcome, although important steps to counter them are being taken in, for example, the revival of *Nordisk judaistik* and the Nordic Network for Jewish Studies. More can, and probably should, be done to further foster a closer association among scholars even as the area's diversity is maintained. There is much to be gained in doing so. But even if scholars remain scattered, and the subject area spread out to the extent that it is impossible to grasp in anything other than its major contours, it is a wellspring of strong research, and it is getting stronger.

Notes

1   This is possible at other universities as well, such as in the case of Jens Carlesson Magalhães, a PhD student in history who specializes on Jewish emancipation in nineteenth-century Sweden.

2   See also the description of his Singer research project: https://www.rj.se/en/gra nts/2021/the-worlds-of-i.b.singer-translation-feuilleton-life-writing.
3   Conference reports were published in the following issues of *Nordisk judaistik – Scandinavian Jewish Studies*: 1 (1), 4 (1), 6 (2), 11 (1–2), 14 (1), 17 (1–2) and 21 (1–2).
4   The unpublished dissertation is being revised for publication at the time of writing. See Hultman (2022) for a case study on building and feeling in a Stockholm synagogue.
5   Thus, for example, the work of sociologist Nina Gren, which focuses more on Palestinian refugees (2015).

References

Åberg, J. (2003), *Det föreställda ghettot. Ultraortodox gränsdragning och identitetskonstruktion i The Jewish Observer 1983–2002*, Lund: Arcus.
Åberg, J. (2005), 'Den judiske björnen', in V. Molnár, G. Paulsson and G. Andersson (eds), *Vetenskapssocieteten i Lund. Årsbok 2005*, 126–36, Lund: Vetenskapssocieteten i Lund.
Åmark. K. (2021), *Förintelsen och antisemitism – en kartläggning av svensk forskning*, Stockholm: Vetenskapsrådet.
Aggestam, K. (1999), *Reframing and Resolving Conflict. Israeli-Palestinian Negotiations 1988–1998*, Lund: Lund University Press.
Aggestam, K., and L. Strömbom (2013), 'Disempowerment and Marginalisation of Peace NGOs: Exposing Peace Gaps in Israel and Palestine', *Peacebuilding* 1 (1): 109–24.
Aggestam, K., L. Strömbom and A. Persson (2014), *Mellan krig och fred i Israel/Palestina*, Lund: Studentlitteratur.
Almbladh, K. (1986), *Studies in the Book of Jonah*, Uppsala: Uppsala University.
Alvstad, E. (2010), *Reading the Dream Text: A Nexus between Dreams and Text in the Rabbinic Literature of Late Antiquity*, Göteborg: University of Gothenburg.
Alvstad, E. (2013), '"The Jew Monster": Religion, satir och judisk identitetsproblematik i en karikatyrteckning av Eli Valley', *Chaos: skandinavisk tidsskrift for religionshistoriske studier* 59: 31–56.
Andersson, L. M. (2000), *En jude är en jude är en jude. Representationer av 'juden' i svensk skämtpress omkring 1900–1930*, Lund: Lunds universitet.
Andersson, L. M., and K. Kvist Geverts, eds (2008), *En problematisk relation? Flyktingpolitik och judiska flyktingar i Sverige 1920–1950*, Uppsala: Uppsala universitet, Historiska institutionen.
Andersson, L. M., and M. Tydén, eds. (2007), *Sverige och Nazityskland. Skuldfrågor och moraldebatt*, Stockholm: Dialogos.
Bachner, H. (2004), *Återkomsten. Antisemitism i Sverige efter 1945*, Stockholm: Natur och Kultur.
Bachner, H., and P. Bevelander (2021), *Antisemitism i Sverige. En jämförelse av attityder och föreställningar 2005 och 2020*, Stockholm: Forum för levande historia.
Bengtsson, H. (2015), *Svenska teologiska institutet. En berättelse från Wien till Jerusalem*, Uppsala: Svenska Kyrkan.
Björk, U. (2018), 'The Eclipse of the Transcendent and the Poetics of Praise: Arendt's Rilke', *Metodo: International Journal of Phenomenology and Philosophy* 6 (1): 99–126.
Björk, U. (2021), 'En annan Arendt', in R. Katz Thor and E. Wallrup (eds), *Blick, rörelse, röst. Festskrift till Cecilia Sjöholm*, 31–7, Huddinge: Södertörns högskola.

Blomqvist, H. (2013), *Myten om judebolsjevismen. Antisemitism och kontrarevolution i svenska ögon.* Stockholm: Carlsson.

Blomqvist, H. (2022), *Socialism in Yiddish: The Jewish Labor Bund in Sweden*, Stockholm: Södertörns högskola.

Brismark, A., and P. Lundqvist (2015), 'A Textile Web: Jewish Immigrants in Gothenburg in the Early Nineteenth Century and Their Impact on the Textile Market', *Scandinavian Journal of History* 40 (4): 485–511.

Carlesson Magalhães, J. (2020), ' "Vårt högsta mål. Judendomens väl": Samfundet I:I Judiska Intresset: 1841–1854', *Nordisk judaistik – Scandinavian Jewish Studies* 31 (1): 23–40. Available online: https://journal.fi/nj/article/download/94886/53696 (accessed 28 March 2023).

Carlsson, C. H. (2011), 'Judisk invandring från Aron Isaac till idag', in H. Müssener (ed.), *Judarna i Sverige – en minoritets historia. Fyra föreläsningar*, 17–54, Uppsala: Uppsala universitet.

Carlsson, C. H. (2021), *Judarnas historia i Sverige*, Stockholm: Natur och Kultur.

Christensen, J. (2021), 'Att inte passa in. Antisemitism och antinazism i Göteborg under 1900-talets första hälft', in J. Christensen, P. Cornell, J. Daun and M. Linde (eds), *Göteborg genom tiderna. Nedslag i stadens sociala och politiska historia*, 343–83, Göteborg: Daidalos.

Christensen, L., and J. Enlund (2021), 'Echoes of Violent Conflict: The Effect of the Israeli-Palestinian Conflict on Hate Crimes in the U.S.', Gothenburg: Working Paper in Economics, University of Gothenburg.

Davidovich, T., and T. Lindqvist (2006), 'Vad är så viktigt med jiddisch?', *Invandrare & minoriteter* 3: 5–10.

Dencik, L. (2011), 'The Dialectics of Diaspora. On the Art of being Jewish in the Swedish Modernity', in J. H. Schoeps and O. Glöckner (eds), *A Road to Nowhere? Jewish Experiences and Uncertainties in the Context of European Unification*, 121–50, Leiden: Brill.

Dencik, L. (2014), 'The Dialectics of Diaspora in Contemporary Modernity', in E. Ben-Rafael, J. Bokser Liwerant and Y. Gorny (eds), *Reconsidering Israel-Diaspora Relations*, 405–28, Leiden: Brill.

Dencik, L. (2020), 'Antisemitisms in the Twenty-First Century. Sweden and Denmark as Forerunners?', in J. Adams and C. Hess (eds), *Antisemitism in the North. History and State of Research*, 231–66, Berlin: De Gruyter.

Dziaczkowska, M. (2020), 'American Judaism and the Second Vatican Council: The Response of the American Jewish Committee to Nostra Aetate', *U.S. Catholic Historian* 38 (3): 25–47.

Dziaczkowska, M., and A. V. Messina, eds (2020), *Jews in Dialogue: Jewish Responses to the Challenges of Multicultural Contemporaneity*, Leiden: Brill.

Flennegård, O. (2022), 'Creating a Youth Ambassador: A Critical Study of a Swedish Project on Teaching and learning about the Holocaust', *Holocaust Studies*, https://doi.org/10.1080/17504902.2022.2136385.

Flennegård, O., and C. Mattson (2023), 'Democratic Pilgrimage: Swedish Students' Understanding of Study Trips to Holocaust Memorial Sites', *Educational Review* 75 (3): 429–46.

Forum for Jewish Studies (n.d.), 'The Forum for Jewish Studies', Uppsala University, Sweden, https://www.teol.uu.se/about-us/the-forum-for-jewish-studies/about-us/ (accessed 14 March 2023).

Forum för levande historia (n.d.), https://www.levandehistoria.se/english (accessed 27 March 2023).

Fredriksen, P., and J. Svartvik, eds (2018), *Krister among the Jews and Gentiles: Essays in Appreciation of the Life and Work of Krister Stendahl*, Mahwah, NJ: Paulist Press.

Gren, N. (2015), *Occupied Lives: Maintaining Integrity in a Palestinian Refugee Camp in the West Bank*, Cairo: The American University in Cairo Press.

Harviainen, T. (1995), 'Levande hebreiska i Norden på 1500–1700-talen', *Nordisk Judaistik – Scandinavian Jewish Studies* 16 (1–2): 75–82.

Hugo Valentine Centre (n.d.), 'The Hugo Valentin Centre', Uppsala University, Sweden, https://www.valentin.uu.se/?languageId=1 (accessed 14 March 2023).

Hultman, M. (2022), 'Atmosphere of the Other: Building and Feeling Stockholm's Orthodox Synagogue', *Emotion, Space and Society* 44, https://doi.org/10.1016/j.emospa.2022.100907.

Ilicki, J. (1988), *Den föränderliga identiteten. Om identitetsförändringar hos den yngre generationen polska judar som invandrade till Sverige under åren 1968–1972*, Åbo: Sällskapet för judaistisk forskning.

Institute for Holocaust Research in Sweden (IHRS) (n.d.), https://ihrs.se/en/ (accessed 27 March 2023).

Ismail, E. (2022), *The Antisemitic Origins of Islamist Violence. A Study of the Muslim Brotherhood and the Islamic State*, Uppsala: Department of Sociology, Uppsala University.

Jansson, E.-M. (1999), *The Message of a Mitsvah: The Mezuza in Rabbinic Literature*, Lund: Sällskapet för judaistisk forskning.

Jick, L. A., J. R. Baskin, A. Greenbaum and S. A. Goldberg (2007), 'Jewish Studies', in F. Skolnik and M. Berenbaum (eds), *Encyclopaedia Judaica*. V. 11, Ja-Kas, 316–27, Detroit: Macmillan Reference USA in association with the Keter Pub. House.

Johnson, B. (1990), 'Professuren i judaistik i Lund', *Nordisk judaistik – Scandinavian Jewish Studies* 11 (1–2): 91–2.

Johnson, B. (2020), *Judendomen – i kristet perspektiv, Andra upplagan*, Lund: Arcus.

Karlsson, K.-G. (2008), *Med folkmord i fokus. Förintelsens plats i den europeiska historiekulturen*, Stockholm: Forum för levande historia.

Karlsson, K.-G., and U. Zander, eds (2003), *Echoes of the Holocaust: Historical Cultures in Contemporary Europe*, Lund: Nordic Academic Press.

Karlsson, K.-G., and U. Zander, eds (2004), *Holocaust Heritage: Inquiries into European Historical Cultures*, Malmö: Sekel.

Karlsson, K.-G., and U. Zander, eds (2006), *The Holocaust on Post-War Battlefields: Genocide as Historical Culture*, Lund: Sekel.

Karlsson, M. (2015), *Cultures of Denial. Comparing Holocaust and Armenian Genocide Denial*, Lund: Department of History, Lund University.

Karlsson, T. (2010), *Götisk kabbala och runisk alkemi: Johannes Bureus och den götiska esoterismen*, Stockholm: Stockholms universitet.

Katz Thor, R. (2018), *Beyond the Witness: Holocaust Representation and the Testimony of Images. Three Films by Yael Hersonski, Harun Farocki and Eyal Sivan*, Stockholm: Art and Theory Publishing.

Katzin, M. (2021), *Skolgårdsrasism, konspirationsteorier och utanförskap*, Malmö: Malmö stad.

Kella, E. (2023), 'From Survivor to Im/Migrant Motherhood and Beyond: Margit Silberstein's Postmemorial Autobiography, Förintelsens Barn', in H. Wahlström

Henriksson, A. Williams and M. Fahlgren (eds), *Narratives of Motherhood and Mothering in Fiction and Life Writing*, 93–114, Cham: Palgrave Macmillan.

Koblik, S. (1988), *The Stones Cry Out. Sweden's Response to the Persecution of Jews 1933–1945*, documents translated by David Mel Paul and Margareta Paul, New York: Holocaust Library.

Ha-Kohen, J. (1981), *Sefer ʿEmeq ha-Bakha (The Vale of Tears) with the chronicle of the anonymous corrector*, Introduction, Critical Edition, Comments by Karin Almbladh, Uppsala: Uppsala University.

Kvist Geverts, K. (2008), *Ett främmande element i nationen. Svensk flyktingpolitik och de judiska flyktingarna 1938–1944*, Uppsala: Uppsala universitet, Historiska institutionen.

Larsson, G. (2017), *Uppbrottet. Andra Moseboken i judisk och kristen tradition*, 2:a reviderade och utökade upplagan, Lund: Arcus.

Levine, P. A. (1996), *From Indifference to Activism. Swedish Diplomacy and the Holocaust, 1938–1944*, Uppsala: Uppsala University.

Liljefors, H. (2022), *Hebreiska bibeln debatterad. En receptionskritisk studie av diskurser om 'Gamla Testamentet' i svenska dagstidningar 1987–2017*, Skellefteå: Artos och Norma bokförlag.

Lindberg, H. (1973), *Svensk flyktingpolitik under internationellt tryck 1936–1941*, Stockholm: Allmänna förlaget.

Lindholm Schulz, H., and M. Schulz, eds (1995), *Visions for a New Middle East. Prospects for Regional Co-Operation and Institution Building in the Context of the Peace Process – Israel, the Palestinian Entity, and Jordan. Proceedings from a One-Day Conference in Jerusalem 1995-04-11*, Göteborg: Padrigu.

Lomfors, I. (1996), *Förlorad barndom – återvunnet liv. De judiska flyktingbarnen från Nazityskland*, Göteborg: Historiska institutionen.

Lund, M. (2013), *Rethinking the Jewish-Comics Connection*, Lund: Lund University, Centre for Theology and Religious Studies.

Lund, M. (2016), *Re-Constructing the Man of Steel. Superman 1938–1941, Jewish American History, and the Invention of the Jewish–Comics Connection*, New York: Palgrave Macmillan.

Lundqvist, P. (2021), 'Tolerans, integration och antisemitism. Judar i 1800-talets Göteborg', in J. Christensen, P. Cornell, J. Daun and M. Linde (eds), *Göteborg genom tiderna. Nedslag i stadens sociala och politiska historia*, 305–42, Göteborg: Daidalos.

Namli, E., J. Svenungsson and A. M. Vincent, eds (2014), *Jewish Thought, Utopia, and Revolution*, Amsterdam: Rodopi.

Nanos, M. D., and M. Zetterholm (2015), *Paul Within Judaism: Restoring the First-Century Context to the Apostle*, Minneapolis: Fortress.

Nordisk Judaistik (n.d), https://journal.fi/nj/about (accessed 27 March 2023).

Nyström, J. (2021), *Reading Romans, Constructing Paul(s). A Conversation between Messianic Jews in Jerusalem and Paul within Judaism Scholars*, Lund: Lund University.

Paideia (n.d.), https://paideia-eu.org/about/ (accessed 27 March 2023).

Persson A. (2020), *EU Diplomacy and the Israeli-Arab Conflict, 1967–2019*, Edinburgh: Edinburgh University Press.

Roos, L. (2002), *The Stranger Who Lives Next Door. Jewish-Christian Relations in Germany during the High Middle Ages*, Uppsala: Swedish Science Press.

Roos, L. (2003), *'Acknowledge Muhammad and Do Not Choose Death!' Some Attitudes to Martyrdom, Conversion and Persecution among Jews Living under Muslim Rule during the Eleventh and Twelfth Centuries*, Uppsala: Swedish Science Press.

Roos, L. (2006), *'God Wants It!' The Ideology of Martyrdom of the Hebrew Crusade Chronicles and Its Jewish and Christian Background*, Turnhout: Brepols.

Roos, L. (2021), 'Building the Third Temple: Jewish and Christian Eschatology in the 21st Century', in C. Grappe (ed.), *La Maison de Dieu. Das Haus Gottes. 7. Symposium Strasbourg, Tübingen, Uppsala*, 351–64, Tübingen: Mohr Siebeck.

Rosengren, H. (2007), *'Judarnas Wagner'. Moses Pergament och den kulturella identifikationens dilemma omkring 1920–1950*, Lund: Sekel.

Rudberg, P. (2017), *The Swedish Jews and the Holocaust*, Abingdon and New York: Routledge.

Schierenbeck, I. (2006), *Det splittrade Israel. Politiska och sociala skiljelinjer*, Lund: Studentlitteratur.

Schwarz, J. (2015), *Survivors and Exiles: Yiddish Culture after the Holocaust*, Detroit: Wayne State University Press.

Segerstedt Institute (n.d.), https://www.gu.se/en/segerstedt-Institute (accessed 28 March 2023).

Skarström Hinojosa, K. (2016), *A Synchronic Approach to the Serek ha Yahad (1QS). From Text to Social and Cultural Context*, Umeå: Institutionen för idé och samhällsstudier, Umeå universitet.

SKMA (n.d.), *Svenska kommittén mot antisemitism [Swedish Committee Against Antisemitism]*, https://skma.se/in-english/ (accessed 31 March 2023).

Sorgenfrei, S. (2022), *'De kommer att vara annorlunda svenskar'. Berättelsen om Sveriges första muslimer*, Stockholm: Norstedts.

Strömbom, L. (2010), *Revisiting the Past: Israeli Identity, Thick Recognition and Conflict Transformation*, Lund: Department of Political Science, Lund University.

Strömbom, L., and J. Mannergren Selimovic (2015), 'Whose Place? Emplaced Narratives and the Politics of Belonging in East Jerusalem's Contested Neighbourhood of Silwan', *Space and Polity* 19 (2): 191–205.

Svanberg, I., and M. Tydén (1997), *Sverige och förintelsen. Debatt och dokument om Europas judar 1933–1945*, Stockholm: Arena.

Svartvik, J. (2011), 'Reading the Epistle to the Hebrews without Presupposing Supersessionism', in P. A. Cunningham, J. Sievers, M. C. Boys, H. H. Henrix and J. Svartvik (eds), *Christ Jesus and the Jewish People Today: New Explorations of Theological Interrelationships*, 77–91, Grand Rapids, MI: William B. Eerdmans.

Thor Tureby, M. (2005), *Hechalutz – en rörelse i tid och rum. Tysk-judiska ungdomars exil i Sverige 1933–1943*, Växjö: Växjö University Press.

Thor Tureby, M. (2012), *Kibbutzer i Sverige. Judiska lantbrukskollektiv i Sverige 1936–1946*, Stockholm: Judiska museet Stockholm.

Thor Tureby, M., and K. Wagrell (2020), *Vittnesmål från Förintelsen och de överlevandes berättelser. Definitioner, insamlingar och användningar, 1939–2020*, Stockholm: Forum för levande historia.

Trautner-Kromann, H. (2001), 'Judaistik', in B. Olsson, G. Bexell and G. Gustafsson (eds), *Theologicum i Lund. Undervisning och forskning i tusen år*, 89–93, Lund: Arcus.

Tydén, M. (1986), *Svensk antisemitism 1880–1930*, Uppsala: Centrum för multietnisk forskning.

Valentin, H. (1924), *Judarnas historia i Sverige*, Stockholm: Bonnier.

Vincent, A. M. (2013), *Making Memory: Jewish and Christian Explorations in Monument, Narrative, and Liturgy*, Eugene: Pickwick.

Vincent, A. M. (2017), 'The Necessity of a Jewish Systematic Theology', *Svensk Teologisk Kvartalskrift* 92 (3–4): 159–70.
Wiese, C. (1999), *Wissenschaft des Judentums und protestantische Theologie im wilhelminischen Deutschland*, Tübingen: Mohr Siebeck.
Wigerfelt A., and B. Wigerfelt (2016), 'Media Images and Experiences of Being a Jew in the Swedish City of Malmö', *SAGE Open* 6 (1), https://doi.org/10.1177/2158244016633739.
Wikander, O. (2014), *Drought, Death, and the Sun in Ugarit and Ancient Israel: A Philological and Comparative Study*, Winona Lake, IN: Eisenbrauns.
Zetterhom, K. H. (2002), *Portrait of a Villain: Laban the Aramean in Rabbinic Literature*, Leiden: Peeters.
Zetterholm, K. H. (2012), *Jewish Interpretation of the Bible: Ancient and Contemporary*, Minneapolis: Fortress Press.
Zetterholm, K. H., A. Runesson, C. Wassén and M. Zetterhom, eds (2022), *Negotiating Identities: Conflict, Conversion, and Consolidation in Early Judaism and Christianity (200 BCE – 600 CE)*, Lanham: Fortress Academic.
Zetterholm, M. (2009), *Approaches to Paul: A Student's Guide to Recent Scholarship*, Minneapolis: Fortress Press.

Chapter 5

ISLAM

Göran Larsson, Susanne Olsson and Simon Sorgenfrei

As in the rest of Europe, the study of Islam and Muslims in Sweden was for a long time primarily the study of Oriental languages, especially Arabic, but also Persian and Turkic languages (i.e. Martin 1995; Nanji 1997). Already in 1624, Arabic is mentioned as one of the languages that the Professor in Hebrew (Hebreae Linguage Professor) was expected to teach at Uppsala University (Malmberg 2007: 19).[1] As pointed out by Håkan Malmberg, Hebrew, and partly also Aramaic and Syriac, were at the forefront, while Arabic was seldom studied neither as a living language nor for its own sake. The Bible and its cultural, linguistic and religious landscapes were the focus. This situation progressively changed, and the Arabic and Turkic languages (including Tataric languages) became essential disciplines for Sweden's diplomatic contacts with the Tatar Khanates and the Ottoman Empire, as well as gradually becoming important for the general study of Oriental languages (Malmberg 2007; on the importance of Swedish diplomatic relations with the wider Muslim world, see Jarring 1987 and Östlund 2020).

As shown by Karl Vilhelm Zetterstéen (1866–1953), the holder of the chair in Semitic languages at Uppsala University between 1903 and 1931, the focus was on philology and rarely, if ever, on Islamic theology (Zetterstéen 1946). Like most other European universities, the study of non-Christian traditions had not yet developed into an independent discipline in Sweden. At the end of the nineteenth century, what we recognize today as the History of Religions was still in its early phase, at least in Sweden. However, the philological study of Arabic and adjacent languages also included translations of parts of the Qur'an. As shown by Christopher Toll (1931–2015), for instance, these were included as specimens for the Magister degree in Oriental languages during the eighteenth century. The oldest example dates from 1786 and contains a translation from Arabic into Latin of Sura 2:253–256 (Toll 2007: 201–2).

A chair in the History of Religions was established at Uppsala University in 1901, its first holder being Professor Nathan Söderblom (1866–1931). It was especially through Professor Tor Andræ (1885–1947) that the study of Islam was developed. Both Söderblom and Andræ were Historians of Religions, but they simultaneously had a close connection with the Church of Sweden as well.

With Professor Torgny Segerstedt (1876–1945) at Stockholm University College (between 1913 and 1917) and Professor Geo Widengren (1907–1996), holder of the chair in Uppsala between 1949 and 1973, a non-confessional study of religions developed in Sweden (on Widengren's significance, see Larsson 2022, 2023). While Segerstedt never conducted any research on Islam, this was one of the many religions on which Widengren published (1955).

That said, Andræ's significance should not be downplayed either. Like most scholars of Islamic Studies in Europe, Andræ mastered the Arabic language, and, with the help of philological methods, he became one of the pioneers in the study of the life of the prophet Muhammad and the formative history of Islam. In several books and essays, he approached the sources of Islam with a critical and comparative gaze. Among his many publications, one could, for instance, mention *Die Person Muhammeds in Lehre und Glauben seiner Gemeinde* (1918) and *Der Ursprung des Islams und das Christentum* (1926). Andræ also made important contributions to the study of early Sufism, focusing especially on the connections between Syriac monastic piety and Sufi theologies and practices. His most important work on early Sufism was published posthumously the year after his death, 1948, and was later translated into English and published as *In the Garden of Myrtles: Studies in Early Islamic Mysticism* (1987).

Irrespective of his close connection with the Church of Sweden and a Christian bias (see Hjärpe 2022a), Andræ is an important scholar for subsequent generations of Historians of Religions, as well as for the study of Islam and Muslims both in Sweden and internationally. Both Widengren and Jan Hjärpe, who became the first holder of a chair in Islamic Studies at the University of Lund, testify that they were influenced by Andræ's way of approaching sources, as well as his contextualization of Islam and Muslim traditions in their wider cultural, linguistic and historical contexts (Widengren 1947). Neither Widengren nor Andræ refrained from comparing Islamic traditions, the life of the prophet Muhammad and the formative history of Islam with earlier Christian (especially Syriac traditions) or other Near Eastern influences. As compared especially to Söderblom (Hedin 1997), but also partly Andræ (Hjärpe 2022a), Widengren was not interested in presenting a judgemental description of Islam or Muslims. For him, like all other religions, Islam was a set of data that should be analysed for its own sake. On this point, Widengren was influenced by Germany's *Religionsgeschichtliche Schule* and those scholars who emphasized that Christianity and the study of the Bible should be placed in a wider Near Eastern context (Rudolph 2005).

Even though Sweden had diplomatic contacts with the larger Muslim world from the sixteenth century onwards, especially with Tatars in Crimea and the Ottoman Empire, but also with the so-called Barbary states in North Africa (Jarring 1987; Östlund 2020), the study of Islam and Muslims was mainly, if not only, focused on texts. Muslims were hardly present in Sweden prior to the Second World War (for some important exceptions, see Sorgenfrei 2022), and even until the late 1960s, the topics of Islam and Muslims were absent from Swedish school curricula and classroom discussions (Kittelmann Flensner and Larsson 2014). However, with the end of the Second World War, the country's demography gradually changed, and in the 1960s and 1970s, substantial numbers of guest workers and migrants with Muslim cultural backgrounds began to arrive in Sweden (Svanberg and Tydén 2005). It was only after the revolution in Iran in 1979 that the Swedish government found it necessary to establish a chair in Islamic Studies at Lund University, and the 1980s saw Islam and Muslims become visible in government debates and state inquiries (Cato 2012). With this development, a second phase in the study of Islam and Muslims began in Sweden. While the first phase had been focused on texts and philological problems, the second phase constituted a break and saw the development of novel approaches, as well as a new empirical focus. It was no longer Islam as a text or as a set of dogmas that was under scrutiny as the main empirical focus, but the lived practices of Muslims.

The Second Phase in the Study of Islam and Muslims in Sweden

One of the most influential Islamic studies scholars in Sweden in the contemporary era has been the Historian of Religion Jan Hjärpe. His doctoral thesis, *Analyse critique des traditions arabes sur les Sabéens harraniens* (1972), was supervised by Widengren in Uppsala. After defending his thesis, Hjärpe came to Lund as an assistant professor in 1977, just before the revolution in Iran. In this position, he was able to introduce the study of contemporary Islam and stress the importance of studying it as a political and social phenomenon as a complement to the historical, or even 'Orientalist', perspective that had previously been dominant. It took some years to convince the university administration in Lund to accept Islamic studies as an important field of research. However, with government support, Hjärpe was given a research post in Islamic Studies, and in 1983, Lund University transformed the post into a chair of Islamic Studies, the first in Sweden, which Hjärpe held until his retirement in 2005 (Hjärpe 2022b).[2]

Islamic Studies in Lund also differed from earlier Swedish research on Islam in that it was defined more broadly as part of the study of religions more generally and included a focus on contemporary issues. This is something that even today dominates the study of Islam and Muslims in Sweden, as we shall see below. For instance, Hjärpe stressed the non-confessional study of Islam and Muslims. Thus, he advocated a distanced and critical approach to the material in order to be able to analyse, explain and understand it, but he also stressed avoiding normative statements.[3] Hjärpe was also engaged in presenting Islam to the broader population. His work was therefore distant from most of his Swedish predecessors, who did not take the present-day situation into account in their research. Apart from striving to understand and explain, Hjärpe also stressed the scholarly duty of giving informed prognoses that could be of benefit to politicians and others, as reflected in his role as a public intellectual. His was the main voice explaining the Muslim world and Islam in the media until his retirement. Prior to his position at Lund University, Hjärpe had also worked closely with the Swedish Ministry of Foreign Affairs.

One of Hjärpe's most influential articles is 'What Will Be Chosen from the Islamic Basket?', which was published in the *European Review* in 1997. In this article, he clarifies how, rather than being a static phenomenon, Islam is continuously being (re)constructed in historical settings, where Muslims draw on Islamic traditions as a resource to legitimate their practices and opinions about what 'true' Islam is. He describes tradition as a basket, which includes an enormous number of different and contradictory elements. Every use of a religious tradition depends on what is selected from the basket. What is of interest, according to Hjärpe, is how the elements making up a religious tradition are used, rather than a static phenomenon labelled as 'Islam', for example. This article is still read by students in Islamic studies and, we dare say, has influenced most Islamic studies scholars in Sweden. 'Hjärpe's basket' is a recurring expression. In his book *Tusen och en natt & den elfte september: Tankar om Islam* (2003), he retrospectively looks at his career and interest in Islamic studies. Here, Hjärpe clarifies that he views religious traditions as language families and that we learn languages to understand people and cultural expressions. Hjärpe stresses the empirical, as well as the need to produce knowledge that will assist us in avoiding stereotypical views on Islam and Muslims.

From the outset, Islamic studies, in the spirit of Hjärpe, questioned three assumptions prevalent in both the media and the wider society: (1) that religious belonging determines how people think and act; (2) that religious traditions are static and unchanging; and (3) that religious people act in accordance with the normative claims of the religious elite, thus making their claims representative for everyone. Such essentialist notions are connected to the previous dominance of theological studies of religion, where studies were meant to prepare students for religious (specifically Christian) service. Such notions follow a theological rather than anthropological view of the study of religions. Hjärpe certainly did not reject studies of normative elites or sources but included aspects that have been labelled as 'lived Islam'. Using this approach, he stressed that it was necessary to study and analyse what so-called ordinary people do and think when they mark something as 'Islamic' or 'Muslim'. Hjärpe stressed that Islamic studies must include psychological, sociological and political perspectives; he was very much influenced by psychology of religion, especially by Hjalmar Sundén (1908–1993; see Lindgren 2014). This gives us non-theological knowledge of Islam and Muslims, where the ever-changing relationships between people and religious traditions are analysed and related to prevailing power structures and claims to authority (Hjärpe 1997, 2003).

Hjärpe (2016) mapped Swedish research on Islam in Sweden, where he concluded that recent and contemporary research included aspects of religious change related to migration and globalization, questions of identity based on psychological and sociological perspectives. Gender roles and gender perspectives on source material, as well as Islam in the media and on the internet, were also covered. Much has changed since Islamic studies was established in Lund. Since then, Swedish Islam has been covered in not only many academic publications, but also popular scientific ones aimed at a larger audience (cf. Larsson 2004). One purpose of many academic and non-academic publications appears to be to show that Islam is not a static phenomenon and that the interpretation of religious traditions changes due to global and local developments, such as, for instance, immigration, and views on and practices of integration, pluralism and violence in the name of Islam. Several PhD theses have covered Swedish Islam and Muslims from different perspectives, including, for example, Islamophobia and media images of Islam. Increasing production is also related to fundamentalist Islam, both from a study of religions perspective and a more security-oriented perspective. A large part of current research thus concerns contemporary material, influenced by public debates and contemporary perspectives on Islam and Muslims, and a lot of the source material is Swedish or European (Olsson and Sorgenfrei 2019). There is thus a decrease in studies of Islam and Muslims elsewhere in the world, as well as on more historical material. The earlier stress on language competence has also declined, making the field of Islamic studies rather contemporary and narrow in scope.

Even though Hjärpe's importance should be stressed, it is fair to say that he was not alone in studying Islam and Muslims in Sweden. Among several academics, one could, for example, mention Gudmar Aneer, who started his academic career by writing a thesis on Mogul India (1973) under the supervision of Geo Widengren in Uppsala but later turned to topics like Shia Islam (1985), religious dialogue and migration (1986), and Sufism. Another example is Christer Hedin (1939–2022), who wrote a thesis in systematic theology that dealt with Muslim missionary work (1988). Hedin has also written several books on Islam and Muslims and on Oriental studies directed to a broader public. Historian of ideas Mohammad Fazlhashemi, now Professor of Islamic Theology and Islamic Philosophy at Uppsala University, wrote a thesis on al-Ghazali (1994) and currently works on modern and contemporary Shiite thought. Important publications on Islam and Muslims have also been edited by David Westerlund and Ingvar Svanberg (1999a, b, 2011, 2016; see also Westerlund 2004). Along with Hjärpe, Åke Sander should be recognized as one of the founding fathers of the study of Islam and Muslims in Europe (1990, 1991; see also Larsson and Sander 2007). With his study of Islam and Muslims in Swedish schoolbooks, Kjell Härenstam is one of the pioneers in the field of Religious Education (1993). Similarly, Eva Evers Rosander (1991, 2015), Sylva Frisk (2004), Jörgen Hellman (2006, 2011) and André Möller (2005), as well as Svanberg and Westerlund, have conducted anthropological studies of Islam in Africa, Indonesia, Java, Malaysia and Eastern Europe (Evers Rosander and Westerlund 1997).

Contemporary Islamic Studies in Sweden

Today, in early 2023, Lund and Linnaeus universities both have Professors in Islamic Studies, and since 2012, Uppsala University has a Professor in Islamic Theology and Philosophy, which falls under the discipline of Systematic Theology. Several other universities, especially Stockholm, Gothenburg, Södertörn and Umeå, have professors in the Study of Religions specializing in the study of

Islam. Important contributions to the study of Islam and Muslims have also been conducted within other disciplines, such as Ethnology, Sociology and Political Science, which, however, will not be described in this chapter.

An overview of theses with a focus on Islam and Muslims at Swedish universities suggests that contemporary issues dominate. Two of the first to defend their theses under the supervision of Hjärpe were Anne Sofie Roald and Leif Stenberg: both took the challenges and possibilities of modernity as their subjects of study. Roald studied *Tarbiya: Education and Politics in Islamic Movements in Jordan and Malaysia* (1994), while Stenberg examined *The Islamization of Science: Four Muslim Positions Developing an Islamic Modernity* (1996). In 2000, Jonas Svensson defended his thesis on *Women's Human Rights and Islam: A Study of Three Attempts at Accommodation* (2000) at the same department.

A focus on contemporary Islam aside, both the geographical spread and the range of subjects are wide. Several projects have, for example, focused on Islamic currents in Indonesia (Kull 2005), Java (Möller 2005) and other parts of Southeast Asia (Johansson 2016). In 2010, Abdel Baten Miaji defended a thesis on women's roles in religious organizations and non-governmental organizations (NGOs) in rural Bangladesh at Lund University, and in 2019, Mattias Dahlkvist's thesis on Maulana Wahiuddin Khan and Islamic peacebuilding in India was defended at Umeå University.

Not surprisingly, the Middle East and North Africa (MENA) region is well represented, with studies on, for example, Philip Halldén's work on the rhetoric of Saudi preachers (2001), David Thurfjell's thesis on Shiite activism in Iran (2003) and Susanne Olsson's thesis on the Egyptian philosopher Hasan Hanafi (2006), Hege Irene Markussen's work on Alevism in contemporary Turkey (2012), Eli Göndör's thesis focusing on the life of Muslim women in contemporary Israel (2012) and Anne Ross Solberg's thesis (2013) concerning the Turkish creationist Harun Yahya. There have also been a few PhD projects focusing on different aspects of Sufism in Bosnia (Gazi 2010), the UK (Stjernholm 2011), the United States and Turkey (Sorgenfrei 2013), as well as South Africa (Eneborg 2020) and Egypt (Brusi 2022).

Following the above-mentioned work by Svensson, further PhD projects have dealt with gender discourses in contemporary Islam. For example, Jesper Petersen (2020) analysed a gender-integrated Danish Mosque, and Erika Li Lundqvist (2013) marginalized sexualities in Lebanon. Nina Jakku (2019) and Vanja Mosbach (2022) dealt with Muslim women's life experiences of being Muslims in a non-Muslim majority country. Both Jakku's and Mosbach's projects were set in contemporary Sweden.

There are further dissertations dealing specifically with Islam and Muslims in Sweden. Jonas Alwall's thesis focused the situation of the Swedish Muslim minority and their relationship with the Swedish state (1998). Jonas Otterbeck studied a Swedish Islamic journal called *Salaam* and the globalization of Islam (2000). Otterbeck's work was later followed by Johan Cato, who in 2012 defended a thesis on discourses on Islam in Swedish public-authority debates. Tomas Lindgren's

(2001) thesis is a comparative study of Swedish Muslim and Christian views and practices of prayer. There have also been studies on conversion to Islam in Sweden, defended by Anna Månsson (2002) and Madelene Sultán Sjöqvist (2006), as well as on Islamic education in Sweden, conducted by Jenny Berglund in her thesis *Teaching Islam: Islamic Religious Education at Three Muslim Schools in Sweden* (2009), and Islamism (Egyptson 2023).

A couple of theses have also focused on contemporary literature, such as Torsten Janson's 2003 dissertation on *da'wah* ('mission, call to Islam') in contemporary Islamic-English children's literature and Mats Bergenhorn's thesis analysing aspects of Salman Rushdie's novel *The Satanic Verses* (2006). In relation to these works on Islam in Europe, mention might also be made to Mattias Gardell's work on African-American Islam and the mission of the Nation of Islam under the leadership of minister Louis Farrakhan (1995), Garbi Schmidt's study of immigrant communities in Chicago (1998) and Anders Ackfeldt's thesis on Islamic semiotic resources in American hip-hop (2019).

There are, however, a few exceptions from the focus on modern developments, for example, Göran Larsson's thesis on religious legitimacy in medieval Spain, *Ibn García's shu'ūbiyya Letter: Ethnic and Theological Tensions in Medieval al-Andalus* (2003), Ulrika Mårtensson's *The True New Testament: Sealing the Heart's Covenant in al-Tabarî's Ta'rîkh al-Rusul wa'l-Mulûk* (2001), Torsten Hylén's thesis *Husayn, the Mediator: A Structural Analysis of the Karbalā' Drama according to Abū Ja'far Muḥammad b. Jarīr al-Ṭabarī* (2007) and Tobias Andersson's thesis in Systematic Theology consisting of a commentary of Sanusi (2022).

In 2023, the Swedish Research Council decided to fund a graduate school in Islamic studies, which includes most professors in the study of religions in Sweden who specialize in Islam. One aim of the school is to make sure that there are future scholars in Islamic studies in Sweden who can act as teachers, researchers and public intellectuals. The graduate school stresses that Islamic studies includes both historical and contemporary material, as well as philological and ethnographic methodologies, but from a non-confessional perspective.

Apart from Lund University, there is no specific centre or research environment for the study of Islam and Muslims linking the past and present. That said, it should be stressed that most universities in Sweden today provide education, and most of them also research, on Islam and Muslim affairs. This chapter has focused on departments of Religious Studies, but as we have indicated, the study of Islam and Muslims is no longer topic solely for scholars of religions. For instance, sociologists, political scientists and linguists have also made important contributions to the field. However, this chapter only deals with the study of religions, and in our case, the study of Islam and Muslims. That said, it should also be emphasized that a growing number of government bodies and NGOs have produced important studies of Islam and Muslims in Sweden. This development shows that the field is thriving and that there is healthy competition over resources and over how to explain and understand Islam and Muslims from both the academic and non-academic points of view.

Notes

1 Sweden's oldest university, established in 1477.
2 See also Prop. 1986/87:80, cf. *Religionen som samhällsfaktor i ett internationellt perspektiv. Material från en Harpsundskonferens med forskningsberedningen* (1987).
3 See Otterbeck (forthcoming) for a detailed presentation and analysis of Hjärpe's production and views on Islam.

References

Alwall, J. (1998), *Muslim Rights and Plights: The Religious Liberty Situation of a Minority in Sweden*, Lund: Lund University
Ackfeldt, A. (2019), *Islamic semiotic Resources in US Hip-Hop Culture*, Lund: Lund University.
Andersson, T. (2022), *Kommentar till Sanusi: En systematisk studie i islamisk teologi*, Uppsala: Uppsala University.
Andræ, T. (1918), *Die Person Muhammeds in Lehre und Glauben seiner Gemeinde*, Stockholm: P.A. Norstedt och söner.
Andræ, T. (1926), *Der Ursprung des Islams und das Christentum*, Uppsala: Almqvist & Wiksell.
Andræ, T. (1987), *In the Garden of Myrtles: Studies in Early Islamic Mysticism*, Albany: State University of New York Press.
Aneer, G. (1973), *Akbar the Great Mogul and His Religious Thoughts*, Uppsala: Uppsala University.
Aneer, G. (1985), *Imām Rūḥullāh Khumainī, Šāh Muḥammad Riẓā Pahlavī and the religious traditions of Iran*. Uppsala: Historia religionum.
Aneer, G. (1986), *Religioners möte. Om kristendom, islam, hinduism och nya religiösa rörelser i Sverige och världen*. Älvsjö: Verbum.
Bergenhorn, M. (2006), *Öppna universum! Slutna traditioner i Salman Rushdies Satansverserna*, Lund: Lund University.
Berglund, J. (2009), *Teaching Islam: Islamic Religious Education at Three Muslim Schools in Sweden*, Uppsala: Uppsala University.
Brusi, F. (2022), *Gracious Traditions: Contemporary Transnational Egyptian Post-Tariqa Sufism*, Stockholm: Stockholm University.
Cato, J. (2012), *När islam blev svenskt: Föreställningar om islam och muslimer i svensk offentlig politik 1975–2010*, Lund: Lund University.
Dahlkvist, M. (2019), *The Politics of Islam, Non-Violence, and Peace: The Thought of Maulana Wahiduddin Khan in Context*, Umeå: Umeå University.
Egyptson, S. (2023), *Global politisk islam: Muslimska brödraskapet & Islamiska förbundet i Sverige*, Lund: Lund University.
Eneborg, Y. M. (2020), *A Sufi for a Secular Age: Reflecting on Muslim Modernity through the Life and Times of Shaykh Fadhlalla Haeri*, Göteborg: University of Gothenburg.
Evers Rosander, E. (1991), *Women in a Borderland: Managing Muslim Identity where Morocco Meets Spain*, Stockholm: Stockholm University.
Evers Rosander, E. (2015), *In Pursuit of Paradise: Senegalese Women, Muridism and Migration*, Uppsala: Nordiska Afrikainstitutet.

Evers Rosander, E., and D. Westerlund, eds (1997), *African Islam and Islam in Africa: Encounters between Sufis and Islamists*, London: Hurst.
Fazlhashemi, M. (1994), *Förändring och kontinuitet: Al-Ghazâlîs politiska omsvängning*, Umeå: Umeå Universitet.
Frisk, S. (2004), *Submitting to God: Women's Islamization in Urban Malaysia*, Göteborg: University of Gothenburg.
Gardell, M. (1995), *Countdown to Armageddon: Minister Farrakhan and the Nation of Islam in the Latter Days*, Stockholm: Stockholm University.
Gaši, A. (2010), *Melamisufism i Bosnien: En dold gemenskap*, Lund: Lund University.
Göndör, E. (2012), *Muslimska kvinnor i Israel: Religionens roll i vardagslivets förflyttningar*, Lund: Lund University.
Halldén, P. (2001), *Islamisk predikan på ljudkassett: En studie i retorik och fonogramologi*, Lund: Lund University.
Hedin, C. (1988). *Alla är födda muslimer: Islam som den naturliga religionen enligt fundamentalistisk apologetik*. Uppsala: Uppsala University.
Hedin, C. (1997), 'Nathan Söderbloms uppfattningar om islam: Exempel på svensk orientalism', *Tidskrift för Mellanösternstudier* 1: 32–62.
Hellman, J. (2006), *Ritual Fasting on West Java: Empowerment, Submission, and Control*, Göteborg: Gothenburg Studies in Social Anthropology.
Hellman, J. (2011), *Förfädernas enträgna närvaro: Pilgrimskap på vänstra Java*, Göteborg: Acta Universitatis Gothoburgensis.
Hjärpe, J. (1972), *Analyse critique des traditions arabes sur les sabéens harraniens*, Uppsala: Uppsala Universitet.
Hjärpe, J. (1997), 'What Will Be Chosen from the Islamic Basket?', *European Review* 5 (3): 267–74.
Hjärpe, J. (2003), *Tusen och en natt & den elfte september: Tankar om Islam*, Stockholm: Prisma.
Hjärpe, J. (2016), 'Islamforskning i Sverige'. Available online: https://www.rj.se/Nyheter/2016/islamforskning-i-sverige/ (accessed 28 February 2023).
Hjärpe, J. (2022a), 'Tor Andræ and Geo Widengren: Perspectives and Purposes of the Study of the History of Religions', in G. Larsson (ed.), *The Legacy, Life and Work of Geo Widengren and the Study of the History of Religions after World War II*, 238–48, Leiden: Brill.
Hjärpe, J. (2022b), *Speech at the inauguration of the new chair in Islamic Studies at Lund University*.
Hylén, T. (2007), *Husayn, the Mediator: A Structural Analysis of the Karbalā' Drama According to Abū Ja'far Muhammad b. Jarīr al-Tabarī (d. 310/923)*, Uppsala: Uppsala University.
Härenstam, K. (1993), *Skolboks-islam: Analys av bilden av islam i läroböcker i religionskunskap*, Göteborg: Acta Universitatis Gothoburgensis.
Jakku, N. (2019), *Muslimska kvinnors mobilitet. Möjligheter och hinder i de liberala idealens Sverige*, Lund: Lund University.
Janson, T. (2003), *Your Cradle is Green: The Islamic Foundation and the Call to Islam in Children's Literature*, Lund: Lund University.
Jarring, G. (1987), 'Sveriges diplomatiska förbindelser med tatarerna på Krim', in M. Berquist, A. W. Johansson and K. Wahlbäck (eds), *Utrikespolitik och historia: Studier tillägnade Wilhelm M. Carlgren den 6 maj 1987*, 83–90, Stockholm: Militärhistoriska förlaget.

Johansson, A. (2016), *Pragmatic Muslim Politics: The Case of Sri Lanka Muslim Congress*, Lund: Lund University.

Kittelmann Flensner, K., and G. Larsson (2014), 'Swedish Religious Education at the End of the 1960s: Classroom Observations, Early Video Ethnography and the National Curriculum of 1962', *British Journal of Religious Education* 36 (2): 202–17.

Kull, A. (2005), *Piety and Politics: Nurcholish Madjid and his Interpretation of Islam in Modern Indonesia*, Lund: Lund University.

Larsson, G. (2003), *Ibn García's shuʿūbiyya Letter: Ethnic and Theological Tensions in Medieval al-Andalus*, Leiden: Brill.

Larsson, G. (2007), *Islam and Muslims in Sweden: Integration or Fragmentation? A Contextual Study*, Münster: LIT Verlag.

Larsson, G. (2004), *Islam och muslimer i Sverige: En kommenterad bibliografi*, Göteborg: Makadam.

Larsson, G. (2023), *Geo Widengren. Stridbar professor i en föränderlig värld*, Stockholm: Langenskiöld.

Larsson, G., ed. (2022), *The Legacy, Life and Work of Geo Widengren and the Study of the History of Religions after World War II*, Leiden: Brill.

Lindgren, T. (2001), *Bön som akt och erfarenhet: En religionspsykologisk studie av bönens uttryck, förutsättningar och funktioner i en muslimsk och kristen kontext*, Uppsala: Uppsala University.

Lindgren, T. (2014), 'Hjalmar Sundén's Impact on the Study of Religion in the Nordic Countries,' *Temenos: Nordic Journal of Comparative Religion* 50 (1): 39–61.

Lundqvist, E. L. (2013), *Gayted Communities: Marginalized Sexualities in Lebanon*, Lund: Lund University.

Malmberg, H. (2007), 'The Professorship of Semitic Languages 400 Years: A Detailed History of the First Three Centuries', in B. Isaksson, M. Eskhult and G. Ramsay (eds), *The Professorship of Semitic Languages at Uppsala University 400 Years: Jubilee Volume from a Symposium Held at the University Hall, 21–23 September 2005*, 11–36, Uppsala: Studia Semitica Upsaliensia 24.

Månsson, A. (2002), *Becoming Muslim: Meanings of Conversion to Islam*, Lund: Lund University.

Markussen, H. I. (2012), *Teaching History, Learning Piety: An Alevi Foundation in Contemporary Turkey*. Lund: Sekel.

Martin, R. C. (1995), 'Islamic Studies: History of the Field', in J. L. Espresso (ed.), *The Oxford Encyclopaedia of the Modern Islamic World*, vol. 2, 325–31, Oxford: Oxford University Press.

Miaji, A. B. (2010), *Rural Women in Bangladesh: The Legal Status of Women and the Relationship between NGOs and Religious Groups*, Lund: Lund University.

Mårtensson, U. (2001), *The True New Testament: Sealing the Heart's Covenant in al-Tabarī's Taʾrīkh al-Rusul waʾl-Mulūk*, Uppsala: Uppsala University.

Möller, A. (2005), *Ramadan in Java: The Joy and Jihad of Ritual Fasting*, Lund: Lund University.

Mosbach, V. (2022), *Voices of Muslim Feminists: Navigating Tradition, Authority and the Debate about Islam*, Uppsala: Uppsala University.

Nanji, A. (1997), *Mapping Islamic Studies: Genealogy, Continuity and Change*, Berlin: Mouton de Gruyter.

Olsson, S. (2006), *Islam and the West in the Ideology of Ḥasan Ḥanafī*, Stockholm: Almqvist & Wiksell International.

Olsson, S., and S. Sorgenfrei (2019) 'Islam and Islamic Studies in Scandinavia', in *Oxford Research Encyclopaedias*, 1–34, online publication April 2019. DOI: 10.1093/acrefore/9780190228637.013.658.

Östlund, J. (2020), *Vid världens ände: Sultanens sändebud och hans berättelse om 1700-talets Sverige*, Lund: Nordic Academic Press.

Otterbeck, J. (2000), *Islam på svenska: Tidskriften Salaam och islams globalisering*, Lund: Lund University.

Otterbeck, J. (forthcoming), in Anders Ackfeldt and Jesper Petersen (eds), *What Did Jan Hjärpe Chose from the Islamic Basket? A Study of the Dominant Voice on Islam in Sweden 1980–2000*.

Petersen, J. (2020), *The Making of the Mariam Mosque: Serendipities and Structures in the Production of Female Authority in Denmark*, Lund: Lund University.

Prop. 1986/87:80, Regeringens proposition 1986/87:80, Om forskning, https://www.riksdagen.se/sv/dokument-lagar/dokument/proposition/om-forskning_GA0380.

Religionen som samhällsfaktor i ett internationellt perspektiv. Material från en Harpsundskonferens med forskningsberedningen (1987), Stockholm: Regeringskansliets offsetscentral.

Roald, A. S. (1994), *Tarbiya: Education and Politics in Islamic Movements in Jordan and Malaysia*, Lund: Lund University.

Ross Solberg, A. (2013), *The Mahdi Wears Armani: An Analysis of the Harun Yahya Enterprise*, Göteborg: University of Gothenburg.

Rudolph, K. (2005), 'Religionsgeschichtliche Schule', in J. Lindsay Jones (ed.), *Encyclopedia of Religion*, vol. 11, 7706–9, New York: Thomson Gale.

Sander, Å. (1990), 'Islam and Muslims in Sweden', *Migration: A European Journal of International Migration and Ethic Relations* 8: 83–134.

Sander, Å. (1991), 'The Road from Musalla to Mosque: The Proess of Integration and Institutionalization of Islam in Sweden', in W. A. R. Shadid and P. S. van Koningsveld (eds), *The Integration of Islam and Hinduism in Western Europe*, 62–88, Kampen: Pharos.

Schmidt, G. (1998), *American Medina: A Study of the Sunni Muslim Immigrant Communities in Chicago*, Lund: Lund University.

Sorgenfrei, S. (2013), *American Dervish: Making Mevlevism in the United States of America*, Göteborg: University of Gothenburg.

Sorgenfrei, S. (2022), *'De kommer att vara annorlunda svenskar': Berättelsen om Sveriges första muslimer*, Stockholm: Norstedts.

Stenberg, L. (1996), *The Islamization of Science: Four Muslim Positions Developing an Islamic Modernity*, Lund: Lund University.

Stjernholm, S. (2011), *Lovers of Muhammad: A Study of Naqshbandi-Haqqani Sufis in the Twenty-First Century*, Lund: Lunds universitet.

Sultán Sjöqvist, M. (2006), *'Vi blev muslimer': Svenska kvinnor berättar. En religionssociologisk studie av konversionsberättelser*, Uppsala: Uppsala Universitet.

Svanberg, I., and M. Tydén (2005), *Tusen år av invandring: En svensk kulturhistoria*, Stockholm: Dialogos.

Svensson, J. (2000), *Women's Human Rights and Islam: A Study of Three Attempts at Accommodation*. Lund: Lund University.

Thurfjell, D. (2003), *Living Shi'ism: Instances of Ritualisation among Islamist Men in Contemporary Iran*. Uppsala: Uppsala University.

Toll, C. (2007), 'The Translation of the Koran into Swedish', in B. Isaksson, M. Eskhult and G. Ramsay (eds), *The Professorship of Semitic Languages at Uppsala University*

400 years. Jubilee Volume from a Symposium held at the University Hall, 21–23 September 2005, 199–217, Uppsala: Studia Semitica Upsaliensia 24.
Westerlund, D., ed. (2004), *Sufism in Europe and North America*, London: Routledge Curzon.
Westerlund, D., and I. Svanberg, eds (1999a), *Islam Outside the Arab world*, Richmond: Curzon.
Westerlund, D., and I. Svanberg, eds (1999b), *Blågul islam? Muslimer I Sverige*. Nora: Nya Doxa.
Westerlund, D., and I. Svanberg (2011), *Islam in the West: Critical Concepts in Islamic Studies*, Milton Park: Routledge.
Westerlund, D., and I. Svanberg, eds (2016), *Muslim Tatar minorities in the Baltic Sea Region*, Leiden: Brill.
Widengren, G. (1947). *Tor Andræ*, Uppsala: Lindblad.
Widengren, G. (1955), *Muhammad: The Apostle of God, and His Ascension*, Uppsala: Uppsala Universitets Årsskrift.
Zettersteen, K. V. (1946). *Arabiska studier i Sverige*, Uppsala: Almqvist & Wiksell.

Chapter 6

INDIAN RELIGIONS

Kristina Myrvold, Katarina Plank and Ferdinando Sardella

'And as long as my spirit dwells in my body, maiden with the serene smile! I will be yours, this is the solemn truth I tell thee.' The quotation is a translation of Otto Fredrik Tullberg's (1802–1853) inscription on a stone in Uppsala. In the 1830s, Tullberg carved out these lines in Sanskrit, derived from the fifth song of the story of Nala and Damayanti in *Mahabharata*, as a declaration of love to his fiancé Sophia Ridderbielke (Bhikhabhai 2016). The Orientalist Tullberg is often recognized as the founder of Indological studies and the first to introduce an interest for Indian religions in Swedish academia.

This chapter provides an overview of the development of the study of Indian religions at Swedish universities, which started in the nineteenth century with an Orientalist and philological study of classical language and texts and evolved into comparative Indo-European languages and Indology. As the discipline of History of Religions was established in the twentieth century, the study of Indian religions was gradually separated from linguistics and came to include theoretical and methodological approaches from humanities and social sciences that combined ethnographic research on contemporary religions with studies of history, languages and texts. The overview illustrates how the fields of research have expanded and diversified to include Hindu, Buddhist, Jain and Sikh traditions which trace their origins to India and historically expanded to greater Asia and later globally through an extensive migration, as well as ideas and practices derived from the Indian traditions in movements that operate transnationally across borders. While the international study of the Asian religions has developed into specialized and interdisciplinary research fields of Hindu, Buddhist, Jaina and Sikh studies, Sweden has never developed corresponding research environments. Rather, the study of Indian religions has been firmly incorporated within the discipline of History and Anthropology of Religion and worked closely with the philological study of Indian languages and texts.

Orientalist Studies and Indology

Long before the academic study of Indian religions developed, knowledge about religions in the East and particular the Buddhist and Hindu traditions were conveyed to Sweden in various ways, such as through missionary letters by Jesuits and travel letters that circulated in Europe during the sixteenth century. As a small monarchy endeavouring to build imperial markets rival to other nations in Europe, the Swedish East India Company (SEIC) was established in 1731 and developed into a large company trading with East-Asia during the eighteenth century. The SEIC never established a trading post in India but used Indian harbours for longer journeys to China, Japan, Malaysia and Indonesia. As a result of these connections, cultural material that described the Indian religions circulated in the Swedish society and gradually became a part of the cultural life. This early material conveyed primarily representations of lived traditions rather than the religious texts which later became the subject for academic work (Offermanns 2002, 2005).

The study of Indian religions in Sweden began with Indological research and the interest for classical languages and texts in the East, much in line with the Orientalist paradigm established by the British philologist William Jones in the end of the eighteenth century.[1] In Sweden, Indology was established at the two larger universities of Uppsala and Lund in the nineteenth century. The study of Sanskrit in Sweden is often claimed to have been launched by Fabian Wilhelm af Ekenstam (1786–1868), who taught philosophy at Lund University and in 1811 published his dissertation on the Sanskrit language in Latin (Ekenstam 1811). The first in-depth study of Sanskrit was conducted at Uppsala University by the philologist Otto Fredrik Tullberg (1802–1853), whom many consider the founder of Indological studies in Sweden. As a Professor of Oriental languages, Tullberg made several travels to Europe to make copies of collected Sanskrit manuscripts for Swedish libraries. One of his students, Carl Fredrik Bergstedt (1817–1903), translated many Sanskrit classics into Swedish, such as the *Savitri* narrative in the *Mahabharata* and the play *Vikramorvasiyam* by the Sanskrit poet Kalidasa (Bergstedt 1844, 1846). Bergstedt also studied Vedanta, and his handwritten notes on this philosophy are preserved in the archive of the Uppsala University Library. The study of Sanskrit was further developed in the 1870s when Axel Erdmann (1843–1926) introduced graduate examinations in Sanskrit and completed numerous studies in the Indo-European languages.

At Lund University, Hjalmar Edgren (1840–1903) was the first to hold an academic title for research on Indian religions when he was appointed Associate Professor of Sanskrit in 1880. Edgren started with a military career and in the 1860s went to North America to participate in the Civil War as a volunteer. After the war, he eventually resigned from the army to focus on an academic career, and in 1874, he obtained a doctoral degree from Yale University. Although Edgren spent most of his time in America and became a Professor of Sanskrit in Lincoln, he laid a foundation for Indology at Lund University. His many publications included translations of the *Nalasaga* from the epic *Mahabharata* and three works by Kalidasa, as well as the only Sanskrit grammar in Swedish at the time (e.g. Edgren 1875, 1877; Tersmeden 2017).

The development of Indology in Sweden became highly influenced by the German Romantic movement and its fondness of translations of Indian classical texts, as well as the emerging comparative study of Indo-European languages (Juntunen 2000: 23). The study of Sanskrit and Indian texts became integrated in comparative Indo-European linguistics in the late nineteenth century. Not all working in this discipline immersed themselves in the Indian languages and texts, but Sanskrit was yet believed to be the oldest surviving Indo-European language, and therefore many took interest in Vedic texts, especially the *Rigveda*. Karl Ferdinand Johansson was the first Professor of Sanskrit and the Indo-European linguistics at Uppsala in 1893. Among other things, he translated a selection of hymns of *Rigveda* and Buddhist *jataka*-stories into Swedish and contributed with translations of Hindu and Buddhist texts to Nathan Söderblom's compilation of religious texts of India published in 1908 (Johansson 1897, 1907; Söderblom 1908). Inspired by Söderblom, Johansson and his students became increasingly interested in Indian religions. One of them was the succeeding Professor Jarl Charpentier (1884–1935), who published widely on the Indian languages, history and literature and was a pioneer in the study of scriptures in the Jain Svetambara tradition (e.g. Charpentier 1920; 1922).

The universities at Lund and Gothenburg followed a similar pattern. At Lund, Nils Flensburg (1855–1926) became the first Professor of Sanskrit and comparative Indo-European languages in 1898, and he studied the *Rigveda* and published on the Vedic mythology (Flensburg 1909). After his professorship, the discipline shifted towards linguistics and away from the broader philological interest for Indian religions and history to become integrated in comparative linguistics (Qvarnström 2006: 46). The University of Gothenburg also established a chair in Comparative Indo-European Linguistics with Sanskrit in 1898. The first professor, Evald Lidén (1862–1939), secured a position as an etymologist through his dissertation on ancient Indic and comparative linguistic history (Lidén 1897). One of his successors, Georg von Munthe af Morgenstierne (1892–1978), had a primary interest for Indo-Iranian languages but started with a dissertation on Sanskrit dramas (Morgenstierne 1921). Other professors holding this chair were Helmer Smith (1882–1956), who was a connoisseur of Pali and edited a dictionary and a grammar in that language, and Gösta Liebert (1916–1998), who published on iconography of Indian deities and collected manuscripts that were later donated to the university library (Liebert 1976; see also Josephson 2001).

During the twentieth century, Indology developed as a discipline at Uppsala and later also at Stockholm University, with a broader study of classical and modern languages and texts in various time periods and areas of the South Asian region. At Uppsala, Nils Simonsson worked to create a separate profile for Indology and was interested in the mechanisms of translation and especially how religious concepts were transmitted in classical texts. His successor, Ruth Walldén, was the first female professor on the chair and raised the study of the Dravidian languages to an international level. Gunilla Gren-Ekholm, who followed and held the chair until the twenty-first century, researched nominal sentences in the *Upanishads* and how the Indian grammar and commentary tradition in the Middle Ages reached Burma with Buddhism (e.g. Gren-Ekholm 1978). As the discipline of Indology at Uppsala transformed into the study of South Asian languages and cultures, the research focus of the subsequent professors focused on modern and regional languages of India. William Smith (1942–2009) studied the grammar on Bengali and religious texts, including the *Ramayana* tradition, in eastern North India (Smith 1988, 1991), whereas the current holder of the chair, Heinz Werner Hessler, is working on early modern and contemporary literature in Hindi and particularly literature by the socially marginalized population of Dalits.

At Stockholm University, a professorship in Indology was established in 1967, initially with a special focus on modern Indian philology but gradually transforming into a broader study of languages and cultures of India. The study programmes were divided into two main orientations: 'Ancient and Middle Indian focus' (Sanskrit, Pali, Prakriti, Tibetan), with primary emphasis on Sanskrit, and 'New Indian focus', with stressing on Hindi and its literature. The first professor on the chair, Siegfried Lienhard, was interested in modern Indian philology such as religious and secular poetry of the Nevars in the Kathmandu Valley (e.g. Lienhard 1974). His successor, Claus Oetke, specialized in Indian and Tibetan Studies and contributed with analyses of *atman* and *anatman* in the Buddhist Pali Canon and in Brahmanical philosophical traditions (Oetke 1988). Carl Suneson focused on translations from Sanskrit (Suneson 1986). By 2014, however, Stockholm University decided to close the section of Indology for various reasons, even if the philological research of Indo-European religions with emphasis on ancient Indian religions remains within the broader study of History of Religions.

Although Rune E. A. Johansson (1918–1981) was not trained as an Indologist but held a licentiate degree in Psychology, he became internationally renowned because of his language skills in Pali. His new ways of interpreting Buddhist Pali texts from psychological perspectives broadened the discipline of psychology, which until then had devoted most of its study of the human psyche based on psychological theories developed in Judaeo-Christian cultural contexts. He translated the *Dhammapada* and the *Sutta Nipata* from Pali into Swedish, wrote a textbook on Pali texts and grammar that came to be used internationally, as well as published two books on the psychology of Buddhism (e.g. Johansson 1969, 1973). In 1972, Johansson established a scholarship foundation, now administered by Uppsala University, to promote research on Buddhism and its ideological content. Over the years, the foundation has been a valuable resource for researchers in philology and the study of religions.

The Study of Indian Religions

If Indology has a long history at Swedish universities and eventually was placed under linguistics, a broader study of historical and contemporary aspects of Indian religions evolved within the disciplines of history and anthropology of religion from the latter part of the twentieth century, influenced by a variety of methodological tools and theoretical frameworks in humanities and social sciences. At Uppsala University, a chair in History of Religions with a special focus on Indian and East Asian religions was held by Eric J. Sharpe (1933–2000) from 1978 and by Peter Schalk from 1983. Sharpe worked on the religious interactions between Christians and Hindus in the nineteenth century and contributed to global perspectives of comparative religion before moving to Sydney to develop the discipline there (Sharpe 1965, 1975). Peter Schalk studied Sanskrit, Pali, Tamil and Sinhala, and through field studies in Sri Lanka (then Ceylon), he developed an interest in Buddhist protective ritual and chanting (Schalk 1972). He later worked on Hinduism and Buddhism in the Khmer Empire during the fourteenth century and developed the research field of Tamil Studies (Schalk 1985, 2004, 2013). Eva Hellman, promoted to Professor of History of Religions in 2012, examined how Hindu concepts and symbols were ideologically and politically utilized in the Hindutva movements with the objective to transform secular India into a Hindu state (Hellman 1993). Focusing on religion and gender, Hellman also studied Hindu constructions of the female gender by looking at goddess worship as a liberating force in relation to the continued subordination of women in Indian society (Hellman 1998).

At Stockholm and Lund, chairs in History of Religions were established in 1913 under which the study of Indian religions was gradually incorporated. Stockholm University maintained the philological interest in ancient languages and religion through the leadership of Ernst Arbman (1937–1958), but in the 1950s Åke Hultkrantz (1958–1986) developed a distinctive anthropological and folkloristic approach that ran parallel with philological endeavours. Erik af Edholm, who initially worked at Uppsala (1983–1995) but later transferred to Stockholm, completed a philological thesis about vision and knowledge in Indian religious thought and became important for the maintenance of Indian languages within History of Religions (Edholm 1989). Peter Jackson Rova continued this with his research on the philological study of Indo-European religions and a particular interest for India and rituals (Jackson and Sjödin 2016). The ethnographic study on contemporary Buddhism evolved with Per-Arne Berglie and his research on ritual obsession and shamanism in the Himalayan region and Buddhist popular religion in Burma (e.g. Berglie 1983). Ferdinando Sardella has been involved in historical and ethnographical studies on Hinduism, and especially Vaishnavism in Bengal and globally (Sardella 2013, Sardella and Wong 2020).

At Lund University, the study of Indian religions was similarly characterized by a broader cultural and historical approach, even though the text-oriented approach and interest for classical texts remained. Sten Rodhe (1915–2014) was the first to present a dissertation with a philological orientation that examined perceptions of liberation and salvation in the Vedic religion (Rodhe 1946). Rodhe can be seen as a forerunner to the theological research orientation which was later developed in Mission Studies and centred on Christian relations and dialogues with Buddhist and Hindu traditions (Qvarnström 2006: 49). Typical for research during the second part of the twentieth century was a continued philological study of manuscripts and historical texts, primarily Hindu and Buddhist. Jan Ergardt (1936–1992), for instance, obtained his doctorate for a study of Buddhism in England during the twentieth century but later took interest in the Buddhist concepts of personality in early Pali and Sanskrit texts, mainly Buddhist treatises (Ergardt 1970; Olsson 1993). Simultaneously, Lund University developed an anthropological approach with emphasis on contemporary lived religious traditions. The study of rituals based on solid ethnographic work started with Carl Gustav Diehl (1906–1995), who analysed contemporary rituals among Hindus in South India and worked as a lecturer before becoming the bishop of Tranquebar for the Evangelical Lutheran Mission in India (Diehl 1956).

The professors holding the chair in History of Religions in the latter part of the twentieth century were highly influenced by the theoretical orientations of functionalism and structuralism in anthropology and sociology. Of note, Tord Olsson (1942–2013) started his career with research on Claude Lévi-Strauss and theorists of totemism but later developed the fields of ritual studies and anthropology of religion, encouraging a methodological approach of combining ethnographies with the study of languages and texts. Although Olsson's empirical field of expertise was African religions, the seminars under his guidance and later his successor Anne-Christine Hornborg, stimulated a generation of students to research lived Buddhist, Hindu and Sikh practices by conducting extensive fieldworks and using theories derived from anthropology and ritual studies as analysing frameworks.

In the early twenty-first century, Lund University invested in research and education on Asia by establishing a master programme in South Asian Studies and supporting the national network, Swedish South Asian Studies Network (SASNET), the latter of which became an important actor for promoting academic studies and exchanges from Lund. For a few years, Kristina Myrvold and Katarina Plank were running the journal *Chakra*, which at the time was the first journal for interdisciplinary research on Indian religions. In 2005, Indic religions, with the study of Hindu, Buddhist, Jain and Sikh traditions, became a research subject within History of Religions, and Olle Qvarnström was appointed as professor to develop a division. Qvarnström retained the philological study of Indian religions with particular interest for Sanskrit texts related to Jain traditions as well as receptions and mutual influences of Buddhist, Hindu and Jain doctrines and philosophies. His translation of the *Yogasastra* of Hemacandra, a twelfth-century Sanskrit treatise on rules and conducts in Svetambara Jainism created by the polymath Hemacandra, was the first of its kind in the English language (Qvarnström 2002).

From 2020, Myrvold continued the study of Indian religions at Lund University as a guest professor for five years. Through her research on the Sikh religion, Myrvold combined contemporary anthropological studies with historical text analysis in research on contemporary religious uses of scriptures and texts, Sikh migration and identity formations in Europe, and historical studies of print culture, scriptures and rituals in colonial Punjab. The development of a new professor programme at Lund University suggested a future investment in religions of East Asia. In 2022, Esther-Maria Guggenmos was appointed Professor in Contemporary Religions with a research focus directed towards divination in Chinese Buddhism and lay Buddhists in Taiwan.

Beside the philological research in Indology, University of Gothenburg established a Department of Religious Studies in the 1970s. Schalk instituted seminars and postgraduate education in the study of religions from 1978. Later in 1983, Schalk moved to Uppsala University to become professor, but two of his students from Gothenburg completed dissertations about Buddhism in Bangladesh and colour symbolism in Mayahana Buddhism (Hockersmith 1985; Slavik 1994). The university did not develop distinct research seminars on Indian religions, like Uppsala and Lund, but engaged in a long-term research and study focus on multiculturalism and religious diversity in which Indian traditions were integrated. As an extension of this interest, Åke Sander organized field-study courses in India which laid the foundation for the project *Go:India* that ran between 2011 and 2017. Through this project, Sander and his colleagues arranged conferences in India, student exchanges and hosted guest researchers from India at Gothenburg (Andersson and Sander 2010).

From 1967, the University of Gothenburg also functioned as a mother branch for the college in Karlstad in order to make it easier for long-distance students in humanities and social sciences to study closer to their homes (Schüllerqvist 2017). As the educational institution at Karlstad matured into an independent college in 1977 and a university in 1999, the study of religions, and especially the Indian traditions, became an integral part of teacher training programmes. From 1987, various types of field trips to Varanasi were arranged, and eight years later, a study centre was established in the city, which gradually became a significant institution to provide Swedish students an opportunity to carry out fieldwork and language studies in India for advanced courses. The centre also assisted students in teacher training programmes and researchers conducting longer fieldworks in India (Fjällsby, Olausson and Ullström 2015).

Although research environments for the study of Indian religions have primarily developed at the larger universities, research and teaching competence is available at most universities with the study of religion, including the universities of Dalarna, Gävle, Jönköping, Linköping, Linnaeus, Malmö, Södertörn, Umeå and, before 2021, also the Mid Sweden University. This is due to the inclusion of Religious Education (RE) as a compulsory subject in the primary and the secondary school and the importance of teacher training programmes for the various school forms. The curricula of RE emphasize teaching on central themes on the world religions and different world views and religious expressions in a national context and in the world.

Main Orientations

Characteristic of research on Indian religions at Swedish universities within the broader study of religion is the continued interweaving of philological, historical and contemporary orientations with the use of diverse methodological and theoretical approaches.

The philological study has continued at the major universities with focus on translations of Hindu, Buddhist and Jain texts in Sanskrit, Prakrit, Tibetan and other languages in studies on religious teachings, practices and mutual influences and conflicts between different traditions. The Vedic religion and ancient Indian texts have attracted continued interest with new questions posed to material on Vedic sacrifices, royal consecrations and conceptions of the soul (Cavallin 2003; Edholm 2016; Norelius 2021). An equal interest has been directed to translations and analyses of Buddhist manuscripts and schools, such as doctrines within the fourth-century *Yogacara* school and auto-commentaries of the sixth-century philosopher Bhavaviveka (Boquist 1993; Qvarnström 1989). The philological study has further examined doxographies and treatises by Jain philosophers, the Hindu divination systems and astrology, and Indian philosophy as represented in the Navya-Nyaya (thirteenth to eighteenth centuries) discourse (e.g. Borgland 2020; Gansten 2003; Qvarnström 2002; Sjödin 2006).

A scholarly challenge for the study of Indian religions during the twentieth century was to position the discipline in relation to the previous entrenchment in Orientalism and the growing number of postcolonial studies questioning Western views and research on India. Ronald Inden's *Imagining India*, for instance, critically surveyed Indology to argue that most scholarship repeatedly denied Indians the power to represent themselves and failed to approach them as rational subjects with agency (Inden 1990). The postcolonial critique influenced a generation of scholars to make the agency of local and regional actors, traditions and practices in India visible and display how imperial ideologies and strategies shaped representations of Indian religions while Indian traditions transformed with Western modernism, migration and globalization.

The text-oriented study incorporated histories of the reception of ideas and practices from Asia in the West, from the time of European colonization during the sixteenth century up to the world wars in the twentieth century. This approach has included specific analyses of the narratives and images of Asian religions by a set of agents: Christian missionaries, traders and travellers within the East India Company, scholars within the academia and theosophists and occult writers (e.g. Eliasson 2022; Nilsson 2020; Offermanns 2002). The historical study of specific religious traditions and regions in India have focused on the most varied topics, such as the Advaita tradition as interpreted by Indian and English philosophers in the nineteenth century, the life and work of the Vaishnava reformer Bhaktisiddhanta Sarasvati, who established a pan-Indian movement for the modern revival of traditional personalist *bhakti* in the early twentieth century, and British colonial politics of using religious scriptures and artefacts to secure loyalty among Punjabi soldiers participating in the First World War (Myrvold and Johansson 2019; Odyniec 2018; Sardella 2013). Historical studies have incorporated studies on the development of material and visual cultures in the religious traditions, like the aniconic art and monuments in the Buddhist tradition (Karlsson 1999; Klint 2021). A special area of research is directed towards Tibetan

Buddhism and includes both historical studies on tantric initiation ritual as well as translations of fifteenth-century texts on mad yogins and female Tibetan masters (Hammar 2005; Larsson 2012, 2018).

Research on contemporary religion has combined ethnographic fieldwork and textual analyses to examine Indian religions in local, national and global settings. A first orientation in this field has been practice-oriented and concentrated on lived Hindu, Buddhist and Sikh practices in South or Southeast Asian contexts. Research on Hindu traditions have included several studies on not only local and transnational contemporary religious movements, such those established around female gurus in India, the modern Advaita and Hindu missions, but also specific orientations like environmental controversies related to religious notions of River Ganga (e.g. Charpentier 2010; Hansson 2001; Sardella 2022; Thorsén 2022). Since the literature on Buddhism was predominantly historical and philological, there was a need to deepen the knowledge about the lived practices and narratives. Ethnographic studies of Buddhism have included various directions and contexts, all from possession rituals in Tibet and Burma to meditation practices (e.g. Barnekow 2003; Berglie 1983). Research on Buddhist traditions has also been leaning towards the social and political sciences by directing attention to social activism, nationalism and politicized religion. This includes studies on nationalism and religion in Burma, Thailand and Japan, among exile Tibetan settlements, as well as Buddhism as a majority religion in Thailand (Foxeus 2011; Larsson 2020; Nilsen 2012; Piltz 2005; Wiktorin 2005). The Sikh tradition, which is the youngest but also the most unexplored religion, received attention through ethnographies on Sikh religious uses of scriptures and lived practices of interpreting religious texts and history (e.g. Myrvold 2007, 2013). Within the South Asian context, research into political dimensions have also embraced studies on Muslim scholars, leaders and political parties (Dahlkvist 2019; Johansson 2016).

Another orientation in the study of contemporary Indian religions has started from sociology of religion and anthropology 'at home' to direct the interest to migration and diaspora communities in Sweden and Europe. Since the early twentieth century, Hindus, Buddhist, Sikhs and Jains have migrated to Europe, but a more regular migration to Sweden began after the world wars and peaked by the early twenty-first century when migrants, especially from India and Thailand, were among the largest immigration groups. Societal developments were accompanied by heightening academic interest for international migration and ethnical relations. However, except for a few introductory works, the prior attention was not on religion, and little was known about Hindu, Buddhist and Sikh groups who had settled in Sweden (Nordin 2023: 22). Previous research in the study of religions had examined minority religions and diaspora communities outside Europe, such as in Hawaii and Bangladesh (e.g. Hamrin 1996; Rosén-Hockersmith 1985).

As an effort to map Asian religions in Sweden, several studies on these groups emerged in the twenty-first century and presented foundational knowledge about migration patterns, the establishment and organization of religious communities and practices, strategies for integration and the transmission of traditions in the

Swedish society (see the chapters by Myrvold, Plank and Rosén-Hockersmith in Andersson and Sander 2005; Myrvold 2011, 2012, 2015; Plank 2011, 2015; Plank, Raddock and Selander 2016; Sardella 2020). In the international study of Indian diaspora communities, Swedish scholars have also contributed with inventories and overviews of the research field both as co-editors and writers for large encyclopaedias and handbooks, such as *Brill's Encyclopedia of Sikhism* and *Handbook of Hinduism in Europe* (Jacobsen et al. 2017; Jacobsen and Sardella 2020, Myrvold 2014). The growing interest in Asian migrants and religions has contributed to the creation of extensive academic research networks for the study of Hindu, Buddhist and Sikh traditions in Nordic and European countries. There are yet many gaps of knowledge on the history of the Asian migration to Sweden, and there is need to update and deepen the understanding of contemporary migrant communities.

A third orientation in the study of contemporary religions has directed attention to Western practitioners and movements that have adopted religious practices that seek origin and legitimacy in the Indian religions. Substantial interest has been directed towards Indian traditions within the broader study of new religious movements and alternative spiritualities. In her study of new religious movements in Sweden, Liselotte Frisk (1959–2020), professor at Dalarna University, examined the movements of Hare Krishna, Bhagwan, Osho, Sathya Sai Baba and Transcendental meditation (e.g. Frisk 1993, 2007). As meditation and mindfulness became incorporated into religious and profane settings in the Swedish society, Plank at Karlstad University explored Buddhist insight meditation (*vipassana*) as well as therapeutic use of mindfulness (Plank 2014). Subsequent research has focused on contemporary forms of yoga, New Age-inspired practices and alternative medicine that derive ideas and practices from the Indian religions (Fitger 2022; Moberg and Ståhle 2014). Many of these studies have contributed to an understanding of how religious practices, ideas and movements operate and transform between local and global settings. This field also include research that examines how new religious practices derived from Asian traditions become implemented in established Christian institutions of the Church of Sweden (Lundgren, Plank and Egnell forthcoming).

Aligned with the study of religion is Psychology of Religion, which has displayed an interest in the religions of the world, particularly meditative and ascetic practices of Buddhist traditions. Hjalmar Sundén, the first professor in the discipline at Uppsala University in 1967, laid the foundation for discipline in Sweden and, among other things, contributed with an analysis of the history and significance of Zen Buddhism in the West from a psychological perspective (Sundén 1995). At Lund University, Antoon Geels extensively studied mystical experiences and traditions in world religions. Geels presented psychological approaches to the study of Tibetan shamanism and later discussed how Buddhist thought could motivate humans for altruistic work (Geels 1990, 2007). In the twenty-first century, the field has shifted focus to the psychology of radicalization and violence, as represented by the research by Tomas Lindgren, professor at Umeå University. Researchers have also developed psychological theories based on textual and anthropological studies of Hindu religious practices and rituals. Run Gröndahl examined the psychological understanding of the relation between psychological assumptions, philosophical theories and ritual phenomena in Hindu Shaktaism and Tantrism (Gröndahl 2000). Based on ethnographic studies in Varanasi, Göran Ståhle developed a theory for a practice-oriented cultural psychology of religion, grounded in a study of a Hindu goddess-temple in Varanasi (Ståhle 2004).

Another prominent research field with focus on the Indian religions is Didactics of Religion which at many institutions became an integral part of the study of religions. A significant orientation within this field has been directed towards representations and stereotypes of Indian religions in Swedish textbooks. Some of the earliest studies in this category examined images of India as a developing country struck by poverty and religion (Olsson 1984, 1988). The first professorship with a special focus on didactics of religion was held by Kjell Härenstam at Karlstad University from 2004. In the early 1990s, Härenstam analysed how Islam was represented in Swedish textbooks in religious education, and this research became widely referenced and highly influential for other studies in didactics, pedagogics and religious studies (Härenstam 1993). Later in his career, Härenstam took a particular interest in Tibetan Buddhism and illustrated how representations of this tradition changed depending upon ideological leanings and significant political events. Influenced by critical research on Orientalism and hermeneutics, he problematized the Christian paradigm and claims of objectivity in religious education to propose an approach that advocated 'learning from' rather than 'learning about' various religious traditions (Härenstam 2000).

Other directions in the field of didactics have been in-depth studies of religious learning practices and religious education in India. Marc Katz at Karlstad University was a pioneer with his ethnographic study on communal inclusive practices and particularly religious rituals, festivals and storytelling in Varanasi as significant means for transferring knowledge and traditions (Katz 1993). Katz produced three films on the festival *Holi*, the fire sacrifice of *Yagya* and the *Muharram* to illustrate how festivals unite different social and religious communities while rituals and text performances bind together devotional traditions (Katz 1996, 2001, 2004). Studies in didactics and sociology of religion have also directed attention to the development of religious education within secular educational institutions in India and used comparative approaches to highlight context-sensitive understandings of concepts like secular and secularism (Cavallin and Sander 2018; Cavallin, Sander and Sitharaman 2020; Niemi 2020).

Considering that many researchers working on Indian religions are often alone with their specialized expertise in a Swedish or even a Nordic context, the field has naturally become international by character. Although many of the early Indologists and Orientalists were desk researchers who never visited India or other Asian countries, many of them operated in international networks of scholars at the time. Contemporary researchers are even more dependent on studies abroad and collaborations with international colleagues for data collection and collegial academic discussions. Given this, researchers studying the Indian religions have naturally worked and published internationally and more often received recognition in academic settings abroad rather than at home, whether this has involved contributions in terms of new translations of ancient manuscripts, historical studies of previously unexplored traditions or ethnographies of religious communities and practices in novel fields.

Looking to the Future

As the above description displays, the study of Indian religions, languages and texts in Sweden has a history that is more than a hundred years long. At most universities, Indian or Asian religions is nowadays a well-established subject area within the broader educational programmes in the study of religions. However, the teaching is generally restricted to Hinduism and Buddhism at the basic level since the study of these traditions is included or can be credited in teacher training programmes. At many places, individual teachers have developed courses on popular themes, such as yoga, modern gurus, minority religions and so on, which run as independent courses. There is currently no bachelor or master programme specifically for the study of Indian or South Asian religions, but at most universities, students can specialize in the field when preparing their theses in religious studies.

Previously, the larger universities in the Nordic countries provided educational programmes in various Indian languages and literature, but university politics and general cutbacks in humanities in the past decades have resulted in a serious decline, reorganization or complete closure of many programmes, particularly those in language studies. In the early 2020s, Uppsala University is the only university that offers a programme in Indology with courses in Hindi and Sanskrit at basic and advanced levels. Consequently, students in Sweden are dependent on universities abroad or language programmes in South Asia, especially if they need to obtain skills in other languages for ethnographic and text-based research. This development has certainly influenced the students' choices of orientations in the study of religions which previously were made within a discipline that operated in tandem with the linguistic and philological programmes.

Previous research at Swedish universities has laid a solid foundation for specialized and cutting-edge research on Indian religions, cultures and languages, but the disciplines and interests have often been maintained by individual researchers. To ensure future in-depth knowledge and competence in different religious traditions, languages, cultural areas and historical periods, there is a need to develop academic infrastructures that can provide long-term research environments for students and researchers early in their career.

Note

1 Jones worked for the East India Company and laid the foundation for Indology by creating the Asiatic Society and discovering relationships between Sanskrit and ancient

European and West Asian languages. For overviews of early Indology in Sweden, see Charpentier (1924) and Juntunen (2000).

References

Andersson, D., and Å. Sander (2010), 'Varför Indien?' in *India on My Mind*, 15–19, Göteborg: Institutionen för litteratur, idéhistoria och religion, Göteborgs universitet.

Andersson, D., and Å. Sander, eds (2005), *Det mångreligiösa Sverige: ett landskap i förändring*, Lund: Studentlitteratur.

Barnekow, S. (2003), *Erfarenheter av Zen*, Lund: Nya Doxa.

Berglie, P.-A. (1983), *Gudarna stiger ned: Rituell besatthet hos sherpas och tibetaner*, Stockholm: Stockholms universitet

Bergstedt, C. F. (1846), *Vikrama och Urvasi eller hjelten och nymfen: Ett indiskt skådespel av Kālidāsa*, Stockholm: I. J. Hjerta.

Bergstedt, C. F. (1844), *Sāvitrī, en episod ur den indiska epopéen Mahâ-bhârata. Från sanskrit-texten metriskt öfversatt jemte inledning och anmärkningar*, Uppsala: Wahlström & Låstbom.

Bhikhabhai, R. (2016), 'Engraved Sanskrit Signatures Deciphered after 180 Years', https://shfstor.blob.core.windows.net/wardsaetra/uploads/file/2016%2007%2028_%20sanskrit%20text%20otto%20tullbergs_RamaB.pdf.

Boquist, Å. (1993), *Trisvabhāva: A Study of the Development of the Three-Nature-Theory in Yogācāra Buddhism*, Stockholm: Almqvist & Wiksell.

Borgland, J. (2020), *Examination into the True Teaching: Vidyānandin's Satyaśāsanaparīkṣā*, Wiesbaden: Harrassowitz Verlag.

Cavallin, C. (2003), *The Efficacy of Sacrifice: Correspondences in the Ṛgvedic Brāhmaṇas*, Göteborg: Institutionen för religionsvetenskap, Göteborgs universitet.

Cavallin, C., Å. Sander and S. Sitharaman (2020), *The Future of Religious Studies in India*, London: Routledge.

Cavallin, C., and Å. Sander (2018), 'Religious Studies in India. Banaras Hindu University: Religion and Universal Human Values', *Journal for the Study of Religions and Ideologies* 17 (50): 30–45.

Charpentier, J. (1920), *Die Suparṇasage: Untersuchungen zur altindischen literatur- und sagengeschichte*, Uppsala: Almqvist & Wiksells.

Charpentier, J. (1922), *The Uttarādhyayanasūtra, Being the first Mūlasūtra of the Śvetāmbara Jains, Edited with an Introduction, Critical Notes and a Commentary*, Uppsala: Appelbergs Boktryckeri AB.

Charpentier, J. (1924), 'Indologiska studier i Sverige', *Svenska Orientsällskapets Årsbok* 2: 55–72.

Charpentier, M.-T. (2010), *Indian Female Gurus in Contemporary Hinduism: A Study of Central Aspects and Expressions of Their Religious Leadership*, Åbo: Åbo Akademi.

Dahlkvist, M. (2019), *The Politics of Islam, Non-Violence, and Peace: The Thought of Maulana Wahiduddin Khan in Context*, Umeå: Umeå universitet.

Diehl, C. G. (1956), *Instrument and Purpose: Studies on Rites and Rituals in South India*, Lund: Gleerup.

Edgren, H. (1875), *Molnbudet (Meghadūta): Ett indiskt skaldestycke*, Malmö: Gumperts bokhandel.

Edgren, H. (1877), *Mālavikā: Ett indiskt skådespel*, Malmö: Gumperts bokhandel.
Edholm, E. af (1989) *Jñānacakṣus: On Vision and Knowledge in Indian Religious Thought*, Uppsala: Uppsala University.
Edholm, K. af (2016), 'Risk, förlust och oviss utgång i vedisk kungaritual', *Chaos: Dansk-norsk tidsskrift for religionshistoriske studier* 65 (1): 149–72.
Ekenstam, F. W. af (1811), *Dissertatio academia, De lingua sanscrit*, Lundae: Literis Berlingianis.
Eliasson, P. (2022), *Towards a New Language: Christology in Early Modern Marathi, Konkani, and Hindustani*, Uppsala: Acta Universitatis Upsaliensis.
Ergardt, J. (1970), *Buddhismen i Västerlandet: undersökning av engelsk buddhism*, Lund: Lund University.
Fitger, M. (2022), *Själens arkitektur: Subtil anatomi som upplevelser, förkroppsligande och självförtåelse, 1875–2020*, Stockholm: Institutionen för etnologi, religionshistoria och genusvetenskap, Stockholms universitet.
Fjällsby, I., P. Olausson and M. Ullström (2015), *Som ringar på vattnet. 25 år av internationellt samarbete*, Karlstad: Karlstad University Press.
Flensburg, N. (1909), *Bidrag till Rigvedas mytologi. Om guden Pūṣan i Rigveda*, Lund: H. Ohlssons boktryckeri.
Foxeus, N. (2011), *The Buddhist World Emperor's Mission: Millenarian Buddhism in Postcolonial Burma*, Stockholm: Department of Ethnology, History of Religions and Gender Studies.
Frisk, L. (2007), *De nya religiösa rörelserna – vart tog de vägen?: en studie av Scientologi-kyrkan, Guds barn, Hare Krishnarörelsen, Moon-rörelsen och Bhagwan-rörelsen och deras utveckling över tid*, Nora: Nya Doxa.
Frisk, L. (1993), *Nya religiösa rörelser i Sverige: relation till samhället/världen, anslutning och engagemang*, Åbo: Åbo Akademis förlag.
Gansten, M. (2003), *Patterns of Destiny: Hindu Nāḍī Astrology*, Stockholm: Almqvist & Wiksell International.
Geels, A. (1990), 'Tibetan Shamanism: A Multi-Dimensional Psychological Approach to the Study of Ecstasy', in N. G. Holm (ed.), *Encounter with India: Studies in Neohinduism*, Åbo: Åbo akademi.
Geels, A. (2007), *Religiös besinning och besinningslös religion: tankar om terror i Guds namn, buddhism och global andlighet*, Nora: Nya Doxa.
Gren-Ekholm, G. (1978), *A Study of Nominal Sentences in the Oldest Upaniṣads*, Studia Indoeuropaea Upsaliensia, Uppsala: Uppsala University.
Gröndahl, R. (2000), *Den gudomliga kroppen: En psykologisk tolkning av hinduisk śāktism och tantrism*, Edsbruk: Akademitryck AB.
Hammar, U. (2005), *Studies in the Kālacakra Tantra: A History of the Kālacakra in Tibet and a Study of the Concept of Ādibuddha, the Fourth Body of the Buddha and the Supreme Unchanging*, Stockholm: Department of Ethnology, History of Religions, and Gender Studies.
Hamrin, T. (1996), *Dansreligionen i japansk immigrantmiljö på Hawai'i: Via helbrägdagörare och Jōdo Shinshū-präster till nationalistisk millennarism*, Stockholm: Almqvist & Wiksell.
Hansson, S. (2001), *Not Just Any Water: Hinduism, Ecology and the Ganges Water Controversy*, Lund: Lund Studies in African and Asian Religions.
Hellman, E. (1998), *Hinduiska gudinnor och kvinnor: En introduktion*, Nora: Nya doxa.
Hellman, E. (1993), *Political Hinduism: The Challenge of the Viśva Hindū Pariṣad*, Uppsala: Uppsala University.

Härenstam, K. (1993), *Skolboks-islam: Analys av bilden av islam i läroböcker i religionskunskap*, Göteborg: Acta Universitatis Gothoburgensis.
Härenstam, K. (2000), *Kan du höra vindhästen? Religionsdidaktik – om konsten att välja kunskap*, Lund: Studentlitteratur.
Inden, R. (1990), *Imagining India*, Cambridge, MA: Basil Blackwell.
Jackson, P., and A.-P. Sjödin, eds (2016), *Philosophy and the End of Sacrifice: Disengaging Ritual in Ancient India, Greece and Beyond*, Sheffield: Equinox.
Jacobsen, K., and F. Sardella, eds (2020), *Handbook of Hindus in Europe*, 2 vols, Leiden: Brill.
Jacobsen, K. A., G. Singh Mann, K. Myrvold and E. Nesbitt, eds (2017), *Brill's Encyclopedia of Sikhism Vol. 1: History, Literature, Society, Beyond Punjab*, Leiden: Brill.
Johansson, A. (2016), *Pragmatic Muslim Politics: The Case of Sri Lanka Muslim Congress*, Cham: Springer.
Johansson, K. F. (1897), *Bidrag till Rigvedas tolkning*, Uppsala: K. Humanistiska vetenskapssamfundet i Uppsala.
Johansson, K. F. (1907), *Indiska sagor 1907*, Stockholm: Aktiebolaget Ljus.
Johansson, R. E. A. (1973), *Pali Buddhist Texts: Explained to the Beginner*, Lund: Studentlitteratur.
Johansson, R. E. A (1969), *The Psychology of Nirvana*, London: George Allen and Unwin.
Josephson, F. (2001), 'Gösta Liebert 1916–1998, Minnesteckning', in P. Hallberg (ed.), *Minnestal hållna på högtidsdagarna 1999–2000*, 37–42, Göteborg: Kungl. Vetenskaps- och Vitterhets-samhället i Göteborg.
Juntunen, M. (2000), 'Indologi och Indienbilder på 1800-talet: Om den svenska indologins historia', *Orientaliska studier* 102: 20–34.
Karlsson, K. (1999), *Face to Face with the Absent Buddha: The Formation of Buddhist Aniconic Art*, Uppsala: Uppsala University.
Katz, M. (1993), *The Children of Assi: The Transference of Religious Traditions and Communal Inclusion in Banaras*, Göteborg: Dept. of Religious Studies.
Katz, M. (1996), *Holi Hey: A Festival of Love, Color, and Life*, Wisconsin: University of Wisconsin-Madison. (Film)
Katz, M. J. (2001), *Tulsidas and the Fire of the Veda*, Wisconsin: University of Wisconsin-Madison. (Film)
Katz, M. J. (2004) *Banaras Muharram and the Coals of Karbala*, Wisconsin: University of Wisconsin-Madison. (Film)
Klint, J. af (2021), *The Barabuḍur: A Synopsis of Buddhism*, Stockholm: Department of Ethnology, History of Religions and Gender Studies.
Larsson, E. (2020), *Rituals of a Secular Nation: Shinto Normativity and the Separation of Religion and State in Postwar Japan*, Uppsala: KPH Trycksaksbolaget AB.
Larsson, S. (2018), *Tsangnyön Herukas sånger: En studie och översättning av en tibetansk buddhistisk yogis religiösa poesi*, Lund: Nordic Academic Press.
Larsson, S. (2012), *Crazy for Wisdom: The Making of a Mad Yogin in Fifteenth-Century Tibet*, Leiden: Brill.
Lidén, E. (1897), *Studien zur altindischen und vergleichenden Sprachgeschichte*, Upsala: Almqvist & Wiksell.
Liebert, G. (1976), *Iconographic Dictionary of the Indian Religions: Hinduism, Buddhism, Jainism*, Leiden: Brill.
Lienhard, S. (1974), *Nevārīgītimañjarī: Religious and Secular Poetry of the Nevars of the Kathmandu Valley*, Stockholm: Almqvist & Wiksell.

Lundgren, L., K. Plank and H. Egnell (2023), 'Nya andliga praktiker i Svenska kyrkan: från exklusiva retreatmiljöer till kyrklig vardagspraktik', *Svensk Teologisk Kvartaltidskrift* 99, no 3.

Moberg, J., and G. Ståhle (2014), *Helig hälsa: Helandemetoder i det mångreligiösa Sverige*, Stockholm: Dialogos Förlag.

Morgenstierne, G. (1921), *Über das Verhältnis zwischen Cārudatta und Mṛcchakaṭikā*, Leipzig: Otto Harrassowitz.

Myrvold, K. (2015), 'Punjabi across Generations: Language Affiliation and Acquisition among Young Swedish Sikhs', in K. A. Jacobsen and K. Myrvold (eds), *Young Sikhs in a Global World: Negotiating Traditions, Identities and Authorities*, 71–96, London: Routledge.

Myrvold, K. (2014), 'Sikhs in Mainland European Countries', in P. Singh and L. E. Fenech (eds), *The Oxford Handbook of Sikh Studies*, 513–23, Oxford: Oxford University Press.

Myrvold, K. (2013), 'Translating the Guru's Words to Local and Global Contexts: Contemporary Katha in the Sikh Religion', in M. Hawley (ed.), *Sikh Diaspora: Theory, Agency, and Experience*, 321–49, Leiden: Brill.

Myrvold, K. (2012), 'Swedish Case Study: Indian Migration and Population in Sweden', *CARIM: Developing a Knowledge Base for Policymaking on India-EU Migration* 6: 1–41.

Myrvold, K. (2011), 'The Swedish Sikhs: Community Building, Representation, and Generational Change', in K. A. Jacobsen and K. Myrvold (eds), *Sikhs in Europe: Migration, Identities and Representations*, 63–94, Farnham: Ashgate.

Myrvold, K. (2007), *Inside the Guru's Gate: Ritual Uses of Texts among the Sikhs in Varanasi*, Lund: Mediatryck.

Myrvold, K., and A. Johansson (2019), 'Miniature Qurans in the First World War: Religious Comforts for Indian Muslim Soldiers', in K. Myrvold and D. M. Parmenter (eds), *Miniature Books: The Format and Function of Tiny Religious Texts*, 132–57, Sheffield: Equinox .

Nilsen, M. (2012), *Negotiating Thainess: Religious and National Identities in Thailand's Southern Conflict*, Lund: Media-tryck.

Niemi, K. (2020), *Religion in Indian Schools: Exploring National Systems of Religious Education through 'Mirroring'*, Stockholm: Universitetsservice US-AB.

Nilsson, J. (2020), *As a Fire beneath the Ashes: The Quest for Chinese Wisdom within Occultism, 1850–1949*, Lund: Centre for Theology and Religious Studies.

Nordin, M. (2023), *Migration, religion och integration*, Stockholm: Delmi kunskapsöversikt.

Norelius, P.-J. (2021), *Soul and Self in Vedic India*, Uppsala: Department of Theology.

Odyniec, P. (2018), *Engaging Advaita: Conceptualising Liberating Knowledge in the Face of Western Modernity*, Uppsala: Acta Universitatis Upsaliensis.

Oetke, C. (1988), *'Ich' und Das Ich: Analytische Untersuchungen zur Buddhistisch-brahmanischen Ātmankontroverse*, Stuttgart: Steiner.

Offermanns, J. (2002), *Der lange Weg des Zen-Buddhismus nach Deutschland: vom 16. Jahrhundert bis Rudolf Otto*, Lund: KFS.

Offermanns, J. (2005), 'Debates on Atheism, Quietism, and Sodomy: The Initial Reception of Buddhism in Europe', *Journal of Global Buddhism* 6: 16–35.

Olsson, T. (1993), 'Jan Ergardt in Memoriam', *Svensk teologisk kvartalsskrift* 69 (2): 84–5.

Olsson, T. (1988), *Folkökning, fattigdom, religion: Objektivitetsproblem i högstadiets läromedel 1960–1985 med särskild inriktning på Indien- och u-landsbilden*, Löberöd: Plus ultra.

Olsson, T. (1984), *Kunskap eller myter: Bilden av Indien i svenska skolböcker*, Lund: Pedagogiska inst.
Piltz, Å. (2005), *Seger åt Tibet!: Den tibetanska diasporan och den tibetanska diasporan och den religiösa nationen*, Lund: Almqvist & Wiksell.
Plank, K. (2015), 'Sacred foodscapes in Thai Buddhist temples in Sweden', *Religion and Food*, Scripta Insituti Donneriani Aboensis, 26: 201-24.
Plank, K., ed. (2014), *Mindfulness: Tradition, tolkning och tillämpning*, Lund: Nordic Academic Press.
Plank, K. (2011), *Insikt och närvaro: Akademiska kontemplationer kring buddhism, meditation och mindfulness*, Göteborg: Makadam förlag.
Plank, K., E. Raddock and P. Selander (2016), 'The Temple Mount of Fredrika: Translocality and Fractured Transnationalism of a Visionary Thai Buddhist Retreat Centre', *Contemporary Buddhism* 17 (2): 405-26.
Qvarnström, O. (2006), 'Från Hampton Roads till Lundagård: Forskning om indiska religioner vid Lunds universitet 1880-2005', in *Vetenskapssocieteten i Lund. Årsbok 2006*, Lund: Vetenskapssocieteten i Lund.
Qvarnström, O. (1989), *Hindu Philosophy in Buddhist Perspective: The Vedāntatattvaviniścaya Chapter of Bhavya's Madhyamakahṛdayakārikā*, Lund: Plus ultra.
Qvarnström, O. (2002), *The Yogaśāstra of Hemacandra: A Twelfth Century Handbook of Śvetāmbara Jainism*, Cambridge, MA: Harvard University Press.
Rodhe, S. (1946), *Deliver Us from Evil: Studies on the Vedic Ideas of Salvation*, Lund: C.W.K. Gleerup.
Rosén-Hockersmith, E. (1985), *Buddhismen i Bangladesh: en studie av en minoritetsreligion*, Uppsala: Religionshistoriska institutionen.
Sardella, F. (2022), 'The History of Mission in Hinduism: The Spread of Bhakti from India to the West', in A. J. Ghiloni (ed.), *World Religions and Their Missions*, 111-38, New York: Peter Lang.
Sardella, F. (2020), 'Hinduism in Sweden', in K. A. Jacobsen and F. Sardella (eds), *Handbook of Hinduism in Europe*, vol. 2, 1466-85, Leiden: Brill.
Sardella, F. (2013), *Modern Hindu Personalism: The History, Life, and Thought of Bhaktisiddhanta Sarasvati*, New York: Oxford University Press.
Sardella, F., and L. Wong, eds (2020), *The Legacy of Vaiṣṇavism in Colonial Bengal*, London: Routledge.
Schalk, P. (2004), *God as a Remover of Obstacles: A Study of Caiva Soteriology among Īḻam Tamil Refugees in Stockholm, Sweden*, Uppsala: Acta Universitatis Upsaliensis.
Schalk, P. (1985), *Studier i Kampucheas historia*, Uppsala: Studies in History of Religions at the Faculty of Arts, Uppsala University.
Schalk, P. (1972), *Der Paritta-Dienst in Ceylon*, Lund: Br. Ekstrand.
Schalk, P., M. Deeg, O. Freiberger, C. Kleine and A. van Nahl, eds (2013), *Religion in Asien?: Studien zur Anwendbarkeit des Religionsbegriffs*, Uppsala: Acta Universitatis Upsaliensis.
Schüllerqvist, B. (2017), 'Varför fick Karlstad en universitetsfilial? Utbildningspolitik, bostadspolitik och samhällsförändring under 1950- och 60-tal', in P. Olausson (ed.), *Universitetsfilialen i Karlstad 1967-1977*, 25-33, Karlstad: Karlstads universitetet.
Sharpe, E. J. (1975), *Comparative Religion: A History*, London: Duckworth.
Sharpe, E. J. (1965), *Not to Destroy but to Fulfil: The Contribution of J. N. Farquhar to Protestant Missionary Thought in India before 1914*, Uppsala: Almqvist & Wiksell.

Sjödin, A.-P. (2006), *The Happening of Tradition: Vallabha on Anumāna in Nyāyalīlāvatī*, Acta Universitatis Upsaliensis, Uppsala: Uppsala University.

Slavik, J. (1994), *Dance of Colours: Basic Patterns of Colour Symbolism in Mahayana Buddhism*, Göteborg: Diss.

Ståhle, G. V. (2004), *Det religiösa självet i praktik vid ett hinduiskt gudinnetempel: Ett kulturpsykologiskt angreppssätt för religionspsykologi*, Uppsala: Religionspsykologi.

Smith, W. L. (1991), *Bengali grammatik: Text & övningar*, Stockholm: Avdeningen för indologi, Stockholms universitet.

Smith, W. L. (1988), *Rāmāyaṇa Traditions in Eastern India: Assam, Bengal, Orissa*, Stockholm: Avdelningen för indologi, Stockholms universitet.

Sundén, H. (1995), *Zen: Historik, analys och betydelse*, Stockholm: Wahlström & Widstrand.

Suneson, C. and Vāsudeva (1986), *Śaurikathodaya: A Yamaka Poem*, Stockholm: Dept. of Indology, Stockholm University.

Söderblom, N. (1908), *Främmande religionsurkunder: i urval och öfversättning*, Stockholm: Geber.

Tersmeden, F. (2017), *Professor, men inte i Lund: Historien om en språkman, soldat och skald på två kontinenter*, Lund: Lunds universitetet, Akademiintendenturen.

Thorsén, E. (2022), *In Search of the Self: A Study of the International Scene of Modern Advaitic Satsang in Present-Day Rishikesh*, Gothenburg: University of Gothenburg.

Wiktorin, P. (2005), *De villkorligt frigivna: relationen mellan munkar och lekfolk i ett nutida Thailand*, Lund: Almqvist & Wiksell.

Chapter 7

WESTERN ESOTERICISM

Henrik Bogdan

Introduction

The study of Western esotericism has, since the 1990s, developed into an important and thriving field of research, particularly within the broader context of religious studies (Hanegraaff 2016; Pasi 2016). The impact and recognition of this new field of research is shown by conferences and organizations being formed on the subject. For example, there are special sections and panels on esotericism at the conferences organized by the International Association for the History of Religions (IAHR), the American Academy of Religions (AAR) and the European Association for the Study of Religion (EASR). Academic organizations devoted to the study of Western esotericism include the Association for the Study of Esotericism (ASE) in the United States and the European Society for the Study of Western Esotericism (ESSWE) here in Europe. These two organizations, among other things, organize international conferences that cover a wide range of esoteric topics. Furthermore, there are several peer-reviewed journals devoted to Western esotericism (or specific aspects of esotericism), of which *Aries: Journal for the Study of Western Esotericism* (E. J. Brill academic publishers) is of special importance. There are also several book series on esotericism published by major publishers, such as Oxford University Press ('Oxford Studies in Western Esotericism'), State University of New York Press (SUNY) ('SUNY Series in Western Esoteric Traditions') and Brill Academic Publishers ('Aries Book Series: Texts and Studies in Western Esotericism'). We can also witness an increasing number of books published about esotericism by leading publishers like Cambridge University Press, University of Chicago Press and University of California Press.

In addition to these organizations and publishing enterprises, a few academic chairs devoted to esotericism have been created. In 1965, a chair in History of Christian Esotericism was established at the *École Pratique des Hautes Études* (Sorbonne). François Secret (1911–2003) held this chair from 1965 to 1979, when he was succeeded by Antoine Faivre (1934–2021), who held the chair from 1979 to 2002. Faivre was, in his turn, succeeded by Jean-Pierre Brach in 2002. From 1979, the chair was entitled History of Esoteric and Mystical Currents in Modern and Contemporary Europe'. In 1999, a chair was established at the University of Amsterdam, devoted to the 'History of Hermetic Philosophy and Related Currents', which is held by Wouter J. Hanegraaff, and a few years later, a chair was established at the University of Exeter, which the late Nicholas Goodrick-Clarke (1953–2012) held until his premature death 2012. Today, courses on esotericism are offered at universities across Europe and in the United States, and there's a steady growth of PhDs awarded on esoteric topics.

Western esotericism is often understood as an umbrella term that covers a wide range of currents, traditions – such as Rosicrucianism, Freemasonry, Theosophy and Occultism – and practices such as alchemy, astrology and magic. The question of what unites all these diverse phenomena lies at the heart of the study of esotericism, and during the first phase of the establishment of this field of research in the 1990s and early 2000s, it was in particular Faivre's definition of Western esotericism as a form of thought (characterized by four constitutive components and two secondary components) that dominated the emergent field. The study of esotericism has, however, come a long way since the days when Faivre's paradigm reigned supreme. While it is impossible to go through all the developments here and now, I will limit myself by just giving a few examples of recent trends in the study of esotericism. First, there has been a major shift towards the study of contemporary esotericism. Some of the fiercest criticism levelled against Faivre and the older generation of scholars has been the apparent disinterest in the contemporary scene. A new generation of scholars have stressed the importance of theories and methods from the social sciences in understanding modern and contemporary forms of esotericism. This trend is, to a certain extent, reflective of a wider trend in religious studies, in which the study of ancient and premodern forms of religions is increasingly diminishing in favour of the study of modern and contemporary forms of religion. Second, the demarcation of Western esotericism as a *western* phenomenon is being questioned at an increasing rate, and scholars such as Kocku von Stuckrad and Julian Strube have criticized the theoretical and methodological reasons for this delimitation. In connection to this, we can also see a re-evaluation of the comparative method, particularly among scholars in the United States, but also here in Europe, who in different ways are advocating a comparative study of esotericism across cultural borders. Third, and perhaps most importantly, esotericism is developing into an interdisciplinary discipline, with scholars using critical theory in order to study questions such as gender, race, class, sexuality and colonialism in esotericism. As will be discussed, some of the leading scholars of these new approaches to esotericism, such as Egil Asprem and Manon Hedenborg White, are affiliated with Swedish universities.

It should be emphasized that the study of esotericism is not limited to religious studies. In fact, some of the most influential pioneers before the field was established in the late 1990s were historians of science, intellectual historians (or historians of ideas) and literature scholars. Many of these early pioneers can be seen as specialists of specific aspects of esotericism, such as alchemy or Swedenborgianism, and it was not until the 1990s with scholars like Faivre that we have more 'generalist' approaches to esotericism, placing subjects like alchemy or magic within the broader frame of Western esotericism. From the 1990s onwards, the study of Western esotericism developed primarily within religious studies, and more specifically the History of Religions. However, as the field gradually became more established across Europe and the United States in the 2000s and 2010s, multidisciplinary approaches were increasingly emphasized and scholars from other fields, such as Art History and Literature Studies, contributed with important perspectives on the study of esotericism. Whilst the same development to a large extent can be traced in Sweden, this chapter will focus on the development of the study of Western esotericism as it has developed within Religious Studies specifically, especially the History of Religions (with two early notable exceptions, Lamm and Lindroth). What follows is thus a selective historical overview of key issues and scholars, followed by a discussion of the impact and international significance of Swedish scholars specializing in Western esotericism.

Historical Overview of the Study of Western Esotericism in Sweden

One of the most influential pioneers in the study of what we today term 'Western esotericism' is the literary scholar Martin Lamm (1880–1950). Lamm became an Associate Professor of Literature (Sw. *docent i estetik med konst- och litteraturhistoria*) at Uppsala University in 1908, and from 1919 to 1945, he held the chair of history of literature (Sw. *litteraturhistoria*) at the University of Stockholm (*Stockholms högskola*). In 1928, Lamm was appointed a member of the Swedish Academy, in which he succeeded Claes Annerstedt (1839–1927) on chair number 2. Lamm holds the distinction of being the first scholar who systematically edited the unpublished papers of August Strindberg (1849–1912), in addition to conducting thorough research on the works of Carl Jonas Love Almquist (1793–1866). Lamm's works in the field of esotericism include a biography of the Swedish visionary mystic Emanuel Swedenborg (1688–1772), *Emanuel Swedenborg. En studie öfver hans utveckling till mystiker och andeskådare* (Emanuel Swedenborg. The Development of His Thought, 1915). Lamm's analysis of Swedenborg's philosophical system and its evolution is considered one of the most influential interpretations of Swedenborg's writings, and the book has had a profound impact on successive generations of scholars working on Swedenborg. Lamm's meticulous investigation into the philosophical and religious influences that shaped Swedenborgian thought sheds light on the enigmatic transformation of Swedenborg from a scientist to a mystic. Lamm convincingly establishes a coherent and logical progression of ideas from Swedenborg's earliest childhood encounters to his most sophisticated theological declarations. Lamm argued that Swedenborg's scientific world view remained intact even after his religious revelations and that his visionary experiences complemented and affirmed his existing understanding of the natural world.[1] Lamm's work on Swedenborg was followed by the two-volume study *Upplysningstidens romantik. Den mystiskt sentimentala strömningen i svensk litteratur* (The Romanticism of the Age of the Enlightenment. The Mystic-Sentimental Current in Swedish Literature, 1918–20).

In this important work, Lamm makes a detailed study of Swedenborgianism and Freemasonry in Sweden during the eighteenth century. The treatment of Freemasonry and esotericism promoted at the court of Gustav III (1746–92) and Charles XIII (1748–1818) was in many ways groundbreaking in that Lamm approached Freemasonry as part of a larger current, which he saw as linked to, yet opposed to and incompatible with, the Enlightenment. [2]

Another pioneer in the study of esotericism worth mentioning here is Sten Lindroth (1914–1980), Professor in History of Ideas (Sw. *Idé- och lärdomshistoria*) at Uppsala University and from 1968 member of the Swedish Academy, on chair number 12. Lindroth was a prolific author, but his main contribution to the field of esotericism was his monumental doctoral dissertation, *Paracelsismen i Sverige till 1600-talets mitt* (Paracelsianism in Sweden to the Mid-17th Century), which he defended in 1943. In this meticulously researched work, Lindroth argued that the philosophical and esoteric teachings of the German mystic Paracelsus, Theophrastus von Hohenheim (c. 1439–1541), had a profound impact upon the intellectual scene in Sweden up until the mid-seventeenth century. Like Lamm, Lindroth approached the object of his analysis as an intellectual current which he placed in the wider context of contemporary Swedish society.

The first Swedish works to deal with esoteric topics from the perspective of religious studies appear in the 1920s, with scholars such as Efraim Breim and Tor Andræ taking the lead. Significantly, these works dealt with modern and contemporary aspects of esotericism, and especially Spiritualism and Theosophy. Efraim Briem (1890–1946) was a historian of religions at Lund University, where he became professor in 1928. Specializing in the Babylonian religion, Briem also published on psychology of religion and contemporary religious traditions and organizations. In his works dealing specifically with esoteric movements, *Spiritismens historia* (The History of Spiritualism, 1922) and *Moderna Religionssurrogat* (Modern Surrogate Religions, 1926), Briem adopted a highly critical and even polemic position towards esoteric movements such as spiritualism and theosophy. The subtitle of the latter work, *Spiritualism, Theosophy, and Christian Science: A Religious Danger* (Sw. *Spiritismen, teosofien och Christian Science, en religiös fara*), is revealing of his purpose with the work: to warn his readers against esoteric movements which by then had established themselves firmly on the Swedish religious landscape. Briem argues that movements like spiritualism and theosophy might look and appear as religions but lack the 'power' of what he considered to be genuine religion (i.e. evangelical Protestantism): 'And they will also thereby constitute a danger to genuine, deep religiosity, a danger no less fatal to real piety than the attacks of the old naturalistic materialism were, more fatal and dangerous because these religious formations appear in the garb of spirituality and idealism' (1926: 9). Briem furthermore criticizes and dismisses the scientific and religious claims of theosophy, anthroposophy and spiritualism, arguing that these claims are either shallow, mistaken or false. However, he does admit that some of the phenomena of spiritualism cannot be dismissed as fraudulent, and he mentions in passing that he has attended several seances: 'I myself have attended several seances, in which the mediums gave real messages about deceased people, of which they had not the slightest knowledge' (1926: 22), although he is unable to offer any explanation of this type of 'genuine' phenomenon. This polemical stance towards modern forms of esotericism is sharply contrasted against his decidedly more positive approach towards Rosicrucianism and Freemasonry, which Briem covered in a later work, *Mysterier och Mysterieförbund* (Mysteries and Mystery Societies, 1932). In this work, Briem argued that secret societies such as Rosicrucianism and, especially, Freemasonry are linked to ancient Babylonian, Egyptian and Greek mystery cults, and that those who join secret societies have always been driven by the same 'desire to unravel the mysteries of existence and find a life that is not ravaged by death but possesses eternal existence' (1932: 416).³

Tor Andræ (1885–1947) was even more dismissive of contemporary esoteric movements like the Theosophical Society than his colleague Briem. Andræ is one of Sweden's most well-known and influential historian of religions. Andræ held the chair of History of Religions at Stockholm University between 1927 and 1929, and he was then appointed the chair of Theological Encyclopaedia (Sw. *teologiska prenotioner och teologisk encyklopedi*) at Uppsala University. Andræ succeeded his mentor Nathan Söderblom as a member of the Swedish Academy in 1932. In 1936, he was appointed Bishop of the Diocese of Linköping. During the same year, he briefly served as the minister of education and ecclesiastical affairs in Prime Minister Axel Pehrsson-Bramstorp's short-lived cabinet. Andræ was highly acclaimed as a scholar of comparative religion, and he made groundbreaking contributions in the field of Islamic studies. Notable works include *Der Ursprung des Islams und das Christentum* (1926) and *Muhammed* (1930). The latter work was highly acclaimed upon its publication and has been translated from Swedish into German, English, Italian and Spanish, hailed as one of the best available biographies of Muhammad. In addition to this, he wrote at length on psychology of religion and in particular on the psychology of mysticism, and it was from this perspective that he approached contemporary esoteric movements like theosophy. In his small monograph *Modern Mystik: En blick på teosofien och den ockulta vetenskapen* (Modern Mysticism: A Look at Theosophy and Occult Science, 1930), Andræ goes at great length to criticize what he called 'modern mysticism'. Andræ argues that theosophy, occultism and spiritualism are lower types of mysticism, compared to the 'higher speculative and religious mysticism' (1930: 9). According to Andræ, this modern or lower type of mysticism is characterized by four features: 'the exotic orientation', 'the strong interest in psychology', 'the anti-puritanical character' and, finally, 'its dual dependence on the popular scientific worldview' (1930: 10–28). The first of these features is marked by the interest in the West for 'remote-living peoples and distant countries' (Andræ 1930: 12). Using the popularity of Inayat Khan (1882–1927) and Rabindranath Tagore (1861–1941) as examples, Andræ argues that the fascination for the Orient and its 'beautifully curly-haired and dark-eyed Eastern prophets' tends to turn into a Western self-contempt. Echoing typical racist and Orientalist sentiments of the 1930s, Andræ stated that 'one does not improve the Nordic beauty by equipping her with the olive complexion of the Portuguese woman and the slanting eyes of the Geisha' (1930: 15). It is in particular theosophy that promotes the fascination of the East, according to Andræ, and the theosophical 'idea of universal brotherhood aims above all at the abolition of the opposition between whites and coloreds' (1930: 14). The second feature, the interest in psychology, is characterized by a preoccupation with matters that deal with the inner life of the human being, or the soul. Hypnosis, suggestion, psychic training, psychoanalysis and parapsychology are examples, according to Andræ, of modern mysticism's focus on psychological explanations of mystical phenomena and experiences. Andræ criticizes the orientation towards psychology in that it reduces mystical experiences to something merely human, and that this separates it from more genuine forms of mysticism with its seriousness and depth. The third feature, the anti-puritanical character of modern mysticism, is essentially a critique of the theosophical appropriation of the Eastern concepts of karma and reincarnation, which, according to Andræ, promotes a naïve optimism of human nature and that humans will ultimately chose good rather than evil. Andræ claims that this is an unnecessary import, which is alien to 'our' spiritual dispositions. Finally, the fourth feature of modern mysticism – its dual dependence on the popular scientific world view – concerns the paradox that while occultists and theosophists criticize materialism and scientific reductionism, they are at the same time trying to emulate or use a scientific language in order to explain religious phenomena and concepts, with words such as rays and vibrations, and, furthermore, that theosophy and occultism are presented as a *science*, or even occult science. Andræ concludes that contemporary occultism in fact is dependent on what it is trying to combat, and that it sails under false colours when it is presenting itself as science:

> But this love for science is an utterly unhappy one, and from the side of true science, it remains entirely unrequited. Without a doubt, this constant sailing under false colors is the most unsympathetic trait of the modern mystical sects. The misuse of the name of science for beliefs, methods, and mindsets that are completely contrary to the spirit of science gives these otherwise well-intentioned movements a touch of charlatanism and humbug. One would not deny them a certain respect if they honestly presented themselves as what they truly are: systems of belief, worldviews, naive attempts at explaining the world. (1930: 27–8)

After the works of Briem and Andræ, surprisingly little was published on esotericism from the perspective of religious studies for very long period. The apparent scholarly lack of interest in esoteric topics could, perhaps, be explained by the fact that esoteric movements from the 1930s onwards gradually declined in Sweden and that the relevance of the study of contemporary esotericism therefore dwindled. In fact, it was not until the early 1970s and the pioneering works on New Religious Movements that esoteric groups began to be studied again, albeit in a cursory manner (see Chapter 8 in this volume). However, as the study of Western esotericism in a strict sense gained momentum in Europe during the late 1990s, collections such as *Att se det dolda: Om New Age och ockultism inför millennieskiftet* (To See the Hidden: On the New Age and Occultism on the Eve of the Millennium, 1998), edited by Owe Wikström, and *Gudars och gudinnors återkomst* (Return of

Gods and Goddesses, 2000), edited by Liselotte Frisk and Carl-Gustav Carlsson, were published and which included chapters on Western esotericism.[4] The first doctoral dissertation in religious studies to be defended at a Swedish university that was clearly anchored in the new field of Western esotericism was Olav Hammer's *Claiming Knowledge: Strategies of Epistemology from Theosophy to the New Age* (2000; later published as Hammer 2001), at Lund University. In this work, Hammer analysed the legitimating strategies in modern Western esotericism, such as the appeal to science, tradition and experience. Hammer went to become one of Sweden's most well-known historian of religions with an international career, first at the Center for History of Hermetic Philosophy and Related Current, University of Amsterdam, and then from 2005 until his retirement in 2023 at the University of Southern Denmark. Hammer has distinguished himself for an international audience as an editor of many important collections and handbooks, such as *Polemical Encounters: Esoteric Discourse and Its Others* (2007) with Kocku von Stuckrad, *Handbook of the Theosophical Current* (2013) with Mikael Rothstein and *Western Esotericism in Scandinavia* (2016) with Henrik Bogdan.

Other dissertations on esotericism defended at Lund University include Lars Steen Larsen, *Western Esotericism: Ultimate Sacred Postulates and Ritual Fields* (2008); Fredrik Gregorius, *Modern Asatro: Att konstruera etnisk och kulturell identitet* (Modern Asatro: Constructing Ethnic and Cultural Identity, 2008); Johan Nilsson, *As a Fire Beneath the Ashes: The Quest for Chinese Wisdom within Occultism, 1850–1949* (2020); and Olivia Cejvan, *Arts and Crafts Divine: Teaching and Learning Ritual Magic in Sodalitas Rosae Crucis* (2023). Gregorius's thesis investigates the contemporary adherents of Asatru in Sweden. At the core of this research lies the examination of Asatru's contemporary manifestation as an ethnic religious practice. The study explores the conceptualization of Asatru as a folk religion among its adherents and its association with the notion of 'Sed'. Linked to the inquiry into ethnic identity and Asatru is the perplexing question of why individuals residing in present-day Sweden establish a profound connection, and self-identify, with a cultural heritage that ceased to exist approximately a millennium ago. Gregorius, now at Linköping University, has continued his research on esotericism and paganism and has published several important articles in these interlinked fields of research. Nilsson's dissertation, on the other hand, delves into the esoteric understanding of Chinese culture as it manifests in articles, ritual directives, paraphrased renditions of Chinese literary works and critical assessments of works authored by influential sinologists. Drawing upon these sources, the thesis examines how occult authors intricately interwove China into narratives that delineate the transmission of historical traditions rooted in ancient wisdom, believed to have persisted from time immemorial to the contemporary era. Nilsson posits that occult writers presaged a profound cultural transformation in the portrayal of China that unfolded during the initial decades of the twentieth century, thereby anticipating elements of the New Age fascination with Chinese spirituality and the utopian interpretation of Chinese society that emerged within European Maoism. Finally, Cejvan's thesis examines the process of teaching and learning within a contemporary esoteric society called the Sodalitas Rosae Crucis

(SRC) in Sweden, which was established in 2002. The SRC carries on the teachings of the Hermetic Order of the Golden Dawn, an influential esoteric society that originated in Victorian London. The SRC employs an initiatory system consisting of multiple degrees, gradually revealing secret teachings and ritual practices. Each degree unlocks new avenues and tools for spiritual attainment, which is the goal of ritual magic in this context. Cejvan's research views elusive and contested concepts like magic, secrecy, ritual and initiation as practical skills that can be taught and learned. The study offers valuable insights into esotericism and the broader realm of spiritual and religious learning. Nilsson and Cejvan have published several articles, and they have taught an introductory course on Occultism and Magic together for several years at Lund University.

In 2003, Henrik Bogdan defended his thesis *From Darkness to Light: Western Esoteric Rituals of Initiation* (published as *Western Esotericism and Rituals of Initiation* in 2007, in French in 2010, and in Ukrainian in 2023) at the University of Gothenburg, with Antoine Faivre as the public opponent. The dissertation traced the development of Masonic rituals of initiation from the Craft degrees of Freemasonry in the early eighteenth century, through the High degrees of Freemasonry in the second half of the eighteenth century and the Hermetic Order of the Golden Dawn towards the end of the nineteenth century, to the modern witchcraft movement in the 1950s. Bogdan has published widely on esotericism, with a special focus on initiatory societies and esoteric New Religious Movements. He has edited works such as *Brother Curwen, Brother Crowley: A Correspondence* by Aleister Crowley and David Curwen (Teitan Press, 2010); *Aleister Crowley and Western Esotericism* with Martin P. Starr (Oxford University Press, 2012), *Occultism in a Global Perspective* with Gordan Djurdjevic (Acumen, 2013), *Sexuality and New Religious Movements* with James R. Lewis (Palgrave Macmillan, 2014), *The Brill Handbook of Freemasonry* with Jan A. M. Snoek (Brill Academic, 2014), and *Western Esotericism in Scandinavia* with Olav Hammer (Brill Academic, 2016). The University of Gothenburg has developed as an important centre for the study of Western esotericism in Sweden, with several courses on esotericism being offered for students both on undergraduate and graduate levels, in addition to a regular seminar series on esotericism that has been running for several years. Other PhD dissertations defended at the University of Gothenburg that deal with aspects of esotericism include Jonathan Peste, *The Poimandres Group in Corpus Hermeticum. Myth, Mysticism and Gnosis in Late Antiquity* (2002); Anna Tessmann, *On the Good Faith: A Fourfold Discursive Construction of Zoroastrianism in Contemporary Russia* (2012); Simon Sorgenfrei, *American Dervish: Making Mevlevism in the United States of America* (2013); Christian Giudice, *Traditionalism and Occultism: Arturo Reghini and the* Antimodern Reaction (2016, published as *Occult Imperium: Arturo Reghini, Roman Traditionalism, and the Anti-Modern Reaction in Fascist Italy* in 2022); and Yusuf Muslim Eneborg, *A Sufi for a Secular Age: Reflecting on Muslim Modernity through the Life and Times of Shaykh Fadhlalla Haeri* (2020). Sorgenfrei has continued to publish widely in the field of religious studies, especially on Sufism in the West, and is now a Professor of Religious Studies at Södertörn University.

Södertörn University in Stockholm has a strong record in the study of esotericism with scholars such as Sorgenfrei, David Thurfjell and, in particular, Per Faxneld, having published widely on esoteric topics. Faxneld defended his thesis *Satanic Feminism: Lucifer as the Liberator of Woman in Nineteenth-Century Culture* at Stockholm University in 2014 (re-published by Oxford University Press in 2017). The dissertation examines how 'Satanic feminism' during the nineteenth century was expressed in a range of esoteric works, autobiographies, pamphlets and magazines, newspaper articles, paintings, sculptures and even consumer culture artefacts such as jewellery. According to Faxneld, four motifs are particularly prominent in the material: (1) reinterpretations of Eve's role in the Fall as something positive, (2) the witch as a proto-feminist, (3) the demon lover transformed into a liberator and (4) a feminized Satan contrasted with an oppressive male God. A fifth and somewhat less central motif is perceptions of Lilith, according to Jewish folk and esoteric traditions, Adam's rebellious wife before the creation of Eve, as the first feminist. The analysis focuses on the intersections between esotericism and the political sphere, as well as the influence that occultism and art have exerted on each other. The theoretical focus lies on counter-readings, counter-discourses and counter-myths, as well as the complex interplay between these and hegemonic discourses aimed at demonizing feminism. A key theme in this context is the boundaries and paradoxes of inversion. Following his dissertation, Faxneld has written and lectured widely on esotericism, in particular on satanism, and the links between esotericism and the visual arts. PhD dissertations on esotericism defended at Södertörn University include Kateryna Zorya, *The Government Used to Hide the Truth, But Now We Can Speak: Contemporary Esotericism in Ukraine 1986–2014* (2023). Zorya's thesis examines how individuals involved in esoteric practices navigated Ukraine between 1986 and 2014. It does so by analysing the content of esoteric publications produced in Ukraine, their geographical distribution and supplementary texts from other post-Soviet countries. The study reveals the existence of two distinct groups of practitioners and highlights how their strategies of self-presentation were influenced by the broader class dynamics that emerged during the Soviet era. The first group, referred to as 'working class esotericists', emerged as a result of the Soviet initiative to quickly train a large number of technical experts. The second group, known as 'intellectual class esotericists', consisted of descendants of pre-Soviet intellectuals who were initially tasked with educating the new wave of technical experts and were eventually expected to be replaced by them.

Stockholm University, located only a short distance from Södertörn University, has developed into a strong centre for the study of esotericism, particularly through the work of Professor Egil Asprem, one of the most well-known, productive and influential scholars in the field of esotericism. Asprem is Professor of the History of Religions, specializing in the study of esotericism, the history of magic, alternative spiritualities and relations between esotericism and science. He defended his doctoral dissertation, *The Problem of Disenchantment: Scientific Naturalism and*

Esoteric Discourse, 1900–1939, in 2012 (published in 2014). The dissertation presents a comprehensive and interdisciplinary approach to understanding the intellectual history of science, religion and the 'occult' during the early twentieth century. Asprem offers a new perspective on Max Weber's well-known concept of a 'disenchantment of the world' and draws upon a diverse range of sources, allowing for an expansive exploration that connects the histories of science, religion, philosophy and Western esotericism. Traditionally, parapsychology, occultism and the modern natural sciences have been regarded as separate cultural phenomena with varying intellectual credibility. However, Asprem reveals that all three have encountered similar intellectual challenges concerning the comprehensibility of nature, the relationship between facts and values, and the interplay of immanence and transcendence. Apart from his dissertation, Asprem has published an impressive number of articles and book chapters, in addition to his monograph *Arguing with Angels: Enochian Magic and Modern Occulture* (2012) and the edited volumes *Contemporary Esotericism* with Kennet Granholm (2013), *Handbook of Conspiracy Theory and Contemporary Religion* with Asbjørn Dyrendal (2018), *New Approaches to the Study of Esotericism* with Julian Strube (2021) and *Religious Dimensions of Conspiracy Theories* with Marco Pasi and Francesco Piraino (2022). Mention should also be made to the Finnish scholar Kennet Granholm, who for several years was affiliated with the University of Stockholm. Granholm was one of the first scholars to use theories and methods of the social sciences in the study of esotericism, and in his doctoral dissertation *Embracing the Dark: The Magic Order of Dragon Rouge, its Practice in Dark Magic and Meaning Making* (published as *Dark Enlightenment: The Historical, Sociological, and Discursive Contexts of Contemporary Esoteric Magic* in 2014), defended at Åbo Academy in 2005, he analysed the discursive strategies of the Swedish initiatory society Dragon Rouge. Apart from the already mentioned doctoral dissertation by Faxneld, dissertations defended at Stockholm University that deal with esotericism include Thomas Karlsson, *Götisk kabbala och runisk alkemi: Johannes Bureus och den götiska esoterismen* (Gothic Kabbalah and Runic Alchemy: Johannes Bureus and the Gothic Esotericism, 2009); Malin Fitger, *Själens arkitektur: Subtil anatomi som upplevelse, förkroppsligande och självförståelse, 1875–2020* (The Architecture of the Soul: Subtle Anatomy as Experience, Embodiment, and Self-Understanding, 1875–2020, published in 2022); Hedda Jansson, *Solbadets Buddha: Buddhism och teosofi i Ellen Keys Livstro* (The Buddha of the Sunbath: Buddhism and Theosophy in Ellen Key's Life Faith, 2023). There are also a few PhD dissertations defended at Stockholm University that deal with esotericism but submitted in other disciplines than religious studies, such as Håkan Lejon, *Historien om den antroposofiska humanismen: den antroposofiska bildningsidén i idéhistoriskt perspektiv 1880–1980* (The History of Anthroposophical Humanism: The Anthroposophical Idea of Education in a Perspective of Intellectual History 1880–1890, published in 1997), and Carl-Michael Edenborg, *Alkemiens skam, den alkemiska traditionens bortstötning ur offentligheten* (The Shame of Alchemy, the Expulsion of the Alchemical Tradition from the Public Sphere, 2002, published in 2003), both submitted in History of Ideas (see also Edenborg 1997 and 2016).

Somewhat surprisingly, the study of Western esotericism has not been established to the same extent as the aforementioned universities at Uppsala University, the oldest university in Sweden, which was founded in 1477. An important exception is the doctoral dissertation defended by Manon Hedenborg White, *The Eloquent Blood: The Goddess Babalon and the Construction of Femininities in Western Esotericism* (2017, published 2020). In her thesis, Hedenborg White examines the evolving perceptions of femininities and feminine sexuality within interpretations of the goddess Babalon, a central deity in Aleister Crowley's (1875–1947) esoteric religion known as Thelema. Traditionally, femininity has been viewed problematically in feminist theory, often associated with notions of lack, artifice and constraint. However, this study takes the perspective that femininities are diverse, not strictly heterosexual or limited to women, and can be constructed in ways that challenge existing gender systems. Drawing from historical and contemporary written sources, qualitative interviews and ethnographic fieldwork in the Anglo-American esoteric community, the study employs Mimi Schippers's model of multiple femininities to analyse the discourse surrounding Babalon from the late nineteenth century until the present, considering the shifting perceptions of femininity and feminine sexuality. Informed by Luce Irigaray's ideas on sexual difference, Rosi Braidotti's concept of feminist figurations and Catherine Waldby's notion of erotic destruction, Hedenborg White set out to answer the following question: Can Babalon serve as a figuration that enables new forms of articulating and inhabiting femininities? By reinterpreting the negative stereotype of the femme fatale, Crowley associated Babalon with an initiatory imperative of ego-annihilation, representing both feminine, erotic otherness and a feminized receptive state required for all seekers. Additionally, Crowley linked Babalon to liberated female sexuality. Other esotericists, such as John W. Parsons and Kenneth Grant, further interpreted Babalon as a feminist revolutionary and as a symbol of non-dual void preceding manifest creation, associating femininity with the dissolution of stable meanings. The growing recognition of feminism and LGBTQ issues in the Anglo-American esoteric community since the 1990s coincides with the increased visibility of female esotericists as contributors to the Babalon discourse. Contemporary discussions surrounding Babalon emphasize the sacred nature of the desiring feminine subject and its connection to the simultaneous potential for both dismantling and affirming bounded subjectivity. This study demonstrates how a previously derogatory feminine stereotype is reimagined over time, simultaneously reproducing and challenging dominant notions of femininity. It argues that Babalon serves as a situated and context-dependent figuration that supports the expression of alternative ways of understanding femininity and feminine sexuality. With this study, Hedenborg White was one of the pioneers in analysing women's roles and gender issues in esotericism, something which she has continued to do in other published works (e.g. Hedenborg White 2021). Hedenborg White is now an Associate Professor at Malmö University, where she has been instrumental in establishing esotericism as a thriving field of research. Finally, in concluding the discussion on the study of esotericism at Uppsala University, mention should be made of Tim Berndtsson's impressive dissertation in Literature Studies, *The Order and the Archive: Freemasonic Archival Culture in Eighteenth-Century Europe* (2018), which examines how European Masons in the eighteenth century established archives and the reciprocal impact of these archives on the Masonic community. The central argument presented here is that archival practices played a pivotal role in two aspects: first, they facilitated the construction of extensive organizational networks capable of strategic endeavours, and, second, they fuelled individual endeavours to attain the coveted 'higher' or esoteric knowledge believed to reside within the Masonic orders.

To wrap up this historical overview of the study of Western esotericism in Sweden, it is worth noting three major research projects that have received funding from the Swedish Research Council. This first project was led by Hedenborg White from 1 July 2018 to 30 June 2021. Entitled 'Power through Closeness? Female Authority and Agency in a Male-Led New Religion', the project examined the various levels of female religious influence and power. It was achieved by studying the life stories of three notable women: Leah Hirsig (1883–1975), Jane Wolfe (1875–1958) and Phyllis Seckler (1917–2004), who held significant positions within the religion known as Thelema which was established in 1904 by the British occultist Crowley. The second project, 'The Roma in the European History of Magic: Transnational Entanglements of Race, Class, gender, and the Occult, *c.* 1417 to 1900', is led by Asprem at Stockholm University and runs from 1 January 2022 to 31 December 2024. The project is described as the first critical and systematic historical study of the Roma's engagement with 'magic' in Europe. Associations of Roma with magic have been a central feature in anti-ziganist stereotypes since the 1400s, but magic practice has also provided an important economic niche, especially for Romani women. Finally, there is the project 'The Neglected Masculine Side of New Age: "Eastern" Spirituality in Martial Arts' led by Faxned. The project, which runs from 1 January 2023 to 31 December 2025, is described as the first major attempt to investigate masculinity in alternative spirituality, thus opening important new venues of research for this field.

International Impact and Significance

Swedish scholars like Egil Asprem, Henrik Bogdan, Per Faxneld, Olav Hammer and Manon Hedenborg White have established themselves on the international scene as leading scholars in esotericism, with a new generation of scholars like Johan Nilsson, Olivia Cejvan and Paulina Gruffman coming along. In terms of publishing, several doctoral dissertations defended at Swedish universities have been published by leading academic publishers like Oxford University Press, SUNY Press and Brill Academic Publishers (e.g. Bogdan 2007, 2010; Faxneld 2017; Giudice 2022; Hammer 2001; Hedenborg White 2020), and, in addition to this, Swedish scholars have published an impressive number of articles, book chapters, monographs and edited volumes on various aspects of esotericism. We can also see that Swedish scholars have assumed important editorial positions and responsibilities for academic journals and book series – for instance, Bogdan is the editor of the Oxford Studies in Western Esotericism and the Palgrave Studies in New Religions and Alternative Spiritualities, and Asprem is the chief editor of *Aries: Journal for the Study if Western Esotericism*.

Furthermore, Asprem, Bogdan and Hedenborg White serve as board members of the leading academic society for the study of esotericism, the European Society for the Study of Western Esotericism (ESSEW), with Asprem acting as treasurer and membership secretary and Bogdan as the secretary of the society. Two Swedish scholars have also served as the editors of the ESSWE newsletter, Faxneld and Giudice. Significantly, Sweden has (as of 2023), together with the UK, the highest number of student members of the ESSWE which indicates a steady growth of the interest in esotericism in Sweden. Several important workshops and conferences on esotericism have been organized in Sweden, of which the Fourth Biennial Conference of the ESSWE at the University of Gothenburg in 2013 and the Ninth Biennial Conference of the ESSWE at Malmö University held 2023 deserve special mention. The latter was the largest ESSWE conference to date, with over two hundred papers on various dimensions of the practice of esotericism and with Linda Woodhead (King's College London), Lawrence Principe (Johns Hopkins University) and Sophie Page (University College London) as keynote speakers. Finally, we can note that Swedish scholars specializing in esotericism are frequent participants at international conferences on esotericism, frequently organizing panels or being part of academic committees. There is furthermore a strong connection between Sweden and the Center for History of Hermetic Philosophy and Related Current at the University of Amsterdam, with Swedish students and scholars having spent time there, for example, Asprem, Bogdan and Hedenborg White.

In sum, the study of (Western) esotericism has firmly established itself as an integral, vocal and dynamic area of research within the broader field of religious studies in Sweden. Over the years, it has evolved from a niche interest into a vibrant academic discipline, capturing the attention of scholars, students and enthusiasts alike. This burgeoning field not only explores the intricate history and development of esoteric traditions, currents and practices but also actively engages in contemporary debates in the Humanities in general and religious studies in particular. As it continues to thrive and expand, the study of esotericism in Sweden stands as a testament to the enthusiasm, dedication and academic rigour of the scholars in the field.

Notes

1 See also Häll (1995).
2 The study of Freemasonry in Sweden is almost exclusively written by historians, often by masons themselves, for example, Dahlgren (1925), Eklund and Svensson (2010), Kinnander (1943), Lekeby (2010) and Lenhammar (1985). See also Bogdan (2016).
3 See Chapter 9 in this volume for a discussion on Briem's works on Psychology of Religion which often covered esoteric topics such as yoga and spiritualism.

Significantly, Briem contributed with a foreword to John Björkhem's pioneering study on parapsychology, *Det ockulta problemet* (The Problem of the Occult 1939).
4   Scholars in other disciplines, such as history of ideas, have also covered esoteric topics, for example, Åkerman (1998), Johannisson (1974), Sanner (1995) and Skott (2000).

References

Åkerman, S. (1998), *Rose Cross Over the Baltic: The Spread of Rosicrucianism in Northern Europe*, Leiden: Brill Academic Publishers.
Andræ, T. (1926), *Der Ursprung des Islams und das Christentum*, Uppsala: Almqvist & Wiksell.
Andræ, T. (1930), *Muhammed: hans liv och hans tro*, Stockholm: Natur och kultur.
Asprem, E. (2012), *Arguing with Angels: Enochian Magic and Modern Occulture*, New York: SUNY Press.
Asprem, E. (2014), *The Problem of Disenchantment: Scientific Naturalism and Esoteric Discourse, 1900–1939*, Leiden: Brill Academic.
Asprem, E., and K. Granholm, eds (2013), *Contemporary Esotericism*, Bristol: Equinox.
Asprem, E., and A. Dyrendal, eds (2018), *Handbook of Conspiracy Theory and Contemporary Religion*, Leiden: Brill Academic.
Asprem, E., and J. Strube (2021), *New Approaches to the Study of Religion*, Leiden: Brill Academic.
Asprem, E., M. Pasi and F. Piraino, eds (2022), *Religious Dimensions of Conspiracy Theories*, London: Routledge.
Berndtsson, T. (2018), *The Order and the Archive: Freemasonic Archival Culture in Eighteenth-Century Europe*, Uppsala: Uppsala University.
Björkhem, J. (1939), *Det occulta problemet: en orientering*, Uppsala, Lindblad.
Bogdan, H., and O. Hammer, eds (2016), *Western Esotericism in Scandinavia*, Leiden: Brill Academic.
Bogdan, H., and J. A. M. Snoek, eds (2014), *The Brill Handbook on Freemasonry*, Leiden: Brill Academic.
Bogdan, H., and J. R. Lewis, eds (2014), *Sexuality and New Religious Movements*, New York: Palgrave Macmillan.
Bogdan, H., and G. Djurdjevic, eds (2013), *Occultism in a Global Perspective*, Durham: Acumen.
Bogdan, H., and M. P. Starr, eds. (2012), *Aleister Crowley and Western Esotericism*, New York: Oxford University Press.
Bogdan, H. (2003), *From Darkness to Light: Western Esoteric Rituals of Initiation*, Gothenburg: University of Gothenburg.
Bogdan, H. (2007), *Western Esotericism and Rituals of Initiation*, Albany: SUNY Press.
Bogdan, H. (2010), *Ésoterisme Occidental et Rituels d'Initiation*, Milan: Arché.
Bogdan, H. (2016), 'Freemasonry in Sweden', in H. Bogdan and O. Hammer (eds), *Western Esotericism in Scandinavia*, 168–81, Leiden: Brill Academic.
Briem, E. (1922), *Spiritismens historia*, Lund: Gleerup.
Briem, E. (1926), *Moderna religionssurrogat. Spiritismen, teosofien och Christian Science, en religiös fara*, Stockholm: Hugo Gebers Förlag.
Briem, E. (1932), *Mysterier och mysterieförbund*, Stockholm: Natur och Kultur.

Cejvan, O. (2023), *Arts and Crafts Divine: Teaching and Learning Ritual Magic in Sodalitas Rosae Crucis*, Lund: Lund University.

Crowley, A., and D. Curwen (2010), *Brother Curwen, Brother Crowley: A Correspondence*, edited by Henrik Bogdan, York Beach, ME: Teitan Press.

Dahlgren, C. (1925), *Frimureriet med tillämpning på Sverige*, Stockholm: H. Klemmings Antikvariat.

Edenborg, C.-M. (1997), *Gull och mull. Den monstruöse greve Gustaf Bonde, upplysningens fiende i frihetstidens Sverige*, Lund: Ellerströms förlag.

Edenborg, C.-M. (2003), *Alkemiens skam, den alkemiska traditionens bortstötning ur offentligheten*, Stockholm: Vertigo förlag.

Edenborg, C.-M. (2016), 'Alchemy in Sweden', in H. Bogdan and O. Hammer (eds), *Western Esotericism in Scandinavia*, 33–42, Leiden: Brill Academic.

Eklund, D., and S. Svensson, eds (2010), *Hertig Carl och det svenska frimureriet*, Uppsala: Forskningslogen Carl Friedrich Eckleff.

Eneborg, Y. M. (2020) *A Sufi for a Secular Age: Reflecting on Muslim Modernity through the Life and Times of Shaykh Fadhlalla Haeri*, Gothenburg: University of Gothenburg.

Faxneld, P. (2014), *Satanic Feminism: Lucifer as the Liberator of Woman in Nineteenth-Century Culture*, Stockholm: Molin & Sorgenfrei.

Faxneld, P. (2017), *Satanic Feminism: Lucifer as the Liberator of Woman in Nineteenth-Century Culture*, New York: Oxford University Press.

Fitger, M. (2022), *Själens arkitektur: Subtil anatomi som upplevelse, förkroppsligande och självförståelse, 1875–2020*, Stockholm: Stockholm University.

Frisk, L., and C.-G. Carlsson, eds (2000), *Gudars och gudinnors återkomst. Studier i nyreligiositet*, Umeå: Institutionen för religionsvetenskap.

Giudice, C. (2016), *Traditionalism and Occultism: Arturo Reghini and the Antimodern Reaction in Early Twentieth Century Italy*, Gothenburg: University of Gothenburg.

Giudice, C. (2022), *Occult Imperium: Arturo Reghini, Roman Traditionalism, and the Anti-Modern Reaction in Fascist Italy*, New York: Oxford University Press.

Granholm, K. (2005), *Embracing the Dark: The Magic Order of Dragon Rouge, its Practice in Dark Magic and Meaning Making*, Åbo: Åbo Akademi.

Granholm, K. (2014), *Dark Enlightenment: The Historical, Sociological, and Discursive Contexts of Contemporary Esoteric Magic*, Leiden: Brill Academic.

Gregorius, F. (2008), *Modern Asatro: Att konstruera etnisk och kulturell identitet*, Lund: Lunds universitet.

Hammer, O. (2001), *Claiming Knowledge: Strategies of Epistemology from Theosophy the New Age*, Leiden: Brill Academic.

Hammer, O., and K. von Stuckrad (2007), *Polemical Encounters: Esoteric Discourse and Its Others*, Leiden: Brill Academic.

Hammer, O., and M. Rothstein (2013), *Handbook of the Theosophical Current*, Leiden: Brill Academic.

Hanegraaff, W. (2016), 'Esotericism Theorized: Major Trends and Approaches to the Study of Esotericism', in April D. DeConick (ed.), *Religion: Secret Religion*, 155–70, Farmington Hills, MI: MacMillan Reference.

Hedenborg White, M. (2017), *The Eloquent Blood: The Goddess Babalon and the Construction of Femininities in Western Esotericism*, Uppsala: Uppsala University.

Hedenborg White, M. (2020), *The Eloquent Blood: The Goddess Babalon and the Construction of Femininities in Western Esotericism*, New York: Oxford University Press.

Hedenborg White, M. (2021), 'Double Toil and Gender Trouble? Performativity and Femininity in the Cauldron of Esotericism Research', in E. Asprem and J. Strube (eds), *New Approaches to the Study of Esotericism*, 182–200, Leiden: Brill Academic.
Häll, J. (1995), *I Swedenborgs labyrint. Studier i de gustavianska swedenborgarnas liv och tänkande*, Stockholm: Atlantis.
Jansson, H. (2023), *Solbadets Buddha: Buddhism och teosofi i Ellen Keys Livstro*, Stockholm: University of Stockholm.
Johannisson, K. (1974), *Magnetisörernas tid. Den animala magnetismen i Sverige*, Uppsala: Almqvist & Wiksell.
Karlsson, T. (2009), *Götisk kabbala och runisk alkemi: Johannes Bureus och den götiska esoterismen*, Stockholm: Stockholms universitet.
Kinnander, M. (1943), *Svenska frimureriets historia*, Stockholm: Natur och Kultur.
Lamm, M. (1915), *Emanuel Swedenborg. En studie öfver hans utveckling till mystiker och andeskådare*, Stockholm: Hugo Gebers Förlag.
Lamm, M. (1918–20), *Upplysningstidens romantik. Den mystiskt sentimentala strömningen i svensk litteratur*, Stockholm: Hugo Gebers Förlag.
Larsen, L. S. (2008), *Western Esotericism: Ultimate Sacred Postulates and Ritual Fields*, Lund: Department of History and Anthropology of Religions, Lund University.
Lejon, H. (1997), *Historien om den antroposofiska humanismen. Den antroposofiska bildningsidén i idéhistoriskt perspektiv 1880–1980*, Stockholm: Almqvist & Wiksell.
Lekeby, K. (2010), *Gustaviansk mystik. Alkemister, kabbalister, magiker, andeskådare, astrologer och skattgrävare i den esoteriska kretsen kring G.A. Reuterholm, hertig Carl och hertiginnan Charlotte 1776–1803*, Sala & Södermalm: Vertigo.
Lenhammar, H. (1985), *Med murslev och svärd. Svenska frimurarorden under 250 år*, Delsbo: Bokförlaget Åsak.
Lindroth, S. (1943), *Paracelsismen i Sverige till 1600-talets mitt*, Stockholm: Almqvist & Wiksell.
Nilsson, J. (2020), *As a Fire Beneath the Ashes: The Quest for Chinese Wisdom within Occultism, 1850–1949*, Lund: Lund University.
Pasi, M. (2016), 'Esotericism Emergent: The Beginning of the Study of Esotericism in the Academy', in April DeConick (ed.), *Religion: Secret Religion*, 143–54, Farmington Hills, MI: MacMillan Reference.
Peste, J. (2002), *The Poimandres Group in Corpus Hermeticum: Myth, Mysticism and Gnosis in Late Antiquity*, Gothenburg: University of Gothenburg.
Sanner, I. (1995), *Att älska sin nästa såsom sig själv: om moraliska utopier under 1800-talet*, Stockholm: Carlsson.
Sorgenfrei, S. (2013), *American Dervish: Making Mevlemism in the United States of America*, Gothenburg: University of Gothenburg.
Skott, F. (2000), *Asatro i tiden*, Gothenburg: Språk- och folkminnesinstitutet.
Tessmann, A. (2012), *On the Good Faith: A Fourfold Discursive Construction of Zoroastrianism in Contemporary Russia*, Gothenburg: University of Gothenburg.
Wikström, O. (1998), *Att se det dolda: Om New Age och ockultism inför millennieskiftet*, Stockholm: Natur & Kultur.
Zorya, K. (2023), *The Government Used to Hide the Truth, But Now We Can Speak: Contemporary Esotericism in Ukraine 1986–2014*, Stockholm: Södertörn University.

Chapter 8

NEW RELIGIOUS MOVEMENTS AND NEW AGE SPIRITUALITY

Peter Åkerbäck and Sanja Nilsson

We will begin this chapter with a comprehensive but not exhaustive overview of publications on the subject of new religious movements and new age spirituality in Sweden prior to the 1990s, when the research field can be said to have been properly established. By recapping the most important publications, we aim at illustrating the backdrop against which it was founded.

Alongside the literature produced on the free churches (the Christian Protestant churches in Sweden not belonging to the Swedish Church), not much was written before the 1970s. The earliest publications are the 1945 study by Gunnar Westin (1890–1967), Professor of Theology at Uppsala University, titled *Trossamfund i Sverige* (Religious Communities in Sweden, 1945) and Erik Nyhlén's (1915–1977) book *Svensk frikyrka* (Swedish Free Church) from 1964; both had a clear focus on the protestant groups and the so-called free churches, Pentecostal movement and so on.

The first major overview featuring new religious movements was published in 1970: *Kulter, sekter, samfund. En studie av religiösa minoriteter i Sverige* (Cults, Sects, Communities. A Study of Religious Minorities in Sweden) by journalist Bo R. Ståhl and pastor and teacher Bertil Persson. The book contains information on seventy-nine different groups, and it constitutes the first detailed descriptions of these groups in Sweden. While the publication lacks an academic stringency, and the different chapters vary from short descriptions to more extended interviews with participants, the general tone of the book is surprisingly positive in its descriptions of the different religious views. Three years later, Ernst Benz's (1907–1978) *Nya religioner* (New Religions, 1973) was translated from German into Swedish and used as course literature on new religious movements well into the 1990s. The book is compelling as it presents a global perspective, including, for instance, Native American churches, Cargo cults and messianic movements in Africa. The greater part of subsequent publications in Sweden has had a focus on the Western countries and cultures. In this early stage of development, theologians were, for the most part, those interested enough to publish a full volume on the subject, and a recurrent feature in this type of literature was to challenge and criticize the groups described, comparing them to Christianity and dismissing them as false heresies. One example is the Uppsala theologian Ingmar Gustafsson, who was engaged early on in questions concerning new religious movements. He produced several books, among them *Tro på villovägar. Om Jehovas vittnen, TM och scientology-kyrkan* (Stray Beliefs. About Jehovah's Witnesses, TM and the Church of Scientology, 1975) and *Guds fruar, Guds barn och andra. Om mormonerna, baháí-religionen och Guds barn* (Wives of God, Children of God and Others. About the Mormons, the Baháí Religion and the Children of God, 1976). Both publications are highly sceptical to the movements they depict. Gustafsson thereafter edited the more nuanced volume *Nyreligiösa rörelser i Sverige* (New Religious Movements in Sweden) which was published in 1983.

Another theologian who wrote one of the earlier books on the new forms of spirituality was the Uppsala priest Lester Wikström (1929–2020), who published a church publication *Nyandligt. En kartläggning och analys av nyreligiösa rörelser med särskild hänsyn till Luleå stift* (New Spirituality. A Mapping and Analysis of New Religious Movements with Special Focus on Luleå Diocese) in 1977. The publication is somewhat critical of the new movements, but it additionally tries to pinpoint and analyse the conflict between the new movements and society as well as put forth questions on how to build tolerance and freedom of religious thought. Wikström further wrote *Nya religioner mitt ibland oss* (New Religions in Our Midst) (1982) and *Trosrörelsen och andra nyandliga rörelser* (The Faith Movement and Other New Spiritual Movements) (1989), both which were highly critical of the movements they were describing, such as Scientology, Children of God, Unification Church and so on.

As mentioned, nearly all publications at this time were produced by theologians and tended to portray the new religious movements in an essentially negative light, contrasting it more or less openly to the 'right' religious view: that of the Swedish Protestant State Church. However, a very interesting and considerably different take on the debate was given by Licentiate Degree Svante Nycander in his 1977 book *De fördömda scientologerna* (The Damned Scientologists). Nycander openly defended Scientology but most of all its sub-organization Narconon, a drug rehabilitating program built on the teachings of the Church of Scientology. Nycander depicts how the program works and its activities in helping drug addicts. He further analyses the opponents to Scientology, problematizing the length to which they were prepared to go in trying to use legislation in order to stop them. The opponents, wrote Nycander, were even going so far as to try to take the scientologists and the equipment they use to court. Nycander's book was followed by the highly negative description of the new religious movements active at the time, presented by the Reverend Erland Sundströms (1908–1988) in his *Nyandliga vindar* (New Spiritual Winds) from 1979. Although an attempt at an academic production, its bias is highly noticeable. The same year, another book was published, *Religionsfrihet – för vem?* (Freedom of Religion – for Whom?), in which the editor, theology candidate Björn Sahlin (1979), was debating the new movements and how they were received by society in Sweden. During this period, it is indisputably clear, the new religious movements were a challenge not only to society but perhaps predominantly to the church and the theological community at the universities in Sweden.

The Field Is Established

One of the most prominent scholars and key persons in the establishment of the field of new religious movements in Sweden is, without a doubt, Professor Liselotte Frisk (1959–2020) of Dalarna University. Professor Frisk's importance and contributions to the research field of new religious movements is comparable to Professor Eileen Barker of the London School of Economics and Political Science (she started one of the first networks on new religious movements in the UK, INFORM (Information Network Focus on Religious Movements)). Frisk commenced her studies in 1980 with a project called 'Alternate Worldviews' at the Department of Psychology in Stockholm University. The project led to a collaboration with fil. dr. Ted Nordquist at Uppsala University. However, Frisk's dissertation on new religious movements, which was a part of the project, was deemed too controversial for the theological department in Uppsala at the time. The topic was not considered to warrant serious study. Nevertheless, Frisk did not give up; she applied and was accepted as a doctoral student at Åbo akademi, Finland, and her dissertation *Nya religiösa rörelser i Sverige. Relation till samhället/världen, anslutning och engagemang* (New Religious Movements in Sweden. Relationship to Society/World, Connection and Commitment) was published in April 1993. It was the first major work on new religious movements in Sweden and included 237 interviews. In a detailed manner, six new religious movements were analysed in relation to sociological theory and key concepts such as conversion, defection, belief and social structure. Besides contributing to an, until then never seen, in-depth study of Anthroposophy, Transcendental Meditation, the Church of Scientology, the International Society for Krishna Consciousness, Siddha Yoga and Neosannyas (the movement of Osho, formerly known as Bhagawan Shree Rajneesh), it provided an impressive overview of the field itself. In addition, it encompassed several interesting methodological discussions.

Frisk subsequently wrote more books on new religious movements with a special focus on Sweden. In *Nyreligiositet i Sverige. Ett religionsvetenskapligt perpektiv* (New Religiosity in Sweden. A Religious Studies Perspective) published in 1998, she expanded the number of movements included to encompass such diverse groups as the Swedish Asatru, the dark magical order Dragon Rouge, Kundalini Yoga and the Family (the Children of God), as well as the Word of Life (from The Faith Movement). The book further presents the concept of New Age and contrasts it to the more organized new religious movements. In her 2007 book *De nya religiösa rörelserna. Vart tog de vägen?* (The New Religious Movements. Where Did They Go?), she followed up on the development of five new religious movements in Sweden, namely, the Church of Scientology, the Children of God, the Hare Krishna Movement, the Moon Movement and the Bhagwan Movement. In this study, like in the dissertation, she presented interview material, including the perspective of the second generation, people who had grown up in the movements.

Although Frisk had discussed the so-called New Age Movement, Olav Hammer, Professor of History of Religions at the University of Southern Denmark, was as early with the first major Swedish study on the New Age movement specifically, with his book *New Age. På spaning efter helheten. En ny folktro?* (New Age. In Search of the Whole. A New Folk Belief?), published in 1997. The book problematized the less organized spiritual milieus and gave it exclusive attention. Starting out in the works of Swedenborg and Mesmer, Hammer followed the divide between medicine and magic and the development of what would be known only in the 1970s as 'new age', in which he details shamanism, healing, UFOs, channelling and a wide collection of other phenomena from the alternative spiritual milieu. Hammer's accessible style of writing and detailed chronology has had a profound impact on alternative spirituality as a research field of its own. Hammer continued his scholarship with *Profeter mot strömmen* (Prophets against the Tide) (1999) and *Claiming Knowledge* (2001), which analyses legitimizing strategies in some new religious movements, and he has since published and edited numerous publications.

Other important publications worth mentioning are, for example, the anthology *Gudars och gudinnors återkomst* (Return of Gods and Goddesses) (2000) which included articles on new religious movements as well as new age and Western esotericism. The book was edited by Frisk and Carl-Gustav Carlsson. Other publications include researcher at the Swedish Church Margareta Skogs's *Det religiösa Sverige* (Religious Sweden) (2001), a survey of the Swedish religious landscape in the form of statistics; and the Swedish version of Christopher Partridge's *Nya Religioner* (New Religions) (2005), which is an encyclopaedia of new religious movements; as well as *Religion i Sverige* (Religions in Sweden) edited by Ingvar Svanberg and David Westerlund (2008). The latter included descriptions of some new religious movements that were not treated earlier in a Swedish context, such as the Raelians. Peter Åkerbäcks's 2008 dissertation *De obeständiga religionerna. Om kollektiva självmord och frälsning i Peoples Temple, Ordre du Temple Solaire och Heaven's Gate* (The Impermanent Religions. On Collective Suicide and Salvation in Peoples Temple, Ordre du Temple Solaire, and Heaven's Gate) was focused on these three major suicide cults, the only one so far to treat these together and trying to offer an explanation on how to understand these three groups.

The Brainwash Discourse and so-called Cult-Wars of the 1970s–1990s

The explosion of new religious movements established primarily in the United States during the 1950s and the 1960s soon found its way to Sweden with the establishment of groups during the early or mid-1970s. With the religious innovative groups came controversy and fear of the unknown manifested in the so-called anti-cult movement. Building on the first anti-cult movement from the United States, the FREECOG (Free Our Children from the Children of God) in

1971, the first anti-cult movements began to appear in Sweden in the mid-1980s. The anti-cult movement began as a group of parents whose children had joined The Children of God, a group which the parents perceived as 'deviant' Christianity and because of which their sons and daughters dropped out of school and society in favour of living communally, often on the roads, and witnessing their new faith to other youngsters. The parents soon united with former members and members of the clergy to publicly protest the existence of the new religious movements, which in their discourse were described as 'cults'.

In Sweden, organizations such as FRI (Föreningen rädda individen), founded in 1978, and ROS (Rådgivning om sekter), founded in 1988, were the main actors. The main focus with regard to the new religious movements was the critique that something must be affecting the young people, given the large numbers that join these groups. The agency of conversion began to be questioned: why would so many young people otherwise join groups that rejected mainstream society? Concepts such as mind control, brainwashing and manipulation techniques were employed to argue that the young were not in these groups out of free will but had been coerced into the new faith and lifestyle. With this assumption came the anti-cult movement with efforts to 'expose the truth of the dangerous cults' in Sweden as well as the rest of the Western world. In focus was Scientology, ISKCON, the Unification Church and the Children of God.

A few academics, predominantly international as well as Swedish scholars of sociology of religion, questioned the scientific base for these claims and with the beginning of the 1990s started what has been called the 'cult-wars', the international conflict between scholars of religion and the anti-cult movement. Within a few years, a small number of defectors entered academia and started studying the new religious movements from a purely psychological perspective. Their findings aligned with the stories of defectors who had been badly treated or otherwise were dissatisfied with their former group, perhaps mainly because the large majority that just joined and left rarely made themselves known. They tended to base their empirical data on 'disgruntled' former members, while sociologists of religion tended to base theirs on current members and/or less dissatisfied defectors. This inevitably led to clashes, as much of what was presented as factual data lacked validity from an academic point of view.

The Establishment of FINYAR

Recognizing the lack of a reliable academic perspective and the need for more data regarding the debate over cults and brainwashing, a few scholars including Frisk, Jonas Alwall, Jenny-Ann Brodin and Åkerbäck established the research network of FINYAR (Forskning och information om nya religiösa rörelser) in 1997, modelled on similar organizations as INFORM in the UK and CESNUR (Centro studi sulle nuove religioni) in Italy. From 2004, FINYAR published an annual peer-reviewed journal, *Aura*, which contained up-to-date research about new religious movements from various perspectives such as sociological, psychological and historical perspectives. Although it initially centred heavily on new religious movements in a Swedish context, the journal developed into a cross-Nordic publication in 2010 and has since then widened the scope to include publications on historical new religious movements, the occurrence of new religiosity in cultural contexts outside of the Nordic Countries and the Western world, and variations of groups within established religions. The publications tend to be written in either Swedish, Norwegian or Danish, but occasionally an article in English is published. As of 2020, *Aura* is published with open access to reach a wider audience.

FINYAR has hosted and participated in several academic conferences throughout the years. FINYAR played an important part in inviting researchers for the state investigation on new religious movements and the publication *I god tro. Samhället och nyandligheten* (In Good Faith. Society and the New Spirituality, SOU 1998: 113), the first politically motivated investigation into the new religious movements. In 2011, a smaller members-only conference took place in Sigtuna, Sweden, and in 2013, a major international conference was co-hosted at Dalarna University together with INFORM and CESNUR. Through the initiative of a few Swedish scholars (including Professor Frisk) as well as other academics, who recognized the need for more publications centring on the issues of new religiosity, the International Society for the Study of New Religions (ISSNR), modelled on FINYAR, was established in 2009 by Frisk, Henrik Bogdan and James R. Lewis (1949–2022). This was a mainly Swedish project, as well as the *International Journal for The Study of New Religions* and the book series 'Palgrave Studies in New Religions and Alternative Spiritualities'. Over the years, the activities of FINYAR have diminished, but the yearly publication *Aura* is still running, a board is still active and its members are active in international conferences.

Issues and Important Academic Contributions

The establishment of *Livets ord* (Word of Life) in Uppsala in 1983 eventually led to more fire on the debate concerning brainwashing. The movement attracted lots of members in the late teens and early twenties; eventually, some of them left the movement, feeling disappointed and disoriented. A suicide among these members raised concern on the dangers of these types of movements, and the anti-cult movement together with concerned relatives asked the government to take action. Tensions ran high, and members from the academic community were often described as cult-apologetics rather than objective.

In 1997, Zenon Panoussis, critical of Scientology, handed over documents from the Church of Scientology to the Swedish government in order to utilize the Swedish Publicity Principle concerning documents handed in to the government, which states that such documents are public and thus open for all citizens to access. The documents were named *The Scientology Bible* but consisted of New Era Dianetics for Operating Thetans (NOTs), documents that the church not only considered having the copyrights to but also wanted to keep secret in order to present them for its members in the correct order according to the spiritual development as a

Scientologist. This led to a long judicial process with different court decisions. In 2015, the Swedish Supreme Administrative Court decided that the documents were to be labelled as confidential. The debate over the new religious movements once again led to heated discussions. Anti-cultists saw the confidentiality as going against the publicity principle, while scholars of religion were trying to nuance the debate by explaining the conflict between an open society and the religious process of initiation and how some religions develop through a step-by-step process.

In 1997, Galina Lindquist (1955–2008) published her dissertation, *Shamanic Performances on the Urban Scene: Neo-Shamanism in Contemporary Sweden*, which was a thorough study of the current craze for shamanism that at the time was a very current theme in the new age milieu.

Two important publications centring on the Swedish Asatru scene were folklorist Fredrik Skott's book *Asatro i tiden* (Aesir Faith in Time) (2000) and Fredrik Gregorius's dissertation *Modern Asatro* (Modern Aesir Faith) (2005). Both sought to present organizations and relate the beliefs and practices to the pre-Christian era while simultaneously analysing Sveriges Asatrosamfund from a modern perspective. Gregorius highlights that the believers try to recreate an often-romanticized version of the old religion as a coherent system of belief, but the milieu rather hosts various ideological connotations and adherence to a multitude of gods. Gregorius has further contributed insights into schisms within the group which led to the establishment of two separate groups. The split resulted in the outspoken anti-racist group Samfundet Forn Sed, while the other, the Nordic Asa Society, has been more inclined towards a nationalist stance. He further elaborated on the controversies surrounding the usage of rune symbols by some far-right groups such as the Nordiska Motståndsrörelsen (the Nordic Resistance movement).

Jenny-Ann Brodin Danell's dissertation *Religion till salu? En sociologisk studie av new age i Sverige* (Religion for Sale? A Sociological Study of New Age in Sweden) (2001) was one of the first studies focused on the commercial aspects of the new spirituality in the new age milieu in relation to its advertisement and the selling of sessions, courses and goods. Presenting a discussion on the economy of new age spirituality, Danell argued that the milieu should be understood as a market where consumers pay for services and products. The use of the Swedish word *Smörgåsbord* to describe the milieu illustrated the display of an endless variety of combination of services and products with little to no exclusivity in regard to other practitioners' products. Hence, the new age practitioner can combine whatever they like and can afford.

Theologian Lars Ahlin was also one of the first scholars in Sweden to highlight the emergence of the so-called new age field. In his book *Pilgrim, turist eller flykting? En studie av individuell religiös rörlighet i senmoderniteten* (Pilgrim, Tourist or Refugee? A Study of Individual Religious Mobility in Late Modernity) (2005), he discussed various phenomena such as TV series where self-proclaimed mediums channelled spirits and prior lives and the sixth sense. By invoking the theories of sociologists Mary Douglas, Zygmunt Bauman and Anthony Giddens, he argued that Swedish society had moved in the direction of neo-libertarian politics which had left large groups of marginalized people. These, he argued, were like pilgrims or tourists on the hunt for meaning. They would take to a variety of spiritual expressions such as healing and astrology, but Ahlin problematized the continuity of the interest: were the practitioners of the new spirituality to be understood as spiritual tourists just temporarily turning to new age for solace, or were they to be understood as pilgrims who had reached a final destination in their search for meaning?

Frisk and Åkerbäck followed up on the study of the new age milieu with their 2013 study, *Den mediterande dalahästen. Religion på nya arenor i samtidens Sverige* (The Meditating Dala Horse. Religion on New Arenas in Contemporary Sweden). The study was inspired by other current studies of this milieu, such as the British Kendall study *The Spiritual Revolution: Why Religion is Giving Way to Spirituality* (2005). The aim of the study was, first, to map all religious and spiritual activities in a designated area of Sweden (Dalacaria), highlighting what kind of practice was being conducted at the time. Second, the study aimed at analysing whether the practitioners and participants in the techniques considered themselves (as well as the researchers) as being religious, spiritual or neither. The findings were that the boundaries for what was considered as constituting religious practice was in a flux. They additionally found that in Sweden, a considerable number of practices was borrowed from a multitude of religious contexts, while still not considered as religious by the practitioners at all.

Another area of the new religious movements that is somewhat understudied is the importance and strategies of sexual practice. A number of the FINYAR's yearly publications was devoted to this subject in 2004. A much more thorough publication of this area is the 2014 *Sexuality and New Religious Movements* edited by Bogdan and Lewis. Bogdan, Professor of Religious Studies at the University of Gothenburg, has also contributed to other publications with important texts on both the Solar Temple and Scientology.

Focus Changes to the Children Growing up in NRMs

Reporter Charlotte Essén's 2008 book *Sektbarn. En bok om de utvalda för paradiset* (Sect Children) brought the issue of children raised in new religious movements to the public debate. This was a clear indication that the focus of the critique had changed. The main concern with the new religious movements was no longer young people getting involved, brainwashed or manipulated; instead, it was the situation for children growing up in these movements. The previously mentioned governmental investigation from 1998 had already indicated such a shift, devoting a substantial chapter to this subject. However, in 2008, it was clear that the problematic view of the new religious movements had definitely shifted. The debate on brainwashing as well as the anti-cult movement was almost non-existent. Instead, a new type of self-help movement consisting of therapists and former members had been organized and had taken over the critical voice. The forum Hjälpkällan (The Help Source) was founded in 2006 and initially directed its help towards young former members of the Jehovah's Witnesses. In time, the organization grew and now caters to former members and critics of a variety of new religious movements.

As an academic response to the shift in focus, Frisk, Åkerbäck and Sanja Nilsson published their book *Guds barnbarn* (God's Grandchildren) in 2017, which is still the single most comprehensive book on the subject of children in new religious movements in Sweden. A fuller version in English titled *Children in Minority Religions: Growing Up in Controversial Religious Groups* was published in 2018. Both publications were the result of a three-year study on children in new religious movements in Sweden. It gathered data from the Hare Krishna movemen the Family International (formerly the Children of God), the Church of Scientology, the Family Federation (formerly the Unification Church), the Knutby Filadelfia congregation (a former Pentecostal group), the Exclusive Brethren and the Jehovah's Witnesses. The material encompasses eighteen in-depth interviews with children aged seven to eighteen and seventy-five in-depth interviews with adult members, former members and leaders for the different groups. The publication problematized the development of accusations from defectors and the anti-cult movement to centre on the best interest of the children, rather than the previous focus on conversion and brainwashing theories. It traced the developments in Sweden and linked it to similar developments internationally; it also discussed the notions of authoritarian parenting styles and freedom of religion for children.

While co-writing the studies mentioned above with Frisk and Åkerbäck, Nilsson wrote her dissertation solely on one of the groups: the Knutby Filadelfia congregation. The group was of particular interest since no academic empirical studies had hitherto been published on them. The group had been a regular Pentecostal congregation up until the mid-1980s when influences of 'The Word of Life', as well as subsequent in-group beliefs that the female charismatic leader Åsa Waldau might be the Bride of Christ in flesh, rendered them the label 'new religious movement' by scholars and 'murderous cult' by the media. The background was a high-profile murder in the group of a pastor's wife in 2004, in which the pastor himself and (one of) his mistresses were convicted of killing the pastor's wife and attempting to murder another member of the congregation. The crime held an unusual aspect: the mistress stated that she had received text messages on her cell phone which she understood to come directly from God, demanding her to carry out the shootings. It was soon revealed that the messages were authored by the pastor himself. Professor of Sociology Eva Lundgren had published her book *Knutbykoden* (The Code to Knutby) in 2008, the same year as the release of Essén's *Sektbarn*. Lundgren's material encompassed over six hundred hours of interviews with the former pastor of the congregation, Helge Fossmo, who was now incarcerated for enticement to the murder in 2004. Lundgren was critical of the congregation, inquiring into the situation of the remaining members, including children and youth. Frisk had, with colleague Professor Susan Palmer of McGill University, Canada, interviewed Fossmo as well. Their article, 'The Life Story of

Helge Fossmo, Former Pastor of Knutby Filadelfia, as Told in Prison: A Narrative Analysis Approach' (2015) was a different approach to the life story presented by Fossmo to Lundgren as it centred less on the crime and the congregation as a 'cult', and more on the religious aspects of the narrative.

Nilsson's dissertation *Performing Perfectly: Childhood in the Knutby Filadelfia before the Dissolution of the Congregation* (2019) contained data from interviews with children and youth within the congregation as well as with leaders and parents. Due to the group splitting up during the time for the data collection, the dissertation holds rare accounts of childhood as understood first-hand by the informants prior to and after the breakup of the congregation. The two narratives were discussed in relation to performances of childhood.

Conclusions

The development of the Swedish religious and spiritual landscape has led to a highly individualized view on spirituality, and practices of spiritual techniques are mainly focused on the health and well-being of the individual. Consequently, the new religious movements have difficulties in acquiring new members and thus find it difficult to grow substantially. Additionally, the more individualized spiritual arena is expanding and growing rapidly. Therefore, current ongoing research in the field is increasingly focused on the health/spirituality arena, with studies on the current tantric movement, the various forms of yoga and the less organized spiritual community in present-day Sweden. One recent good example of this is Malin Fitger's 2022 dissertation *Själens arkitektur. Subtil anatomi som upplevelse, förkroppsligande och självförståelse, 1875–2020* (The Architecture of the Soul. Subtle Anatomy as Experience, Embodiment, and Self-understanding, 1875–2020).

The field of new religious movements in Sweden can be described as having clear and fast progress. Starting with the new religious movements being established in the late 1960s early 1970s, it was followed by a debate on their presence and the debate on brainwashing and young people joining the groups. As young people stopped joining the groups, at least in any noticeable numbers, the focus shifted to the children growing up in the new religious movements. At the same time, the individualized society in Sweden has developed, perhaps further than in any other Western country, which has resulted in a highly individualized view on religion and spirituality. Future studies on new religious movements and new spirituality in Sweden have a variety of challenging but also exciting possibilities with many points of departure. Religious milieus which need to be explored in research is the ageing communities of the new religious movements of the 1960s. Similarly, because of the expansion of migration, the field is opening up to research fringe religious groups originating in the Middle East and the African continent, as well as the growing number of self-help gurus advocating spiritual solutions within the health and medical field.

References

Ahlin, L. (2005), *Pilgrim, turist eller flykting? En studie av individuell religiös rörlighet i senmoderniteten*, Eslöv: Symposium.
Åkerbäck, P. (2008), *De obeständiga religionerna. Om kollektiva självmord och frälsning i Peoples Temple, Ordre du Temple Solaire och Heaven's Gate*, Stockholm: Stockholms universitet.
Benz, E. (1973), *Nya religioner*, trans. P. Wiking, Stockholm: Natur och kultur.
Bogdan, H., and J. R. Lewis, eds (2014), *Sexuality and New Religious Movements*, New York: Palgrave Macmillan.
Brodin, J.-A. D. (2001), *Religion till salu? En sociologisk studie av new age i Sverige*, Stockholm: Stockholms universitet.
Essén, C. (2008), *Sektbarn. En bok om de utvalda för paradiset*, Stockholm: Bonnier.
Fitger, M. (2022), *Själens arkitektur. Subtil anatomi som upplevelse, förkroppsligande och självförståelse, 1875–2020*, Stockholm: Stockholms universitet.
Frisk, L. (1993), *Nya religiösa rörelser i Sverige. Relation till samhället/världen, anslutning och engagemang*, Åbo: Åbo akademis förlag.
Frisk, L. (1998), *Nyreligiositet i Sverige. Ett religionsvetenskapligt perspektiv*, Nora: Nya Doxa.
Frisk, L. (2007), *De nya religiösa rörelserna. Vart tog de vägen? En studie av Scientologi-kyrkan, Guds Barn, Hare Krishna-rörelsen, Moon-rörelsen och Bhagwan-rörelsen och deras utveckling över tid*, Nora: Nya Doxa.
Frisk, L., and C.-G. Carlsson, eds (2000), *Gudars och gulinnors återkomst. Studier i nyreligiositet*, Umeå: Institutionen för religionsvetenskap.
Frisk, L., and P. Åkerbäck (2013), *Den mediterande dalahästen. Religion på nya arenor i samtidens Sverige*, Stockholm: Dialogos.
Frisk, L., P. Åkerbäck and S. Nilsson (2017), *Guds nya barnbarn. Att växa upp i kontroversiella religiösa grupper*, trans. B. Johansson, Stockholm: Dialogos.
Frisk, L., P. Åkerbäck and S. Nilsson (2018), *Children in Minority Religions: Growing Up in Controversial Religious Groups*, Bristol: Equinox.
Frisk, L., and S. Palmer (2015), 'The Life Story of Helge Fossmo, Former Pastor of Knutby Filadelfia, as Told in Prison: A Narrative Analysis Approach', *International Journal for the Study of New Religions* 6 (1): 51–73.
Gregorius, F. (2005), *Modern Asatro. Att konstruera etnisk och kulturell identitet*, Lund: Lunds universitet.
Gustafsson, I. (1975), *Tro på villovägar. Om Jehovas vittnen, TM och scientology-kyrkan*, Stockholm: Gummesson.
Gustafsson, I. (1976), *Guds fruar, Guds barn och andra. Om mormonerna, bahái-religionen och Guds barn*, Stockholm: Gummesson.
Gustafsson, I., B. Samuelsson and P. Sundberg (1983), *Nyreligiösa rörelser i Sverige. En kort presentation*, Stockholm: Norman.
Hammer, O. (1997), *New Age. På spaning efter helheten. En ny folktro?*, Stockholm: Wahlström & Widstrand.
Hammer, O. (1999), *Profeter mot strömmen. Essäer om mystiker, medier och magiker i vår tid*, Stockholm: Wahlström & Widstrand.
Hammer, O. (2001), *Claiming Knowledge: Strategies of Epistemology from Theosophy to the New Age*, Boston: Brill.

Heelas, P., and L. Woodhead (2005), *The spiritual revolution. Why religion is giving way to spirituality*, Malden, Mass: Blackwell
Lindquist, G. (1997), *Shamanic Performances on the Urban Scene: Neo-shamanism in Contemporary Sweden*, Stockholm: Stockholm University.
Lundgren, E. (2008), *Knutbykoden*, trans. S. Lundgren, Stockholm: Modernista.
Nilsson, S. (2019), *Performing Perfectly. Childhood in Knutby Filadelfia before the Dissolution of the congregation*, Göteborg: Department of Literature, History of Ideas, and Religion, University of Gothenburg.
Nycander, S. (1977), *De fördömda scientologerna. Ett debattinlägg om de religiöst avvikande och om narkomanvårdsprogrammet Narconon*, Stockholm: Proprius.
Nyhlén, E. (1964), *Svensk frikyrka*, Stockholm: Prisma.
Partridge, C., ed. (2005), *Nya religioner. En uppslagsbok om andliga rörelser, sekter och alternativ andlighet*, Örebro: Libris.
Sahlin, B., ed. (1979), *Religionsfrihet – för vem? Nya religioner möter samhället*, Stockholm: Proprius.
Skott, F. (2000), *Asatro i tiden*, Göteborg: Språk- och folkminnesinstitutet.
Sundström, E. (1979), *Nyandliga vindar. Varifrån och varthän?*, Stockholm: Gummesson.
Skog, M. (2001), *Det religiösa Sverige. Gudstjänst- och andaktsliv under ett veckoslut kring millennieskiftet*, Örebro: Libris.
SOU (1998), *I god tro. samhället och nyandligheten: betänkande av Utredningen om samhällets stöd till människor som av särskilda skäl befinner sig i psykiska kristillstånd*, Statens offentliga utredningar, 1998:13, Stockholm: Fritzes offentliga publikationer.
Ståhl, B. R., and B. Persson (1970), *Kulter, sekter, samfund. En studie av religiösa minoriteter i Sverige*, Örebro: NBV-service.
Svanberg, I., and D. Westerlund, eds (2008), *Religion i Sverige*, Stockholm: Dialogos.
Westin, G. (1945), *Trossamfund i Sverige*, Uppsala: Lindblad.
Wikström, L. (1977), *Nyandligt. En kartläggning och analys av nyreligiösa rörelser med särskild hänsyn till Luleå stift*, Stockholm: Verbum.
Wikström, L. (1982), *Nya religioner mitt ibland oss. En liten handbok om nyandliga strömningar i 80-talets Sverige*, Älvsjö: Verbum.
Wikström, L. (1989), *Trosrörelsen och andra nyandliga rörelser*, Uppsala: MEF

Internet sources:

CESNUR
https://www.cesnur.org/
FINYAR
https://finyar.org/
Hjälpkällan
https://hjalpkallan.nu/
INFORM
https://inform.ac/

Part II

SOCIAL SCIENTIFIC APPROACHES

Chapter 9

PSYCHOLOGY OF RELIGION

Göran Ståhle and Tomas Lindgren

Psychology of religion in Sweden developed as a distinct area of study at the beginning of the twentieth century in the theological faculties of the universities of Uppsala and Lund. It initially featured as part of a subject called 'Theological Prenotions and Theological Encyclopaedia'. This was later renamed 'History and Psychology of Religion' at Uppsala (from 1938) and 'History of Religions with Psychology of Religion' at Lund (from 1947). Both of these new names emphasize the close relationship between the history of religion and psychology of religion, and also that psychological perspectives were intended to be an important supplement to historical-philological research on religion.

This emphasis can be traced to Nathan Söderblom (1866–1931), who was appointed Professor of Theological Prenotions and Theological Encyclopaedia at Uppsala University in 1901. As a liberal theologian, Söderblom viewed religious experience – or more precisely, the experience of the holy – as the foundation of all historical expressions of religion (Jonsson 2014; Kippenberg 2002). Therefore, he argued that the academic study of religion should take psychology as its point of reference. In Söderblom's own words, 'the history of religion cannot be written without psychology. The psychology of religion, for its part, always presupposes some history' (1916: 9).

The psychological perspective implied a focus on the individual and lived religion. In his summary of the research conducted during these years, Hans Åkerberg (1935–1994), Associate Professor of History of Religions with Psychology of Religion at Lund University, defines this approach as a 'near-life' (*livsnära*) perspective (1974). Söderblom, who conducted several case studies based on personal documents, describes his approach as 'concentrating on the deep spirits and individual geniuses in the realm of piety' (1916: 63).

Many of Söderblom's students adopted his approach to religion. These include Knut B. Westman (1881–1967), who was appointed Professor of Church History at Uppsala University in 1930, and Emilia Fogelklou (1878–1972), the first woman to obtain an academic degree in theology in Sweden. In 1940, she also applied for the chair in History of Religions with the Psychology of Religion at Uppsala University, but the position went to Geo Widengren (1907–1996) (on

Widengren, see Larsson 2022). Fogelklou was a prolific lecturer and writer outside of the academy, introducing psychological perspectives to a Swedish audience, addressing education, mental health issues and pastoral psychology (Gieser 2009). Söderblom's approach was also adopted by Tor Andræ (1885–1947) and Efraim Briem (1890–1946).

Tor Andræ was appointed Professor of History of Religions at Stockholm University College in 1927, and two years later he succeeded Edgar Reuterskiöld (1872–1932) as Professor of Theological Prenotions and Theological Encyclopaedia at Uppsala University. Andræ – whom Eric Sharpe (1986: 201) describes as a 'psychologist of religion and Islamist' – wrote several psychologically informed studies that were translated into various languages and earned him an international reputation (Widengren 1947). These include his 'masterly study' of the Prophet Muhammad (Schimmel 1985: 7), *Muhammed: Hans liv och hans tro* (1930), and his 'classic discussion' of mystical Islam (Schimmel 1983: 10), *I myrtenträdgården: Studier i sufisk mystik* (1947).

Efraim Briem, who was appointed Professor of Theological Prenotions and Theological Encyclopaedia at Lund University in 1928, was a specialist on Babylonian and Assyrian religion as well as psychology of religion. He published several books on religious experiences; for example, *Den religiösa upplevelsen i dess kristna huvudformer* (1930), *Gudstro och gudsupplevelse i historisk och psykologisk belysning* (1933) and *Helgon och helgonliv* (1942). Briem edited a book series with the aim of introducing psychology of religion to a Swedish audience. It included seven volumes, published between 1926 and 1933, and was called *Modern religionspsykologi* (Modern Psychology of Religion). The first titles were translations of works by distinguished scholars, such as Robert H. Thouless's *Religionspsykologi i översiktlig framställning* (1926), Vilhelm Grønbech's *Mystik i Österland och Västerland* (1926) and Jacob Peter Bang's *De stora väckelserörelserna, en historisk och psykologisk framställning* (1926). One title in the series is a contribution by Briem himself, *Stigmatisationer och visioner* (1929), which presents a selection of historical case studies of stigmatization and provides explanations in terms of hysteria and suggestion.

Perhaps the most well-known publication in the series, however, is Andræ's *Mystikens psykologi* (1926), which is based on lectures he gave at Stockholm University College. It explores the then current research on mysticism, with a focus on possession and inspiration. A typology is developed, resting upon case studies, mainly from Christian contexts but also from Islam, Ancient Greek philosophy, yoga, shamanism and spiritualism. Andræ interprets mysticism in terms of subconscious processes and depersonalization. Notably, by way of these comparative studies, he considers religious experiences to be of the same nature as other manifestations of the 'human spirit' (*själsliv*), for example, artistic inspiration and psychopathological conditions. In concordance, he argues against a *sui generis* understanding of religious experiences and the idea that there exists an innate 'religious sentiment' (Andræ 1926: 8).

Andræ also made contributions to the introduction of depth psychology in the Swedish context, including the psychologies of Sigmund Freud (1856–1939) and

Carl Gustav Jung (1875-1961). His publication *Psykoanalys och religion* (1927) aimed to be an 'unbiased' investigation into a then current academic debate on the relations of these 'new' psychologies to religion. This debate was initiated by the above-mentioned Fogelklou and medical doctor Poul Bjerre (1876-1964) at seminars held at Sigtunastiftelsen in 1919. At issue was how the practice of psychotherapy related to pastoral psychology and to the respective professions of medical doctors and priests (Gieser 2009). It also included a debate in 1927 in the newspaper *Stockholms Dagblad* involving, among others, the theologian Arvid Runestam (1887-1962), as summarized in his pamphlet *Psykoanalys och kristendom* (1928).

Another member of the circles around Andræ was Ivar Alm (1897-1973), who was central to the introduction of Jungian psychology in Sweden. He wrote several articles on Jung and translated some of his more central works into Swedish. Alm was a student of Andræ, and his doctoral dissertation, *Den religiösa funktionen i människosjälen* (1936), compares Freud's and Jung's views on religion. Late in life, Alm published the widely read *Från Freud till Jung: Några kapitel ur djuppsykologins historia* (1973), which was admired for its intellectual clarity (Gieser 2009).

At the same time, Indologists and Sanskritists began to employ psychological theories to explain various religious phenomena. Karl Sigurd Lindquist (1895-1943), for example, who earned a PhD in Sanskrit in 1932, specializing in the study of yoga and Indian philosophy, related them to hypnosis and suggestion in his treatise *Die Methoden des Yoga* (1932). A year after his appointment as Associate Professor in the Psychology of Religion and the History of Religion at Uppsala University in 1934, he published a comprehensive study of mysticism, *Mystikens väg och mål*.

Ernst Arbman (1891-1959), who earned a PhD in Sanskrit from Uppsala University in 1922 and was appointed Professor of the History of Religion at Stockholm University College in 1937, had a particular interest in Indic religions, ethnic religions, Norse religions and psychology of religion. His magnum opus is a posthumously published three-volume study of ecstasy/religious trance from phenomenological and psychological points of view, *Ecstasy or Religious Trance* (1963, 1968, 1970). In accordance with Arbman's will, it was edited by the professor who succeeded him, Åke Hultkrantz (1920-2006), from the accumulated manuscripts of almost twenty years of work.

Thus, psychology of religion in Sweden in the early twentieth century was characterized by a focus on intense experiences and altered states of consciousness, including a broad range of anomalous experiences. In this regard, John Björkhem (1910-1963) must be mentioned. He was a remarkable interdisciplinary scholar, holding doctorates in both theology and psychology, who was a pioneering figure in Swedish research on hypnosis and parapsychological phenomena. He was part of the circle around Andræ and completed his doctorate in theology in 1940 on an in-depth case study on the Flemish mystic Antoinette Bourignon (1616-1680). Andræ wrote the foreword to one of Björkhem's most well-known publications, *Det ockulta problemet* (1939), which was a popular depiction of parapsychological research.

The Establishment of Psychology of Religion

Hjalmar Sundén (1908–1993), who was awarded a personal professorship in Psychology of Religion at Uppsala University in 1967, the first of its kind in Scandinavia, had a great influence on the psychological study of religion in Sweden from the 1970s through to the early 1990s. Sundén, like Söderblom, studied in Paris at the end of the 1930s and defended his doctoral dissertation on the philosopher Henri Bergson (1859–1941), *La théorie bergsonienne de la religion*, at the Sorbonne in 1940. After his return to Sweden, he was employed as a teacher in an upper-secondary school and taught psychology at the police academy in Stockholm. 'There [at the police academy] I did my best work in psychology,' he said. He continued,

> It was extremely interesting: what can psychology do with statements made in court, maintaining that this or that happened? About what happened in fact, one only has statements. (It's also like this in the psychology of religion: people experience things; statements are made about their experiences.) For 10 years I worked with the most unbelievable cases. And I understood that people can experience the most incredible things perceptually. (Sundén 2012: 236)

Even during these years, he was active as a researcher, with a primary focus on the psychological aspects of religion. In 1959, the first edition of his magnum opus, *Religionen och rollerna*, was published, and three years later it was translated into German.

Sundén's definition of psychology of religion as 'the study of religious experiences and behaviors' (1981a: 22), which is derived from standard definitions of mainstream psychology, underscores that it is an interdisciplinary field, comprising the history of religions and psychology. In the same manner as Andræ and Widengren, Professor of the History of Religions at Uppsala University from 1940 to 1973 (Larsson 2022), Sundén argued that

> anyone who seeks to practice the psychology of religion must first acquire a sound knowledge of the history of religions; this is really the first prerequisite. The second is that one must also be well versed in modern psychological methods. (Sundén 2012: 241)

Sundén primarily used qualitative methods in his research and borrowed concepts from various subfields of psychology – such as cognitive psychology, symbolic interactionism, psychoanalytical theory and analytical psychology – arguing that no single psychological perspective can explain all aspects of religion, and that the character of the specific religious phenomenon under scrutiny will determine which psychological perspective is to be used. He was a prolific scholar and author, whose literary production includes about thirty books and more than two hundred articles spanning a wide range of topics, including psychobiographical studies of extraordinary individuals (Sundén 1959, 1966, 1969, 1973, 1981b, 1987, 1983), psychological studies of poetry and fiction (Sundén 1981b), a study of Zen Buddhism (Sundén 1970) and a book on children and religion, *Barn och religion* (Sundén 1974).

An important part of Sundén's legacy is his so-called role theory, a sociocognitive theory that aims to answer the question of how religious experiences are psychologically possible. For Sundén, who claimed to have had several such experiences himself, including an apparition of 'an angel dressed in blue, just as I had seen in a book' when he was a child (Sundén 2012: 241), religious experiences are a type of perceptual experiences which are relational in character and depend upon a familiarity with religious narratives.

Thus, in contrast to scholars who considered religious experience to be a *sui generis* phenomenon that, to borrow an apt phrase by Ann Taves, 'cannot or should not be explained in anything other than religious terms' (2009: 18), Sundén contends that religious experiences are imaginative second-order experiences that cannot be independent of their context, and indeed that they are at least partly, if not entirely, social and cultural constructions. Religious experiences are thus 'unthinkable without religious reference systems, without religious tradition, without myth and ritual' (Sundén 1959: 65).

Although Sundén claimed, late in life, that he 'didn't want to work with an American understanding of the role concept' (2012: 237), the main concepts of his theory are unmistakably influenced by American scholars like George Herbert Mead (1863–1931), Ralph Linton (1893–1953), Theodore R. Sarbin (1911–2005) and Theodore Newcomb (1903–1984): for example, Mead's idea that role-taking is to imagine oneself in other people's shoes in order to anticipate how they will behave in specific situations. In Sundén's version of role theory, the concept of role refers to a model of behaviour, including expectations of certain interactions, related to a specific position in an interactive social system. Roles can thus function as both behavioural and perceptual patterns (Sundén 1969).

Sundén's role theory generated much empirical research in Sweden during the 1970s and 1980s. It was employed in studies of religious conversions (Åkerberg 1975; Källstad 1974), prayer experiences (Hillerdal 1985; Källstad 1984; Wiedel 1984), meditation (Källstad 1978), mystical experiences (Källstad 1987), apparitions (Hillerdal and Gustafsson 1973; Hjärpe 1977), experiences of God's guidance (Wikström 1975) and glossolalia and baptism in the Holy Spirit (Holm 1976). It is mainly in these texts, not in his own writings, that Sundén's ideas and observations are systematized, applied, revised and presented as a (relatively) coherent theory. Some of these scholars developed the theory's implicit connections to symbolic interactionism, such as Karl Geyer's study of religious education (1989), Desmond Ayim-Aboagye's (1993) study of experiences of healing in West Africa and Linda Vikdahl's (2014) symbolic interactionist study of experiences of participation in the Church of Sweden among people with intellectual disabilities. Moreover, Nils G. Holm (2014) has created an integrated role theory that includes interactionist concepts.

The Expansion of Psychology of Religion

The 1980s and 1990s marked a period during which psychology of religion expanded as a separate discipline within the field of religious studies. Professorships were established at both Uppsala and Lund universities, but they developed in two different directions. At Uppsala, Sundén's impact could be seen in the combination of a broad spectrum of theories and qualitative methods and their intimate relationship to the History of Religions. At Lund, the research was oriented towards academic psychology, and therefore a quantitative methodology was preferred.

Thorvald Källstad (1918–1989) was appointed Professor of Psychology of Religion at Uppsala University after Sundén's retirement in 1975, and he remained in this capacity until 1984, when he was succeeded by Owe Wikström (b. 1945). Both of them conducted qualitative research – including in-depth case studies – employed role theory and focused on religious experiences. Wikström also focused on the relationship between religion and psychopathology (Wikström 1980), and hypnosis, possession and healing (Wikström 1984). In his later career, he wrote several popular books and essays, which apply psychology of religion to literature, art and music, such as the widely read *Långsamhetens lov* (2001).

A more quantitative tradition was introduced at Lund University when Kurt Bergling (b. 1936) was appointed Professor of Psychology of Religion in 1989. Bergling is an expert on moral development (e.g. Bergling 1981), and he oriented the department's research towards mainstream psychology. Several of his students followed the same path and used quantitative methods in their research, such as Antti Oksanen's (1994) meta-analysis of religious conversions; Marcus Koskinen-Hagman's (1999) quantitative study of the intrinsic, extrinsic and quest scales; Yvonne Petersson Bouin's (2000) meta-analysis of the effects of meditation on respiration and the temporal lobes; and Jonas Eek's (2001) quasi-experimental study of pilgrims to the Taizé community in France. Bergling also initiated a translation into Swedish of a textbook on psychology of religion by American Professor of Psychology David M. Wulff. It was entitled *Religionspsykologi* and published in two volumes (1993a,b). Significantly, the first volume is a comprehensive overview of quantitative psychological research on religion.

However, the qualitative tradition was furthered by other scholars at Lund University, such as Åkerberg and Antoon Geels (1946–2020). Åkerberg published a doctoral dissertation on Söderblom in 1975, *Omvändelse och kamp: En empirisk religionspsykologisk undersökning av den unge Nathan Söderbloms religiösa utveckling 1866–1894*. In 1976, he was appointed Associate Professor in the History of Religions with Psychology of Religions at Lund University. Åkerberg was a productive researcher, making both empirical and theoretical contributions to psychology of religion. Arguing for an interpretative and phenomenological methodology (1980, 1981), he gave prominence to humanistic research on empirical grounds, with reference to scholars such as Danish historian of religion Grønbech (1873–1948) and American psychologist William James (1842–1910).

Åkerberg held that historical material and literature studies can make an important contribution to psychology of religion, although this ran counter to the quantitative methodologies of mainstream psychology. Åkerberg could trace this tradition in the Swedish psychology of religion back to Söderblom (see Pettersson and Åkerberg 1980) and to James (Åkerberg 1972, 1974). Åkerberg applied this approach to in-depth case studies, including on Swedish author Sven Stolpe (1905–1996) (1985b), on Swedish poet Dan Andersson (1888–1920) (1985a) and on Swedish bishop Bo Giertz (1905–1998) (1985c). Åkerberg published two widely read books, based upon this same methodology, on existential crisis, suffering and death, *Kamp och kris* (1983a) and *Tillvaron och religionen* (1985d). Following in the same humanistic tradition, Jan Hermansson published a doctoral dissertation (1997) on Gordon W. Allport's (1897–1967) writings on religion, at Lund University.

Geels, who was appointed Professor of the History of Religions with Psychology of Religion at Lund University in 1999, was a widely recognized authority on intense religious experiences and mysticism. He published numerous books and articles on these themes, such as his in-depth case studies of the mystic Hjalmar Ekström (1885–1962) (1980) and the artist Violet Tengberg (1920–2014) (1989), and his empirical study of apparitions in contemporary Sweden (1991). In a series of books on mysticism in Judaism, Christianity and Islam, he combined comparative and historical studies with psychological interpretations (Geels 1998, 1999, 2001). The interpretative perspectives employed were primarily taken from psychodynamic theories, but he also combined these with ideas from cognitive psychology. Together with Wikström, Geels also authored an introductory textbook *Den religiösa människan* (1984), which was published several times between 1984 and 2017 in various revised editions. Significantly, in the tradition of Sundén, it mainly rests on social psychological and psychodynamic perspectives on religious experiences and behaviours.

The frequent use of psychodynamic theories in the Swedish study of religion and spirituality is another illustration of Sundén's impact (Åkerberg 1983b). Psychodynamic theories and methods were refined during the 1990s, for example, in works by Wikström (1990, 1997) and Valerie DeMarinis (1997), where the ideas of clinical psychologist Paul Pruyser (1916–1987) are prominent. Object relations theory has been employed in several studies, such as in Lisbeth Rubensson's (1996) study of the Swedish author Gunnar Edman (1915–1995) and in Petra Junus's application of feminist-inspired psychodynamic theories in conjunction with Argentinian psychotherapist Ana-Maria Rizzuto's (b. 1932) theory of 'God representations', in a study of women's use of feminine representations of the divine (Junus 1995).

Other scholars picked up Sundén's interest in analytical psychology (e.g. Sundén 1981b), such as Wikström's Jungian interpretation of Fyodor Dostoyevsky's novel *Crime and Punishment* (1982), Torbjörn Lengborn's study of the Swedish author Sven Lidman (1882–1960) (1988), Åke Tilander's studies of various aspects of Jung's psychology (Tilander 1990) and Febe Orest's study of popular culture from a Jungian perspective (Orest 2009).

Contemporary Psychology of Religion

Contemporary psychology of religion in Sweden has primarily focused on themes such as health, migration and violence, as well as perspectives like meaning-making, coping, attachment and the cognitive science of religion. Religion and health, a multidisciplinary research field related to the clinical psychology of religion, has become a major theme since the appointment of Valerie DeMarinis (b. 1954) as Professor of Psychology of Religion at Uppsala University in 2000. DeMarinis trained as a clinical psychologist, with a PhD from Harvard University and a Master of Divinity degree from Princeton University in the United States. She preferred mixed methodologies, had a special interest in meaning-making and existential health (for overviews, see DeMarinis, Wikström and Cetrez 2011; DeMarinis 2013), established cooperative endeavours with the public health sciences and was later also appointed Professor at the Department of Public Health and Clinical Medicine at Umeå University. Several studies have been published in Sweden that use mixed methodologies and focus on meaning-making processes and existential health, such as DeMarinis's (2003) and Cecilia Melder's (2011) studies on the existential dimensions of public health, Christina Lloyd's (2018) study of existential issues among young women in psychiatric treatment, Åsa Schumann's (2018) study of meaning-making processes among pupils at primary school and Maria Liljas Stålhandske and colleagues' (2011) study of existential issues in relation to induced abortion.

Another major perspective in the contemporary study of religion and health is coping theory, as in Marianne Ekedahl's (2001) study of religious coping and pastoral care, Mikael Lundmark's (2017) study of religious coping in life situations changed by cancer and in several studies by Fereshteh Ahmadi and her colleagues on religious coping and cancer treatment (e.g. Ahmadi and Ahmadi 2018). Other research relating to the theme of religion and health includes, for example, Gustaf Ståhlberg's (2000) study of the psychological dimensions of pastoral care, Lennart Belfrage's (2009) psychological exploration of stress-related burnout among clergy in the Church of Sweden and Lisa Rudolfsson's (2015) study of pastoral care for victims of sexual abuse.

DeMarinis and other Swedish scholars have also explored meaning-making in relation to migration, as in DeMarinis's (1998) study on transcultural care in Sweden and in Åsa Löwén's (2006) study of meaning-making among child refugees in Sweden. Önver Cetrez (b. 1970), who was appointed Professor of Psychology of Religion at Uppsala University in 2022, has published extensively on migration, as with several studies on meaning-making among Assyrian/Syriac migrants in Sweden (e.g. 2011, 2021a) and Turkey (e.g. 2017), and on Iraqi refugees in Sweden (2021b). Victor Dudas's (2020) study of identity development among Assyrian/Syriac adolescents in Sweden is another example.

There has also been interest in culture and ritual, as with DeMarinis's studies on the health-promoting function of ritual in different cultural contexts (1997, 2013). This is furthered in Liljas Stålhandske's (2005) research on ritual invention and mental health in contemporary Sweden, Göran Ståhle's cultural-psychological study on Hindu rituals in India (2004) and studies on the practice of Ayurveda in Sweden (2011). Also of note is Yukako Nahlbom's (2018) study of meaning-making in the context of the 2011 earthquake in Japan.

Pehr Granqvist (b. 1973), Professor of Psychology at Stockholm University, has published extensively on the connection between attachment processes and relationships with superhuman agents, and he is probably the most frequently cited Swedish psychologist of religion in recent years. In the literature, attachment bonds are divided into secure and insecure (avoidant and resistant/anxious/ambivalent), and two primary hypotheses have been suggested to describe the link between attachment to caregivers (or attachment figures) and relationships to superhuman agents: the correspondence hypothesis –which predicts that relationships to superhuman agents mirror attachment style – and the compensation hypothesis – which predicts that relationships with supernatural agents are compensations for insecure attachments (Kirkpatrick 2005: 128). In a series of studies, Granqvist and colleagues have found some support for both hypotheses (e.g. Granqvist Hagekull 1999). Thus, securely attached individuals 'often adopt religious or nonreligious standards that are similar to those held by their sensitive attachment figures in childhood', while insecurely attached individuals 'may find in God or other religious entities a surrogate (or alternative) attachment figure, one who may aid in compensating for states of insecurity and other unsatisfactory attachments' (Granqvist 2020: 123, 154). Interestingly, they have also found a positive association between insecure attachment and a propensity for mystical experiences and a predilection for a New Age type of religiosity (e.g. Granqvist and Hagekull 2001; Granqvist et al. 2007). Moreover, in a recent study of psychological security in welfare states, Joel Gruneau Brulin could not find any support for the idea that the welfare state provides a secure base in the same way as religion does, 'but through the security that the welfare state provides there is nonetheless less need to turn to religion' (Gruneau Brulin 2021: 77).

Tomas Lindgren (b. 1963), who was appointed Professor of Psychology of Religion at Umeå University in 2015, has focused primarily on the intersection of religion and violence, such as his (and his colleagues') studies of the psychological dimensions of religious conflicts, terrorism, radicalism and radicalization (e.g. Lindgren 2014, 2016, 2023; Lindgren, Sonnenschein and Eriksson 2022; Sonnenschein and Lindgren 2020), which is referred to elsewhere in this book.

There has also been continuing interest in case studies and narrative analysis, which was initiated by Sundén, but this has now become qualified in relation to recent theory in narrative psychology (see Belzen and Geels 2008). This is exemplified by Lindgren's psychobiographies of the Swedish ambassador Mohammed Knut Bernström (Lindgren 2004) and the Islamic scholar Wahiduddin Khan (Lindgren 2018), as well as his narrative study of Muslim prayer experiences (Lindgren 2005).

Another field related to psychology of religion that has generated much research is the cognitive science of religion, a multidisciplinary field of study that is covered in Chapter 11 of this volume.

Conclusions

In Sweden, three phases in the history of the psychological study of religion can be identified. The first phase was characterized by Nathan Söderblom's focus upon religious experiences, defined in the broad sense of including anomalous experiences. In this approach, psychology offered a 'near-life' perspective as part of the comparative and historical study of religion. In the second phase, the impact of Hjalmar Sundén was evident, with the appearance of a broad spectrum of qualitative psychological perspectives. During this period, the subject became institutionalized as a separate academic discipline. The third phase is characterized by a specialization in different fields of research, such as religion and health or the cognitive science of religion. These fields are recognized as multidisciplinary and no longer united in an academic discipline called 'the Psychology of Religion'. The situation that pertained during the earlier twentieth century has returned, whereby psychological research on religion is part of the broader study of religion, not a separate academic discipline.

References

Ahmadi, F., and N. Ahmadi (2018), *Meaning-Making Methods for Coping with Serious Illness*, Abingdon: Taylor & Francis.
Åkerberg, H. (1985a). *Diktaren och arvet: några Dan Andersson-studier*, Göteborg: Zinderman.
Åkerberg, H. (1985b), *Sven Stolpe och Sigtunaupplevelsen: en psykologisk studie av ett livsavgörande utvecklingssteg*, Stockholm: Legenda.
Åkerberg, H. (1985c), *Teologin i Stengrunden: själavård och homiletik: en psykologisk studie*, Stockholm: Petra.
Åkerberg, H. (1985d), *Tillßvaron och religionen: Psykologiska studier kring personlighet och mystik*, Stockholm: Almqvist & Wiksell International.
Åkerberg, H. (1983a), *Kamp och kris: Två psykologiska och livsåskådningsvetenskapliga kristeorier*, Stockholm: Almqvist & Wiksell International.
Åkerberg, H., ed. (1983b), *Djuppsykologi och religion: Religionspsykologiska studier till belysning av huvudriktningar inom djuppsykologin*, Stockholm: Almqvist & Wiksell International.
Åkerberg, H. (1981), *Tolkning och förståelse: metodfrågor, data och tolkningar för religionspsykologiska interpretationsövningar*, Lund: Studentlitteratur.
Åkerberg, H. (1980), *Några religionspsykologiska principfrågor*, Lund: Studentlitteratur.
Åkerberg, H. (1975), *Omvändelse och kamp: En empirisk religionspsykologisk undersökning av den unge Nathan Söderbloms religiösa utveckling 1866–1894*, Lund: Lund University.
Åkerberg, H. (1974), '"Livsnära religionspsykologi": Ett arv och ett program', *Svensk teologisk kvartalsskrift* 2: 76–89.
Alm, I. (1973), *Från Freud till Jung: Några kapitel ur djuppsykologiens historia*, Stockholm: Almqvist & Wiksell.

Alm, I. (1936), *Den religiösa funktionen i människosjälen: Studier till frågan om religionens innebörd och människans väsen i modern psykologi, särskilt hos Freud och Jung*, Uppsala: Uppsala Universitet.
Andræ, T. (1947), *I myrtenträdgården: Studier i sufisk mystik*, Stockholm: Bonniers.
Andræ, T. (1930), *Muhammed: Hans liv och hans tro*, Stockholm: Natur och kultur.
Andræ, T. (1927), *Psykoanalys och religion*, Stockholm: Bonnier.
Andræ, T. (1926), *Mystikens psykologi: Besatthet och inspiration*, Stockholm: Sveriges kristliga studentrörelse.
Arbman, E. (1970), *Ecstasy or Religious Trance: In the Experience of the Ecstatics and from the Psychological Point of View. Vol. 3 Ecstasy and Psychopathological States*, Stockholm: Svenska bokförlaget.
Arbman, E. (1968), *Ecstasy or Religious Trance: In the Experience of the Ecstatics and from the Psychological Point of View. Vol. 2 Essence and Forms of Ecstasy*, Stockholm: Svenska bokförlaget.
Arbman, E. (1963), *Ecstasy or Religious Trance: In the Experience of the Ecstatics and from the Psychological Point of View. Vol. 1 Vision and Ecstasy*, Stockholm: Svenska bokförlaget.
Ayim-Aboagye, D. (1993), *The Function of Myth in Akan Healing Experience: A Psychological Inquiry into Two Traditional Akan Healing Communities*, dissertation, Uppsala: Uppsala University.
Bang, J. P. (1926), *De stora väckelserörelserna: En historisk och psykologisk framställning*, Stockholm: Sveriges kristliga studentrörelses förlag.
Belfrage, L. (2009), *Clergy Existence Challenged: An Existential Psychological Exploration of Meaning-Making and Burnout Related to the Church of Sweden*, Uppsala: Uppsala universitet.
Belzen, J. A. van, and A. Geels, eds (2008), *Autobiography and the Psychological Study of Religious Lives*, Amsterdam: Rodopi.
Bergling, K. (1981), *Moral Development: The Validity of Kohlberg's Theory*, Stockholm: Almqvist & Wiksell.
Björkhem, J. (1939), *Det ockulta problemet: En orientering*, Uppsala: Lindblad.
Briem, E. (1942), *Helgon och helgonliv*, Lund: Gleerup.
Briem, E. (1933), *Gudstro och gudsupplevelse i historisk och psykologisk belysning*, Lund: Gleerup.
Briem, E. (1930), *Den religiösa upplevelsen i dess kristna huvudformer*, Lund: Gleerup.
Briem, E. (1929), *Stigmatisationer och visioner*, Stockholm: Sveriges kristliga studentrörelse.
Cetrez, Ö., A. Maluk and M. A. Rajon (2021a). *Syrian Migrants in Sweden: A Survey on Experiences of Migration and Integration*, Global Migration: Consequences and Responses - RESPOND Working Paper Series, 2021/84, Uppsala.
Cetrez, Ö. A., V. DeMarinis, M. Sundvall, M. Fernandez-Gonzalez, L. Borisova and D. Titelman (2021b), 'A Public Mental Health Study Among Iraqi Refugees in Sweden: Social Determinants, Resilience, Gender, and Cultural Context', *Frontiers in Sociology* 6. doi: 10.3389/fsoc.2021.551105.
Cetrez, Ö., and V. DeMarinis (2017), 'A Psychosocial, Spiritual, and Physical Health Study among Assyrian-Syrian Refugees in Istanbul', *Middle East Journal of Refugee Studies* 2 (2): 227.
Cetrez, Ö. A. (2011), 'The Next Generation Assyrians in Sweden: Religiosity as a Functioning System of Meaning within the Process of Acculturation', *Mental Health, Religion and Culture* 14 (5): 473–87.

DeMarinis, V. (2013), 'Existential Meaning-Making and Ritualizing for Understanding Mental Health Function in Cultural Context', in Herman Westerink (ed.), *Constructs of Meaning and Religious Transformation*, 207–22, Göttingen: V&R Unipress.

DeMarinis, V. (2003), *Pastoral Care, Existential Health, and Existential Epidemiology*, Stockholm: Verbum.

DeMarinis, V. (1998), *Tvärkulturell vård i livets slutskede: att möta äldre personermed invandrarbakgrund*, Lund: Studentlitteratur.

DeMarinis, V. (1997), 'Religious Ritual Function and the Illusionistic World', *Archive for the Psychology of Religion* 22: 166–81.

DeMarinis, V., O. Wikström and Ö. Cetrez, eds (2011), *Inspiration till religionspsykologin: Kultur, hälsa och mening*, Stockholm: Natur & kultur.

Dudas, V. (2020), *Exploring the Identity of a Group of Assyrian/Syriac Young Adolescents in Sweden: A Mixed-Methods Study within the Discipline of Psychology Religion and the Research Field of Identity Development*, Uppsala: Uppsala University.

Eek, J. (2001), *Religious Facilitation through Intense Liturgical Participation: A Quasi-Experimental Study of Swedish Pilgrims to Taizé*, Lund: Lund University Press.

Ekedahl, M. A. (2001), *Hur orkar man i det svåraste? Copingprocesser hos sjukhussjälavårdare i möte med existentiell problematik: en religionspsykologisk studie*, Uppsala: Acta Universitatis Upsaliensis.

Geels, A. (2001), *Kristen mystik: ur psykologisk synvinkel*, Skellefteå: Norma.

Geels, A. (1999), *Muslimsk mystik: ur psykologisk synvinkel*, Skellefteå: Artos & Norma.

Geels, A. (1998), *Judisk mystik: ur psykologisk synvinkel*, Skellefteå: Norma.

Geels, A. (1991), *Att möta Gud i kaos: religiösa visioner i dagens Sverige*, Stockholm: Norstedts.

Geels, A. (1989), *Skapande mystik: En psykologisk undersökning av Violet Tengbergs religiösa visioner och konstnärliga skapande*, Löberöd: Plus Ultra.

Geels, A. (1980), *Mystikern Hjalmar Ekström: En religionspsykologisk studie av hans religiösa utveckling*, Lund: Doxa.

Geels, A., and O. Wikström (1984), *Den religiösa människan: En introduktion till religionspsykologin*, Helsingborg: Plus ultra.

Geyer, K. (1989), *Att dana människor: Om kvalitet i livsfrågeorienterad verksamhet, en diskussion i George Herbert Meads anda*, Uppsala: Uppsala universitet.

Gieser, S. (2009), *Psykoterapins pionjärer i Sverige*, Stockholm: Proprius.

Granqvist, P. (2020), *Attachment in Religion and Spirituality: A Wider View*, New York: Guilford Publications.

Granqvist, P., and B. Hagekull, B. (1999), 'Religiousness and Perceived Childhood Attachment: Profiling Socialized Correspondence and Emotional Compensation', *Journal for the Scientific Study of Religion* 38 (2): 254–73.

Granqvist, P., and B. Hagekull (2001), 'Seeking Security in the New Age: On Attachment and Emotional Compensation', *Journal for the Scientific Study of Religion* 40 (3): 527–45.

Granqvist, P., T. Ivarsson, A. G. Broberg and B. Hagekull (2007), 'Examining Relations among Attachment, Religiosity, and New Age Spirituality Using the Adult Attachment Interview', *Developmental Psychology* 43 (3): 590–601.

Gruneau Brulin, J. (2021), *Security in the welfare state: Attachment, religion and secularity*, Stockholm: Stockholms universitet.

Grønbech, V. (1926), *Mystik i Österland och Västerland: Förra delen Indien*, Stockholm: Sveriges kristliga studentrörelses förlag.

Hermanson, J. (1997), *The Interplay of Social Science and Personal Belief in Gordon W. Allport's Psychology of Religion*, Lund: Lund University.
Hillerdal, G. (1985), *Bönhörelse: Utsagor i vår tid*, Stockholm: Proprius förlag.
Hillerdal, G., and B. Gustafsson (1973), *De såg och hörde Jesus: Om kristusuppenbarelser i vår tid*, Stockholm: Verbum.
Hjärpe, J. (1977), 'Rollernas Muhammed', *Religion och Bibel* 36: 63–72.
Holm, N. G. (1976), *Tungotal och andedop: En religionspsykologisk undersökning av glossolali hos finlandssvenska pingstvänner*, Uppsala: Uppsala universitet.
Holm, N. G. (2014), *The Human Symbolic Construction of Reality: A Psycho-Phenomenological Study*, Berlin: LIT Verlag.
Jonsson, J. (2014), *'Jag är bara Nathan Söderblom satt till tjänst': En biografi*, Stockholm: Verbum.
Junus, P. (1995), *Den levande gudinnan: Kvinnoidentitet och religiositet som förändringsprocess*, Nora: Bokförlaget Nya Doxa.
Källstad, T. (1974), *John Wesley and the Bible: A Psychological Study*, Stockholm: Nya bokförings AB.
Källstad, T. (1978), 'Ignatius Loyala, and the Spiritual Exercises: A Psychological Study', in T. Källstad (ed.), *Psychological Studies on Religious Man*, 13–45, Uppsala: Uppsala University.
Källstad, T. (1984), 'Bönens Psykologi', *Svensk Teologisk Kvartalstidskrift* 3:107–13.
Källstad, T. (1987), *Levande mystik: En psykologisk undersökning av Ruth Dahléns religiösa upplevelser*, Delsbo: Åsak.
Kippenberg, H. G. (2002), *Discovering Religious History in the Modern Age*, Princeton: Princeton University Press.
Kirkpatrick, L. A. (2005), *Attachment, Evolution, and the Psychology of Religion*, New York: The Guilford Press.
Koskinen-Hagman, M. (1999), *Latent Trait Models of Intrinsic, Extrinsic, and Quest Religious Orientations*, Lund: Lund University Press.
Larsson, G., ed. (2022), *The Legacy, Life and Work of Geo Widengren and the Study of the History of Religions after World War II*, Leiden: Brill.
Lengborn, T. (1988), *Sven Lidmans omvändelse: frälsningsupplevelse och omvändelseprocess 1915–1921: en religionspsykologisk studie*, Uppsala: Uppsala Universitet.
Liljas Stålhandske, M. (2005), *Ritual Invention: A Play Perspective on Existential Ritual and Mental Health in Late Modern Sweden*, Uppsala: Uppsala universitet.
Liljas Stålhandske, M., M. Ekstrand and T. Tydén (2011), 'Existential Experiences and Strategies in Relation to Induced Abortion, an Interview Study With 24 Swedish Women', *Archive for the Psychology of Religion/ Archiv für Religionspsychologie* 33 (3): 345–70.
Lindgren, T. (2004), 'The Narrative Construction of Muslim identity: A Single Case Study', *Archive for the Psychology of Religion* 26: 51–73.
Lindgren, T. (2005), 'The Narrative Construction of Muslim Prayer Experiences', *International Journal for the Psychology of Religion* 2: 159–74.
Lindgren, T. (2014), 'Hjalmar Sundén's Impact on the Study of Religion in the Nordic Countries', *Temenos* 52: 39–61.
Lindgren, T. (2016), 'The Psychological Study of Religious Violence: A Theoretical and Methodological Study', *Al-Albab* 5: 155–74.

Lindgren, T. (2018), 'A Nonviolent Identity: A Psychobiographical Study of an Islamic Scholar', in A. Village and R. Hood Jr. (eds), *Research in the Social Scientific Study of Religion*, 96–122, Leiden: Brill.
Lindgren, T. (2023), *Fundamentalism och helig terror: Religionspsykologi för vår tid*, Lund: Studentlitteratur.
Lindgren, T., H. Sonnenschein and J. Eriksson (2022), 'Moderate and Radical Muslims, but for Whom and for What Purpose?', in R. Hood Jr. and S. Cheruvallil-Contractor (eds), *Research in the Social Scientific Study of Religion*, 78–100, Leiden: Brill.
Lindquist, K. S. (1935), *Mystikens väg och mål.: En religionspsykologisk studie till kristen och utomkristen mystik*, Uppsala: Uppsala University.
Lindquist, K. S. (1932), *Die Methoden des Yoga: Inauguraldissertation*, dissertation, Lund: Lund University.
Lloyd, C. (2018), *Moments of Meaning – Towards an Assessment of Protective and Risk Factors for Existential Vulnerability among Young Women with Mental Ill-Health Concerns: A Mixed Methods Project in Clinical Psychology of Religion and Existential Health*, Uppsala: Uppsala universitet.
Lundmark, M. (2017), *Religiositet och coping: Religionspsykologiska studier av kristna med cancer*, Umeå: Umeå universitet.
Löwén, Å. (2006), *Asylexistensens villkor: Resurser och problem i meningsskapande hos asylsökande barn i Sverige*, Uppsala: Uppsala universitet.
Melder, C. A. (2011), *Vilsenhetens epidemiologi: En religionspsykologisk studie i existentiell folkhälsa*, Uppsala: Uppsala universitet.
Nahlbom, Y. (2018), *Existential Meaning-Making in the Midst of Meaninglessness and Suffering: Studying the Function of Religion and Religious Organizations in the Reconstruction and Development of Existential Meaning and Psychosocial Well-Being after the 2011 Great East Japan Earthquake and Tsunami*, Uppsala: Uppsala universitet.
Oksanen, A. (1994), *Religious Conversion: A Meta-Analytic Study*, Lund: Lund University Press.
Orést, F. (2009), *Ondska – individuell och kulturell projektion: filmupplevelser analyserade enligt den analytiska psykologin*, Åbo: Åbo Akademis förlag.
Petersson Bouin, Y. (2000), *Effects of Meditation on Respiration and the Temporal Lobes: An Exploratory and Meta-Analytic Study*, Lund: Lund University Press.
Pettersson, O., and H. Åkerberg, eds (1980), *William James då och nu: Några religionspsykologiska studier*, Lund: Doxa.
Rubensson, L. (1996), *Ögonblicket - det förvandlande: En religionspsykologisk studie av en livsavgörande gudsupplevelse i Gunnar Edmans liv*, dissertation, Uppsala: Uppsala University.
Rudolfsson, L. (2015), *Walk with Me: Pastoral Care for Victims of Sexual Abuse Viewed through Existential Psychology*, Göteborg: Göteborgs universitet.
Runestam, A. (1928), *Psykoanalys och kristendom*, Stockholm: Sveriges kristliga studentrörelses förlag.
Schimmel, A. (1983), *Mystical Dimensions of Islam*, Chapel Hill: University of North California Press.
Schimmel, A. (1985), *And Muhammad Is His Messenger: The Veneration of the Prophet in Islamic Piety*, Chapel Hill: University of North California Press.
Schumann, Å. (2018), *Vilken mening!?: en blandad metodstudie i religionspsykologi av meningsskapandets betydelse för skolungdomar*, Uppsala: Uppsala universitet.
Sharpe, E. J. (1986), *Comparative Religion: A History*, London: Duckworth.

Sonnenschein, H., and T. Lindgren (2020), 'The Shapeshifting Self: Narrative Pathways into Political Violence', *Religions* 11 (464), https://doi.org/10.3390/rel11090464.
Ståhlberg, G. (2000), *Psykologin som utmanare och hjälpreda för själavården: Om själavårdsarbetets psykologiska förutsättningar i teori och praxis*, Umeå: Umeå Universitet.
Ståhle, G. (2004), *Det religiösa självet i praktik vid ett hinduiskt gudinnetempel: Ett kulturpsykologiskt angreppssätt för religionspsykologi*, Uppsala: Uppsala universitet.
Ståhle, G. (2011), 'Coaching a Healthy Lifestyle: Positioning Ayurveda in a Late Modern Context', *International Journal for the Study of New Religions* 1 (2): 243–60.
Sundén, H. (1940), *La théorie bergsonienne de la religion*, dissertation, Uppsala: Uppsala University.
Sundén, H. (1959), *Religionen och rollerna*, Stockholm: Svenska kyrkans diakonistyrelses förlag.
Sundén, H. (1966), *Kristusmeditationer i Dag Hammarskjölds vägmärken*, Stockholm: Diakonistyrelsens bokförlag.
Sundén, H. (1969), *Älgskyttar, helgon och exegeter: Några religionspsykologiska Essäer*, Stockholm: Wahlström & Widstrand.
Sundén, H. (1970), *Zen: Historisk, analys och betydelse (andra upplagan)*, Stockholm: Wahlström & Widstrand.
Sundén, H. (1973), *Den heliga Birgitta: Ormungens moder som blev Kristi brud*, Stockholm: Wahlström & Widstrand.
Sundén, H. (1974), *Barn och religion (andra utvidgade upplagan)*, Stockholm: Verbum.
Sundén, H. (1981a), *Religionspsykologi*, Stockholm: Proprius.
Sundén, H. (1981b), *Persona och anima: En tillämpning av C. G. Jungs psykologi på sex författare*, Stockholm: Proprius.
Sundén, H. (1983), *Konungen och riket: Om den gudomliga världsstyrelsen*, Stockholm: Proprius.
Sundén, H. (1987), 'Saint Augustine and the Psalter in the Light of Role-Psychology', *Journal for the Scientific Study of Religion* 26: 375–82.
Sundén, H. (2012), "From the History of Religion to the Psychology of Religion", in Belzen, J. A. (ed.), *Psychology of Religion: Autobiographical Approaches*, 233–42, New York: Springer.
Söderblom, N. (1916), *Studiet av religionen*, Stockholm: Norstedt.
Taves, A. (2009), *Religious Experience Reconsidered: A Building-Block Approach to the Study of Religion and Other Special Things*, Princeton: Princeton University Press.
Tilander, Å. (1990), *A Theme in C. G. Jung's Psychohistory: An Analysis of the Origin and Development of a Complex*, Uppsala: Uppsala University.
Thouless, R. H. (1926), *Religionspsykologi i översiktlig framställning*, Stockholm: Sveriges kristliga studentrörelses förlag.
Vikdahl, L. (2014), *Jag vill också vara en ängel: om upplevelser av delaktighet i Svenska kyrkan hos personer med utvecklingsstörning*, dissertation, Umeå: Umeå universitet.
Watts, F. (2017), *Psychology, Religion, and Spirituality: Concepts and Applications*, Cambridge: Cambridge University Press.
Widengren, G. (1947), *Tor Andræ*, Uppsala: J. A. Lindblads förlag.
Wiedel, B. (1984), *Bön och Tradition: En empirisk religionspsykologisk undersökning av gudsbild och gudsförhållande i samband med bönens form och funktion inom Svenska Alliansmissionen*, Lund: Studentlitteratur.

Wikström, O. (1975), *Guds ledning: En explorativ religionspsykologisk studie av fromheten hos ett antal västerbottniska åldringar, med särskild hänsyn tagen till upplevelsen av Guds ledning*, Stockholm: Almquist & Wiksell.
Wikström, O. (1980), *Stöd eller börda? Religionens roll i psykiatri och psykoterapi: en religonspsykologisk studie*, Älvsjö: Skeab/Verbum.
Wikström, O. (1982), *Raskolnikov: Om den kluvnes väg mot helhet i Dostojevskijs Brott och straff: en religionspsykologisk studie*, Bodafors: Doxa.
Wikström, O. (1984), *Hypnos, symboldrama och religion: Religionspsykologiska studier kring 'spontan religiositet', besatthet-exorcism och 'inre helande'*, Åbo: Åbo Akademi.
Wikström, O. (1990), *Den outgrundliga människan: Livsfrågor, psykoterapi och själavård*, Stockholm: Natur och kultur.
Wikström, O. (1997), *Det bländande mörkret: Om andlig vägledning och psykologi i vår tid*, Örebro: Libris.
Wikström, O. (2001), *Långsamhetens lov: Eller vådan av att åka moped genom Louvren*, Stockholm: Natur och kultur.
Wulff, D. M. (1993a), *Religionspsykologi 1*, Lund: Studentlitteratur.
Wulff, D. M. (1993b), *Religionspsykologi 2*, Lund: Studentlitteratur

Chapter 10

SOCIOLOGY OF RELIGION

Mia Lövheim and Magdalena Nordin

Sociology of religion in Sweden has evolved from a strong focus on and connection with the national Lutheran Church, quantitative methods and theories of secularization towards a broader range of areas of study, methods and theories. This development has run parallel to changes in Swedish society since the 1980s. These concern the gradual separation of the Swedish Lutheran Church from the state and the subsequent changes in laws and policy concerning state governance of religious communities. This includes changes in the Swedish welfare system that have allowed for the expansion of private as well as civil society actors. Finally, increased globalization and migration from non-European countries has brought a larger religious and cultural diversity to Swedish society. This challenges previous models of accommodating religion within a secular society, which is much debated in media and political discourse.

As will be presented below, studies of changes in worship and life cycle rituals within the Church of Sweden has remained a topic of research over time, but new areas have become more prominent, such as the diversification of religious beliefs and of the role of religious organizations in society, as well as debates on religious diversity in media and politics. From an international perspective, Sweden has remained an intriguing case due to the seemingly paradoxical coexistence of low levels of religiosity in terms of belief and active participation in religious congregations, but persistent membership in the national Lutheran Church – what has been referred to as 'believing in belonging' (Bäckström 1993). In recent years, new theoretical perspectives and methods have been introduced in order to better grasp the new 'religious complexity' in contemporary Sweden (Furseth 2018; Lövheim and Nordin 2022).

The broadening of the field of studies in Swedish sociology of religion is also related to organizational changes within the universities, where the theology and religious studies departments at Lund and Uppsala universities have been complemented by more recently established university departments and university colleges. Thus, sociology of religion can today be characterized as an interdisciplinary research field where researchers from disciplines such as psychology of religion, sociology, practical theology, Islamic studies, Church history, anthropology, media studies, law studies and political science cooperate.

Brief Historical Overview

Sociology of religion constitutes one of the more recently established research areas in the Swedish university system with regard to religious studies and theology. The discipline was institutionalized in Sweden in the 1960s through a combination of political and personal initiatives (Bexell 2021; Dahlgren 2021; Davidsson Bremborg, Gustafsson and Karlsson Hallonsten 2009; Gustafsson 2013; Näsström 2013; Skog 1976). In 1958, a commission of inquiry regarding the relation between the Church of Sweden and the Swedish state constituted a first step in this process. A key point in the directives for the commission was the need to investigate, using social scientific methods, the significance of religion (here mainly referring to Christianity) for the formation of modern society. The chairperson for the appointed group of researchers to pursue this task was the Associate Professor (docent) in Church History at Lund University, Berndt Gustafsson (1920–1975). The result of this work was published in the commission report SOU 1963:26. Religionens betydelse som samhällsfaktor: Möjligheter och metoder för en sociologisk undersökning. This task gave Gustafsson the incentive and resources to act as the principal initiator of sociology of religion in Sweden (Bäckström 2023; Gustafsson 2013; Skog 1976).

In 1962, Gustafsson established the Research Institute for Sociology of Religion in Stockholm (*Religionssociologiska Insitutet*, RSI)[1] as a way to facilitate, foremost, research on the conditions for and consequences of the ongoing political process of separating the Lutheran Church of Sweden and the state. Even though Gustafsson died in 1975 –only fifty-five years old – the institute remained active until 1991 and produced several studies related to Church and state relations and on religion in contemporary Sweden more broadly (Dahlgren 2021; Gustafsson 2013; Nordin 2021). In total, the institute was responsible for more than five hundred research publications involving around two hundred researchers (Gustafsson 2013). In 1990, the institute was incorporated into the Department for Research in the Church of Sweden. Moreover, Gustafsson's book *Religionssociologi* from 1965 is to be seen as the first Swedish textbook on the sociology of religion.

Parallel to this process, sociology of religion was also established as a research area within the universities in Sweden. The initiative for a broadening of religious studies to include sociology and psychology of religion came from the faculties of Theology in Lund and Uppsala,[2] who approached the Swedish Higher Education Authority with this request in 1966. In 1967, a commission was established with the task of investigating a reorganization of studies of religion at the theological faculties in Sweden from the training of ministers for the Church of Sweden and moving towards greater relevance for wider society. In 1971, the commission recommended a professorship in sociology of religion with national responsibilities, based in Lund. The decision was formalized by the Swedish parliament in 1975.

The argument for this proposal was the need to strengthen existing research on religion by including perspectives and methods needed for an increasing diversity of religious and cultural expressions in Swedish society (Bäckström 2023).

The aforementioned Berndt Gustafsson applied for the professorship in sociology of religion but passed away before the hiring process was completed. His colleague at the Department of Sociology at Lund University, Göran Gustafsson (1936–2018, PhD in sociology), became the first Professor in Sociology of Religion in 1977, a post which he held until 2001 when he retired (Dahlgren and Straarup 2020). Further political initiatives to strengthen social scientific research for measuring religious beliefs and world views resulted in a government decision on a chair for sociology of religion at Uppsala University in 1988. Thorleif Pettersson (1940–2010), who had a PhD in comparative religion and psychology of religion, was appointed to this position until 2007. When Pettersson retired, Anders Bäckström, who had a background in practical theology, served as professor until 2010, after which Mia Lövheim was appointed Professor in Sociology of Religion. Curt Dahlgren, who in 1982 defended the first thesis in the newly established research area, served as Professor in Sociology of Religion at Lund University from 2002 to 2008.

Since 1982, around fifty PhD theses has been defended in the research area of sociology of religion at the faculties in Uppsala and Lund. The first woman to defend a thesis in sociology of religion was Eva Hamberg in 1990 (Hamberg 1990). Doctoral theses related to sociology of religion have also been completed in the faculties of humanities and social sciences at the universities in Gothenburg, Lund, Uppsala and Umeå (Hammarström and Ekerwald 2022; Näsström 2013; see, for example, Gelfgren 2003; Ilicki 1988; Liedgren 2007; Lundberg 2005; Nilsson 2019; Palm 1982; Rosenius 2015; Sjödin 2011; Willander 2014). As a result of organizational changes in the last decades, sociology of religion no longer exists as an independent research area at the universities in Lund (since 2006) and Uppsala (since 2020). However, sociology of religion continues to be a specialization for PhD studies within a broader research area in several universities in Sweden. The Berndt Gustafsson Memorial Foundation, established in 1990, and the Association of Sociology of Religion in Sweden support and organize researchers of various affiliations who conduct sociological research on religion.

Key Issues and Scholars

Quantitative studies of religion and social change were characteristic of the first decades of research within sociology of religion in Sweden. Professors Göran Gustafsson and Thorleif Pettersson conducted several projects initiated by the government on relations between the state and the Church of Sweden, as well as Nordic comparative projects on religious change and religious and moral pluralism at national and local levels (Gustafsson 1985, 1987; Pettersson and Halman 2002). These projects, and the unique access to longitudinal data on religious beliefs and behaviour collected through the Church of Sweden's yearly membership studies (Pettersson 1988), enabled the development of methods for the collection and sophisticated statistical analysis of survey and register data on topics ranging from habits of Bible reading (Gustafsson 1990), incentives for leaving the Church and the role of religion in crisis (Bromander 2005, 2011; Dahlgren 2008; see also below). The data was also used to test and critically review the applicability of theories stemming from an Anglo-American context (Gustafsson 1994).

The focus on the Church of Sweden was also continued during the decades that followed in more qualitative-based studies, for example, regarding Church engagements in foreign aid (Rubin 2000), the Church as a service supplier (Pettersson 2000), the priest as occupation and office (Ohlsson 2012), education in the Church (Straarup and Ekberg 2012) and local responses to changes in the Church after the separation from the state (Rosenius 2015).

Values and Value Changes

Studies of changes in religious beliefs, world views and values has, as described above, been a central theme in Swedish sociology of religion since the 1960s. This research has been carried out in cooperation with the Church of Sweden as well as through international longitudinal surveys such as International Social Survey Programme (ISSP), European Value Systems Study Group (EVSSG) and the World Values Survey (WVS). By using data from the WVS studies, Pettersson critically discussed Ronald Inglehart's theory of a generational value change from materialist to post-materialist values, which has granted Sweden the epithet 'the most secularised country in the world' because of high levels of secular-rational and self-expression values in the population (Pettersson 1994). Pettersson and Hamberg also used WVS data to analyse the validity of theories of individual rational choice and organisational supply for participation in organised religious activities (Hamberg and Pettersson 1994, 1997).

Studies of the connection between changes in religious beliefs and values and societal transformation using survey data from Christian Churches as well as other religious denominations have continued through the work of Jonas Bromander, Eva Hamberg and Erika Willander (Bromander 2011; Hamberg 2000; Willander 2014; Willander and Thurfjell 2021). These issues have also been further pursued in survey and mixed-method studies of youth, conducted by Mia Lövheim, Jonas Bromander, Anders Sjöborg and Maria Klingenberg at Uppsala University. These studies have contributed to a deeper understanding of the complex role of religion in highly secularized countries, and how religiosity interplays with opinions, activities and life conditions related to areas such as school, media, family, health, politics and migration (Lövheim and Bromander 2012; Klingenberg 2019; Klingenberg and Lövheim 2019;).

Religious Practices and Life Cycle Rituals

Another path that the sociology of religion took by the end of the 1990s was an increased focus on religious practices and rituals. This started to some degree with

Göran Gustafsson's quantitative studies of what he chose to label as 'ceremony religiosity' (*förrättningsreligiositet*) in the Swedish population. These studies showed how life cycle rituals in the Church of Sweden still attracted people to a higher degree than participation in Sunday services (Gustafsson 1997). Parallel to this, and from a more critical perspective, research explored the reasons for and implications of this persistent pattern of nominal membership in the Church of Sweden, exploring whether this pattern of 'believing in belonging' could be seen as a particular case of the British sociologist Grace Davie's expression 'believing without belonging' (1990; Bäckström 1993; Pettersson and Gustafsson 1990).[3] Other studies revealed that motifs connected to cultural belonging and tradition, rather than religious belief or religious socialization, were important to remaining a member of the Church (Bromander 2005, 2011; Dahlgren 2008).

Qualitative studies about life cycle rituals, such as baptism within the Church of Sweden, demonstrated how these practices had religious importance for the parents of the baptised child but were also driven by social factors, such as being included in the congregation (Reimers 1995; see also Sjölin 1999). The significance of community and tradition, rather than religious belief, were also shown to explain the relatively high interest in singing in church choirs (Bromander 2002).

Besides the significance of tradition and a social context, research has shown how increased possibilities for personalizing rituals, such as weddings, were also of importance for couples choosing to be married in the Church of Sweden (Jarnkvist 2011). Research on official rituals in catastrophes, such as the shipwreck of *Estonia* in 1994, and on pilgrimage in Sweden underscored how a combination of individual choice and the provision of traditional frames and social context seem to explain the continued connection to the Church of Sweden among a majority of the population (Davidsson Bremborg 2008; Gustafsson 1995; Pettersson 1995).

Quantitative studies of rituals also continued alongside these qualitative studies, especially regarding rituals related to death and funerals.[4] These studies substantiated the trend of not only individualization in religious practice in Sweden (Avelin et al. 2012; Dahlgren 2000; see also Gustafsson 2003) but also of privatization of religion; that is, practices are taking place in the private sphere (Davidsson Bremborg 2012; Davidsson Bremborg and Rådestad 2013, 2014).

Spirituality and New Religious Movements

The focus on trends of individualization and religious privatization that influenced international sociology of religion in the 1980s and 1990s became visible among Swedish scholars in a shift towards research on new religious movements and non-organized religiosity. This, in Sweden, worked in some studies as a bridge between former research on religiosity in the Church of Sweden and studies of religiosity and value changes in a more diverse religious landscape in Sweden (Bråkenhielm 2001; Gustafsson 1995; Hamberg 1990; Jeffner 1988).

In the research, it is argued that engagement in religious organizations among individuals in Sweden had changed from active membership in one established religious organization towards a selective connection to several religious groups and organizations, from which an individual mix of beliefs and practices were formed in accordance with needs developing over the lifespan (Ahlin 2001, 2005; Dahlgren 1982; Frisk 1993, 1998; Frohm 1995; Löwendahl 2002). This trend of religiosity expressed as an individual mix of religious symbols and affiliations was also reflected in obituaries in the daily press (Dahlgren 2000). More recent studies in Sweden have focused on negotiations between individual spirituality, authority and social stigma within charismatic Christian denominations (e.g. Moberg 2013; Nilsson 2019).

Religious Diversity and Migration

At the end of the 1990s, research in sociology of religion came to focus on increased religious diversity in Swedish society as a consequence of immigration to Sweden from non-Nordic countries (Nordin 2023a; Nordin and Otterbeck 2023).[5] Also, in this area, quantitative studies were the starting point. Professor Hamberg, at the Department of Theology at Lund University, followed up the former research on value changes with a study on changes in values, including religious practices, among Swedish Hungarians. She demonstrated that values changed as a result of migration, from more to less religiously grounded, thus becoming more similar to values and religiosity among the majority population (Hamberg 2000). Later studies have shown a similar trend for Swedish Chileans (Nordin 2004) and refugees from Syria and Somalia (Puranen 2019). Research on changes in religious traditions related to integration in the Syriac Orthodox Church in Sweden (Nordin 2023b; Nordin and Westergren 2023) and on religiosity and secularization among Muslims in Sweden (Thurfjell and Willander 2021) also confirms the early findings of how the religious beliefs, values and practices of immigrants on an individual level, as well as in organized religious communities, over time come to resemble the levels of religious beliefs, values and practices of the majority population.

Among the early studies on Muslims in Sweden (see Chapter 5 of this volume), there was one example that was, strictly speaking, in the research area of sociology of religion (Alwall 1998). This study was also innovative in its focus on the religious organizations and in the use of not only interviews but also observations. One major result from the study was that, despite a high degree of freedom of religion in Sweden, Muslim organizations experienced various tensions in the establishment process (see also Mosbach 2022). Furthermore, several other studies in the field of religion and immigration from adjacent fields have also been influenced by sociological theories (e.g. Bang 1990; Cato 2012; Dencik 2006; Deniz 1999; Hammarström 2007; Karlsson Minganti 2007; Månsson 2002; Otterbeck 2010).

Finally, studies of increased religious diversity in Sweden have also focused on changes in the state-governing of religious groups. These studies have analysed changes in the Swedish state's perception and handling of minority religious communities since the 1950s (Lundgren 2021) and on interreligious groups (Axelson and Strier 2020; Lund Liebmann, Nordin and Paulson Galal 2018; Nordin 2020). The analysis shows that the dominant political approach to religion in Sweden is characterized by pragmatic secularism (Bäckström 2013), which, in comparison to, for example, the French situation, leads to a lack of overarching strategies for the regulation of religious diversity.

Churches as Welfare Providers

Changes in the religious landscape of Sweden in the late 1990s inspired a new interest in studying religious organizations as part of civil society. Studies of churches and religious denominations as suppliers of welfare services have been a strong theme in research conducted at Uppsala University. Anders Bäckström has initiated several international comparative studies focusing on a new role for Christian churches as actors in welfare and social work through the EU-funded projects, 'Welfare and Religion in a European Perspective' (WREP) and 'Welfare and Values in Europe: Transitions related to Religion, Minorities and Gender' (WaVE) (Bäckström et al. 2010, 2011). Other studies have focused on the changing role of the Church of Sweden in contemporary society through theories of service production (Pettersson 2000) and implications of the increased focus on diaconal work for the identity and organization of the Church (Engel 2006). Comparisons have also been made between Christian churches as welfare providers in Sweden and Germany (Leis-Peters 2004), Britain (Middlemiss LéMon 2009) and Tanzania (Sundqvist 2017). In recent years studies of changes in other parts of state-funded social services have also been undertaken, such as regulations for religious chaplaincy within healthcare institutions and universities (Hoeg et al. 2019; Nordin 2018).

Media and Politics

Swedish and Nordic studies show that the media has become the most frequent arena for encountering religion, rather than within the family or religious organisations (Klingenberg and Lövheim 2019; Lövheim et al. 2018). Furthermore, public debates on religion have increased in recent decades, also in highly secularized societies like Sweden. Research by Swedish sociologists of religion have showed an increased diversity in the coverage of religion in the secular media, with a particular focus on Islam since the early 1990s. In editorials and opinion articles in the daily press, a shift can be discerned from handling religion as a non-issue to religion as a central theme in debates between various political and value-based standpoints concerning the future of democracy (Axner 2013; Linderman and Lövheim 2016; Lövheim 2019). Several of these studies have taken place within the Nordic Network on Media and Religion, where theories on mediatization, or long-term relations between media change and social and cultural change, have been central.

These studies have also analysed intersections between the mediatization and politicization of religion as religion becomes increasingly contested in public and political debate. The connections between media debates and new political cleavages and actors in the Nordic countries, in particular nationalist populist parties, from 1988 to 2010 have been analysed through party programmes and parliamentary debates (Lindberg 2015; Lövheim et al. 2018). Studies of mediated religion within Swedish sociology of religion has also concerned the uses of televised religious worship services (Linderman 1993) and fiction film as resources for individual and collective meaning making (Axelson 2008). The use of digital media platforms in the construction of religious identity, authority and community has been explored among youth (Lövheim 2004; Sjöborg 2006), Muslims in diaspora (Larsson 2011) and Conservative Christian communities (Gelfgren 2012). Several PhD projects in sociology of religion in Sweden have continued this tradition, with studies of religion and well-being in popular magazines (Kardemark 2012; Winell 2016), the formation and negotiation of atheist identity, gender and race on YouTube (Lundmark 2019), and discussions about religion and politics in hybrid media (Jensdotter 2021).

New Areas in Recent Research

A core issue in recent public debates concerns the relation between democratic values such as gender equality and freedom of expression, and values connected to religious communities. This calls for research on how religion is perceived and practised outside as well as inside organized religious communities, as well as new theoretical perspectives and methods. One such area for research is religious education. Surveys conducted by Swedish sociologists of religion has shown that, besides various forms of media, school is where young people primarily encounter religious worldviews (Löfstedt and Sjöborg 2020). Studies of how pupils in upper secondary high school reflect on religious diversity in school and the media and develop 'religious literacy' have been conducted at Uppsala University (Wrammert 2021). Furthermore, research on the experiences of religious education teachers in handling discussions on religious and secular values in school has been conducted within the project 'Teaching Religion in Late Modern Sweden' (Broberg 2019; Löfstedt and Sjöborg 2020; see also Chapter 12 of this volume).

The critique against secularization as the primary theory for analysing the interplay between modernity and religion, and debates on the 'post-secular condition' (Habermas 2006), in international studies of religion has also influenced sociology of religion in Sweden. In recent decades, theories of lived religion and religion as social practice (Ammerman 2021) have been used in sociology of religion research, focusing on people's everyday life (Enstedt and Plank 2018; see also Chapter 15 of this volume). These studies add new knowledge about how religion influences everyday life in multiple ways, even in societies where organised religion is in decline.

This change of focus from macro- and meso-level analyses to studies of individual practice can also be seen in studies of the construction of agency for women and non-binary persons within gender-conservative religious traditions. Recent PhD studies within sociology of religion have, drawing on analysis of Muslim women in Sweden (Mosbach 2022) and transsexual Orthodox Jews in North America and Israel (Poveda 2017), argued for an understanding of religious agency as a process of navigating between self-expression, religious tradition and public debates on gender and religion. This research contributes to a questioning of the hypothesis of increased individualization and privatization of religion as an outcome of secularization and brings new insights on the complex intersections between individual agency, social position and power in contemporary society (see also Jarnkvist 2021).

Impact and International Significance

As the above presentation of key issues in research within sociology of religion in Sweden shows, studies have often been conducted within Nordic comparative research projects. Göran Gustafsson's and Thorleif Pettersson's early studies on changes in religiosity and values have continued through Nordic comparative projects such as 'The Role of Religion in the Public Sphere' (NOREL, Furseth 2018) and 'Engaging with Conflicts in Mediatised Religious Environments' (CoMRel, Lundby 2018). A recurring Nordic research collaboration is the 'Nordic Conference in the Sociology of Religion', held every second year in a Nordic country since the beginning of the 1970s.

In European and wider international research, Pettersson played a key role as the Swedish representative in the establishment of the WVS in the 1990s, under the leadership of Professor Ronald Inglehart (1934–1921). Bäckström launched the EU-funded comparative studies WREP and WaVE, amongst others. In studies of media and religion, the first conference for the International Society for Media, Religion and Culture Research (ISMRC) was held in Uppsala in 1993 and cooperation continues through the Nordic Network on Media and Religion. Today, sociology of religion-oriented researchers are continuously involved in various collaborations with colleagues in the Nordic and other European countries. Some examples are research on human rights, values and religion (Botvar and Sjöborg 2012); young adults, values and religion in a cross-cultural, global comparative perspective (Klingenberg and Sjö 2019); and networks for funeral research, religion in public institutions and the complexity in studies of religiosity (Middlemiss LéMon, Nordin and Broo 2023).[6]

Sweden continues to be an intriguing case for international studies of social and religious change. Scholars working within sociology of religion have contributed to international studies through a critical discussion and refinement of the secularization thesis, using a combination of quantitative and qualitative data. The seemingly paradoxical trends of religious and social change in Sweden show that secularization cannot be seen as a linear process but rather involves more complex patterns where continuous decline in religious belief and participation in religious congregations exist simultaneously with a continued support for Christianity as culture and tradition, and increased debate on the place of religion in a secular, democratic and culturally diverse society. A further example is how Swedish researchers have contributed through an approach to mediatization of religion as a dynamic process shaped by the affordances of media technology and practices and the ways in which these are used by religious actors (Larsson 2011; Linderman 1996; Lövheim 2014, 2013).

Political challenges that followed from increased religious diversity in Europe towards the end of the twentieth century contributed to the funding of several large, interdisciplinary research programmes on religion and society (Davie 2016). In Uppsala, the centre of excellence and research programme 'The Impact of Religion: Challenges for Society, Law and Democracy' provided a platform for research and international cooperation from 2009 to 2019. The Centre for Multi-Disciplinary Research on Religion and Society established at Uppsala University during these years has continued to serve as a node for international and interdisciplinary research on changes in values and religiosity in highly secularized societies during the early twenty-first century.

Conclusions

As the brief historical overview in this chapter shows, the close connections between political initiatives to handle changes in Swedish society, changes within the Church of Sweden and developments within the universities have been instrumental in the formation of sociology of religion as a research area. The Sociology of Religion Institute, RSI, served as a connecting point for research on these issues and also between the first three professors in sociology of religion: Berndt Gustafsson, Göran Gustafsson and Thorleif Pettersson. In recent years, sociology of religion has transformed from a discipline closely connected to the Church of Sweden and located in theological faculties to a research field where scholars with varying disciplinary backgrounds use and contribute to the development of sociological theory and methods for studying contemporary religion. Furthermore, the methods and (to some extent) theories used and developed within sociology of religion, such as surveys and interviews, are increasingly being used by scholars in other disciplines, for example, History of Religion and Practical Theology.

The main contribution from sociology of religion in Sweden to international studies of religion has, we argue, concerned a refinement of the secularization thesis from empirical data that shows a coexistence of low levels of religiosity in terms of belief and active participation in religious congregations with persistent membership in the national Lutheran Church and participation in life cycle rituals. Early quantitative analysis contributed to a critical development of theories about secularization, where Swedish data since the 1980s have been used to argue for an understanding of religious change as a process of simultaneous but seemingly paradoxical trends. Research conducted by sociologists of religion today continues to explore how these paradoxical trends unfold in a situation of wider diversity and contestation of religion. These studies indicate continued secularization in terms of beliefs and participation in organized religion among the majority population as well as more newly arrived religious groups in Sweden, and a renegotiation of religion as belonging through culture and tradition, which has expanded beyond churches into the fields of media, welfare, education, culture and political debate.

Notes

1 The RSI was established as a private and independent foundation.
2 This differentiates Sweden from the other Nordic countries, in which sociology of religion has also been and is an established part of departments of sociology or a department within humanities.
3 Part of the so-called *Kyrkolivsanalysprojektet* (the Church Analysis Project) (KYLA), 1987–90.
4 Part of a research project on funerals at the Department of Theology at Lund University, 1997–2002.
5 This societal change had been going on since the 1970s but has been little researched among migration scholars in Sweden (Nordin 2013, 2023a).
6 See Department of Cross-Cultural and Regional Studies (n.d.).

References

Ahlin, L. (2001), *New age: Konsumtionsvara eller värden att kämpa för? Hemmets Journal och Idagsidan i Svenska Dagbladet analyserat utifrån Mary Douglas grid/group-modell och Pierre Bourdieus fältteori*, Lund: Lund University.

Ahlin, L. (2005), *Pilgrim, turist eller flyktning? En studie av individuell religiös rörlighet i senmoderniteten*, Stockholm: Symposium.

Alwall, J. (1998), *Muslim Rights and Plights: The Religious Liberty Situation of a Minority in Sweden*, Lund: Studia Theologica Lundensia.

Ammerman, N. T. (2021), *Studying Lived Religion: Context and Practices*, New York: NYU Press.

Avelin, P., K. Erlandsson, I. Hildingsson, A. Davidsson Bremborg and I. Rådestad (2012), 'Make the Stillborn Baby and the Loss Real for the Siblings: Parents' Advice on How the Siblings of a Stillborn Baby Can Be Supported', *Journal of Perinatal Education* 21 (2): 90–8.

Axelson, T. (2008), *Film och mening. En receptionsstudie om spelfilm, filmpublik och existentiella frågor*, Uppsala: Acta Universitatis Upsaliensis: Psychologia et Sociologia Religionum.

Axelson, T., and J. Strier (2020), 'Religions – a Janus-Faced Phenomenon in Local Politics: A Swedish Interreligious council and Participants' Views on Religions as a Possible Asset for Societal Cohesion in the Local Community', *Interreligious Studies and Intercultural Theology* 4 (2): 224–46.

Axner, M. (2013), *Public Religions in Swedish Media: A Study of Religious Actors on Three Newspaper Debate Pages 2001–2011*, Uppsala: Acta Universitatis Upsaliensis: Studies in Religion & Society, 11.

Bäckström, A. (1993), 'Believing in Belonging: The Swedish Way of Being Religious', in R. Ryökäs and E. Ryökäs (eds), *Urban Faith 2000*, 31–42, Helsinki: Publications of Church Sociology A8.

Bäckström, A., G. Davie, N. Edgardh and P. Pettersson (2010), *Welfare and Religion in 21st Century Europe: Volume 1. Configuring the Connections*, Farnham: Ashgate.

Bäckström, A., G. Davie, N. Edgardh and P. Pettersson (2011), *Welfare and Values in 21st Century Europa: Volume 2. Gendered, Religious and Social Change*, Farnham: Ashgate.

Bäckström, A. (2013), 'Religion mellan det privata och det offentliga – om religion och välfärd', in H. Stenström (ed.), *Religionens offentlighet. Om religionens plats i samhället*, 27–46, Stockholm: Artos & Norma bokförlag.

Bäckström, A. (2023), *Religionssociologins pionjärer i Sverige*. Skellefteå: Artos & Norma.

Bang, H. (1990), *Religious Identity over Two Generations: Roman Catholic Immigrant and Convert Families*, Stockholm: Stockholm University.

Bexell, O. (2021), *Teologiska fakulteten vid Uppsala universitet 1916–2000. Historiska studier*, Uppsala: Acta Universitatis Upsaliensis. Skrifter rörande Uppsala universitet C. Organisation och Historia, 120.

Bromander, J. (2005), *Medlem I Svenska kyrkan. En studie kring samtid och framtid*, Stockholm: Verbum förlag.

Botvar, P. K., and A. Sjöborg (2012), 'Views on Human Rights among Christian, Muslim and Non-Religious Youth in Norway and Sweden', *Nordic Journal of Religion and Society* 1: 67–81.

Bråkenhielm, C. R., ed. (2001), *Världsbild och mening. En empirisk studie av livsåskådningar i dagens Sverige*, Nora: Nya Doxa.

Broberg, M. (2019), *'Stay A while and Listen': Understanding the Dynamics of Mediatization, Authority, and Literacy in Swedish Religious Education*, Uppsala: Acta Universitatis Upsaliensis: Studies in Religion & Society, 17.

Bromander, J. (2002), *Rum för röster. Sociologiska analyser av musiklivet inom Svenska kyrkan, som det uppfattas av kyrkobesökare, kyrkomusiker samt kyrkokorister*. Uppsala: Verbum.

Bromander, J. (2011), *Svenska kyrkans medlemmar*, Stockholm: Verbum.

Cato, J. (2012), *När islam blev svenskt: föreställningar om islam och muslimer i svensk offentlig politik 1975–2010*, Lund: Lund University.

Dahlgren, C. (1982), *Maranata. En sociologisk studie av en sektrörelses uppkomst och utveckling*, Lund: Lund University.

Dahlgren, C. (2000), *När döden skiljer oss åt... Anonymitet och individualisering i dödsannonser: 1945–1999*, Stockholm: Databokförlaget.

Dahlgren, C. (2008), *Att lämna sitt trossamfund. Några sociologiska perspektiv*, Lund: Arcus.

Dahlgren C., and J. Straarup (2020), 'Gustafsson, Göran', in A. Possamai and A. J. Blasi (eds), *The SAGE Encyclopedia of the Sociology of Religion*, 331–2, Thousand Oaks, CA: Sage.

Dahlgren, C., ed. (2021), *Religionssociologisk mångfald. Texter till minne av Berndt Gustafsson, grundare av religionssociologi i Sverige*. Lund: Lunds Studies in Sociology of Religion, vol 13.

Davidsson Bremborg, A. (2008), 'Spirituality in Silence and Nature: Motivations, Experiences, and Impressions among Swedish Pilgrims', *Journal of Empirical Theology* 21 (2): 149–65.

Davidsson Bremborg, A., G. Gustafson and G. Karlsson Hallonsten, eds (2009), *Religionssociologi i brytningstider*, Lund: Lunds Studies in Sociology of Religion.

Davidsson Bremborg, A. (2012), 'The Memorialization of Stillbirth in the Internet Age', in S. Earle C. Komaromy and L. Layne (eds), *Understanding Reproductive Loss. Perspectives on Life, Death and Fertility*, 155–66, Surrey: Ashgate.

Davidsson Bremborg, A., and J. Rådestad (2013), 'Memory Triggers and Anniversaries of Stillborn Children', *Nordic Journal of Religion and Society* 26 (2): 157–74.

Davidsson Bremborg, A., and I. Rådestad (2014), 'Home Memorials after Stillbirths in Sweden', in M. Rotar, A. Teodorescu and C. Rotar (eds), *Dying and Death in 18th–21st Century Europe: Vol. 2*, 457–68, Newcastle upon Tyne: Cambridge Scholars.

Davie, G. (1990), 'Believing without Belonging: Is This the Future of Religion in Britain?', *Social Compass* 37 (4): 455–69.

Davie, G. (2016), 'Afterword: The Big Picture', in A.-S. Lind, M. Lövheim and U. Zackariasson (eds), *Reconsidering Religion, Law, and Democracy: New Challenges for Society and Research*, 255–64, Lund: Nordic Academic Press.

Dencik, L. (2006), *Judendom i Sverige. En sociologisk belysning*, Uppsala: Swedish Science Press.

Deniz, F. (1999), *En minoritets odyssé: Upprätthållande och transformation av etnisk identitet i förhållande till moderniseringsprocesser: det assyriska exemplet*, Uppsala: Uppsala University.

Department of Cross-Cultural and Regional Studies (n.d.), 'Complexity and Beyond in Studies of Religiosity in the Nordic Countries (CBSR)', University of Copenhagen, https://ccrs.ku.dk/research/centres-and-projects/complexity-and-beyond-in-stud ies-of-religiosity-in-the-nordic-countries/ (accessed 17 April 2023).

Engel, C. (2006), *Svenska kyrkans sociala arbete – för vem och varför? En religionssociologisk studie av ett diakonalt dilemma*. Stockholm: Ersta Sköndal högskola, 26.

Enstedt, D., and K. Plank, eds (2018), *Levd religion: Det heliga i vardagen*, Lund: Nordic Academic Press.

Frisk, L. (1993), *Nya religiösa rörelser i Sverige: Relation till samhället/världen, anslutning och engagemang*, Åbo: Åbo Akademy.

Frisk, L. (1998), *Nyreligiositet i Sverige: Ett religionsvetenskapligt perspektiv*, Örebro: Nya Doxa.

Frohm, K. (1995), *Livsstil eller Organisation. En studie av några kristna gemenskapsgrupper i 1980-talet Sverige*, Lund: Lund University.

Furseth, I., ed. (2018), *Religious Complexity in the Public Sphere – Comparing Nordic Countries*, Basingstoke: Palgrave MacMillian.

Gelfgren, S. (2003), *Ett utvalt släkte: väckelse och sekularisering. Evangeliska fosterlands- stiftelsen 1856–1910*, Umeå: Umeå University.

Gelfgren, S. (2012), '"Let There Be Digital Networks and God Will Provide Growth?": Comparing Aims and Hopes of 19th Century and Post Millennial Christianity', in P. Cheong, C. Ess, S. Gelfgren and P. Fisher-Nielsen (eds), *Digital Religion, Social Media and Culture: Perspectives, Practices and Futures*, 227–42, New York: Peter Lang.

Gustafsson, B. (1965), *Religionssociologi*, Scandinavian University Books, Stockholm: Svenska bokförlaget, Bonniers.

Gustafsson, G. (1985), *Religiös förändring i Norden 1930–1980*, Malmö: Liber förlag.

Gustafsson, G. (1987), 'Religious Change in the Five Nordic Countries 1930–1980', *Comparative Social Research* 10: 145–81.

Gustafsson, G. (1990), *Förkunnarna, församlingarna och Bibeln*, Örebro: Libris.

Gustafsson, G. (1994), 'Marknadsutbudet bestämmer den religiösa aktiviteten. En religionssociologisk teori för 1990-talet?', in J. Straarup (ed.), *Perspektiv på Svenska kyrkans statistik 1993*, 29–52, Uppsala: Svenska kyrkans forskningsråd.

Gustafsson, G. (1995), 'Svenska folket, Estonia och religionen', in *Två undersökningar om Estonia och religionen*, Lund: Religionssociologiska studier.

Gustafsson, G. (1997), *Tro samfund och samhälle. Sociologiska perspektiv*, Örebro: Libris.
Gustafsson, G. (2003), *När det sociala kapitalet växlas in. Om begravningar och deltagandet i begravningar*, Lund: Centrum för teologi och religionsvetenskap, Lunds universitet.
Gustafsson, G. (2013), *Religionssociologiska Intsitutets publikationer*, Lund: Lunds Studies in Sociology of Religion.
Habermas, J. (2006), 'Religion in the Public Sphere', *European Journal of Philosophy* 14 (1): 1–25.
Hamberg, E. (1990), *Studies in the Prevalence of Religious Beliefs and Religious Practice in Contemporary Sweden*, Uppsala: Acta Universitatis Upsaliensis. Psychologia et Sociologia Religionum.
Hamberg, E. (2000), *Livsåskådningar religion och värderingar i en invandrargrupp. En studie av sverigeungrare*, CEIFOs skriftserie, nr 85, Stockholm: CEIFO.
Hamberg, E., and T. Pettersson (1994), 'The Religious Market: Denominational Competition and Religious Participation in Contemporary Sweden', *Journal for the Scientific Study of Religion* 33: 205–16.
Hamberg, E., and T. Pettersson (1997), 'Short-Term Changes in Religious Supply and Church Attendance in Contemporary Sweden', *Journal for the Scientific Study of Religion* 8: 35–51.
Hammarström, G., and H. Ekerwald (2022), 'Avhandlingar for doktorsexamen, 1969–2022', in G. Hammarström and H. Ekerwald (eds), *Sociologiska institutionen vid Uppsala universitet 75 år, 1947–2022*, 150–9, Uppsala: Uppsala universitet.
Hammarström, P. (2007), *Nationens styvbarn: judisk samhällsintegration i några Norrlandsstäder 1870–1940*, Stockholm: Carlsson.
Hoeg, I. M., L. Kühle, M. Nordin and H. Reintoft Christensen (2019), 'Rooms of Silence at Three Universities in Scandinavia', *Sociology of Religion: A Quarterly Review* 80 (3): 299–322.
Ilicki, J. (1988), *Den föränderliga identiteten. Om identitetsförändringar hos den yngre generationen polska judar som invandrade till Sverige under åren 1968–1972*, Åbo: Sällskapet för judaistisk forskning.
Jarnkvist, K. (2011), *När jag gifter mig ska jag göra det på riktigt. Berättelser om barn, brudar och bröllop*, Umeå: Umeå idé och samhällstudier
Jarnkvist, K. (2021), 'Using Intersectional Perspectives in the Studies of Non-Religion Ritualization', *Religions* 12 (1), https://doi.org/10.3390/rel12010002.
Jeffner, A. (1988), *Livsåskådningar i Sverige. Inledande projektpresentation och översiktlig resultatredovisning*, Uppsala: Rapport från Teologiska institutionen, Uppsala universitet.
Jensdotter, L. (2021), *Religion och politik i hybrida mediemiljöer. En analys av kommentarer till nyheter om Miljöpartiet, Kristdemokraterna och Sverigedemokraterna på Facebook*, Uppsala: Acta Universitatis Upsaliensis: Studies in Religion & Society.
Kardemark, W. (2012), *När livet tar rätt form: om människosyn i svenska hälsotidskrifter 1910–13 och 2009*, Göteborg: University of Gothenburg.
Karlsson Minganti, P. (2007), *Muslima: Islamisk väckelse och unga muslimska kvinnors förhandlingar om genus i det samtida Sverige*, Stockholm: Carlssons bokförlag.
Klingenberg, M. (2019), 'Youth and Religion in Sweden: Orientations to Religion amongst "Believers," "Atheists" and "the Uninterested" ', *Nordic Journal of Religion and Society* 32 (2): 148–67.
Klingenberg, M., and M. Lövheim (2019), *Unga och Religion. Troende, ointresserade eller neutrala?*, Malmö: Gleerups förlag.

Klingenberg, M., and S. Sjö (2019), 'Theorizing Religious Socialization: A Critical Assessment', *Religion* 2: 163–78.

Larsson, G. (2011), *Muslims and the New Media: Historical and Contemporary Debates*, London: Routledge.

Leis-Peters, A. (2004), *Den kyrkliga diakonins roll inom ramen för två välfärdssystem. En jämförande fallstudie av två diakoniinstitutioner i Sverige och Tyskland*, Uppsala: Diakonivetenskapliga institutets skriftserie.

Liedgren Dobronravoff, P. (2007), *Att bli, att vara och att ha varit – om ingångar i och utgångar ur Jehovas vittnen i Sverige*, Lund: Lund University.

Lindberg, J. (2015), *Religion in Nordic Politics as a Means to Social Cohesion: An Empirical Study on Party Platforms and Parliamentary Debates 1988–2012*, Uppsala: Acta Universitatis Upsaliensis: Studies in Religion & Society.

Linderman, A. G. (1993), *Religious Broadcasting in the United States and Sweden. A Comparative Analysis of the History of Religious Broadcasting with Emphasis on Religious Television*, Licentiate dissertation, Lund: Lund University.

Linderman, A., and M. Lövheim (2016), 'Measuring Resurgence of Religion? Methodological Considerations in a Study of Swedish Editorials', *Nordicom Review* 37: 101–14.

Lundberg, A. P. (2005), *Om gemenskap. En sociologisk betraktelse*, Lund: Lund University.

Lundgren, L. (2021), *A Risk or a Resource? A Study of the Swedish State's Shifting Perception and Handling of Minority Religious Communities between 1952–2019*, Stockholm: Ersta Sköndal Bräcke högskola.

Löfstedt, M., and A. Sjöborg (2020), 'Tolerance and Criticism within Religious Education', in M. Lövheim and M. Stenmark (eds), *A Constructive Critique of Religion: Encounters between Christianity, Islam, and Non-religion in Secular Societies*, 135–47, London: Bloomsbury Academic.

Lövheim. M. (2004), *Intersecting Identities: Young People, Religion and Interaction on the Internet*, Uppsala: Uppsala University: Department of Theology.

Lövheim, M., and J. Bromander, eds (2012), *Religion som resurs? Existentiella frågor och värderingar i unga svenskars liv*, Skellefteå: Artos & Norma.

Lövheim, M., ed. (2013), *Media, Religion and Gender: Key Issues and New Challenges*, London: Routledge.

Lövheim, M. (2014), 'Mediatization and Religion', in K. Lundby (ed.), *Mediatization of Communication*, 547–71, Berlin: De Gruyter Mounton.

Lövheim, M., J. Lindberg, P. K. Botvar, H. Reintoft Christensen, K. Niemelä and A. Bäckström (2018), 'Religion on the Political Agenda', in I. Furseth (ed.), *Religious Complexity in the Public Sphere – Comparing Nordic Countries*, 137–91, Basingstoke: Palgrave MacMillian.

Lövheim, M. (2019), '"The Swedish Condition": Representations of Religion in the Swedish Press 1988–2018', *Temenos* 55 (2): 271–92.

Lövheim, M., and M. Nordin, eds (2022), *Sociologiska perspektiv på religion i Sverige*, 2nd edn, Malmö: Gleerups.

Löwendahl, L. (2002), *Med kroppen som instrument. En studie an new age med focus på hälsa, kroppslighet och genus*, Lund: Lund University.

Lund Liebmann, L., M. Nordin and L. Paulsen Galal (2018), 'Routes and Relations in Scandinavian Interfaith Forums: Governance of Religious Diversity by States and Majority Churches', *Social Compass* 65 (3): 329–45.

Lundby, K., ed. (2018), *Contesting Religion: The Media Dynamics of Cultural Conflicts in Scandinavia*, Berlin: De Gruyter.

Lundmark, E. (2019),'This Is the Face of an Atheist': Performing Private Truths in Precarious Publics, Uppsala: Uppsala University: Department of Theology.
Månsson, A. (2002), Becoming Muslim: Meanings of Conversion to Islam, Lund: Lund University.
Middlemiss LéMon, M. (2009), The In-Between Church: A Study of the Church of England's Role in Society through the Prism of Welfare, Uppsala: Uppsala: Acta Universitatis Upsaliensis.
Middlemiss LéMon, M., M. Nordin and M. Broo, eds (2023), 'Funerals in the North of Europe: Similarities and Differences', Approaching Religion 13 (1): 1–4.
Moberg, J. (2013), Piety, Intimacy and Mobility: A Case Study of Charismatic Christianity in Present-Day Stockholm, Stockholm: Huddinge: Södertörn högskola.
Mosbach, V. (2022), Voices of Muslim Feminists: Navigating Tradition, Authority and the Debate about Islam, Uppsala: Acta Universitatis Upsaliensis: Studies in Religion & Society.
Näsström, B.-M. (2013), 'Religionsvetenskap (1973–2002)', in Personliga tillbakablickar över ämnesområden vid Göteborgs universitet, 54–6, Göteborg: Göteborgs universitet.
Nilsson, S. (2019), Performing Perfectly: Presentations of Childhood in Knutby Filadelfia before and after the Dissolution of the Congregation, Göteborg: University of Gothenburg.
Nordin, M. (2004), Religiositet bland migranter. Sverige-chilenares förhållande till religion och samfund, Lund: Lund Studies in Sociology of Religion, Lund University.
Nordin, M. (2013), 'Religion och migration', in B. Petersson and C. Johansson (eds), IMER idag, 112–33, Stockholm: Liber.
Nordin, M. (2018), 'Blurred Religion in Contemporary Sweden – Health Care Institutions as an Empirical Example', Journal of Religion in Europe 11 (2–3): 161–85.
Nordin, M. (2020), 'How to Understand Interreligious Dialogue in Sweden in Relation to the Socio-Cultural Context', Interdisciplinary Journal for Religion and Transformation in Contemporary Society 6 (2): 429–47.
Nordin, M. (2021), 'Institutets tidiga studier av "religiösa organisationer bland invandrare"', in C. Dahlgren (ed.), Religionssociologisk mångfald. Texter till minne av Berndt Gustafsson, grundare av religionssociologi i Sverige, Lunds Studies in Sociology of Religion, vol. 13, 107–26, Lund: Lund University.
Nordin, M. (2023a), Kunskapsöversikt om migration, religion och integration, Stockholm: DELMI.
Nordin, M. (2023), 'Family and the Transmission of Traditions in the Syriac Orthodox Church in Sweden', Nordic Journal of Religion and Society 36 (1): 19–32.
Nordin, M., and J. Otterbeck (2023), Migration and Religion, IMISCOE Short Readers, Springer, https://doi.org/10.1007/978-3-031-30766-9.
Nordin, M., and A. Westergren (2023), 'Veiled Integration: The Use of Headscarves among a Christian Minority in Sweden', International Journal of Religion 4 (1): 3–18.
Ohlsson, G. (2012), Från ämbetsman till ämbetsbärare. Förändringar speglade i anmälningar mot präster under tre brytningstider, Lunds Studies in Sociology of Religion, vol 11, Lund: Lund universitet.
Otterbeck, J. (2010), Samtidsislam. Unga muslimer i Malmö och Köpenhamn, Stockholm: Carlsson.
Palm, I. (1982), Frikyrkorna, arbetarfrågan och klasskampen. Frikyrkorörelsens hållning till arbetarnas fackliga och politiska kamp åren kring sekelskiftet, Uppsala: Uppsala University.

Pettersson, P. (1995), *Svenska kyrkan och Estonia-katastrofen, Redovisning av externt och internt utvärderingsarbete*, Karlstad: Karlstads universitet: Fakulteten för ekonomi, kommunikation och IT, Centrum för tjänsteforskning.
Pettersson, P. (2000), *Kvalitet i livslånga tjänsterelationer. Svenska kyrkan ur tjänsteteoretiskt och religionssociologiskt perspektiv*, Stockholm: Verbum.
Pettersson, T. (1988), 'Swedish Church Statistics: Unique data for Sociological Research', *Social Compass* 35: 15–31.
Pettersson, T., and G. Gustafsson (1990), *Församlingsstrategier och den kyrkliga sedens styrka. En rapport från projektet Kyrkolivsanalys*, Stockholm: Religionssociologiska Institutet.
Pettersson, T. (1994), 'Culture Shift and Generational Population Replacement: Individualism, Secularization and Moral Value Change in Contemporary Scandinavia', in T. Pettersson and O. Riis (eds), *Scandinavian Values. Religion and Morality in the Nordic Countries*, 197–212, Uppsala: Acta Universitatis Upsaliensis, Psychologia et Sociologia Religionum.
Pettersson, T., and L. Halman (2002), 'Moral Pluralism in Contemporary Europe: Evidence from the Project Religious and Moral Pluralism (RAMP)', *Research in the Social Scientific Study of Religion* 13: 173–204.
Poveda, O. (2017), *According to Whose Will: The Entanglements of Gender & Religion in the Lives of Transgender Jews with an Orthodox Background*, Uppsala: Acta Universitatis Upsaliensis: Studies in Religion & Society.
Puranen, B. (2019), *Med migranters röst. Den subjektiva integrationen*, Forskningsrapport 2019/2, Stockholm: Institutet för framtidsstudier.
Reimers, E. (1995), *Dopet som kult och kultur: bilder av dopet I dopsamtal och föräldraintervjuer*, Stockholm: Verbum.
Rosenius, M. (2015), *Svenska kyrkan samma kyrka? Ecklesiologi före och efter relationsförändringarna mellan kyrka och stat*, Umeå: Umeå University, Idé- och samhällsstudier.
Rubin, L. (2000), *Engagemang i Lutherhjälpen. Studier av motiv och drivkrafter hos frivilliga aktiva*, Lund: Lund University.
Sjöborg, A. (2006), *Bibeln på mina egna villkor. En studie av medierade kontakter med bibeln med särskilt avseende på ungdomar*, Uppsala: Acta Universitatis Upsaliensis. Psychologia et Sociologia Religionum.
Sjödin, D. (2011), *Tryggare kan ingen vara. Migration, religion och integration i en segregerad omgivning*, Lund: Lund University.
Sjölin, I. (1999), *Dopsed i förändring. Studier av Örebro pastorat 1710–1910*, Lund: Lund University.
Skog, M., ed. (1976), *Berndt Gustafsson-Forskare och visionär*, Stockholm: Propius.
SOU 1963:26 (1963), *Religionens betydelse som samhällsfaktor: Möjligheter och metoder för en sociologisk undersökning*, Stockholm: AB Wilhelmssons Boktryckeri.
Straarup, J., and M. Ekberg (2012), *Den sorglöst försumliga kyrkan. Belyst norrifrån*, Skellefteå: Artos & Norma bokförlag.
Sundqvist, J. (2017), *Beyond an Instrumental Approach to Religion and Development: Challenges for Church-Based Healthcare in Tanzania*, Uppsala: Acta Universitatis Upsaliensis: Studies in Religion & Society.
Thurfjell, D., and E. Willander (2021), 'Muslims by Ascription: On Post-Lutheran Secularity and Muslim Immigrants', *Numen* 68 (4): 307–35.
Willander, E. (2014), *What Counts as Religion in Sociology? The Problem of Religiosity in Sociological Methodology*, Uppsala: Uppsala University.

Winell, A. (2016), *'Godis för kropp och själ'. Välbefinnande och vardagsandlighet i tre svenska kvinnotidningar*, Uppsala: Acta Universitatis Upsaliensis: Studies in Religion & Society.

Wrammert, A. (2021), *Med(ie)vetenhet, motstånd och engagemang: Gymnasieungdomars tal om och erfarenheter av religion*, Uppsala: Acta Universitatis Upsaliensis: Studies in Religion and Society.

Chapter 11

THE COGNITIVE SCIENCE OF RELIGION

Jonas Svensson and Egil Asprem

The cognitive science of religion (CSR) has become an increasingly established part of the international religious studies landscape. In this chapter, we present and discuss the hitherto quite limited presence of CSR in the Swedish religious studies context.

To situate our discussion in a broader perspective, a brief chronology of CSR is warranted. The so-called cognitive revolution first began as a reaction against behaviourism in the 1950s, particularly in linguistics and psychology (Miller 2003). The reaction was premised on the notion that the human mind is neither an impenetrable black box, about which nothing meaningful can be said, nor a passive blank slate, upon which culture is written. Instead, humans come equipped with specific capacities that shape how they sense, perceive, feel and ultimately think about the world and about themselves and other people. Moreover, these capacities, or modules, are the products of evolution by natural selection. Through the second half of the twentieth century, this view had repercussions in fields ranging from psychology and linguistics to philosophy and anthropology (Miller 2003).

The cognitive science of religion is a late child of this development. Akin to cognitive turns in other fields, it is interested in how the rapidly increasing knowledge about the nuts and bolts of human cognition, that is to say, how the human mind processes information and the consequences of such processing in terms of recurring patterns in human behaviour, can help us explain aspects of those cultural phenomena we tend to classify as 'religion'. As such, CSR scholars have addressed most aspects that other branches of religious studies are interested in, including the emergence and persistence of beliefs in superhuman agents, ritual, practice, morality and ethics, emotions and experience, social cohesion, cooperation, group identity and violence, but have sought to ground these aspects in evolved cognitive traits that are common to the species. Often, this has meant a focus on how religious phenomena exploit traits that had evolved for quite different purposes – in other words, religion is seen as a by-product of evolution rather than an adaptive phenomenon in its own right.

The pioneers of CSR were, to a large extent, anthropologists (such as Stewart Guthrie, Dan Sperber, Pascal Boyer, Harvey Whitehouse and Scott Atran), religious studies scholars (E. Thomas Lawson, Luther H. Martin and Armin Geertz) and philosophers (Robert McCauley). Only a few of the early contributors were trained in psychology (e.g. Justin Barrett and Jesse Bering). More recently, however, CSR has started to attract and train scholars with a solid footing in experimental psychology or cognitive neuroscience on a larger scale.

In a simplified manner, we may divide the development of CSR into three phases. The first phase of *pioneering* includes foundational works by the likes of Stewart Guthrie (e.g. Guthrie 1992) and E. Thomas Lawson and Robert McCauley (e.g. Lawson and McCauley 1990), among others. Lawson and McCauley's *Rethinking Religion: Connecting Cognition and Culture* in particular was a programmatic call for complementing interpretative approaches with explanatory ones and for grounding the study of religion in the study of the mind as a culture-creating capacity.

A second phase of *consolidation* began around the year 2000, marked by the appearance of high-profile publications directed at a wider audience, such as Boyer's *Religion Explained* (2001), Atran's *In Gods We Trust* (2002), Barrett's *Why Would Anyone Believe in God* (2004) and Whitehouse's *Modes of Religiosity* (2004), and a push towards institutionalization through the founding of journals and scholarly societies. The *Journal of Cognition and Culture* was launched in 2001 (with Lawson and Boyer as editors), and the International Association for the Cognitive Science of Religion, IACSR, was founded in 2006. The cognitive science of religion had by this time gained a clear theoretical grounding in evolutionary psychology and memory research, which was reflected in central concepts such as those of minimal counter-intuitiveness (MCI theory), the hyperactive agency detection device (HADD) and Theory of Mind or mentalization.

After 2010, and a much-debated convention by the International Association for the Study of the History of Religions in Toronto where CSR was heavily represented, a third phase of *maturation* began. This was characterized by tighter interdisciplinary collaborations with trained psychologists and cognitive neuroscientists, an emphasis on experimental testing and critique of earlier theories and hypotheses, renewed attention to questions about religion, cooperation, violence and identity (e.g. Norenzayan 2013), and the integration of explanatory frameworks that are grounded more in the philosophy of mind (e.g. embodied cognition, enactivism) and cognitive neuroscience (e.g. predictive processing) than in evolutionary psychology. New journals like *Religion, Brain and Behavior* (est. 2011) have been crucial to this development.

Viewed from Sweden, it is noteworthy that the Religion, Cognition and Culture Unit at Aarhus University in Denmark was also instrumental in this third phase. Notably, Armin Geertz has criticized not only 'neurotheology' (2009) but also earlier 'mentalistic' CSR models as well (2010), calling for a robust biocultural theory of religion as embrained, embodied, encultured and enacted. Researchers at the centre have contributed to incorporating cognitive neuroscience in fruitful ways in CSR and developing new experimental paradigms (e.g. Andersen et al.

2014, 2017; Schjødt et al. 2011). The centre has been particularly important in embracing and developing the theoretical framework of predictive processing (cf. Schjødt 2019).

CSR in Sweden: Slow on the Uptake, Gradually Gaining Momentum

It is easy to conclude that CSR never took hold in Sweden and Norway like it did in Denmark, or for that matter Finland, which can boast of CSR scholarship like that of Ilkka Pyysiäinen (2001). Instead, it is perhaps noteworthy that one of the most thorough *critiques* of CSR in an international context was produced by Professor Håkan Rydving (2008), a Swedish historian of religion based in Norway.

Since we are dealing with small fields in countries with small population sizes, it may be pointless to seek explanations of this difference, which might be coincidental. Nevertheless, we offer a few speculations as to why CSR has been a tough sell in the Swedish religious studies context.

First, we note the internal disciplinary divisions in the study of religion in Sweden, particularly between the History of Religions (*religionshistoria*) and the broader religious studies (*religionsvetenskap*), which includes behavioural science approaches, and (although this is under vigorous and continuous debate) theology. The former has historically pioneered the non-confessional, *humanistic* study of religion, defending its identity against both theology and social and behavioural science approaches. The cognitive science of religion, with its affiliations with experimental psychology and the natural sciences (particularly perspectives from evolutionary science), may have appeared suspect as both a form of non-humanistic scientism (e.g. going against a well-established norm of anti-reductionism) and, with its claims to general relevance, a form of crypto-theology, promoting essentialist, universalist and specifically Western notions of religion. Indeed, Rydving's 2008 critique focused both on CSR's claims to being 'scientific' and its perceived naturalization and generalization of a culture-specific 'Western folk category' (i.e. 'religion').

Second, psychology of religion has long been a well-established branch of *religionsvetenskap* in Sweden, with dedicated chairs at Lund, Uppsala and Umeå (see Chapter 9 of this volume). Because of its focus on the human mind, CSR may have been seen as a competitor, or as a superfluous and even misguided newcomer, with its apparent focus on the strictly cognitive dimension of human psychology. Moreover, CSR's generalistic, explanatory approach and reliance on the results from experimental research do not rhyme well with a preference in the Swedish tradition of psychology of religion for individual case studies, diversity of religious experience, mental health, mysticism and humanistic, interpretive approaches focusing individual meaning making. For such approaches, the classical works of William James (1842–1910) or the psychoanalytic and psychodynamic tradition remained a better fit.

However, it should be noted that even in the history of psychology of religion in Sweden, there have been examples of perspectives that came close to prefiguring a

CSR approach. Most notably, perhaps, are some of the works of its first professor, Hjalmar Sundén (1908–1993) (see Lindgren 2014). Sundén's greatest 'claim to fame', the so-called role theory, addresses the issue of the constructive role of basic mechanisms of the mind for human perception, a main theme in CSR, asking the basic question of how religion is psychologically possible (Sundén 1966). In the introductory essay to his published collection *Älgskyttar och exegeter* (Moose Hunters and Exegetes) entitled 'Varseblivning och religiös erfarenhet' ('Perception and Religious Experience'), Sundén addressed the role of even more basic structures of the human mind in perception, regardless of internalized cultural beliefs, otherwise a central theme in his role theory (Sundén 1969). However, he did not pursue this line of thought any further.

Regardless of the history, one can note that there have been clear signs of change during the last decade and a half. The steps taken have been small, and much of the output has appeared in Swedish and transmitted through academically less prestigious channels.

The first signs of this shift can be seen in the inclusion of CSR in two textbooks for undergraduate students, both published in 2010. The Open Access textbook, *Människor och makter 2.0* (Humans and Powers 2.0, 2010), edited by Stefan Arvidsson and Jonas Svensson, included a chapter on cognitive theories of religion (Olsson 2010). Olav Hammer and Jesper Sørensen's (2010) textbook, *Religion i människors medvetande och samhälle* (Religion in Human Minds and Society), devoted half of the text matter to CSR. In its 2017 revised edition, the dominant Swedish handbook on psychology of religion, *Den religiösa människan* (The Religious Human) (Geels and Wikström 2017), included three new chapters clearly connected to research within CSR: on evolutionary psychology (Lindgren 2017), moral psychology (Svensson 2017) and on CSR as such (Geels 2017). More recently, a new textbook on theory and method in the History of Religions (*Religionshistoria. En introduktion till teori och metod*) (Asprem and Sundqvist 2021) included a chapter on CSR (Asprem 2021). This textbook did not include any chapter on psychology of religion, which is particularly noteworthy. In a 2016 national symposium for the Swedish Association for the History of Religion (SSRF), a question posed in one of the panels was 'Has CSR made the psychology of religion obsolete?'.

One can also note a growing presence of CSR in scholarly works directed at the general public. A 2016 collection of essays entitled *Varför finns religion* (Why Is There Religion?) included two chapters providing answers to that question from CSR (Svensson 2016) and evolutionary theory (Lindenfors 2016), respectively. A more recent, general introduction to the concept 'religion' devoted roughly a quarter of the text matter to key theoretical insights and concepts taken from CSR (Larsson and Sorgenfrei 2019).

There have also, during the last decade, been some efforts towards establishing new networks for a slowly growing number of scholars of religion, including PhD students, interested in CSR approaches. In 2018, Jonas Svensson, Göran Larsson and Andreas Nordin arranged a workshop in Växjö with Ann Taves and her collaborator Egil Asprem (who had relocated to Sweden from the US in 2016), focused on the building-block approach to religion, which explicitly addresses the problem of combining humanistic with science-based research (for the resulting publication, see Larsson, Svensson and Nordin 2020). In 2019, the Nordic Network for the Cognitive Science of Religion held a conference in Stockholm organized by Asprem and Ingela Visuri, proving particularly attractive to PhD candidates in Sweden and Finland. This was the first time the NNCSR met outside Aarhus.

Some Contemporary Examples

Given the fact that the cognitive science of religion has a short history, and an even shorter one in Swedish academia, we have perhaps a simpler task than our colleagues writing other chapters in this volume. We do not have to summarize a long history of an academic discipline, and we have room to cover the works of most of the relatively few scholars in Sweden that have taken an interest in the field. A somewhat delicate problem, however, is that we both are part of this small group and are in the less enviable situation of having to write about our own work from a third-person perspective.

While it is generally true, as stated above, that it is only in the last decade that CSR has had any noticeable impact on the study of religions in Sweden, there are noticeable exceptions.

In his dissertation *Behaving as a Christ-Believer: A Cognitive Perspective on Identity and Behavior Norms in Ephesians* (2009; revised edition published in 2021) New Testament scholar Rikard Roitto explored the potential of a theoretical CSR perspective to provide insight into the norms, behaviours and social identity of early Christian communities, with a case study of the first-century Christ believers in Ephesos. Citing key researchers from the first and second phases of the development of CSR, Roitto sided with a tendency within biblical studies of theoretical expansion into this field in the first half of the 2000s. Even earlier, Peter J. Södergård's dissertation in the History of Religions in Uppsala, *The Hermetic Piety of the Mind: A Semiotic and Cognitive Study of the Discourse of Hermes Trismegistos* (2003), pursued the somewhat less-trodden path within CSR of cognitive linguistics, drawing on conceptual blending and cognitive metaphor theory (but cf. Sørensen 2006).

Theologian Lotta Knutson Bråkenhielm published her dissertation *Religion – evolutionens missfoster eller kärleksbarn* (Religion – the Freak Child or (Illegitimate) Love Child of Evolution) in 2016, in which she provided a detailed outline of some of the main themes within CSR in its first two phases as described above. Citing Barrett, Atran, Boyer and Bering, the focus was on the 'religion as a natural by-product of evolution' hypothesis in CSR. Thematically, it focused on the aspect of religious beliefs rather than ritual and social organization.

The dissertation was defended as a work of philosophy of religion at a theological faculty. The aspect of CSR that it addressed was also one that had appeared particularly problematic for this branch of academia, namely that it reduces, and even explains away, religion through providing naturalistic explanations for certain types of beliefs and practices. On the proximate level, these beliefs and practices are nothing but by-products of how the human mind in general works. On a distant level, they are the result of a long process of evolution of the human mental apparatus by natural selection. According to Bråkenhielm, this theory poses a real problem for theism and notions of a personal godhead with intentions, active in the unfolding of events in the world. Bråkenhielm's theological goal is to search for and construct a rationally more tenable image of the divine (presumably in a theistic, perhaps even limited, Christian context), which eventually turns out to be a deistic notion of 'something', an abstract and distant god. Such an image of the divine, incidentally much in line with the Church of Sweden, becomes the only option compatible with the critical scrutiny, and reductionism, of CSR.

From the perspective of someone less concerned with the theological implications of CSR and more with its value as an analytical tool for the study of Islam, one of the authors of the current chapter, Jonas Svensson, published the book *Människans Muhammad* in 2015. The main objective was, as in the case of Bråkenhielm, to introduce aspects of CSR more generally into the study of religion in Sweden. This was done by applying a CSR framework to a specific theme: Muslim perceptions of Prophet Muhammad and the consequences of such perceptions in the development of dogma, rituals and social organization throughout history.

The method used in the book was to isolate what previous research had identified as phenomena in need of explanation, and exploring to what extent recent theoretical claims within CSR could offer such explanations. Basically, it involved substituting previous references to human 'beliefs', 'intentions', 'strategies' and 'needs' as causal forces in relation to the phenomena under study, with the concept of pan-human psychological 'proclivities' and their cumulative cultural effects. A similar approach has been applied by Svensson in several publications before and after *Människans Muhammed*, using a CSR framework and addressing, for example, Muslim discourses on HIV/AIDS, the cult of relics, Salafism, Qur'an desecration and religious violence in the wake of reactions to caricatures images of Muhammad (see e.g. Svensson 2014, 2018, 2021).

The other author of this chapter, Egil Asprem, has not only applied existing CSR theories to problems in his area of specialization but also contributed to new theoretical developments in line with the third phase of CSR discussed above. A central aspect of his work, developed together with the American scholar Ann Taves, has been the so-called building-block approach to the study of religion (e.g. Taves 2009; Taves and Asprem 2020). Religion is seen as a complex cultural concept that mobilizes various aspects of human cognition and psychology. With Taves, Asprem has applied this approach to the study of 'religious experience', the study of experience narratives in texts and the concept of 'worldviews' (Asprem and Taves 2021; Taves and Asprem 2017; Taves, Asprem and Ihm 2018).

In single-authored work, Asprem has applied CSR perspectives to the study of esotericism and new religious movements. In a metatheoretical article (Asprem 2016a), he argued that the study of esotericism is primarily concerned with practices focused on 'knowledge deemed special', identifying five definitional clusters in the literature which, in turn, can be broken down and approached in terms of three types of basic processes (building blocks) having to do with metarepresentations, (ritual) actions and event cognition. In more applied work, he has used MCI theory to explain the selective use of scientific representations in new religious contexts (Asprem 2016b) and has contributed to explaining the use of the imagination in esoteric practices by drawing on predictive processing, a central theory in the third phase of CSR (Asprem 2017).

In 2019, Ingela Visuri presented her thesis on religious experiences, beliefs and practices among young Swedes diagnosed with non-neurotypical disorders on the autism spectrum, aspects of which were soon after published in the leading journal *Religion, Brain & Behavior* (Visuri 2020a). The research relates to a longer discussion within CSR concerning autism and religious belief, based on the assumption that defective functioning of the ability for 'mentalisation', or Theory of Mind, among people on the autism spectrum would result in certain groups of people being less prone to hold beliefs concerning culturally postulated superhuman agents with intentions.

Visuri's findings, arrived at through a series of qualitative research interventions, shows a need for nuancing previous assumptions and experimental results. A general assumption that people with high-functioning autism would be less prone than others to construct mental images of invisible, but active, agents does not find support in her material. In fact, it turned out that Visuri's informants had vivid inner worlds populated by imaginary actors, which they also found less problematic to interact with than other, social actors whose body language as well as minds must be interpreted. The imaginary worlds, and their inhabitants, constructed by the informants, often built upon contemporary pop-cultural input (film, videogames, etc.) and served as a coping strategy, a way to construct and entertain 'parasocial' relationships, for persons for whom everyday social relationships are difficult to navigate and uphold (Visuri 2019, 2020a,b).

Visuri convincingly argues that the methodologies hitherto used to evaluate the impact of cognitive disorders on religiosity, mainly autism, have been blind to inbuilt biases in the neurotypical control group, answering questions in vignettes in a way that was influenced by a desire to not deviate from the socially acceptable, a bias not present in the target group. Visuri thus also advocates for the importance of qualitative research methods in CSR.

While CSR cannot be said to have had a large influence on psychology of religion in Sweden as a discipline, there are exceptions. Tomas Lindgren, Professor in Psychology of Religion at Umeå University, has repeatedly, over the last two decades, attached his own research to key concepts and key theoretical takes within CSR with a particular orientation to social psychology and evolutionary psychology. His primary area of research, religiously motivated violence and non-violence, does enter into dialogue with key researchers in CSR, including scholars such as Atran and Boyer (e.g. Lindgren and Sonnenschein 2021). More importantly, Lindgren has questioned the assumption in studies of religion and violence that religious beliefs are a causal factor in certain violent actions performed by individuals and groups, citing the well-researched human tendency towards post-rationalization of both their own behaviour and the behaviour of others, a key theme in the strand within CSR that adhere to the by-product notion of religious phenomena (see also Chapter 17 in this volume on religion and violence). As mentioned above, Lindgren is also one of the few scholars of religious studies in Sweden who has tried to integrate evolutionary psychology in his own work. The forthcoming revision of his 2009 book *Fundamentalism och helig terror* will, in his own words, contain a 'substantial updating' of the CSR and evolutionary-psychological perspectives.

It should be noted that while the focus here is on CSR within different branches of the study of religions, there are researchers with other academic affiliations that have also been part of the development in recent decades. These include internationally renowned psychologist Pehr Granqvist, who also acted as Visuri's co-advisor. A specialist on attachment, his thorough research on an evolved human attachment bias and its cultural effects on religious beliefs and practices in different religions is an important contribution to CSR research and its basic assumptions: that human beings possess (evolved) mental capacities and proclivities that can causally account for cultural phenomena usually studied by researchers under the umbrella term 'religion' (for recent examples, see Cherniak et al. 2021 and Granqvist 2020, 2023).

Another researcher, formally outside religious studies proper, but at the same time one of the more persistent champions of CSR in Sweden, is anthropologist Andreas Nordin. Nordin has meticulously striven to apply core concepts of CSR to material gathered primarily (but not exclusively) through field work on religious beliefs, experiences and practices among Nepalese Hindus. In this, he has contributed, also from an international perspective, with a much welcome cross-cultural, empirical exploration of the usefulness of the CSR framework outside of a WEIRD (Western, Educated, Industrialized, Rich and Democratic) context.

In his dissertation at the University of Gothenburg from 2006, Nordin applies a series of theoretical concepts and explanatory frameworks from CSR on a particular cultural phenomenon: pilgrimages to Hindu sacred places in the Nepalese Himalayas, with material gathered through extensive fieldwork. This empirical focus on Nepal is also kept in a series of later publications. Nordin has applied CSR in an anthropological take on the issue of honour culture, and perceptions of honour, and also to morality in general (e.g. Nordin 2013, 2015). More recently, Nordin has published several works that address the issue of religious dreams and religious dream content from the perspective of CSR, drawing on the notion of counter-intuitiveness (e.g. Nordin and Bjälkebring 2021; Nordin 2023).

Finally, yet another scholar from outside religious studies may be mentioned, the zoologist Patrik Lindenfors, who, mainly in a series of works directed at a general public, has explored human thinking and its role in trajectories of cultural evolution, including the emergence and development of religious beliefs and practices. His latest book, *Äckel* (Disgust) (2023), touches upon recurring themes in CSR, such as the analysis of religious ritual and notions of contagion, religion and sexuality, religious dehumanization and religious conflict.

Although researchers in the study of religions in Sweden have been slow to take up CSR approaches, there are signs, apart from the examples given above, that a change is underway, especially among emerging scholars. In the very recent years, we have witnessed several dissertation projects and completed dissertations that engage with CSR in a productive manner. Among the completed dissertations, we can note philosopher of religion Ingrid Malm Lindberg's *The Multifaceted Role of Imagination in Science and Religion* (2021), which explores the role of structures of human perception, conceptual blending and rituals in processes of imagination. Another recent example is historian of religion Malin Fitger's dissertation, *Själens arkitektur. Subtil anatomi som upplevelse, förkroppsligande och självförståelse, 1875–2020* (2022), studying how concepts such as 'energy' and 'soul' are understood by practitioners of new religious movements, New Age and yoga. The dissertation makes use of conceptual blending theory and, in particular, theories on embodied cognition, much addressed in the third phase of CSR noted above. Finally, Olivia Cejvan's (2023) dissertation, an ethnographic study of educational strategies in an initiatory esoteric order, draws on Asprem's (2017) predictive processing theory of imagination-based practices as one of its tools for explaining how initiates learn to remould their inner worlds. This can be seen as a further sign that CSR perspectives, including home-grown ones, are becoming part of the regular toolkit of historians of religion in Sweden.

Concluding Remarks

As can be noted from the review above, the way in which CSR has been explored by scholars in various sub-branches of the study of religions in Sweden and incorporated in their works is diverse, ranging from Psychology of Religion to philosophy, anthropology, religious education, History of Religions and Islamic studies. Although the number of scholars in Sweden who have taken an active interest in CSR remains small, they display between themselves a diversity of ways of approaching the field, both empirically and methodologically. A noticeable trend is that the development appears to have gone beyond introducing and justifying the use of CSR as a 'new' perspective within the study of religions, to incorporating it as just another means, among others, to bring a deeper understanding of cultural phenomena placed under the umbrella term 'religion'. The lack of undergraduate and graduate courses as well as research units dedicated specifically to CSR remains a challenge to the continued growth of the field. Nevertheless, some of the suspicion that met CSR in the beginning is perhaps, and from our perspective hopefully, fading away.

References

Andersen, M., U. Schjødt, K. L. Nielbo and J. Sørensen (2014), 'Mystical Experience in the Lab', *Method & Theory in the Study of Religion* 26 (3): 217–45.

Andersen, M., T. Pfeiffer, S. Müller and U. Schjoedt (2017), 'Agency Detection in Predictive Minds: A Virtual Reality Study', *Religion, Brain & Behavior* 9 (1): 52–64.

Asprem, E., and O. Sundqvist, eds (2021), *Religionshistoria: en ntroduction till teori och metod*, Lund: Studentlitteratur.

Asprem, E., and A. Taves (2021), 'Event Model Analysis', in S. Engler and M. Stausberg (eds), *Routledge Handbook of Research Methods in the Study of Religion*, 532–41, London: Routledge.

Asprem, E. (2016a), 'Reverse Engineering Esotericism: How to Prepare a Complex Cultural Concept for the Cognitive Science of Religion', *Religion* 46 (2): 158–85.

Asprem, E. (2016b), 'How Schrödinger's Cat Became a Zombie: On the Epidemiology of Science-Based Representations in Popular and Religious Contexts', *Method & Theory in the Study of Religion* 28 (2): 113–40.

Asprem, E. (2017), 'Explaining the Esoteric Imagination: Towards a Theory of Kataphatic Practice', *Aries* 17 (1): 17–50.

Asprem, E. (2021), 'Kognitionsvetenskapliga perspektiv', in E. Asprem and O. Sundqvist (eds), *Religionshistoria: en introduktion till teori och metod*, 121–42, Lund: Studentlitteratur.

Atran, S. (2002), *In Gods We Trust: The Evolutionary Landscape of Religion*, Oxford: Oxford University Press.

Arvidsson, S., and J. Svensson, eds (2010), *Människor och makter 2.0: En ntroduction till religionsvetenskap*, Halmstad, Högskolan I Halmstad.

Barrett, J. L. (2004), *Why Would Anyone Believe in God?*, Walnut Creek: AltaMira Press.

Boyer, P. (2001), *Religion Explained: The Human Instincts That Fashion Gods, Spirits and Ancestors*, London: Vintage.

Cejvan, O. (2023), *Arts and Crafts Divine: Teaching and Learning Ritual Magic in Sodalitas Rosae Crucis*, Lund: Faculty of Theology and Humanities.

Cherniak, A. D., M. Mikulincer, P. R. Shaver and P. Granqvist (2021), 'Attachment Theory and Religion', *Current Opinion in Psychology* 40: 126–30.

Fitger, M. (2022), *Själens arkitektur: Subtil anatomi som upplevelse, förkroppsligande och självförståelse, 1875–2020*, Stockholm: Faculty of Humanities, Stockholm University.

Geels, A. (2017), 'Kognitionsvetenskaplig religionspsykologi', in A. Geels and O. Wikström (eds), *Den religiösa människan*, 537–63, Stockholm: Liber.

Geels, A., and O. Wikström, eds (2017), *Den religiösa människan: Enntroductionn till religionspsykologin*, Stockholm: Natur & kultur.

Geertz, A. W. (2009), 'When Cognitive Scientists Become Religious, Science Is in Trouble: On Neurotheology from a Philosophy of Science Perspective', *Religion* 39 (4): 319–24.

Geertz, A. W. (2010), 'Brain, Body and Culture: A Biocultural Theory of Religion', *Method & Theory in the Study of Religion* 22: 304–21.

Granqvist, P. (2020), *Attachment in Religion and Spirituality: A Wider View*, New York: Guilford Publications.

Granqvist, P. (2023), *Tryggare kan ingen vara? Anknytning, religion, andlighet och sekularitet*, Stockholm: Fri tanke.

Guthrie, S. (1992), *Faces in the Clouds: A New Theory of Religion*, Oxford: Oxford University Press.

Hammer, O., and J. Sørensen (2010), *Religion: I människors medvetanden och samhällen*, Lund: Studentlitteratur.

Knutsson Bråkenhielm, L. (2016), *Religion – evolutionens missfoster eller kärleksbarn?: kognitionsvetenskaplig religionsforskning och dess relevans för religiösa trosföreställningars rationalitet*, Uppsala: Uppsala University, Faculty of Theology.

Larsson, G., and S. Sorgenfrei (2019), *Religion*, Stockholm: Liber.

Larsson, G., J. Svensson and A. Nordin, eds (2020), *Building Blocks of Religion: Critical Applications and Future Prospects*, Sheffield: Equinox.

Lawson, E. T., and R. N. McCauley (1990), *Rethinking Religion: Connecting Cognition and Culture*, Cambridge: Cambridge University Press.

Lindenfors, P. (2016), 'Evolutionära förklaringar av religion', in D. Thurfjell (ed.), *Varför finns religion?*, 2–22, Stockholm: Molin & Sorgenfrei.

Lindenfors, P. (2023), *Äckel: Smitta, synd, samhälle*, Stockholm: Ordfront förlag.

Lindgren, T. (2009), *Fundamentalism och helig terror: Religionspsykologi för vår tid*, Lund: Studentlitteratur.

Lindgren, T. (2014), 'Hjalmar Sundén's Impact on the Study of Religion in the Nordic Countries', *Temenos* 50 (1): 39–62.

Lindgren, T. (2017), 'Evolutionspsykologi och religion', in A. Geels and O. Wikström (eds), *Den religiösa människan*, 483–504, Stockholm: Liber.

Lindgren, T., and H. Sonnenschein (2021), 'Bloody, Intense, and Durable: The Politics of "Religious Conflict"', *Temenos* 57(1): 59–80.

Malm Lindberg, I. (2021), *The Multifaceted Role of Imagination in Science and Religion: A Critical Examination of Its Epistemic, Creative and Meaning-Making Functions*, Uppsala: Uppsala University, Faculty of Theology.

Miller, G. A. (2003), 'The Cognitive Revolution: A Historical Perspective', *Trends in Cognitive Science* 7 (3): 141–4.

Nordin, A. (2013), 'Evolved Cognition and Cultural Transmission of Honour Concepts', *Journal of cognition and culture* 13 (1–2): 111–27.

Nordin, A. (2015), 'Indirect Reciprocity and Reputation Management in Religious Morality Relating to Concepts of Supernatural Agents', *Journal for the Cognitive Science of Religion* 3 (2): 125–53.

Nordin, A. (2023), 'Gauging Oneiromancy – the Cognition of Dream Content and Cultural Transmission of (Supernatural) Divination', *Religion, Brain & Behavior*. doi: 10.1080/2153599X.2023.2172068.

Nordin, A., and P. Bjälkebring (2021), 'The Counterintuitiveness of Supernatural Dreams and Religiosity', *Journal of Cognition and Culture* 21 (3–4): 309–30.

Norenzayan A. (2013), *Big Gods: How Religion Transformed Cooperation and Conflict*, Princeton: Princeton University Press.

Olsson, S. (2010), 'Kognitiva teorier', in S. Arvidsson and J. Svensson (eds), *Människor och makter 2.0: En introduktion till religionsvetenskap*, 116–21, Halmstad: Halmstad University.

Pyysiäinen, I. (2001), *How Religion Works: Towards a New Cognitive Science of Religion*, Leiden: Brill.

Roitto, R. (2009), *Behaving as a Christ-Believer: A Cognitive Perspective on Identity and Behavior Norms in Ephesians*, Linköping: Linköping University.

Roitto, R. (2021), *Behaving as a Christ-Believer: A Cognitive Perspective on Identity and Behavior Norms in Ephesians*, Stockholm: Enskilda Högskolan.

Rydving, H. (2008), 'A Western Folk Category of Mind?', *Temenos* 44 (1): 73–99.

Schjødt, U. (2019), 'Predictive Coding in the Study of Religion: A Believer's Testimony', in A. Klostergaard Petersen, I. S. Gilhus, L. M. Martin, J. Sinding Jensen and J. Sørensen, J. (eds), *Evolution, Cognition, and the History of Religion: A New Synthesis*, 364–79, Leiden: Brill.

Schjødt, U., H. Stødkilde-Jørgensen, A. Geertz, T. E. Lund and A. Roepstorff (2011), 'The Power of Charisma: Perceived Charisma Inhibits the Frontal Executive Network of Believers in Intercessory Prayer', *Cognitive Affective Neuroscience* 6 (1): 119–27.

Sundén, H. (1966), *Religionen och rollerna*, Uppsala: Svenska Kyrkans Diakonistyrelse.
Sundén, H. (1969), *Älgskyttar, helgon och exegeter: Några religionspsykologiska essäer*, Stockholm: Wahlström & Widstrand.
Svensson, J. (2014), 'God's Rage: Muslim Representations of HIV/AIDS as a Divine Punishment from the Perspective of the Cognitive Science of Religion', *Numen* 61 (5–6): 569–93.
Svensson, J. (2015), *Människans Muhammed*, Stockholm: Molin & Sorgenfrei.
Svensson, J. (2016), 'Kognitionsvetenskapliga svar', in D. Thurfjell (ed.), *Varför finns religion?*, 44–69, Stockholm: Molin & Sorgenfrei.
Svensson, J. (2017). 'Moralpsykologi och religion', in A. Geels and O. Wikström (eds), *Den religiösa människan*, 505–36, Stockholm: Liber.
Svensson, J. (2018), 'Vi har hämnats Profeten!: Kognitionsvetenskaplig religionsforskning i analys av reaktioner på Muhammedkarikatyrer', *DIN: tidsskrift for religion og kultur* 1:158–83.
Svensson, J. (2021). 'The Contagious Muhammad: Addressing Prophetic Relics in Islam from the Perspective of the Cognitive Science of Religion', *Journal for the Cognitive Science of Religion* 5 (2): 187–204.
Södergård, P. (2003), *The Hermetic Piety of the Mind: A Semiotic and Cognitive Study of the Discourse of Hermes Trismegistos*, Uppsala: Uppsala University, Faculty of Theology.
Sørensen, J. (2006), *A Cognitive Theory of Magic*, Walnut Creek: AltaMira Press.
Taves, A. (2009), *Religious Experience Reconsidered: A building-Block Approach to the Study of Religion and Other Special Things*, Princeton: Princeton University Press.
Taves, A., and E. Asprem (2017), 'Experience as Event: Event Cognition and the Study of (Religious) Experiences', *Religion, Brain & Behavior* 7 (1): 43–62.
Taves, A., and E. Asprem (2020), 'The Building Block Approach: An Overview', in G. Larsson, J. Svensson and A. Nordin (eds), *Building Blocks of Religion: Critical Applications and Future Prospects*, 5–25, London: Equinox.
Taves, A., W. Asprem and E. Ihm (2018), 'Psychology, Meaning Making, and the Study of Worldviews: Beyond Religion and Non-Religion', *Psychology of Religion and Spirituality* 10 (3): 207–17.
Thurfjell, D., ed. (2016), *Varför finns religion?*, Stockholm: Molin & Sorgenfrei.
Visuri, I. (2019), *Varieties of Supernatural Experience: The Case of High-Functioning Autism*, Huddinge: Södertörn University.
Visuri, I. (2020a), 'Sensory Supernatural Experiences in Autism', *Religion, Brain & Behavior* 10 (2): 151–65.
Visuri, I. (2020b), 'Invisible Hands and Sacred Unicorns: Occulture as a Schema for Supernatural Ascriptions in the Millennial Generation', in G. Larsson, J. Svensson and A. Nordin (eds), *Building Blocks of Religion: Critical Applications and Future Prospect*, 71–81, London: Equinox.
Whitehouse, H. (2004), *Modes of Religiosity: A Cognitive Theory of Religious Transmission*, Walnut Creek: AltaMira Press.

Chapter 12

RELIGIOUS EDUCATION

Christina Osbeck and Olof Franck

Like the other chapters in this volume, the purpose of our text is to give a general presentation of a specific topic – in this case, religious education (RE) in Sweden. However, this is a task that is not that easily carried out. The term 'religious education' is used internationally both for the subject taught in schools and also for research in relation to educational practices concerning religions, world views and ethics. We, the authors of this chapter, are both professors of subject matter education with a focus on social studies (*ämnesdidaktik med inriktning mot de samhällsorienterande ämnena*), but we have almost exclusively written about religions, world views and ethics, and have backgrounds as associate professors in religious studies and the philosophy of religion, respectively. In Sweden today, RE is not an established academic discipline, like *Religionspädagogik* or *Religionsdidaktik* in Germany, for instance. Nevertheless, *religionsdidaktik* or *religionspedagogik* are often the Swedish terms used in practice for research in relation to education concerning religion, world views and ethics, and they have perhaps previously had stronger formal positions as disciplines – depending on one's point of view. The Swedish school subject *religionskunskap* translates literally as 'knowledge of religions', stressing the objective character of the studies, which has been central since the 1960s. The subject has, especially from the curricula of 1980 onwards, been taught in close cooperation with history, civics and geography. Together, the four subjects are called social studies, in Swedish, *samhällsorienterande ämnen* (literally 'subjects orienting towards society'), which is why one can identify as a researcher in *religionsdidaktik* and yet have a position in subject matter education with a focus on social studies, as in the University of Gothenburg. In other universities, such positions may be called something else that often indicates a broader area like *pedagogical work* but can also, as at Stockholm University, be called *religionsdidaktik*. The examples illustrate the ambiguous nature of *religionsdidaktik*, which can be understood both as a disadvantage and an advantage, a fact that will be discussed below.

To solve the challenges that the ambiguity of the subject creates for this text, we have chosen to start by presenting the school subject, its history and its situation today. Thereafter, we will mainly concentrate on research in relation to the school subject, which we will refer to here as *religionsdidaktik* or RE research. Consequently, the school subject will be referred to as religious education or using the abbreviation RE. The presentation will focus both on the development of the field of RE research and on the more contemporary situation. In the concluding discussion, we will examine possible criteria for being considered a research field and will assess *religionsdidaktik* in relation to these criteria.

The History of RE as a School Subject in Sweden

Perhaps 'learning from history', to use an expression taken from today's primary school curriculum, can be interpreted in terms of 'understanding that the people of each age must be judged on the terms and values of their time'. By becoming familiar as far as possible with how historians, politicians, educators and theologians thought and argued about the place and role of religion in school, education and teaching, a picture can emerge where we and our beliefs and discussions can be reflected in the light of something that is outside our own context. We can see lines going back in time, lines that almost never run completely straight or without breaks and oscillations, but, nevertheless, lines that provide today's conversations with a background and perhaps also a context that can become deeper and wider.

Four Steps in the History of Swedish RE

Sven Hartman (2002) suggests an analytical perspective where what has happened within RE, regarding its place, role, structure and content, between the introduction of the School Act in 1842 and today's non-denominational subject is divided into four stages.

For much of the Swedish compulsory school's 180-year history, RE, referred to as Christianity, was a major subject. When the 1842 School Act gave Sweden a public school system, this was an expression of both continuity and change in terms of the place and role of religion in society and school. According to the Church Act of 1686, it was the responsibility of parents and householders to teach children and servants to read. This was, as Hartman points out, a two-step responsibility. Those responsible had a duty to teach, but it was up to the priests to check the results of this teaching in *husförhör* (house hearings/examinations). Even after 1842, the teaching of Christianity was at the centre of education, with a focus on catechism knowledge and biblical history. The correct doctrine was to be guaranteed by the use of Luther's catechism as a textbook, and those who taught about, and within, this doctrine were priests, who had theological, rather than educational, training.

One can, according to Hartman, identify four stages or 'turning points' in the history of the subject. The first can be traced to the decades before the 1883 curriculum (*normalplan*), when the old educational system, in which the teaching obligation was centred on the home, was dismantled. Responsibility for teaching was transferred to the school and its teachers, and this also applied to religious education.

This was, as Hartman points out, even though 'religion began to be regarded more and more as something that lay within the private sphere' (2002: 216).¹

The second turning point came with the introduction of the 1919 school curriculum. Liberal and social democratic challenges to a more conservative view of teaching was paying off. More child-friendly teaching was mandated, and students were expected to play a more active role in classrooms. The long-standing teaching of Luther's catechism disappeared, and thus the tradition that religious education in school should be confessionally linked to the Church of Sweden was also broken. Here began an era in which the teaching of Christianity became non-denominational (Hartman 2002: 216). An important role in this process was played by the Free Churches as strong representatives of a wider Christian context where the state church is no longer an obvious or sole bearer of Christian faith and tradition.

A third turning point was a new step in the process in which the content and goals of the topic of Christianity become the subject of critical discussion in the Swedish parliament as well as among representatives of the Free Churches. This turning point was constituted by the demands for 'objectivity' put forward in the school curriculum of 1962. This requirement was the subject of debate and of different interpretations.

The fourth and final turning point is linked to the 1969 curriculum, where a subject-centred teaching was replaced by a more student-centred one, and it was also at that time that a focus on 'existential questions' (*livsfrågor*) was introduced (Hartman 2002: 216). The subject name 'Christianity' was replaced by 'religious education' (e.g. Larsson and Kittelmann Flensner 2014).

Looking at Today's RE with Historical Glasses

Today in Sweden, the subject of religious education, like all other subjects, should, according to the educational policy documents, involve non-confessional teaching. The common image of Swedish society is that secularization is a fundamental characteristic, an image that is inspired by, among other things, the studies conducted within the World Values Survey and its well-known cultural map, where Sweden has a special place, far in the upper-right corner, with a combination of a focus on secular-rational and on self-expression values (WVS 2023).

As has often been pointed out, this image needs to be problematized (Davie 2002; Thurfjell 2015), even if it captures something significant. In societal discourse regarding this issue, a non-confessional RE appears to be natural. It needs to be pointed out, however, that this does not mean that teaching about religion would be considered unimportant. Rather, in the Swedish multicultural societal discourse, RE is associated with the responsibility for raising ethical and existential issues in relation to both traditional religions and world views, as well as about children's and young people's perspectives on 'life issues' (Franck and Thalén 2018; Osbeck et al. 2018; Sporre, Lotz-Sisitka and Osbeck 2022).

RE in Sweden, like other subjects, is subject to the requirement that teaching must be factual, comprehensive and non-confessional (Skolverket 2022), a requirement that can be seen to be in line with the position, mentioned earlier, regarding objectivity, which came to be discussed and applied early in the history of the subject. For RE, this means, more precisely, that the teaching of the subject should provide students with the preconditions for developing knowledge of religions and other beliefs, as well as of different interpretations and varying practices in RE in Sweden. Further, abilities to critically examine issues related to the relationship between religion and society, and to reason about ethics, moral issues and life issues from different perspectives, are emphasized in the curriculum (Skolverket 2022), where a critical approach is advocated, alongside the development of an understanding of religious and philosophical diversity, just as the study of ethics should create opportunities for reasoning and discussing ethics, morality and life issues.

RE Research in Sweden, 1960–2000

Research Related to the School Subject RE

In Sweden, the interest in religious education can be said to have been reawakened with the changes in the school subject in the 1960s, with the requirements for objectivity, which was unique in Europe at that time. The changes also affected the Church of Sweden, which up to that point had understood RE teaching in school as a sort of preparation for the sacrament of confirmation. There were debates about how to understand the new subject, concerning both its starting points and aim, and what assumptions were possible to be made about the subject. Gradually, the idea of existential questions as foundational for the new RE subject became established. People may have different philosophies of life, but there are basic existential questions that all people have. Their different views on life can be regarded as different answers to the same questions. Not surprisingly, one central and continuous strand in the landscape of empirical RE research in Sweden has concerned what kind of existential questions children have, since the teaching of religions can be framed as answers to these questions (Skolöverstyrelsen, Lindskog and Ronnås 1969). Within this tradition, research by Hartman and his colleagues can be considered as having the most central position, even if there are other researchers who have contributed to accumulated knowledge in this area, where the recurrent questions concern relationships, inclusion and exclusion (e.g. Eriksson 1999; Falkevall 2010; Hartman 1986).

Research Related to Education for Upper Secondary School Teachers

If the organization of the school, the RE subject and the teaching of RE can be understood as affecting the direction of RE research, it is also possible to see that the organization of teacher education – the questions that are in focus in these contexts – has affected the conditions for RE research and also the directions it has taken. At the beginning of the 1970s, the religious studies and theology education in Lund and Uppsala went through large structural changes. At that time, priests and subject teachers for older students (aged thirteen and upwards) studied on these courses together. One of the starting points for these changes was criticism of the university education at the time, among other things, for a lack of societal relevance (Universitetskanslersämbetet 1971: 74). From this starting point, larger changes took place concerning disciplines, divisions of disciplines and designations of disciplines. 'Science of religious behaviour' (*religionsbeteendevetenskap*) was established as a discipline and consisted of science of religious education (*religionspedagogik*), as well as psychology and sociology of religion (the last two subdisciplines are covered in Chapters 9 and 10 in this volume).

Even though a professorial position was not created for *religionspedagogik*, as was the case for psychology and sociology of religion, it became a subject within religious studies in 1973 (Larsson 1992: 11). Central figures in this work for the status of the subject as a scientific discipline were Kurt Bergling in Uppsala and Rune Larsson in Lund.

As part of this work, these researchers formulated definitions of the discipline. Bergling's was the earlier of the two, which gave Larsson the opportunity not only to relate to Bergling's formulation but also to criticize it. Bergling understood the area of religious educational research as consisting of 'the behavioural scientific empirical study of issues related to the emergence and development of religious and worldview concepts, religious thinking and religious maturity, as well as the mediation of religious and worldview interpretations of the human life situation during upbringing, education, teaching and other influences" (1977: 97). In his criticism of Bergling's definition, Larsson focuses on what he considers a narrow individual perspective, and he stresses that the focus of the subject 'can almost be described as educational psychology applied to religious material [and can be said to leave out] the fundamental issues, the questions relating to goals, content and evaluation' (Larsson 1992: 15). In contrast, Larsson defines *religionspedagogik* as 'a scientific discipline that deals with the problems associated with the acquisition of knowledge, values and patterns of action of a religious and worldview nature' (1992: 17), which is a broader, but at the same time less precise, definition. Also, a tighter focus is shown in Bergling's work in comparison to Larsson. While Bergling has had a special interest in developmental psychology with a focus on the theories of Jean Piaget (1896–1980) and Lawrence Kohlberg (1927–1987), especially in moral development, Larsson has had a broader interest, starting his career with a dissertation on German curricula. While Bergling's professorship was in psychology of religion and he left the RE scene, Larsson stayed in the field for a longer period and devoted time to introducing international RE scholars to the Swedish audience, for example, through translated publications. In this task, his strong engagement in international RE networks, such as the Nordic Conference on Religious Education (NCRE) and the International Seminar on Religious Education and Values (ISREV), has been of great value.

Research Related to Education for Primary School Teachers

In 1977, the education for teachers in primary school (up to twelve years old) became a part of university education. Gradually, the demands for a scientifically based education increased. This concerned in particular the teaching related to specific subjects and the teaching about the more practical parts of teaching (*metodik*). With regard to theory of teaching and learning, and empirically derived knowledge of this kind (*pedagogik*), the scientific base was stronger. Here, the scientific tradition that was made central was the continental European tradition of *didaktik* (Kroksmark 1989). In this tradition, there is an interest in knowledge where questions of content, methods and aims are kept together and the relationships between teacher, students and content are focused on the same time (e.g. Osbeck, Ingerman and Claesson 2018). Pioneering work in the field was done by the Gothenburg-based Professor in Science of Education (*pedagogik*), Ference Marton, who brought together educational scholars from different theoretical traditions and content areas for discussions on *fackdidaktik* (from *Fachdidaktik* in Germany; later *ämnesdidaktik* in Sweden), its possibilities and central strands. The work was published as a book series, where the chapter on RE was written by Henry Cöster. As his background was in systematic theology with a strong critical, emancipatory, hermeneutical and narrative interest, the focus, and title, of the chapter was 'Critical-Didactical Examination of the RE Subject', with a historical approach. In his examination, he uses his understanding of the Christian tradition as a critical corrective in the interpretation of religion in a school context where teaching and learning can carry the risk of making achievement and knowledge into values in themselves (Cöster 1986).

Much research and development work in RE was also done in relation to practical aspects of teacher education. One example of such an arena, where Cöster was also active, was the teacher education in Karlstad. At the end of the 1970s and beginning of the 1980s, in the FöRe project (*Försöksundervisning Religionskunskap* (Explorative Teaching in Religious Education)), Cöster, together with his colleagues Ingrid Emanuelson and Björn Skogar, developed a narrative-based rationale and approach for teaching religion in school (Cöster 1982). A central theme in this project was RE as contributing to children's life understanding through repertoires of life interpretative stories, where critical emancipatory perspectives constitute recurrent themes. Together, Emanuelson and Skogar wrote paraphrases of Bible stories (1981) and tried out different methods of working with frame stories to find ways to come closer to students' life worlds, making Bible stories more accessible to young people (cf. Goldman 1978). Besides the FöRe project, several other influential RE contributions have come from the Karlstad group. For example, Emanuelson's dissertation on potential life interpretation contributions in hymns and further reception studies on children's interpretations of biblical stories should be mentioned in this context (Emanuelson 1990). Skogar's work on the nature of the RE subject and its life interpretative aim in school (2000) should also be mentioned. Skogar also became a central figure in establishing national cooperation both in terms of early anthologies in the field (Almén et al. 2000) and in shaping a critical and creative network for RE scholars together with, among others, Hartman (Nfred). In addition, a fourth Karlstad colleague, Kjell Härenstam, paved the way for further development of the text-book research tradition in the RE field. For example, his work on Islam in Swedish schoolbooks has been quite influential in the Swedish RE field and, among other things, points out how prejudices can be spread through the seemingly neutral textbooks and can paradoxically be related to how central values in the curriculum are stressed (Härenstam 1993).

Summing Up: Four Types of RE Research, 1960–2000

The presentation of RE research given above has been structured in terms of three arenas affecting the development of RE research, that is, the RE school subject in compulsory school, research related to education for upper secondary school teachers and research related to education for primary school teachers. In the examples above, four kinds of RE research have been described. The first of these concerns *the aim of the subject*. This research can be both descriptive in relation to, for instance, analyses of curricula, and prescriptive in relation to, for example, teacher education (e.g. Buchardt 2004: 120). The second kind of research involves studies on *factors relevant to children's learning*, such as children's existential questions. The third type of research relates to *content-oriented studies* in the form of curriculum, textbook and hymn studies, and the fourth type relates to *reception studies*, concerning impacts of teaching,

When comparing this with systematic analyses of Swedish RE publications (Osbeck and Lied 2012), one can see that one category of publications, which has been rather common over the course of years, is lacking in the above description. This category could be called *expert studies for teachers* and consists of publications written for RE teachers about a theme that the text authors can be understood as experts on, a theme that can also be considered as being of interest to RE teachers in school. This category does not necessarily have to be understood as an RE research category, as most of the authors primarily identify themselves as researchers in other fields of religious studies than RE.

One can also see from the above-mentioned publication analysis that Swedish RE research before 2010 to a large extent lacked studies of ongoing teaching and learning processes such as, for instance, classroom studies.

RE Research in Sweden after the Millennium

In our description of contemporary RE, we have chosen to point out two arenas in which influential RE research is conducted. These are, first, theses for the PhD examination, and second, research funded by the national research council (Vetenskapsrådet, VR). Since we have previously conducted research reviews on these materials, we will sum up these findings here (Osbeck and Franck 2020).

Three Tendencies in RE PhD Studies

Based on PhD theses defended between 2000 and 2020, three changes in current RE research, in comparison to the previous forty years or so, can be identified

(Osbeck and Franck 2020). First, more *classroom studies* have been carried out during this period. One example of this is Karin Kittelmann Flensner's thesis (2015), in which she identifies a dominant secularist discourse in RE classroom practice, where religion and religious people appear as outdated.

Second, current empirical RE research has stressed *contextual processes and informal processes* as being important for learning. For instance, multicultural schools have been shown to have strong opportunities and resources for RE learning that are, however, not necessarily taken into account, due to a 'Swedish' hegemonic norm (von Brömssen 2003). Moreover, studies have pointed towards how students' life understandings and life interpretations are formed by informal contexts in school that interact with their formal RE learning, without attention necessarily being paid to this (Osbeck 2006; Risenfors 2011).

Third, studies have given insight into *new RE practices*, or RE connected practices, that have emerged during this period. One such example is Islamic Religious Education (IRE), which Jenny Berglund describes in her thesis (2009). Another example is the optional subject *livskunskap* (life competencies education/ life skills education) that emerged at the beginning of the twenty-first century, a subject that has focused on values education in particular (e.g. Löf 2011; see also other kinds of texts that discuss *livskunskap* more explicitly in relation to the RE subject e.g. Zetterqvist and Skeie 2014).

Four Traits in VR-funded RE Research

If we shift our focus from dissertations towards the research funded by the national research council (VR) after the millennium, an important question concerns what else can be learned about RE research during this period. At least four traits in the identified research projects on religion and ethics in education stand out (Osbeck and Franck 2020). First, not much of the VR-funded educational research during this period has addressed religion or ethics. Second, of the funded projects, few have been focused on religions or ethics as content or knowledge. Even fewer have been directed towards how knowledge of religion/ ethics is taught and learned. One such project, on global conflicts, was led by Kittelmann Flensner (see, for instance, K. Flensner, Larsson and Säljö 2019). Another project, led by Karin Sporre, prioritizes children's existential questions. Third, quite a few of the projects concerning religion/ethics, rather than focusing on these in terms of knowledge for teaching and learning, have instead focused on socialization processes. Here, RE plays the role of an arena for such processes (cf. Larsson's discussion of Bergling's definition of *religionspedagogik*), for example, concerning femininities and masculinities as in the VR project led by Sharon Todd (Osbeck and Franck 2020). Fourth, little of the conducted research seems to have an impact on curriculum development. Quite the opposite: current RE research focuses seem to have been affected by curricula, for example, the strong emphasis on fundamental values in the curriculum has motivated research on this topic, as in, for instance, the VR-funded research by Edgar Almén (Osbeck and Franck 2020).

While considering these four traits of RE research funded by the VR, one could add that other RE research has also been conducted during these years, funded in other ways. An influential research category is constituted by the studies funded through the European Union. During the current period, the largest international RE projects have probably been the REDCo project (Religion, Education, Dialogue and Conflict; see e.g. ter Avest et al. 2009) and the TRES project (Teaching Religion in a Multicultural European Society) where, among other things, European teachers' aims with their RE teaching have been explored empirically (Riegel and Ziebertz 2009; Pettersson and Osbeck 2009).

Conclusions

As stated at the beginning of this chapter, Religious Education in Sweden can be understood as an ambiguous knowledge field. Religious Education is being researched in many different academic disciplines. What that fact may mean for RE knowledge (re)production, that is, how academic disciplines work as frames for research contributions, has been explored by RE researchers from the Nordic countries (e.g. Buchardt and Osbeck 2017), and both advantages and disadvantages of this situation have been identified. The variety of relevant disciplines from which knowledge contributions may come makes space for academic freedom and creativity, but it also makes it more difficult to discuss and ensure quality in RE research. Critical discussion may not arise, and contributions could be understood as parallel rather than related to each other. When an established discipline is absent, scaffolding for cumulative knowledge development seems to be lacking.

If, then, the subject is so ambiguous and the academic disciplines for RE knowledge development are so varied, can RE research in Sweden really be understood as a field of research? As always, this is the kind of question that depends on what one means by 'a field of research'. Here, we will discuss this question with help of a definition by Peter Fensham (2003), who considers the question to be related to: (1) *the structure of the field and the external criteria*; (2) *the research and its internal criteria* and (3) to *the results of the research*.

Among the structural criteria, he stresses the function of *professorships* in establishing the field. So, once more, one could ask the question of what it might mean that the field is so fragmented and that *religionsdidaktik* is not recognized as a subject in its own right but placed within broader fields such as subject matter education with a focus on social studies, or as at Stockholm University, recognized as a specific field in the name of a professorship but not in the name of the research subject. Furthermore, the existence of *research journals* is, according to Fensham, important, and here both the range of journals and the number of articles have increased nationally and internationally. While some journals relate to RE alone, for example, the *British Journal of Religious Education*, other journals treat RE as a part of a larger area such as the subject of social studies, for example, *Nordidactica*. Furthermore, it seems that RE, in comparison to other humanistic and social science areas of subject matter education, had established rather vital *professional organizations and conferences* at quite an early stage. Often, these are combined and work both as professional research organizations and as conferences, such as the national NFR (Nationellt Forum för Religionsdidaktisk/-pedagogisk forskning), Nordic NCRE (Nordic Conference on Religious Education) and the international ISREV (International Seminar on Religious Education and Values). The number of scholars contributing internationally has increased over the years. Moreover, at some universities in Sweden, there are opportunities for conducting advanced studies and research in relation to the RE subject at postgraduate level but seldom or never within what might be called an academic RE discipline. Instead, the studies are conducted in other disciplines, such as subject matter education, religious studies, pedagogical work and so on.

Concerning the internal criteria of research, Fensham points at the importance of *recognition of knowledge in the specific content field*. In the RE research field, which often attracts primary education teachers, this has been a debated issue, that is, how deep a disciplinary knowledge in the content field is necessary or reasonable to require for religious *education* research. The next set of criteria concern the recognition of specific *research questions, concepts and theories, methods, and progression in the field*. Here, it is once again clear that the international RE research field is also fragmented and that progression is being hindered by the low amount of research in general, and particularly when it comes to replication studies or cumulative studies, where studies draw closely on each other. It seems to be more the case that studies are 'living their own lives', recognizing other studies as existing but not affected by them to any great extent. Consequently, what Fensham speaks of as model publications or seminal publications seem to be almost invisible in RE.

The final group of criteria is, for Fensham, constituted by the results: whether research findings have consequences for practice is an important factor in determining what constitutes a research field. The status of RE research is, in this respect, perhaps one which is shared with other educational fields. There seem to be some distance between research and practice, even though the Education Act of 2010 stresses that education should be based on research, and popular science journals that attract both teachers and researchers exist in the field (e.g. *Religion & Livsfrågor*). However, many new forms of funding, with the aim of bringing researchers and teachers closer together in cooperation, have also been open to RE scholars and teachers (e.g. *Skolforskningsinstitutet*, ULF), which has benefited the field of educational research generally in Sweden. To what extent this has also concretely facilitated RE research is a question for further empirical research. It can, however, be stated that both the national and local investments in research schools for practising teachers have been most valuable and have contributed new knowledge, which hopefully has also influenced and will continue to influence RE practice (e.g. Holmqvist Lidh 2016; Kittelmann Flensner 2015).

Note

1 All quotations are translated from Swedish to English by the authors of this chapter.

References

Avest, I. t., D. P. Jozsa, T. Knauth, J. Rosón and G. Skeie, eds (2009), *Dialogue and Conflict on Religion: Studies of Classroom Interaction in European Countries*, Münster: Waxmann Verlag.

Almén, E., R. Furenhed, S. G. Hartman and B. Skogar (2000), *Livstolkning och värdegrund. Att undervisa om religion, livsfrågor och etik*, Linköping: Linköpings universitet.

Bergling, K. (1977), 'Religionspedagogisk forskning. Ett i Sverige nytt teologiskt forskningsfält', *Svensk teologisk kvartalstidskrift* 3: 96–109.

Berglund, J. (2009), *Teaching Islam: Islamic Religious Education at Three Muslim Schools in Sweden*, Uppsala: Uppsala universitet.

von Brömssen, K. (2003), *Tolkningar, förhandlingar och tystnader. Elevers tal om religion i det mångkulturella och postkoloniala rummet*, Göteborg: Acta universitatis gothoburgensis.

Buchardt, M. (2004), 'Religious Education in School: Approaches in School Practice and Research in Denmark', in R. Larsson and C. Gustavsson (eds), *Towards a European Perspective on Religious Education*, 117–26, Skellefteå: Artos & Norma bokförlag.

Buchardt, M., and C. Osbeck (2017), 'Epistemologies of Religious Education Research in the Nordic Welfare States', *Nordidactica* 2017 (1): i–vii.

Cöster, H. (1982), *Berättelsen befriar: Teologisk hermeneutik*, Karlstad: Högskolan i Karlstad.

Cöster, H. (1986), 'En kritisk-didaktisk granskning av religionskunskapsämnet', in F. Marton (ed.), *Fackdidaktik. Vol. 2. Svenska och främmande språk, samhällsorienterande ämnen*, 101–15, Lund: Studentlitteratur.

Davie, G. (2002), *Europe: The Exceptional Case: Parameters of Faith in the Modern World*, London: Darton, Longmann and Todd.

Emanuelson, I. (1990), *Livstolkning i den obligatoriska skolans urval av psalmer och religiösa sånger 1889–1980*, Uppsala: Acta universitatis upsaliensis.

Emanuelson, I., and B. Skogar (1981), *Rufus berättar för Joram*, Karlstad: Högskolan i Karlstad.

Eriksson, K. (1999), *På spaning efter livets mening: Om livsfrågor och livsåskådning hos äldre grundskoleelever i en undervisningsmiljö som befrämjar kunskapande*, Malmö: Lärarhögskolan i Malmö.

Falkevall, B. (2010), *Livsfrågor och religionskunskap: En belysning av ett centralt begrepp i svensk religionsdidaktik*, Stockholm: Stockholms universitet.

Fensham, P. J. (2003), *Defining an identity: the evolution of science education as a field of research*, Dordrecht: Kluwer Academic.

Flensner, K., G. Larsson and R. Säljö (2019), 'Jihadists and Refugees at the Theatre: Global Conflicts in Classroom Practices in Sweden', *Education Sciences* 9 (2): 80, https://doi.org/10.3390/educsci9020080.

Franck, O., and P. Thalén (2018), *Interkulturell religionsdidaktik – utmaningar och möjligheter*, Lund: Studentlitteratur.

Goldman, R. (1978), *Readiness for Religion: A Basis for Developmental Religious Education*, London: Routledge.
Hartman, S. G. (1986), *Barns tankar om livet*, Stockholm: Natur och kultur.
Hartman, S. (2002), 'Hur religionsämnet formades', in E. Almén, R. Furenhed, S. G. Hartman and B. Skogar (eds), *Livstolkning och värdegrund. Att undervisa om religion, livsfrågor och etik*, 212–51, Linköping: Linköpings universitet.
Härenstam, K. (1993), *Skolboks-islam. Analys av bilden av islam i läroböcker i religionskunskap*, Göteborg: Acta universitatis gothoburgensis.
Holmqvist Lidh, C. (2016). *Representera och bli representerad: elever med religiös positionering talar om skolans religionskunskapsundervisning*, Karlstad: Karlstads universitet.
Kittelmann Flensner, K. (2015), *Religious Education in Contemporary Pluralistic Sweden*, Gothenburg: University of Gothenburg.
Kroksmark, T. (1989), *Didaktiska strövtåg. Didaktiska idéer från Comenius till fenomenografisk didaktik*, Göteborg: Daidalos.
Larsson, R. (1992), *Introduktion till religionspedagogiken*, Lund: Lunds universitet.
Larsson, G., and K. Kittelmann Flensner (2014), 'Swedish Religious Education at the End of the 1960s: Classroom Observations, Early Video Ethnography and the National Curriculum of 1962', *British Journal of Religious Education* 36 (2): 202–17.
Löf, C. (2011), *Med livet på schemat: Om skolämnet livskunskap och den riskfyllda barndomen*, Lund: Lunds universitet.
Osbeck, C. (2006), *Kränkningens livsförståelse. En religionsdidaktisk studie av livsförståelselärande i skolan*, Karlstad: Karlstads universitet.
Osbeck, C., and O. Franck (2020), 'Funded RE Research and Its Impact on Curricula Development – Tendencies in Sweden 2000–2020', *Religions* 11 (10): 521, https://doi.org/10.3390/rel11100521.
Osbeck, C., and S. Lied (2012), 'RE Research in Hamar and Karlstad in a Subject Didactical and International Context', in S. Lied and C. Osbeck (eds), *Religionsdidaktisk arbeid pågår! Religionsdidaktikk i Hamar og Karlstad*, Vallset: Oplandske Bokforlag.
Osbeck, C., Å. Ingerman and S. Claesson (2018), *Didactic Classroom Studies—A Potential Research Direction*, Lund: Nordic Academic Press.
Osbeck, C., O. Franck, A. Lilja, K. Sporre and J. Tykesson (2018), 'Abilities, Knowledge Requirements and national tests in RE: The Swedish Case as an Example in the Outcome-Focused School and Society of Today', *Zeitschrift für Pädagogik und Theologie* 70 (4): 397–408.
Osbeck, C., and P. Pettersson (2009), 'Non-Confessional and Confessional Education: Religious Education in Public Schools and in the Church of Sweden", in U. Riegel and H.-G. Ziebertz (eds), *How Teachers in Europe Teach Religion: An International Empirical Study in 16 Countries*, 211–27, Münster: LIT-Verlag.
Riegel, U., and H.-G. Ziebertz (2009), *How Teachers in Europe Teach Religion: An International Empirical Study in 16 Countries*, Münster: LIT-Verlag.
Risenfors, S. (2011), *Gymnasieungdomars livstolkande*, Göteborg: Göteborgs universitet.
Skogar, B. (2000), 'Religionsdidaktikens kärnproblem', in M. Linnarud (ed.), *På spaning efter ämnets kärna: didaktiska tankar kring några skolämnen*, 29–43, Karlstad: Universitetstryckeriet.
Skolverket (2022), *Läroplan för grundskolan, förskoleklassen och fritidshemmet 2022*, Stockholm: Skolverket.

Skolöverstyrelsen, O. Lindskog and J. Ronnås (1969), *Tonåringen och livsfrågorna. Elevattityder och undervisningen i livsåskådning och etik på grundskolans högstadium. Elevundersökningar och metodiska förslag av en arbetsgrupp inom skolöverstyrelsen*, Stockholm: SÖ-förlag.

Sporre, K., H. Lotz-Sisitka and C. Osbeck (2022), 'Taking the Moral Authorship of Children and Youth Seriously in Times of the Anthropocene', *Ethics and Education* 17 (1): 101–16.

Thurfjell, D. (2015), *Det gudlösa folket. De postkristna svenskarna och religionen*, Stockholm: Molin & Sorgenfrei.

Universitetskanslersämbetet (1971), *Betänkande avgivet av utredningen angående den religionsvetenskapliga utbildningens mål och organisation (RUMO)*, Stockholm: Universitetskanslersämbetet.

World Values Survey (WVS) (2023), worldvaluessurvey.org (accessed 6 September 2023).

Zetterqvist, K. G., and G. Skeie (2014), 'Religion i skolen; her, der og hvor-som-helst?', *Norsk pedagogisk tidsskrift* 98 (5): 305–15.

Part III

THEMES IN THE STUDY OF RELIGION IN SWEDEN

Chapter 13

COMPARATIVE STUDIES

Stefan Arvidsson and Peter Jackson Rova

To compare is a basic cognitive function, used by everyone on an everyday basis.[1] We cannot not compare. Nevertheless, the act of comparison has gained an unusual prominence in the scholarly study of religion. The discipline today known either as the History of Religions or the study of religions has occasionally been labelled comparative religion (Lincoln 2018; Sharpe 1975; Smith 1990, 2004, especially chapter 8; and on the methodology of comparison in a more technical sense, see Freiberger 2019).

The historical circumstances rendering religion(s) comparable in Western Europe by the beginning of the early modern period coincides, on the one hand, with the Humanist critique of a religious discourse previously dominated by ecclesiastical interests and, on the other hand, with the rapidly expanding ethnographic knowledge to result from overseas explorations. As a result of these circumstances, discussions about the spiritual legacy of humankind were no longer exclusively dictated by Biblical narrative nor by the official teachings of the Church. A more recent historical explanation for the emphasis on comparison in the History of Religions is the fact that it emerged amid colonialism and missionary activities in the 1870s. Since then, the incentives for the history/study of religions have changed to the same extent as the methodology of comparison has been treated with increasing analytical care. More recently still, discussions have come to revolve around the many technical and epistemological challenges of the comparative act itself, with a recurrent ambition to revise and ultimately defend the comparative enterprise against various strands of postmodern scepticism. By contrast, debates during the twentieth century tended to concern the overall paradigm (or historiographic setting) behind comparisons.

If one were to outline the shifting styles and preferences of comparison among Swedish historians of religions from the early twentieth century onwards, it would be adequate to distinguish two dominant paradigms. The first paradigm was specifically aimed at a historical contextualization of the classical heritage with a particular emphasis on Indo-Iranian comparanda, whereas the second aimed at ethnographic and ecological contextualizations of religion with a particular emphasis on the hunter-gatherers of northern Eurasia and America. These trends can, in turn, be linked to a group of dominant figures who left a long-standing mark on the practice of the discipline, both in Sweden and internationally. It is on these trends and figures that we intend to focus in this chapter, leaving only brief attention to more recent developments.

Nathan Söderblom and His Legacy

Conventionally, Friedrich Max Müller (1823–1900) is heralded as the founder of the comparative study of religion (Bosch 2002; Davis and Nicholls 2017). The overall or historiographic framework that he worked within was a combination of romantic notions of ancient Aryan times and Protestant complacency. Müller immersed himself in the History of Religions with an attempt to help revitalize the spirit of ancient civilizations and thereby facilitate the reformation of contemporary religions entrenched in medieval theologies and ethics. His translations, editions and theoretical proposals strengthened, he thought, the good faith, namely Protestantism defended by Kantian philosophy.

Sweden's first historian of religions in a strict academic sense, Nathan Söderblom (1866–1931), pursued his research within the same liberal Protestant framework as Müller (Jonson 2014; Lange 2014). Having defended his doctoral dissertation in 1901 at the pioneering fifth section of the *École Pratiques des Hautes Études* in Paris, Söderblom was almost immediately appointed to the chair of Theological Prenotions and Theological Encyclopedia (later renamed 'History of Religions and Psychology of Religions') in Uppsala. He also came to hold the first chair of the History of Religions at the newly founded *Religionsgeschichtliches Seminar* in Leipzig from 1912 before accepting the appointment as archbishop of the Church of Sweden in 1914. In this latter capacity, he is especially recognized for his ecumenical work and as the initiator of the World Conference of Life and Work (*Stora ekumeniska mötet*) in Stockholm in 1925.

Söderblom came to have an enduring influence over the study of religion in Sweden during the first half of the twentieth century. His collection of religious texts in four volumes, *Främmande religionsurkunder. I urval och öfversättning* (1908), became the obvious reference corpus for generations of Swedish students. He also prepared a series of revised German versions (between 1903 and 1931) of the Dutch historian of religions Cornelius Petrus Tiele's (1830–1901) compendium, known in German as *Kompendium der Religionsgeschichte*, which long served as a standard introduction to the field.

As clearly indicated in the preface to the last revised edition of the compendium, Söderblom was keen to delineate the historical study of religion in non-theological terms. At the same time, however, his categorization of similarities between religions reveals a theological tendency. Similarities, he asserts, are grounded not only in external historical contact or mere analogy, but in certain cases also in what he rather vaguely terms 'fundamental-essential agreement' (*Grundwesentliche Übereinstimmung*) (Tiele and Söderblom 1931: 6).

Söderblom was succeeded by Tor Andræ (1885–1947), a specialist in Islam (see Chapter 5 in this volume) who had previously been the second holder of the endowed chair of History of Religions at Stockholm University College (later to become Stockholm University) (Widengren 1947). Established in 1913, the Stockholm chair was intended (according to the explicit wish of its anonymous donor(s)) to provide a secular, humanistic alternative to the study of religion at the old Theological Faculties of Uppsala and Lund. The comparative aim to cover 'the gradually occurring transformations of religious rites and notions' ([D]e religiösa riternas och föreställningarnas gradvis skeende omgestningar), as stated in the board minutes of the Philosophical Faculty's deliberations, should speak for itself. It was in this secular, humanistic environment that Geo Widengren (1907–1986) received his first training before eventually succeeding Andræ on the Uppsala chair (Larsson 2022a,b). It was also in this environment that the earlier Uppsala-based scholar Ernst Arbman (1891–1959) was to pursue his continuous academic career as the successor of Andræ between 1937 and 1958. This castling move of scholarly exchange between Uppsala and Stockholm had an interesting bearing on the two trends of comparison that we shall try to disentangle in the following.

'Vayu Theosophy', or Comparative Indo-European Religion

By choosing the spiritual beings known as *fravashis* as the topic of his doctoral dissertation, Söderblom initiated a long-standing Swedish tradition of studies in Indo-Iranian religions (1899). The early succession included scholars such as H. S. Nyberg, Kasten Rönnow, Widengren, Stig Wikander (all in Uppsala) and Sven S. Hartman (Lund). Nevertheless, the 'Iranophilia' of early Swedish historians of religion neither was a uniquely local manifestation of scholarly interests during this period, nor was it always driven by the same intellectual tenets. A reason for Söderblom's initial interest in ancient Iranian religion seems to have been the idea of treating Zarathushtra as a genuine exponent to the same divine revelation as the Mosaic and Israelite prophets. This idea was emphatically contested by Nyberg (1889–1974) in *Irans forntida religioner*, published in 1937, a few years after Söderblom's death (Kahle 1991). According to Nyberg, the figure of Zarathushtra was not truly analogous to the Semitic prophets; it should rather be considered 'a professional ecstatic' ('en professionell extatiker', Nyberg 1937: 296).

Nyberg's remark is a significant example of a fascination for religious ecstasy that was to remain a dominant theoretical concern in Swedish comparative religion for decades. It is a theme that deserves particular attention since it helps us better understand how the above-mentioned trends of comparative historical and ethnographic contextualization could emerge out of a once less diversified scholarly milieu. A mediating key figure in this foundational drama was, as we shall see, Arbman. Before turning to him, however, a few further notes on the ecstatic predilections of Nyberg and his circle are in order.

Nyberg believed that Zoroastrianism had developed as a syncretistic mix of cultic elements from two once-distinct religious communities: the so-called

Mithra community and the community to which Zarathushtra had himself belonged (the so-called Gāthā community). Apart from an emphasis in the first community on Mithra, the god of the social contract, Nyberg also identified the wind god Vayu/Vāyu (or Vāta) as a bleak and once more prominent figure associated with death and ambiguous sovereignty (Nyberg 1937: 82–3). He also considered ecstatic techniques and experiences to have had a crucial impact on Zarathustra's poetic compositions (Nyberg 1937: 163ff.).

In a posthumously published article ('Zagreus och Dionysos', 1943) and an unpublished manuscript (*Dionysos and Orpheus*), the Uppsala-based Indologist Rönnow (1897–1943) sought to reassemble traces of an ecstatic and heterodox sacrificial religiosity in ancient India and Iran (known as *Vāyureligionen*) which included the same kind of cosmological-sacrificial speculation that had given rise to the Dionysiac mysteries in ancient Greece. The god Vayu had also been a primary concern of Wikander (1908–1983), who edited and translated the two extant Avestan hymns to Vayu (Wikander 1941) with plans on a separate commentary. In the first preface (co-written with Rönnow), we are told that the *Vāyu-Vāta-religion* – since it is also believed to have left traces among Italic and Germanic groups – must have once formed part of an Indo-European religious heritage (Wikander 1941). In making such claims, Wikander acknowledges the influence from two scholars, who were the then leading figures of the organization SS Ahnenerbe, Otto Höfler and Walter Wüst, to suggest that his understanding of the Vāyu-religion as a characteristic blend of theosophical speculation and ecstatic frenzy was also resonating with prominent currents of Nazi ideology by the same period (Wikander 1941).

It is a delicate task to decide if, for whom and to what extent the scholarly discourse of Indo-Iranian ecstasy among students of comparative religion in Uppsala and Lund really entailed covert political sympathies (cf. Junginger 2008). Even if Wikander would seem to be the most apparent candidate, his scholarly exchange with Höfler and Wüst – in spite of the fact that it took place at a particularly critical phase of ideological re-education in Nazi Germany – should not be validated as a mere argumentum ad hominem, but had better been treated in more detail as a separate case (Arvidsson 2002; Timuş 2008).

Another figure who was once clearly participating in the emergent discourse of Indo-Iranian ecstasy from an early date on – with his 1922 dissertation on the Vedic god Rudra (*Rudra. Untersuchungen zum altindischen Glauben und Kultus*) and a follow-up monograph on conceptions of the soul in ancient India from 1926 (*Untersuchungen zur primitiven Seelenvorstellung mit besonderer Rücksicht auf Indien*) – was Arbman. His interests in ecstasy and conceptions of the soul were, however, to lead him in another direction. As the third holder of the chair in Stockholm from 1937, he was to become a seminal figure in the second paradigm of Swedish comparative religion that we have chosen to label 'ethnographic' (see below).

A personal dedication to Arbman in the characteristically tidy handwriting of Carl-Martin Edsman (1911–2010) on the title page of Anders Olerud's dissertation *L'idée de macrocosmos et de microcosmos dans le Timée de Platon. Étude de mythologie compareée* from 1951 complains: 'With worried regards from the innocent godfather, the last fruit of the Vayu theosophy is herewith submitted' ('Med en bekymrad hälsning från den oskyldige faddern översändes härmed Vayuteosofiens sista frukt'). In his formal capacity as Olerud's *Doktorvater*, Edsman renounces, as it were, responsibility of his spiritual child. Whereas Arbman and Edsman were apparently on good terms, the hostility between Edsman and Widengren is notorious. Alongside those of Albrecht Götze and Richard Reitzenstein, the works by Widengren, Wikander and Rönnow are treated with particular respect by Olerud as pioneering keys to the oriental origins of macro-microcosmic speculation. If Edsman ever had a particular group of founding figures in mind when referring to the 'Vayu theosophy', it would have been these three.

Åke Hultkrantz's 'Ecology of Religion'

A rival theory to Müllers's and Söderblom's liberal Protestant understanding of the History of Religions was formed already during the last decades of the nineteenth century. Evolutionism, ignited by Charles Darwin's historization of nature, became the paradigm à la mode. In contrast to the romantic sentiments blossoming among liberal Protestants – idealizing ancient beliefs (be it 'the simple teaching' of Jesus, or Vedic monotheism) – the evolutionists celebrated modernity. In their view, everything – not only science, technology and social organization but also the arts and spirituality – evolved towards something higher and better. In order to understand the evolutionary processes, and as a remainder of nineteenth-century historicism, the evolutionist scholars of religions went back beyond, as they saw it, the time of the ancient civilizations to examine the most primitive forms of religion. An early exponent of this trend in Sweden was Torgny Segerstedt (1876–1945). In 1903, Segerstedt defended a much-criticized dissertation in Uppsala, replete with references to figures such as Herbert Spencer, Andrew Lang and E. B. Tylor (*Till frågan om polyteismens uppkomst* (On the Question of the Origin of Polytheism)) (Benzow 1948). It is commonly assumed that Segerstedt's ensuing status as an unwanted presence at the Theological Faculties in Uppsala and Lund was a contributing factor to the creation of the professorship in Stockholm (see above), which he was the first to hold between 1913 and 1917 before embarking on a new career as a publicist in Gothenburg.

In books such as *The Mycenaean Origin of Greek Mythology* (1932) and *Greek Popular Religion* (1940; *Greek Folk Religion* in 1961), the Swedish classicist Martin P. Nilsson (1874–1967) revolutionized the study of ancient religion by searching for primitive forms of religion that had preceded, but still were traceable in, classical mythology. Beneath Greek and Roman mythology, loved by educated people in Europe since the Renaissance, Nilsson detected crude rituals addressing beings belonging to a 'lower mythology' comparable to the religious world of primitive peoples in Oceania and Africa.

As Nilsson himself intimated, his preoccupation with primitive rituals, often of the fertility variety, might have had something to do with him descending from a long line of farmers (Nilsson 1961: vii). Other scholars with a more typical middle-class background soon found Nilsson's evolutionism overdue and boring. He was indeed a late blossom on the evolutionary tree. The evolutionist paradigm had gone hand in hand with the general optimism of the nineteenth century and thus with progressive and humanist sentiments, distinctly expressed by Nilsson in his book *Straff och sällhet i den andra världen i förkristen religion* (1937; later editions under the title *Helvetets förhistoria*). Regarding stories and images of eternal punishment in the underworld, Nilsson laconically comments, 'One loses the wish to describe them' ('man tappar lusten att beskriva dem'; Nilsson 1963: 7).

With the First World War, the progressive and humanist optimism of the nineteenth century declined. Scholars now started to abandon evolutionism and turned instead to sociological models such as functionalism, promising to explain that strange and apparently malfunctioning thing called 'society'. Harsh criticism was raised against schematic evolutionism. In 1946, Widengren published a booklet, *Religionens ursprung: En kort framställning av de evolutionistiska religionsteorierna och kritiken mot dessa*, summarizing the main criticism. A decade or so later, being partial to evolutionist theories was seen as something of an embarrassment. That was also true for Lund University, where the History of Religions is said to have begun as colloquia in Nilsson's parlour.

One aspect of evolutionism did survive the otherwise devastating criticism: the interest in the relationship between religious ideas and the natural environment. In contrast to a traditional historicist framework, in which the thinking, decisions and doings of conscious and (potentially) intelligent humans was in focus, evolutionism portrayed humans as feeble victims to natural forces. This theme – religious man amid nature – linked the history of religions to ethnography and historical geography. At Stockholm University, Arbman picked up an interest in psychological interpretations of 'primitive' (in this case, pre-Vedic) beliefs about the soul. Studies in this vein were later undertaken at the same university by Arbman's students and predecessors Hultkrantz (North America), Louise Bäckman (Saami religion) and Per-Arne Berglie (South Asia).

A determinant change of paradigm came with Hultkrantz (1920–2006). Combining the evolutionist attention to the natural conditions of humanity with Arbman's interest in conceptions of the soul and with emic understandings of the mind among 'primitive' people, Hultkrantz launched in seminal articles in 1966 and 1974 what he called 'the ecology of religion'. Even if Hultkrantz did not reject the idea of people creating history wilfully, and thus acknowledged the historical perspective as significant, the ecology of religions nevertheless paid due notice to the forming forces of nature. The chaotic diversity of religions could best be understood, he suggested, by explaining their differences and peculiarities by references to their natural environments. The basic idea was to show how religions 'make use of environment and adapt themselves to it' (Hultkrantz 1979: 221). Hultkrantz's own trademark became the concept 'circumpolar religions'. The similarities he found between different ethnic religions across the Arctic Circle should thus *not* be explained by historical diffusion, or by being on the same evolutionary stage, but with shared natural conditions.

Even if the ecology of religions comes across as solid materialism, something of the liberal-theologian approach lingers in Hultkrantz's work:

> Ecology of religion helps us to achieve a deeper perspective on religious dynamics. We perceive that the forms and patterns of religion often depend on exterior conditions and that much of what we usually conceive to be genuine expressions of religious content are actually fortuitous manifestations. ... Ecology of religion thus diverts religion of its fortuitous forms; it shows what is the casual expression and the genuine belief. By removing the external attributes of a religion, suggested by environmental adaptation and historical process, we may arrive at the basic ideas and values of that religion. A more profound view of the intrinsic values of so-called primitive religions will, I think, provide us with a key to the understanding of those great religious traditions that are dominant today. (Hultkrantz 1979: 236)

Later Developments in Comparative Indo-European Religion

As mentioned above, the comparative study of Indo-Iranian religions, the religions of classical antiquity and the Germanic world would lead some Swedish Indologists and historians of religions (especially Rönnow, Wikander and Åke V. Ström) to theorize more broadly about an ancestral Indo-European religion. This paradigm can be considered to grow out of what Müller and scholars after him inaccurately labelled 'Aryan religion'.[2] It had remained an enduring habitus among historians of religion already from the nineteenth century onwards to bring Aryan/Indo-European religion, race and culture in contrast with Semitic equivalents. This is evident, for instance, from the structure of *Tiele-Söderbloms Kompendium*, which distinguishes between three Near Eastern cultural complexes (i.e. Egyptians, Semites and Hittites) in its third section and then turns to the 'Religions of the Aryan Cultures of Asia including Buddhism'. Helmer Ringgren and Ström's *Religionerna i historia och nutid* ('Religions in Past and Present') – arguably by far the most widely used textbook in the History of Religions in Sweden, first published in 1957 and continuously revised and reprinted until the early 1990s – retains the distinction between religions among Indo-European and Semitic peoples where one would today rather have expected cultural-geographical areas (such as the Mediterranean world, Mesopotamia or South Asia) to form the basis of such distinctions, leaving the discussion of ancestral linguistic communities to a separate section.

While the degree of pro-Aryan sentiments among Swedish historians of religion is not the prime focus of this chapter, it is worth noting that the emergent scholarly milieu around Nyberg and his students (especially the young Widengren and Wikander) in Uppsala by the early 1930s was to have a deep impact on George Dumézil's rehabilitation of Indo-European mythology during his formative years as a lecturer in French in Uppsala from 1931 to 1933.

From the 1960s until the 1990s, Mircea Eliade (1907–1986) was almost unanimously hailed as the leading scholar of comparative religion. Sweden was no exception. Eliade wrote books that were extremely comprehensive, trying, in fact, to seize the whole world of religions in a few categories and at the same time uncovering the existential dimensions in religious traditions. This combination made books such as *The Sacred and the Profane: The Nature of Religion* (1961; Swedish translation 1968) and *The Myth of the Eternal Return: Cosmos and History* (1971; Swedish translation 2002) popular among scholars, students and ordinary readers alike. That said, it is debatable whether Eliade's 'phenomenology of religions' functioned more as a stimulus for the interest in comparative religion in general than as a template for scholars. There are at least few works by Swedish scholars which can be safely labelled 'Eliadian' in the same sense as there are 'Dumézilian' works (notably those of Ström and the late Wikander). The closest we get to a scholar building on Eliade might be Edsman, an Uppsala historian of religions famously not on good terms with Widengren and colleagues.

Today, in Sweden, Eliade is read only as a classic. The decline of his popularity began in the 1980s and was paralleled by a similar deprecation of Dumézil's work. In both cases, their youthful involvement in national-conservative politics (and the allegations that these involvements influenced their scholarly views) became a liability in the eyes of many scholars. The main cause to their loss of prestige was, however, the criticism, launched by postmodernists, against *any* form of (large-scale) comparison. When knowledge is revealed as, at its core, a means to power and the exclamation of the day is 'Vive la différence!', systematic comparisons are easily seen as a blatant and crude encroachment to a fluid, multifaceted reality.

If the tradition of comparative religion, especially the once-blossoming study of Indo-European religions, should live on, it needed to be rethought and reformulated. Bruce Lincoln, a student of Eliade and an expert on Indo-European religions, took on the task. Adopting for his dissertation *Priests, Warriors, and Cattle: A Study in the Ecology of Religions* (1981) the perspective of Hultkrantz, Lincoln hoped to ground (Indo-European) comparative religion in some sort of materialism. In retrospect, the materialist approach in the dissertation was perhaps more of the Marxist variety than part of the 'ecology of religions' outlined by Hultkrantz.

Oddly enough, this feasibility to ground comparisons not in cultural-historical developments, evolutionary stages or natural environments but in class relations had been foreshadowed by a dissertation submitted at Stockholm University in 1949. Using not only evidence from Indian caste ideology but also comparanda from other parts of the globe, Per Meurling (1906–1984) in *De fyra väderstrecken: En jämförande religionshistorisk undersökning* (1949) relates conceptualizations of the directions to social classes. Had Meurling's dissertation been submitted twenty years later, it would surely have found the right audience. Instead, it now fell into oblivion (arguably assisted into that state by the author's controversial persona as communist, spy, pornographer, etc.).

From the 1990s onwards, the tradition of comparative religion based on Indo-European languages and culture (and race) struggled in Sweden, as in most countries throughout the world, with the task to rethink its premises. The work of Lincoln, influenced by theoretical criticism raised by Ulf Drobin in his dissertation *Om teori och empiri i religionshistorisk forskning* (1983), had a strong impact on several Swedish scholars. It promised a way forward by proving that Indo-European religion could still be studied seriously, even after the downfall of Dumézil and Eliade, by adopting theories from the social sciences and comparative poetics. Due mainly to advances in these fields and the bourgeoning field of archaeogenetics, the interest in Indo-European languages and culture (not race) has recently started to reconstitute itself, as proven by the formation of Swedish research group Languages and Myths of Prehistory (LAMP).

Ragnarök, Shamanism and a Book on Methodology

Among the Swedish historians/scholars of religion of the nineteenth and twentieth centuries that gained an international reputation, only the work by Söderblom, Widengren and Hultkrantz contributed profoundly to comparative religion in a narrow sense. The methodologies and theories of these scholars varied greatly and testify to the changing knowledge interests (to use Jürgen Habermas's term) that have shaped the field. While today the theological knowledge interests that once informed Söderblom are now confined to the prestigious Faculties of Theology in Uppsala and Lund, the concerns, research questions and methodologies that guided Widengren's historical-philological and Hultkrantz's ethnographic studies continue, but with new perspectives and theories.

As examples of two recent and equally pathfinding contributions, we would like to mention Anders Hultgård's grand-scale comparative approach to Old Norse eschatology (*The End of the World in Scandinavian Mythology: A Comparative Perspective on Ragnarök*, published in 2022) and a critical examination of the global categories of 'shaman' and 'shamanism'. While the two contributions are very different in terms of both their scale and empirical scope, they ensue from a scholarly tradition insisting on linguistic competence as a necessary key to unlocking religious traditions. Hultgård makes use of his linguistic competence to put Old Norse eschatological traditions in a new comparative perspective, whereas Håkan Rydving (2011) does so by addressing the apparent shortcomings of comparative approaches to the circumpolar religious traditions of Eurasia by treating the categories of 'shaman' and 'shamanism' (in contrast to the vernacular category of *šaman* among the Siberian Evenks) as proper objects of research only insofar as the persons or groups at stake (whether indigenous or not) participate in this modern scholarly formation. Linguistically informed arguments about the merits and shortcomings of cross-cultural comparison need not contradict each other; they can be equally successful, and they depend largely on the empirical and epistemological problems we are facing.

Before wrapping up, there is one more book that deserves to be mentioned – a non-empirical study. In 1973, Hultkrantz published *Metodvägar inom den jämförande religionsforskningen* (roughly: *Methods in Comparative Religions*). Besides a conventional description of the source material relevant for a comparative religion enterprise, Hultkrantz shrewdly compares the comparisons. He brings to the fore, among others, diachronic versus synchronic comparisons, philological versus anthropological, historical versus geographical and phenomenological versus structuralist. It is often said about scholars writing in a language that is not English, German or French that if the book had been translated, it would probably have had a huge impact. For *Metodvägar inom den jämförande religionsforskningen*, it is tempting to use this overused claim.

As often is the case in academia, a too shining luminary – and like Söderblom, Nilsson and Widengren, Hultkrantz became internationally renowned – may cast a shadow over potential successors. It is true that Stockholm scholars such as Bäckman and Berglie worked with similar themes as Hultkrantz, but it is probably fair to say that the influence of his theories on Swedish comparative religion have been very limited during the last thirty years. This is even more remarkable considering the fact that the impending climate crisis has impelled scholars to take questions about 'religion and ecology' more seriously than ever.

Conclusions

The comparative study of ancient texts and languages has lost much of its dominant role in the History of Religion, and so has the ethnographic approach, once considered its most promising alternative. Scholars of religion are no longer required to master at least three ancient languages, to conduct fieldwork in inaccessible areas or to peruse a vast corpus of ethnographic reports from various parts of the world. In their place, scholars of religions in Sweden have, like their colleagues around the globe, turned either to empirical specializations within area studies or to rather gnomic theorizations. For the History of Religions, this is an unfortunate turn. Not only has the History of Religions been the leading humanistic field in developing self-reflective and critical ideas around the inevitable cognitive act of comparing, but the withdrawal from comparative studies also has curbed our capability to come up with hypotheses and narratives that have the potential to arouse the interest of the non-scholarly public. This is an endangerment not only for the History of Religion but also for the humanities at large.

Notes

1 We would like to thank Bruce Lincoln (University of Chicago) for sharing with us his thoughts on some crucial concerns of this exposé, not least based on his experiences as a visiting fellow in Uppsala in the mid-1980s. We also wish to thank Erik af Edholm (Stockholm University) for supplying valuable information about the so-called 'Vayu theosophy' based on a handwritten dedication from Carl-Martin Edsman on Ernst Arban's copy of Anders Olerud's 1951 doctoral dissertation (see the section '"Vayu Theosophy", or Comparative Indo-European Religion).
2 A self-designation among ancient speakers of Indian and Iranian languages, the term 'Aryan' has also been used idiosyncratically from the mid-nineteenth century as a

synonym of the more inclusive and less ambiguous linguistic term 'Indo-European' (German *indogermanisch*). As regards the all-inclusive sense of 'Aryan', the emphasis typically lies in the cultural spirit and racial character of these speakers rather than in their linguistic affinities.

References

Arbman, E. (1922), *Rudra. Untersuchungen zum altindischen Glauben und Kultus*, Uppsala: Uppsala University.
Arbman, E. (1926), *Untersuchungen zur primitiven Seelenvorstellung mit besonderer Rücksicht auf Indien*, Uppsala: Uppsala University.
Arvidsson, S. (2002), 'Stig Wikander och forskningen om ariska mannaförbund', *Chaos: Dansk-norsk tidsskrift for religionshistoriske studier* 38: 55–68.
Benzow, K. (1948), *Torgny Segerstedt som religionsforskare*, Göteborg: Göteborgs kungl. vetenskaps- och vitterhets-samhälles handlingar.
Bosch, L. P. van den (2002), *Friedrich Max Müller: A Life Devoted to the Humanities*, Leiden: Brill.
Davis, J. R., and A. Nicholls (2017), *Friedrich Max Müller and the Role of Philology in Victorian Thought*, Abingdon: Routledge.
Drobin, U. (1983), *Om teori och empiri i religionshistorisk forskning*, Stockholm: Stockholm University.
Eliade, M. (1961), *The Sacred and the Profane: The Nature of Religion*, New York: Harper & Brothers.
Eliade, M. (1971), *The Myth of the Eternal Return: Cosmos and History*, Princeton: Princeton University Press.
Freiberger, O. (2019), *Considering Comparison: A Method for Religious Studies*, New York: Oxford University Press.
Hultgård, A. (2022), *The End of the World in Scandinavian Mythology: A Comparative Perspective on Ragnarök*, New York: Oxford University Press.
Hultkrantz, Å. (1966), 'An Ecological Approach to Religion', *Ethnos* 31: 1–4.
Hultkrantz, Å. (1979), 'Ecology of Religion: Its Scope and Methodology'", in L. Honko (ed.), *Science of Religion. Studies in Methodology: Proceedings of the Study Conference of the International Association for the History of Religions, held in Turku, Finland, August 27-31, 1973*, 221–36, Berlin: De Gruyter.
Hultkrantz, Å. (1973), *Metodvägar inom den jämförande religionsforskningen*, Stockholm: Esselte studium.
Jonson, J. (2014), *Jag är bara Nathan Söderblom satt till tjänst: En biografi*, Stockholm: Verbum.
Junginger, H., ed. (2008), *The Study of Religion under the Impact of Fascism*, Leiden: Brill.
Kahle, S. (1991), *H.S. Nyberg: En vetenskapsmans biografi*, Stockholm: Norstedt.
Lange, D. (2014), *Nathan Söderblom och hans tid*, Skellefteå: Artos & Norma.
Larsson, G., ed. (2022a), *The Legacy, Life and Work of Geo Widengren and the Study of the History of Religions after World War II*, Leiden: Brill.
Larsson, G. (2022b), 'Pondering the Legacy of Geo Widengren: Isolated Genius, or Uncritical Supporter of a Band of Brothers?', *Method and Theory in the Study of Religion*, https://doi.org/10.1163/15700682-bja10093.

Lincoln, B. (1981), *Priests, Warriors, and Cattle: A Study in the Ecology of Religions*, Berkeley: University of California Press.
Lincoln, B. (2018), *Apples and Oranges: Explorations in, on, and with Comparison*, Chicago: University of Chicago Press.
Meurling, P. (1949), *De fyra väderstrecken: En jämförande religionshistorisk undersökning*, Stockholm: Stockholms högskola.
Nilsson, M. P. (1932), *The Mycenaean Origin of Greek Mythology*, Cambridge: Cambridge University Press.
Nilsson, M. P. (1940), *Greek Popular Religion*, New York: Columbia University Press.
Nilsson, M. P. (1961), *Greek Folk Religion*, New York: Harper.
Nilsson, M. P. (1963), *Helvetets förhistoria. Straff och sällhet i den andra världen i förkristen religion*, Stockholm: Aldus/Bonnier.
Nyberg, H. S. (1937), *Irans forntida religioner. Olaus-Petri-föreläsningar vid Uppsala universitet*, Stockholm: Svenska kyrkans diakonistyrelse.
Ringgren, H., and Å. V. Ström (1957), *Religionerna i historia och nutid*, Stockholm: Diakonistyrelse.
Rönnow, K. (1943), 'Zagreus och Dionysos', *Religion och Bibel* II: 15–48.
Rydving, H. (2011), 'Le chamanismne aujourd'hui: constructions et déconstructions d'une illusion scientifique', *Études Mongoles et sibériennes, centralasiatiques et tibétaines* 43: 1–15.
Segerstedt, T. (1903), *Till frågan om polyteismens uppkomst: En religionshistorisk undersökning*, Uppsala: Uppsala University.
Sharpe, E. J. (1975), *Comparative Religion: A History*, London: Duckworth.
Smith, J. Z. (1990), *Drudgery Divine: On the Comparison of Early Christianities and the Religions of Late Antiquity*, Chicago: University of Chicago Press.
Smith, J. Z. (2004), *Relating Religion: Essays in the Study of Religion*, Chicago: University of Chicago Press.
Söderblom, N. (1899), *Les fravashis: Étude sur les traces dans le mazdéisme d'une ancienne conception sur la survivance des morts*, Paris: Leroux.
Söderblom, N., ed. (1908), *Främmande religionsurkunder. I urval och öfversättning*, Stockholm: Geber.
Tiele, K. P., and N. Söderblom (1931), *Tiele-Söderbloms Kompendium der Religionsgeschichte*, Berlin: Theophil Biller's Verlag.
Timuş, M. (2008), 'Quand l'Allemagne était leur Mecque… La science des religions chez Stig Wikander (1935–1944)', in H. Junginger (ed.), *The Study of Religion under the Impact of Fascism*, 205–28, Leiden: Brill.
Widengren, G. (1946), *Religionens ursprung: En kort framställning av de evolutionistiska religionsteorierna och kritiken mot dessa*, Stockholm: Diakonistyrelse.
Widengren, G. (1947), *Tor Andræ*, Uppsala: Lindblad.
Wikander, S. (1941), *Vayu: Texte und Untersuchungen zur indo-iranischen Religionsgeschichte: T. 1. Texte*, Uppsala: Lundequistska bokhandel.

Chapter 14

RITUAL STUDIES

Anne-Christine Hornborg

This chapter presents some early Swedish publications on ritual and the international inspiration derived from the entry of the field of Ritual Studies into Sweden, in part through an interdisciplinary conference at Lund University in 2005 discussing the multifaceted ways of approaching rituals within different disciplines. The chapter then reviews some publications on different ritual contexts (Sweden, Canada, Peru) which look at concepts such as embodiment, interrituality, ritual ontology, objects and agency, rituals as environmental practices and as conciliatory practices. Several examples are also provided of the increasing number of Swedish publications focusing on rituals in recent years, which in different ways develop the research within this field.

There have long been Swedish researchers with an interest in rituals, for example, Åke Hultkrantz (1920–2006), former Professor in History of Religion at Stockholm University. He was an expert on North American Natives and carried out many years of field research with the Shoshoni in Wyoming. Among his many publications on rituals is *Belief and Worship in Native North America* (1981), a collection of fifteen essays on the religious attitudes and practices of various North American Native communities. Topics include the importance of myths and rituals, the cult of the dead, the Spirit Lodge, the Sun Dance Lodge, the Ghost Dance and the spread of the Peyote Cult. Another publication is *Shamanic Healing and Ritual Drama: Health and Medicine in the Native North American Religious Traditions* (1992), in which he offers a detailed survey of Native American practices and beliefs regarding health, medicine and religion. In contrast to the sharp Euro-American division between medicine and religion, Hultkrantz proposed that Native American medical beliefs and practices only can be assessed in relation to their religious ideas.

Another researcher with an early interest in rituals is Britt-Mari Näsström, Professor Emerita in History of Religions at the University of Gothenburg. Among her publication could be mentioned *The Abhorrence of Love: Studies in Rituals and Mystic Aspects in Catullus' Poem of Attis* (1989). This publication examines the peculiar rites belonging to the mysteries of Cybele and Attis and concentrates on the initiation of the Attis priest. Another publication, *Blot – tro och offer i det förkristna Norden* (2002), examines sacrifice as central in pre-Christian society. In *Blot*, Näsström describes how the sacrificial rituals were conducted and how the phenomenon of sacrifice was anchored in the world of religious imagination.

Tord Olsson (1942–2013), former Professor in History of Religion at Lund University, inspired a new generation of ritual researchers. His guidance over several years created a 'Lund school', with several theses focusing on the study of rituals. Olsson was a diligent fieldworker and visited the Maasai people in Kenya and the Bambara in Mali. Based on his encounters with rituals during several years of fieldwork in Mali, he argues that traditional religious life in the small Bambara village of Gwanyebugu cannot be described as a coherent system of rites, myths, traditions and beliefs (Olsson 2010). In the village, three ritual-mythical fields can be distinguished at the same time, while people, often the same individuals, move between these fields. Olsson proposes that the myths emanate and draw their power from what he calls 'ritual fields'. He also spent time in Turkey with Sufi dervishes to study and participate in their rituals to describe the spiritual, bodily and emotional experience that they conveyed. In one article (Olsson 2001), he describes the setting where the 'whirling dervishes' perform their dancing. Music plays an important part; some Muslims reject music as leading people to destruction, while others praise music for its possibility to search for divine love or religious intoxication. The Cerrahi Sufis' rituals in Istanbul are described from the perspective of participant observation. These rituals contain several elements which cannot easily be converted into language. Olsson writes that one explanation for why people devote themselves to religious symbols can be found precisely in the fact that they form a kind of non-linguistic representation which conveys physical and mental experiences and cultural and social values in a way that other media cannot.

Although there was an interest in rituals and ritual practice in earlier research in Sweden, it would increase as Swedish researchers followed the international development in this field. The establishment of the approach of Ritual Studies became an important source of inspiration that broadened the earlier study of rituals.

The Emergence of Ritual Studies and Its Introduction in Sweden

The increased interest in rituals as objects of study is reflected in the American Academy of Religion's call in 1977 for more systematic research on the subject. Ritual Studies as a specific interdisciplinary subject strengthened its position in 1982, when the Ritual Studies Group was formed. One of those setting the tone was Ronald Grimes, director of Ritual Studies International and Professor of Religion and Culture at Wilfrid Laurier University. The journal *Religious Studies Review* showed the versatility of the new study of ritual, and in 1987, the *Journal of Ritual Studies* was established. In 2013, Grimes was awarded an honorary doctorate at the Lund Faculty of Theology in Sweden for his inspiration (see e.g. Grimes 1990, 2014) for the ongoing work of the study of rituals at the department.

Ritual Studies made it possible to bind together several scholarly disciplines to focus on a topic that ranges from normative concerns in theology and liturgy to more descriptive and socio-analytic theories. At Uppsala University, a seminar was held in the spring of 2000 to discuss the innovative ways in which rituals were being addressed (Stausberg, Sundqvist and Svalaskog 2002). Later, in 2003, Ritual Studies as a specific subject was formally introduced in Sweden at the Center for Theology and Religious Studies at Lund University through the establishment of a four-year assistant professorship in History of Religions to further develop ritual research. The initiator was Professor Olsson, whose research and inspiring guidance over several years had created a 'Lund school' with several theses focusing on rituals.

One of these theses dealt with the Mi'kmaq First Nation people in Canada (Nova Scotia) and their defence of a mountain that they considered sacred, Kluskap's Mountain, which was threatened by large-scale mining (Hornborg 2001). The thesis discussed sacred sites, colonialism, historiography, ethnicity and various political/religious groupings. Although the rituals were constantly present, Hornborg probably made the mistake many do when studying these practices: they are reduced to mere expressions of thoughts and ideologies. But in 2003 Hornborg was granted the above-mentioned four-year assistant professorship to develop the field of Ritual Studies, and these years changed her research. From now on, the concept of ritual became a topic of its own, inspiring the pursuit of a language for understanding and analysing ritual practices. This pursuit has since permeated two decades of research and supervising doctoral students, often inspired by Ritual Studies.

To investigate the currently ongoing interdisciplinary study of rituals, a conference was arranged in Lund in 2005, inviting researchers from different disciplines to discuss multidisciplinary perspectives on the various kinds of formalized behaviour categorized as rituals. The participating researchers presented their approaches to questions such as: How does ritual differ from other action? Which theories do we need? How can we use experiences from other disciplines? The archaeologists Liv Nilsson Stutz and Åsa Berggren (2010: 53–64) showed how ritual studies and ritual theory have been a great source of inspiration in archaeologists' work on reconstructing and contextualizing rituals in the past. The ethnologists Professor Lynn Åkesson and Assistant Professor Karin Salomonsson (2010: 53–64) discussed Catherine Bell's observation (1997) that we are today facing a new ritual paradigm, in which the individual is at the centre of these new practices, rather than ideology, belief or the collective. Stephan Borgehammar, Professor in Practical Theology, saw both similarities and differences between what he calls the younger sister Ritual Studies and the older sister Liturgical Studies (2010: 65–78). Rikard Loman, from the Department of Literature, analysed the relationship between ritual and theatre (2010: 79–96). Based on results in current memory psychology research, Professor Carl Martin Allwood, from the Department of Psychology, demonstrated how the 'distributed cognition' approach contributes to increasing our understanding of rituals (2010: 97–114). Tord Olsson Professor in History of Religions, discussed encounters with rituals during his multi-year fieldwork in Mali (2010: 115–50). Anne-Christine

Hornborg's (2010b: 151–69) presentation discussed the new ritualized contexts that are said to promote the individual's well-being and health, and which have become a rapidly growing market in contemporary Sweden. The interdisciplinary discussion at the conference provided the foundation for a publication on the use of rituals in different disciplines: *Den rituella människan – flervetenskapliga perspektiv* (Hornborg 2010a).

The Versatility of Ritual as an Opening to Multidisciplinary Perspectives

New ways of conceptualizing ritual language, performances and structure, some based on influences from other scholarly disciplines, henceforth inspired Swedish researchers. In what follows, we turn to some examples from publications that discuss central concepts and focus on ritual practice and performance rather than merely on ritual as a display of faith.

In analysing the design of new healing practices that have rapidly developed in Sweden in recent years, it has been useful to apply terminology from Ritual Studies (Hornborg 2012, 2021a,b). By focusing on the 'ritual language' and on how intense emotions and feelings of transformation are created through performances, similarities can be observed between the new healing therapies and how Pentecostal preachers and world-leading coaches like Anthony Robbins (Robbins.youtube) in like manner very consciously design ritual acts into full-scale experiences. In these acts, happiness and feelings of fulfilment are highlighted, a state of mind which Abraham Maslow (1964) has described as 'peak experience' (Robbins markets himself as a 'Peak Performer Strategist'). The article 'Rebranding the Soul: Designing Rituals for the Well-Made Man in Market Society' (Hornborg 2021b) discusses how these new practices reveal a clear, secular prosperity theology with conversion narratives about a new, better life, including missionary injunctions to redeem others.

The dissolution of colonialism and the awakened interest among indigenous peoples in their history have also generated new forms of rituals that are difficult to classify. The article '"I'm Inca": The Fiesta of Mamacha Carmen in the Andean village of Pisac' (Hornborg 2007) examines the communication of identity in ritual dancing during the Fiesta de Virgen del Carmen in Pisac, a village in the Peruvian Andes. In framing an arena for representation and interpretation of local lifeworlds, the fiesta is endowed with profoundly existential significance for the participants. In performing the different characters, the dancers are given opportunities to renegotiate social and economic structures. By using their bodies to transcend their everyday practices and habitus, and to infuse them with new meanings, the dancers articulate new and politically transformative messages about tradition, power and social hierarchy. An interesting question is if the newly created Inca ceremonies in front of the Sun Temple of Coricancha in the old Inca capital of Cuzco should be seen as modern Peruvians' way of creating continuity and pride in their traditions or be dismissed as simply a tourist spectacle. The article describes how one local Quechua spectator proudly declared: 'I'm Inca!'

Another interdisciplinary approach is to look at similarities in textual and ritual studies. Like texts, rituals can be classified into different genres, but more with regard to the actions than the content. The stylistic literary figure of parallelism can be found in the structure of the ritual acts (Tambiah 1985), and the use of intertextuality can be transformed into inter*rituality* in the construction of new rituals. By reusing minor ritual acts or objects from other established rituals classified as 'tradition', newly invented performances can also be experienced as tradition. The article 'Interrituality as a Means to Perform the Art of Building New Rituals' (Hornborg 2017) closely examines ritual creativity and invention by a Mi'kmaq pipe carrier in his staging of a *kekunit*, a godparent ritual, performed in a Mi'kmaq First Nations Reserve in Nova Scotia, Canada. The use of interrituality – borrowing minor ritual acts or elements including objects found in other rituals – becomes important in creating a sense of established ritual and to frame an invented rite as traditional and familiar. Interrituality thus authorizes the new performance and contributes to giving the participants feelings of being Mi'kmaq and following the traditional path.

Ritual is also an embodied way of communication, as Thomas Csordas has shown in his classical article 'Somatic Modes of Attention' (1993). Following his discussion, the article 'Eloquent Bodies: Rituals in the Context of Alleviating Suffering' (Hornborg 2005) examines how the revitalization of traditional rituals has been an effective way of developing a new embodiment and identity. The ability of the Canadian Mi'kmaq to rework the cultural body, historically imposed on them by the dominant society, opens the way to weeding out destructive patterns unconsciously or consciously embedded historically in their bodies. The ritual gives them opportunities to explore a new *habitus* and to employ the body in a domain shared with like-minded peers so as to facilitate new ways of approaching the world. The rituals thus provide redemptive opportunities for bodies that have been disempowered by hegemonic contexts and simultaneously offer social affirmation of the new way of being in the world.

A much-discussed topic today is the concept of animism and how to cleanse it from historical and evolutionary narratives classifying it as a primitive world view. A more interesting approach is to look at how specific ontologies are created in rituals as basic social acts (Rappaport 1999), based on acceptance and social consequences for the participants beyond displaying their world view or beliefs. Are, for example, Catholics cannibalistic creatures because they eat a man's body and drink his blood? Or is communion performed at a societal level, creating a specific ritual ontology rather than reflecting the participants everyday belief? The article 'Objects as Subjects: Agency, and Performativity in Rituals' (Hornborg 2016) looks deeper into how objects in the ritual ontology are transformed into subjects with social consequences that may even effect ordinary life when the ritual is over. In ritual theory, objects have mostly been discussed in terms of symbols and interpretations. However, material objects that are employed in rituals are not merely passive carriers of attached cultural meanings. Objects do not only become animated in rituals but as such are also ascribed agency, thus further animating the ritual field. As ritual agents, they achieve important performative functions in the field of transformations. The smoke of burning sage in a ritual setting is not like an everyday smoke but sacred, and it not only symbolizes a purification process for the participants, but – as a performative agent – it 'actually' cleanses them of bad spirits in their ongoing lives. Thus, this animation has social consequences even beyond the ritual, regardless of the individual belief or unbelief. In attributing personhood and agency to objects, it is thus more useful to discuss the phenomenology of animism and ritual objects as forms of relational epistemology than as cases of epistemological fallacies indicating a childish or 'primitive' world view.

Rituals can also be employed in the service of environmental issues. This is discussed in 'Protecting Earth? Rappaport's Vision of Rituals as Environmental Practices' (Hornborg 2008), which refers to Roy Rappaport's general theory of ritual. It starts by discussing technology as a kind of ritual product of science and then briefly presents Rappaport's ritual theory as an aid in understanding how Mi'kmaq have employed rituals in their efforts to protect a sacred mountain from being turned into a superquarry. The Mi'kmaq communicated an important message in their rituals: this issue concerned the meaning of places, Mi'kmaq traditions and non-negotiable values. Turning the protest actions into ritual acts amounted to the strategic use of a specific practice which the authorities and the mining company could not deal with (How do you argue with a song?). It thus affected political decisions and in the long run also protected the environment. It was through the use of eagle feathers, sweetgrass, drums and the concept of Mother Earth that the mountain was protected from technological impact and thus saved for coming generations.

Another way of looking into the ritual language is to study how it reconciles different and seemingly contradictory practices, such as being a Catholic and a First Nation traditionalist. The article 'Ritual Practice as Power Play or Redemptive Hegemony: The Mi'kmaq Appropriation of Catholicism' (Hornborg 2004; see also Hornborg 2002), discusses how the annual celebration of St. Anne's Day (the mother of Mary) has become such an integral part of Mi'kmaq life that they refer to it as Mi'kmaq tradition. If neo-traditionalism has meant a revival of ancient traditions like the sweat lodge, most Mi'kmaq will still join the Catholic St. Anne's Day event, which has been celebrated at Chapel Island since the eighteenth century. Performed in a Mi'kmaq context, the ritual works as 'redemptive hegemony' (Bell 1997: 2), reconciling two traditions.

Finally, there are researchers who themselves have become ritual innovators and practitioners (e.g. Harner ([1980]1990). An example of a Swedish scholar who also combined her research with self-composed rituals for others is Maria Liljas Stålhandske. Inspired by ritual scholars such as Bell (1992, 1997), Arnold Van Gennep (1960) and Victor Turner (1974, 1982, 1986), she not only describes the theories relevant to her discussions in *Ritual Invention: A Play Perspective on Existential Ritual and Mental Health in Late Modern Sweden* (2005) but also puts them to work by creating rituals for healing. Her work points to the transitional mode of relating, which balances distance and absorption, as a mood that can be related to a liminal process and to the promotion of mental health. The health-promoting ritual process is described as offering a moment in which the boundaries between self and other, between bodily experience and cultural communication, are resolved.

Further Development of Putting Ritual in Focus in Swedish Publications

As mentioned above, ritual phenomena are now increasingly visible in several Swedish publications and dissertation projects. A first scholar to mention is Henrik Bogdan, Professor in Religious Studies at the University of Gothenburg, who addresses alternative religious traditions and practices, such as Western esotericism, new religious movements and initiatory societies and orders. His *Western Esotericism and Rituals of Initiation* ([2003]2007) explores three hundred years' practice of Masonic rituals of initiation which have been part of Western culture, spreading far beyond the boundaries of traditional Freemasonry, and the historical development of these rituals and their relationship with Western esotericism.

André Möller's book *Ramadan in Java: The Joy and Jihad of Ritual Fasting* (2005) provides its readers with ways of approaching and understanding Ramadan – and various different Islamic phenomena – in Indonesia and in other parts of the Muslim world. It is argued that we may approach Islam from three different angles, that is, to discuss it from the normative, the written and the lived perspectives, respectively. In this study, thorough attention is thus directed not only to the classical and normative Islamic texts and the lived reality in Java but also to the popular and contemporary Indonesian literature on Ramadan.

Martin Modéus (since December 2022 the archbishop of Sweden) chose to study the Biblical *shelamim* in *Sacrifice and Symbol: Biblical Shelamim in a Ritual Perspective* (2005) and suggests that an investigation of ritual issues should start with the situation that creates the need for the performance, not in an analysis of the ritual's form or content. He suggests that the term *shelamim* entered the texts through glossation, in order to specify the slaughtered sacrifice, the *zebah*, of the legitimate cult. Most probably, the need for this specification began to be felt when the centralization of the cult in effect divided the old, slaughtered sacrifice in two: a domestic slaughter of lesser ritual value and a solemn cultic performance in the only legitimate cult site, the temple of Jerusalem.

Professor David Thurfjell, of Södertörn University, has examined ritual processes in contemporary Islam: *Living Shi'ism: Instances of Ritualisation Among Islamic Men in Contemporary Iran* (2006). This book is about Iranian Islamism at the grass-roots level. It provides a vivid, near-life portrait of young activist men who uphold the movement through their zealous support of revolutionary ideals and the present regime. By focusing on beliefs and rituals of individual persons, it gives a unique picture of the shifting motifs behind Islamist engagement in today's Iran. The book contextualizes the interviewed individuals within the wider framework of Iranian society and relates their stories to a discussion on ritual, emotion, embodiment and authority.

In Kristina Myrvold's *Inside the Guru's Gate: Ritual Uses of Texts among the Sikhs in Varanasi* (2007), the focus is on the holy scripture Guru Granth Sahib and the rituals for taking care of the book. The scripture is installed daily on an elevated throne like a royal sovereign who/which admits worshippers and at nightfall is ceremonially taken to a special bedroom for rest. In religious services, the Sikhs daily recite and sing hymns from the scripture and explore its semantic contents for guidance in their social life.

In her studies of women's groups in England, *Cultivating the Sacred: Ritual Creativity and Practice among Women in Contemporary Europe* (2010), Åsa Trulsson analyzes how ritual creativity may seem like a contradiction in terms, yet the religious landscape in contemporary Euro-America is permeated with experimentation of ritual forms, different modalities of action, imagination and play as routes to authenticity. Her study examines different settings in Europe involved in such ritual creativity, which would commonly be classified as postmodern spirituality, new age or paganism.

Another example focused on rituals is Jessica Moberg's work *Piety, Intimacy and Mobility: A Case Study of Charismatic Christianity in Present-Day Stockholm* (2013), which deals with Pentecostal Christianity, where ritual is constantly present. Moberg describes how practitioners cultivate a form of charismatic piety characterized by certain embodied orientations, patterns of ritualization and narrative genres. To shed further light on this process, the book draws upon a variety of theories concerning ritualization, embodiment, performance, narratives and materiality.

In *American Dervish: Making Mevlevism in the United States of America* (2013), Simon Sorgenfrei, professor at Södertörn University, describes results of fieldwork carried out among Mevlevi Order of America (MOA) circles in the United States and Europe between 2008 and 2010. He focuses on the use of narratives, documents, garments and rituals in informant's Mevlevi-making. Primarily, the study set out to examine how members of the MOA practice and authorize what they define as being Mevlevi Sufism.

Tao Thykier Makeeff's *Do Satyrs Wear Sneakers? Hellenic Polytheism and the Reception of Antiquity in Contemporary Greece – a Study in Serious Play* (2019), describes contemporary Hellenic polytheist rituals and discusses how and why they are designed and performed. The author underlines the importance of understanding ritual as play, but often serious play, and emphasizes the importance of religious musicality and improvisation as a key to understanding the dynamics of ritual and ritual change.

Martina Prosén's work, *A Rhythm That Connects My Heart with God: Worship, Ritual and Pentecostal Spirituality as Theology* (2021), seeks to shed light on Pentecostal theology and spirituality through an investigation of worship as it is practiced in two urban Pentecostal-charismatic churches in Nairobi, Kenya. The study combines insights from Pentecostal studies, more specifically Pentecostal theology, and ritual studies, particularly performance theory. The analysis is indebted to ritual theorists and their understanding of ritual as embodied action, functioning in complex ways to create meaning, attune bodies and enact transformation. By utilizing a performance perspective on ritual, the study highlights the way worship is enacted in time and space.

Henrik Ohlsson at Södertörn University conducted field research in Sweden and Finland between 2017 and 2022, and his work *Facing Nature: Cultivating Experience in the Nature Connection Movement* (2022) follows a burgeoning social movement in which connection with nature is seen as a means of both personal well-being and ecological sustainability at the societal level. The thesis describes and analyses ideas, practices, organizations and literature in a contemporary cultural context in the borderland between health practice, environmental activism and spirituality. It also examines participants' personal experiences and understands both the practice and its social milieu as a cultivation of experience, whereby experiences of nature as being alive and communicative are maintained and enhanced.

Ive Brissman discusses similar 'green' themes in *Wild Enchantment in the Anthropocene: Exploring the Wild in Narratives, Practices and Place in Dark Green Spirituality* (2021). Her concept of 'negotiating baselines' refers to practices that work to read landscapes, to restore the lost memories, and relate to deep time perspectives. In exploring various workshops, she found that narrative, practice and place form a node, which together offer ways how to cultivate wild enchantment.

Olivia Cejvan puts pedagogy and ritual at the center in *Arts and Crafts Divine: Teaching and Learning Ritual Magic in Sodalitas Rosae Crucis* (2023). Focusing on practices and learning environments, from large, formal initiation ceremonies to playful rituals in intimate social situations, the study explores a variety of didactical tools and the reasons for, and effects of, their use. It maps how teaching and learning unfold in scaffolding, assessment and reiteration practices, with attention to teachings and informal storytelling, small talk and the diverse uses of secrecy which characterize teaching and learning in Sodalitas Rosae Crucis.

The above list could be extended, but it highlights some important contributions to the study of rituals as it has been established and continues to engage researchers in Swedish religious studies.

Conclusions

This chapter discusses how new perspectives on studying rituals in all their diversity and contexts have found their way into Swedish research. When Ritual Studies as a subject was formally introduced at Lund University in 2003, an interdisciplinary conference in 2005 discussed how different disciplines have adopted the ritual language and how bridges might be built. The chapter presents several Swedish researchers who have focused on rituals, and it reviews some specific concepts that are discussed in their different publications. A focus on rituals is now deeply embedded in Swedish religious studies and will certainly continue in future research and publications.

References

Allwood, C. M. (2010), 'Ritualer: självförverkligande eller tvångsupprepning?', in A-C. Hornborg (ed.), *Den rituella människan – flervetenskapliga perspektiv*, 97–114, Linköping University Electronic Press: http://liu.diva-portal.org/smash/get/diva2:347184/.

Bell, C. (1992), *Ritual Theory, Ritual Practice*, New York: Oxford University Press.
Bell, C. (1997), *Ritual: Perspectives and Dimensions*, New York: Oxford University Press.
Berggren, Å., and L. Nilsson Stutz (2010), 'Ett utmanat koncept? Ritualbegreppets möte med arkeologin', in A.-C. Hornborg (ed.), *Den rituella människan – flervetenskapliga perspektiv*, 25–52, Linköping University Electronic Press: http://liu.diva-portal.org/smash/get/diva2:347097/FULLTEXT01.pdf.
Bogdan, H. ([2003]2007), *Western Esotericism and Rituals of Initiation*, Albany: State University of New York Press.
Borgehammar, S. (2010), 'Den äldre systern – en kort introduktion till Liturgivetenskapen', in A.-C. Hornborg (ed.), *Den rituella människan – flervetenskapliga perspektiv*, 65–78, Linköping University Electronic Press: http://liu.diva-portal.org/smash/get/diva2:347184/.
Brissman, I. (2021), *Wild Enchantment in the Anthropocene: Exploring the Wild in Narratives, Practices and Place in Dark Green Spirituality*, thesis, Lund University: Media-Tryck.
Cejvan, O. (2023), *Arts and Crafts Divine: Teaching and Learning Ritual Magic in Sodalitas Rosae Crucis*, thesis, Lund University: Media-Tryck.
Csordas, T. J. (1993), 'Somatic Modes of Attention', *Cultural Anthropology* 8 (2): 135–56.
Grimes, R. L. (1990), *Ritual Criticism: Case Studies in Its Practice, Essays on Its Theory*, Columbia: University of South Carolina Press.
Grimes, R. L. (2014), *The Craft of Ritual Studies*, New York: Oxford University Press.
Harner, M. ([1980]1990), *The Way of the Shaman*, New York: HarperCollins.
Hornborg, A.-C. (2001), *A Landscape of Left-Overs: Changing Conceptions of Place and Environment among Mi'kmaq Indians of Eastern Canada*, thesis, Lund: Almqvist & Wiksell International.
Hornborg, A.-C. (2002), 'St Anne's Day – A Time to "Turn Home" for the Canadian Mi'kmaq Indians', *International Review of Mission* XCI (361): 237–55.
Hornborg, A.-C. (2004), 'Ritual Practice as Power Play or Redemptive Hegemony: The Mi'kmaq Appropriation of Catholicism', *Swedish Missiological Themes* (92) 2:169–93.
Hornborg, A.-C. (2005), 'Eloquent bodies: Rituals in the Context of Alleviating Suffering', *Numen* 52 (3): 356–94.
Hornborg, A.-C. (2007), ' "I'm Inca": The Fiesta of Mamacha Carmen in the Andean village of Pisac', *Journal of Ritual Studies* 21 (2): 46–56.
Hornborg, A.-C. (2008), 'Protecting Earth? Rappaport's Vision of Rituals as Environmental Practices', *Journal of Human Ecology* 24 (4): 275–83.
Hornborg, A.-C., ed. (2010a). *Den rituella människan – flervetenskapliga perspektiv*, Linköping University Electronic Press: http://urn.kb.se/resolve?urn=urn:nbn:se:liu:diva-58921.
Hornborg, A.-C. (2010b), 'Marknadsföring av natur, hälsa och rituellt helande i det senmoderna Sverige', in A-C. Hornborg (ed.), *Den rituella människan – flervetenskapliga perspektiv*, Linköping University Electronic Press: http://liu.diva-portal.org/smash/get/diva2:347193/FULLTEXT01.
Hornborg, A.-C. (2012), *Coaching och lekmannaterapi – en modern väckelse*, Falun: Dialogos.
Hornborg, A.-C. (2016), 'Objects as Subjects: Agency, and Performativity in Rituals', in M. Broo, T. Hovi, P. Ingman and T. Utriainen (eds), *The Relational Dynamics of Enchantment and Sacralization: Changing the Terms of the Religion vs Science Debate*, International Association for the History of Religions book series, 27–44, Bristol, CT: Equinox.

Hornborg, A.-C. (2017), 'Interrituality as the Mean to Perform the Art of Building New Rituals', *Journal of Ritual Studies* 31 (2): 17–27.

Hornborg, A.-C. (2021a), 'Designing Enchanted Rituals for Modern Man', in P. J. Stewart and A. Strathern (eds), *The Palgrave Handbook of Anthropological Ritual Studies*, 255–74, Palgrave: Macmillan.

Hornborg, A.-C. (2021b), 'Rebranding the Soul: Designing Rituals for the Well-made Man in Market Society', in J. Cornelio, F. Gauthier, T. Martikainen and L. Woodhead (eds), *Routledge International Handbook of Religion in Global Society*, 52–62, London: Routledge.

Hultkrantz, Å. (1981), *Belief and Worship in Native North America*, New York: Syracuse University Press.

Hultkrantz, Å. (1992), *Shamanic Healing & Ritual Drama: Health & Medicine in the Native North American Religious Tradition*, New York: Crossroad.

Liljas Stålhandske, M. (2005), *Ritual Invention: A Play Perspective on Existential Ritual and Mental Health in Late Modern Sweden*, thesis, Uppsala: Diakonivetenskapliga institutet.

Loman, R. (2010), 'Västerländsk teater ur ett ritperspektiv', in A.-C. Hornborg (ed.), *Den rituella människan – flervetenskapliga perspektiv*, 79–96, Linköping University Electronic Press: http://urn.kb.se/resolve?urn=urn:nbn:se:liu:diva-58921.

Makeeff, T. Thykier (2019), *Do Satyrs Wear Sneakers? Hellenic Polytheism and the Reception of Antiquity in Contemporary Greece – a Study in Serious Play*, thesis, Lund University: Media-Tryck.

Maslow, A. (1964), *Religions, Values, and Peak Experiences* (Kappa Delta Pi Lecture Series), Ohio: Ohio State University Press.

Moberg, J. (2013), *Piety, Intimacy and Mobility: A Case Study of Charismatic Christianity in Present-Day Stockholm*, Huddinge: Södertörns högskola.

Modéus, M. (2005), *Sacrifice and Symbol: Biblical Shelamim in a Ritual Perspective*, Coniectanea Biblica Old Testament Series 52, thesis, Stockholm: Almqvist & Wiksell International.

Myrvold, K. (2007), *Inside the Guru's Gate: Ritual Uses of Texts among the Sikhs in Varanasi*, Lund Studies in African and Asian Religions, vol. 17, Department of History and Anthropology of Religions, thesis, Lund University: Media-Tryck.

Möller, A. (2005), *Ramadan in Java: The Joy and Jihad of Ritual Fasting*, Lund Studies in History of Religion, vol. 20, thesis, Stockholm: Almqvist & Wiksell International.

Näsström, B.-M. (1989), *The Abhorrence of Love: Studies in Rituals and Mystic Aspects in Catullus' Poem of Attis*, Stockholm: Almqvist & Wiksell International.

Näsström, B.-M. (2002), *Blot – tro och offer i det förkristna Norden*, Stockholm: Norstedts.

Ohlsson, H. (2022), *Facing Nature: Cultivating Experience in the Nature Connection Movement*, Huddinge: Södertörns högskola.

Olsson, T. (2001), 'Rituell musik och islamsk musik, det mesta i Turkiet', *Svenskt Gudstjänstliv* 76: 65–76.

Olsson, T. (2010), 'Den dubbla blicken: en berättelse om konsten att frammana rituell närvaro hos bambarafolket i Mali', in A.-C. Hornborg (ed.), *Den rituella människan – flervetenskapliga perspektiv*, 115–50, Linköping University Electronic Press: http://liu.diva-portal.org/smash/get/diva2:347191/FULLTEXT01.pdf.

Prosén, M. (2021), *A Rhythm that Connects my Heart with God: Worship, Ritual and Pentecostal Spirituality as Theology*, thesis, Lund: Media-Tryck.

Rappaport, R. (1999), *Ritual and Religion in the Making of Humanity*, Cambridge: Cambridge University Press.

Salomonsson, K., and L. Åkesson (2010), 'Ritualernas marknad: etnologisk forskning om livscykelriter och upplevelseindustrin', in A.-C. Hornborg (ed.), *Den rituella människan – flervetenskapliga perspektiv*, 53–64, Linköping University Electronic Press: http://liu.diva-portal.org/smash/get/diva2:347156/FULLTEXT01.pdf.

Sorgenfrei, S. (2013), *American Dervish: Making Mevlevism in the United States of America*, Gothenburg: Department of Literature, History of Ideas, and Religion, University of Gothenburg.

Stausberg, M., O. Sundqvist and A. L. Svalaskog, eds (2002), *Riter och ritteorier: Religionshistoriska diskussioner och teoretiska ansatser*. Nora: Nya Doxa.

Tambiah, S. J. (1985), *A Performative Approach to Ritual: An Anthropological Perspective*, Cambridge, MA: Harvard University Press.

Thurfjell, D. (2006), *Living Shi'ism: Instances of Ritualisation Among Islamic Men in Contemporary Iran*, New York: Brill.

Trulsson, Å. (2010), *Cultivating the Sacred: Ritual Creativity and Practice among Women in Contemporary Europe*, thesis, Lund: Media-Tryck.

Turner, V. W. (1974), *Dramas, Fields, and Metaphors: Symbolic Action in Human Society*, Ithaca: Cornell University Press.

Turner, V. W. (1982), *From Ritual to Theatre: The Human Seriousness of Play*, New York: PAJP.

Turner, V. W. (1986), *The Anthropology of Performance*, New York: PAJP.

Van Gennep, A. (1960), *The Rites of Passage*, trans. M. B. Vizedon and G. Caffee, Chicago: Chicago University Press.

YouTube clip:

Robbins.youtube: www.youtube.com/watch?v=zjm10gcqOKg&list=PL6BE9764C303DB0A6&index=2 (accessed 5 October 2015).

Chapter 15

LIVED RELIGION

Daniel Enstedt, Jessica Moberg and Katarina Plank

Lived Religion as an Emerging Research Field

In the late 1990s and early 2000s, a line of scholars in religious studies called into question taken-for-granted perspectives and categories and sought to renew the discipline by suggesting new approaches and new ways forward. In the process, concepts such as ritual (Bell 1992, 1997; Grimes 2014) and even religion itself were scrutinized (Asad 1993; Fitzgerald 2000; McCutcheon 1995; cf. Wiebe 1988). Scholars who criticized belief-centred research and an over-emphasis on official religion explored perspectives that foregrounded narrative and memory (Hervieu-Léger 2000), material culture (McDannell 1995; see also Morgan 2010a,b), emotions (Riis and Woodhead 2010) and previously neglected arenas of religious practice (Smith 2004). Lived religion, which was established as a field of research in the 1990s, is one outcome of this critical enterprise, especially driven by sociologists of religion. One starting point of lived religion research is the criticism of an assumed one-sided focus on religious organizations, representatives, texts and beliefs – that is, the *sola scriptura* and *sola fide* aspects of religious studies. As an alternative, lived religion research emphasizes 'how religion and spirituality are practiced, experienced and expressed by ordinary people (rather than official spokespersons) in the context of their everyday lives', as one of the field's leading figures, Meredith B. McGuire (2008: 12), put it. In light of McGuire's reasoning, it can be said that the tension between *lived* and *prescribed* religion is central in lived religion research, as is the assumption that there is rarely, if ever, any immediate agreement between what religious institutions, groups and leaders advocate and what people believe and practise. Moreover, research on the religious life and practice of individuals needs to be highlighted in relation to the established religious dogmas, norms and values of *prescribed* religion as well as to the social context in which such practice is embedded.

A rather simple, but effective, distinction between *lived religion, represented religion* and *reported religion* (Gregg and Scholfield 2015) notes the importance of focusing not only on the official level of religion or on varied media coverage, which would risk giving a misleading picture of people's religiosity and religious traditions, and not only on the individual but also on the aggregated, collective level. To better understand religion, scholars of lived religion stress the need to consider how people actually practise, participate in and live their religion in everyday life arenas and locations. In this way, we can discern orders and patterns that may differ from those prescribed and those that cross boundaries of religious traditions. This does not mean that the prescribed notions of how a person should live life are to be entirely set aside, but rather that they should be seen in relation to lived religion and the contexts in which it is practised. This perspective is not new, being an established ideal in the anthropology of religion, but for sociologists of religion and sometimes also historians of religion, the lived religion perspective serves as a gentle reminder of the importance of designing research projects, exploring a field and working with data 'bottom-up'.

To discern patterns of religion in everyday life, Nancy T. Ammerman, another key scholar in the field, has argued that we must pay 'attention to the nonexperts [and] put away the biases about "real religion" that have often characterized scientific attempts at explanation' (2014: 5). Instead, we should turn to the layperson's reception, negotiation and renegotiation of imperatives from religious leaders, authorities and institutions, as well as to other sources of knowledge, such as the media and popular culture. From such a viewpoint, prescribed religion does not determine adherents' religious beliefs and practices but may influence them to different degrees and in different ways. Nonetheless, as Ammerman's (1997; cf. Moberg 2013) research illustrates, people's religious practices and beliefs are rarely haphazard but follow patterns within the framework of a religion's official practice, on its fringes and in everyday life. In other words, the nature of the relationship between the lived religious practice and the official, prescribed one, as well as the underlying patterns in religious practice, need to be examined empirically (McGuire 2008; Nyhagen 2017).

Brief Historical Overview

Sketching the contours of a research field is not always easy, particularly with regard to its historical background: Which forerunners and studies are to be included, and how should the boundaries be drawn with respect to neighbouring fields? With the field lived religion, we need to account for its contemporary American history, before turning to the developments in Sweden.[1]

American researchers were influential in initiating the field, although the concept of 'lived religion' is taken from the French *la religion vécue* and French anthropology of religion focusing on folk forms of religion (Croq and Garrioch 2013).[2] David Hall's *Lived Religion in America* (1997) marked a starting point of the research field. Both religious scholars and historians contributed chapters, and Hall emphasized the importance of studying people's beliefs and actions in everyday life, in the past as well as in the present. The anthology also included studies of groups that had been marginalized in research, such as migrants, women, people of colour, sexual minorities and religious laypeople. While *Lived*

Religion in America marked a starting point, there were forerunners to it. One was Robert Orsi's (1985) *The Madonna of 115th Street: Faith and Community in Italian Harlem, 1880–1950*, which examines migration stories, rituals and meaning-making among Italian immigrants in New York. An emphasis on everyday life and the religious practices of individuals has also been high on the agenda of field-based sociological, anthropological and ethnological research. Another important reference text is Courtney Bender's *Heaven's Kitchen*, a 2003 field-based study of unpaid volunteers in New York who provide meals to people suffering from AIDS. With McGuire's *Lived Religion* (2008) and Ammerman's anthology *Everyday Religion* (2007) and *Sacred Stories, Spiritual Tribes* (2014), the sociology of religion received three standard works in the field of lived religion. Ammerman's more recent *Studying Lived Religion* (2021) draws on a wide range of previous studies, not always explicitly in the field of lived religion, as she sought to characterize the field in more detail (see more below). A new channel for lived religion publications was created in 2017, when Palgrave Macmillan published the first volume in a series dedicated to lived religion: *Palgrave Studies in Lived Religion and Societal Challenges*.

Returning to the question of historical influences, one might question to what extent lived religion offers something new – or whether it is, in fact, a matter of religious scholars, primarily sociologists, 'discovering' what anthropologists have always taken for granted. Obviously, there is something to the idea that 'novelties' are rarely completely new. Quite often, there are predecessors and sources of inspiration beyond those mentioned in reference lists. Lived religion is no exception. Focusing on practice and materiality is hardly new in the anthropology of religion, where scholars are trained to study societies other than their own. In anthropology, the tradition extending from Marcel Mauss (1935) via Pierre Bourdieu (1977) to Saba Mahmood (2005) has also explored the body, discipline and training. Among the historical studies, we find the French Annales School, which has emphasized studying micro-history and popular beliefs and practices in contrast to those of the educated elite (Febvre 1953; Ginzburg 1976; Le Roy Ladurie 1975). Nonetheless, we do believe that lived religion has brought about some important novelties, beyond turning an 'anthropological gaze' on contemporary, often Western, societies and their religion. In the resulting amalgamation, a special view of religion has crystallized in which places such as the home have reappeared (Ammerman 2007) and themes such as practice and the body have emerged, and there has been an influx of methods from sociology. This last matter is important. One example of this is how Ammerman (1997, 2014) has investigated patterns of religiosity beyond the official through combining survey studies with semi-structured interviews.

Lived religion has continued to influence religious studies and neighbouring disciplines in other parts of the world. The large-scale project 'Lived Ancient Religion: Questioning "Cults" and "Polis Religion"' (2012–17) – hosted by Erfurt University and led by Jörg Rüpke – testifies to its impact on the History of Religion. This project, which explored materiality, experiences, the body and ritual action in Antiquity, was interdisciplinary and used both historical and archaeological materials and methods (Gasparini et al. 2020; Rüpke 2016). Lived religion has also influenced practical theology (Ammerman 2016; Ganzevoort and Roeland 2014), although such studies are rare in Sweden.[3]

In Sweden, lived religion is still an emerging research field. Although there has certainly been much previous research – in the history, anthropology, sociology and psychology of religion – that could be labelled 'lived religion', the research field has not been established for long. Lived religion made its way to Sweden at the turn of the millennium, in a national context in which similar perspectives and methods were already being developed in different academic milieus. Lived religion also tapped into and became part of a larger current in religious studies: increased interest in contemporary religion, practice and ethnographic methods. Along with ritual studies, vernacular religion and material religion, lived religion became part of this current. As we illustrate below, Sweden has been home to vibrant research milieus that approach religion in ways like those we find in lived religion research but without having ties to key figures and texts in the field. We also find contexts in which lived religion perspectives are combined with those of neighbouring fields of research. Naturally, this makes it difficult to distinguish between 'lived religion research' and research in related areas in anthropology, psychology or the sociology of religion. Perhaps unsurprisingly, boundaries between lived religion research and research in similar fields are as blurred as the boundaries between different religious traditions can be on the level of everyday practice.

One milieu that should be mentioned is the history and anthropology of religion at Lund University, which, under the leadership of the late Professor Emeritus Tord Olsson (1942–2013), specialized in ethnographic studies of ritual practice in different settings around the world. This environment, which drew inspiration from *ritual studies*, has been a breeding ground for field-based publications and dissertations. Among these are Anne-Christine Hornborg's dissertation on the Mi'kmaq Indians in Canada (2001) and her introduction to ritual analysis *Den rituella människan* (2010); André Möller's (2005) studies of ritual fasting during Ramadan in Java; Kristina Myrvold's inquiries into the ritual use of texts among Sikhs in India in her dissertation *Inside the Guru's Gate* (2007); Åsa Trulsson's dissertation *Cultivating the Sacred* (2010), in which she analysed ritual practice and innovation among neo-pagan women in Europe; and Katarina Plank's research on lay meditation practices among Buddhist converts in Sweden in her dissertation *Insikt och närvaro* (2011).

Lund University also proved important in training new researchers with a strong interest in religious practice and rituals, who have continued to exert influence on other universities with an ongoing emphasis on empirical field research. Two examples of this are, yet again, Plank and Hornborg.

At Stockholm University, the History of Religion has had a broad research profile that includes both historical and philological studies as well as ethnographic and anthropological studies. Professor Emeritus Per-Arne Berglie developed an interest in spiritual possession and folk religion in Southeast Asia and inspired several generations of scholars to work with anthropological approaches. Among those researchers involved in the study of lived religion at Stockholm University is Marja-Liisa Keinänen, who has studied women in Karelia and questions of gender, food and folk beliefs. Keinänen's thesis examined childbirth practices in pre-modern Karelia (Keinänen 2003). Also meriting mention is Frederic Brusi, who examines sanctified Muslim men and women and their resting places, and how these places are used religiously in everyday life.[4]

At the turn of the millennium, religious studies at Södertörn University College developed a profile focused on contemporary religion, practice and field studies. In this environment, lived religion perspectives were mixed and integrated with analytical approaches from embodiment theory, ritual studies and new materiality. When Hornborg became a professor there, she further developed ritual and embodiment perspectives and conducted studies of ritual innovation in new spiritualities (Hornborg 2012). Two examples of lived religion perspectives being blended with embodiment and ritual perspectives are the doctoral dissertations of Jessica Moberg (2013) and Simon Sorgenfrei (2013), which focused on the cultivation of neo-Pentecostal religiosity in Sweden and the practical aspects of dervish life in the United States. Ann af Burén's 2015 dissertation, in which she scrutinized semi-secular Swedes' use of the word 'religion', is another example of how lived religion perspectives can be mixed with those from neighbouring fields.[5] Other relevant publications include David Thurfjell's *Living Shi'ism* (2006)[6] and his study of Pentecostal revival among the Kaale Roma (2013).

The University of Gothenburg became a creative meeting place, resulting in several projects between 2012 and 2016. One was carried out by Göran Larsson and Daniel Enstedt on leaving religion (Enstedt 2018a,b; Enstedt, Larsson and Mantsinen 2019; Larsson 2018), a second was conducted by Katarina Plank, who studied Thai Buddhists in Sweden, and a third by Jessica Moberg, who explored how media and popular culture fuel ritual transformation in new spiritualities (Moberg 2016, 2018, 2019; Plank 2013, 2014b, 2015, 2017; Plank, Raddock and Selander 2016). In 2015, Enstedt, Plank and Moberg initiated the Network for the Study of Lived Religion and Society. Since then, the organizers of the Network have held seminars and produced the volume *Levd religion* (2018), edited by Enstedt and Plank, attempting to introduce the international research field in Sweden, particularly for students, and highlighting existing research. The people involved in the Network have initiated both smaller and larger research projects: Moberg and Wilhelm Kardemark have carried out pilot studies of 'lived Christian sports culture' and lived religion in cemeteries in Gothenburg (Kardemark and Moberg 2017; Moberg and Kardemark 2022). In 2019, Enstedt and Plank were awarded a research grant from the Swedish Research Council for the project 'Lived Religion and Social Mobility among Migrants in Sweden' (2020-4). Enstedt has also initiated an ongoing project about Qigong in Sweden, and in 2020, Plank was awarded a research grant from *Riksbankens Jubileumsfond* for the project 'New Faces of the Folk Church: Lived Religion, New Spiritual Practices and Theological Legitimation' (2021-4).

We also note several recent publications in diverse areas in religious studies, with an emphasis on contemporary fieldwork-based studies. One example is Julia Kuhlin's doctoral dissertation on lived Pentecostalism among middle-class women in India (2022) carried out at Uppsala University.

Lived religion perspectives have also been developed in sociology, in which Erica Willander (2020) works with quantitative methods; in historical disciplines such as church history, in which the Reformation has been explored from a lay perspective (Heiding and Nyman 2016); and in history, in which the research project 'Mapping Lived Religion: Medieval Cults of Saints in Sweden and Finland' hosted by Linnaeus University is one indication of a growing interest in lived religion perspectives, as is the special issue of *Scandia: tidskrift för historisk forskning* (2022) entitled *Levd religion i det förmoderna Nordeuropa*.

Lived religion has also been discussed in relation to education, and the perspective has been implemented in the curricula of primary and secondary school.[7] The former has resulted in an increased number of didactical publications in the 2010s and 2020s, written by scholars critical of the stereotypical representations of religion in religious education in Swedish schools and presenting lived religion as a way of addressing such shortcomings (Berglund 2021; Enstedt 2022; Hall and Liljefors Persson 2021; Halvarson Britton 2019; see also Kittelmann Flensner 2015). In higher education, the lived religion perspective can benefit students of religious studies. Kristian Niemi at Karlstad University argues that 'lived religion' can be understood as a threshold concept, serving as a key that helps unlock the academic subject of religious studies. Niemi further argues that the perspective enables a more nuanced understanding of the complexity of religious life and binds together a multitude of perspectives that students encounter through their education (Niemi 2018). In addition, scholars such as Enstedt and Plank have begun to develop methods for teaching religion that are inspired by lived religion (Enstedt 2020; Enstedt and Plank 2021; Plank 2014a). Over the last ten years or so, lived religion has influenced higher education, with several universities having developed courses on lived religion or with a distinct lived religion profile. Among them are Södertörn University College (*Levd religion, genus och sexualitet*), Lund University (*Religionshistoria: Levd religion – traditionella och nyskapande ritualer*),[8] the University of Gothenburg (*Levd religion and Religion i Göteborg*) and Linköping University (*Religionshistoria II: Levd religion i samtiden*, 15 credits). At Karlstad University and Södertörn University College, lived religion perspectives are integral to most education, and at the University of Gothenburg they are included in the teacher training programme.

Key Issues in the Study of Lived Religion

Lived religion today is a maturing field of research, as indicated by the sometimes-critical inventories of previous studies and discussions of future directions. In this connection, Kim Knibbe and Helena Kupari (2020) have called for theoretical developments within lived religion research. Similarly, Gustavo Morello and Silvia Fernandes have pointed out and sought to address a geographical imbalance in the field – that is, a strong focus on the Global North – by including cases from the Global South.[9]

Pointing to the future, Ammerman (2016: 89) has suggested that the study of lived religion should be 'organized around domains of life where sacred things are being produced, encountered, and shared' (original partly italicized). Ammerman has identified seven dimensions – which she also describes as building blocks and analytical perspectives – according to which one can study lived religion. These dimensions are the spiritual, embodiment, materiality, emotions, aesthetics, morality and narrative (Ammerman 2021). These dimensions, which often overlap, should be understood as analytical categories that assist the gaze of the lived religion researcher during fieldwork. In addition, Ammerman argues for the importance of including intersectional perspectives in the analysis, with intersectionality not constituting a separate dimension but rather a more comprehensive framework. Additionally, she proposes that 'studying lived religion means paying attention to the social patterning at all three levels – interacting individuals, structuring institutions, and overarching cultural resources' (Ammerman 2021: 181). In *Levd religion: Det heliga i vardagen*, Enstedt and Plank (2018: 13–16) similarly suggested seven dimensions of lived religion: materiality, embodiment, religious practice, relationships, power, spatiality and narratives. Enstedt and Plank's description of these seven dimensions overlaps with Ammerman's (2021) in *Studying Lived Religion*. As we see it, both volumes testify to today's concern with analytical development, perhaps also indicating something of a consensus concerning key issues in the field.

Conclusions

Lived religion research in Sweden stands out internationally in three ways. First, Swedish scholars have started to move beyond the micro-studies that have been characteristic of the field and started to explore developments on the macro and meso levels.[10] One example of the former is Erika Willander's (2020) lived religion interpretation of secularization patterns in Sweden (see also Willander 2018). Swedish researchers have also initiated studies of institutions such as hospitals (Nordin 2018) and non-traditional practices in the Church of Sweden (Lundgren, Plank and Egnell 2023). Second, the lived religion perspective is becoming integral to teacher training courses and to primary and secondary school curricula. Third, lived religion has been introduced into the neighbouring discipline of history, where it has been employed in studies of premodern Christianity and folk religion (Ellis Nilsson, Kolbe and Zachrisson 2022).

Finally, we would like to suggest some directions for future studies within lived religion. As we have pointed out, the tendency has been to conduct field-based studies in contemporary religious settings. On the one hand, qualitative field studies can be deepened by including types of materials and analyses other than those that use narrative material; for instance, different perspectives on rituals, materiality and spatiality would be potentially stimulating directions for future exploration. On the other hand, lived religion could become more dynamic as a field if other methods and studies were included. Its predominantly contemporary focus could be supplemented with different types of historical studies: archival studies and historical material, not least based on folk memory archives and the like, and in relation to archaeological remains and historical studies (cf. Berntson 2016). In *Lived Religion in America* (1997), Hall in fact stressed the importance of historical studies, but historical studies have been rare internationally. Beyond qualitative research, we see potential in well-designed quantitative studies that explore everyday lived religion on a more general level. This would naturally demand considerable effort to create proper tools for gathering and analysing material, which leads us to the next issue.

Lived religion research has usually applied an inductive grassroots perspective and paid attention to individuals' religious practices in everyday life. Such a starting point entails a risk of losing oneself in individual examples and case descriptions and thus missing more general patterns. Lived religion research also provides space for macro perspectives, such as studying lived religion in relation to utopian urban planning (Bender 2016) or from the roof of a skyscraper in New York (Certeau 1984). In this way, other dimensions of the spatial conditions of lived religion can also be considered in a productive way.

An approach that has come to the fore concerns new forms of religiosity in the digital age in which we live. In such an existence, we need to examine 'digital religion', a term coined by Heidi Campbell (2013) to capture 'the technological and cultural space evoked in talking about how online and offline religious spheres become blended or integrated' (Campbell 2017: 229). In such an approach, online ethnography research (i.e. *netnography*) can be combined with other methods, opening the field for the study of popular culture and media and their importance for lived religion.

As mentioned above, lived religion research has often ignored religious institutions, doctrines, dogmas, representatives and leaders. The time may now be ripe to return to these aspects of religiosity. In addition, an increased interest in cultural spheres beyond the North Atlantic may provide new perspectives on lived religion that further loosen the Eurocentric understanding of religion that has shaped the field of research for so long (cf. Kuhlin 2022; Thorsén 2022).

Somewhat simplified, it can be said that the study of lived religion has emphasized religious practices linked to everyday life rather than beliefs linked to religious traditions. It has also meant that individual people's personal religious experiences have been highlighted, rather than more typical forms of religion at the group or aggregate level. The field's specific focus has led to new ways of thinking, while clear trends in research design have emerged, which are now being problematized in a needed way. The research field is in an exciting phase in which new analytical concepts and models are being developed (e.g. Enstedt and Moberg 2023). This suggests that there is much more to discover and learn, and as we see it, the future of the field is ripe with possibilities.

Notes

1 This presentation of the research field of lived religion is based on our previous publications in Swedish, especially Enstedt and Plank (2018, 2021).

2   For background on the rise of the anthropology of religion, from which several aspects incorporated into the field of lived religion have emerged, see Sir Edmund Leach's still relevant text 'Anthropology of Religion: British and French Schools' (1985).
3   Ritual studies, which has several points of contact with lived religion, has inspired theological studies, such as Martina Prosén's (2021) thesis, in which she highlights the ritual life among Pentecostal Christians in Kenya.
4   https://www.su.se/forskning/forsknings%C3%A4mnen/religionshistoria/levd-religion (accessed 3 February 2023).
5   af Burén, Moberg and Sorgenfrei were officially enrolled at the University of Gothenburg but mainly worked and were active at Södertörn University College.
6   This was the book version of his doctoral dissertation from Uppsala University.
7   Current developments within the Swedish National Agency for Education suggest that lived religion could become integral to teacher education programmes in the future. Today, the Agency's *Commentary Material on the Syllabus* in religious studies (Skolverket 2022: 6) explicitly states that it is important that pupils become 'aware of *how people within different religious traditions live with, and express, their religion and beliefs in different ways*'. The Agency further explains that pupils 'should become aware that the way people practice and understand their religion in everyday life may differ significantly from the image of religion that official advocates – priests, theologians, and spiritual leaders – give. The reason for highlighting this in teaching is to counteract stereotypical images and a predetermined view of religion in relation to people's actual values and actions' (Skolverket 2022: 6). In this, the Agency reflects common perceptions in lived religion research: the discrepancy between lived and learned religion, the diversity of everyday-life religion and the potential of lived religion research to counteract prejudices and stereotypes, correct misconceptions and undermine conflicts.
8   In this case, lived religion appears to be a matter of buzzwords, as the reading list covers ritual studies rather than lived religion literature.
9   https://www.mdpi.com/journal/religions/special_issues/Lived_Religions (accessed 3 February 2023).
10 Ammerman's (1997, 2014) use of quantitative methods and statistical analysis is an exception to this general trend in lived religion research.

References

Ammerman, N. T. (1997), 'Golden Rule Christianity: Lived Religion in the American Mainstream', in D. Hall (ed.), *Lived Religion in America: Toward a History of Practice*, 196–216, Princeton: Princeton University Press.

Ammerman, N. T., ed. (2007), *Everyday Religion: Observing Modern Religious Lives*, New York: Oxford University Press.

Ammerman, N. T. (2014), *Sacred Stories, Spiritual Tribes: Finding Religion in Everyday Life*, Oxford: Oxford University Press.

Ammerman, N. T. (2016), 'Lived Religion as an Emerging Field: An Assessment of Its Contours and Frontiers', *Nordic Journal of Religion and Society* 29 (2): 83–99.

Ammerman, N. T. (2021), *Studying Lived Religion: Contexts and Practices*, New York: New York University Press.

Asad, T. (1993), *Genealogies of Religion: Discipline and Reasons of Power in Christianity and Islam*, Baltimore: Johns Hopkins University Press.
Bell, C. (1992), *Ritual Theory, Ritual Practice*, New York: Oxford University Press.
Bell, C. (1997), *Ritual: Perspectives and Dimensions*, New York: Oxford University Press.
Bender, C. (2016), 'How and Why to Study Up: Frank Lloyd Wright's Broadacre City and the Study of Lived Religion', *Nordic Journal of Religion and Society* 29 (2): 100–16.
Bender, C. (2003), *Heaven's Kitchen: Living Religion at God's Love We Deliver*, Chicago: University of Chicago Press.
Berglund, J. (2021), 'Ett fokus på levd islam bortanför maximalistiska representationer', in M. von der Lippe (ed.), *Fordommer i skolen: Gruppekonstruksjoner, utenforskap og inkludering*, 183–97, Oslo: Universitetsforlaget.
Berntson, M. (2016), 'Popular Belief and the Disruption of Religious Practices in Reformation Sweden', in T. Lehtonen and L. Kaljundi (eds), *Re-Forming Texts, Music, and Church Art in the Early Modern North*, 43–68, Amsterdam: Amsterdam University Press.
Bourdieu, P. (1977), *Outline of a Theory of Practice*, Cambridge: Cambridge University Press.
Burén, A. af (2015), *Living Simultaneity: On Religion among Semi-Secular Swedes*, Göteborg: University of Gothenburg.
Campbell, H. ed. (2013), *Digital Religion: Understanding Religious Practice in New Media Worlds*, London: Routledge.
Campbell, H. (2017), 'Religious Communication and Technology', *Annals of the International Communication Association* 41 (3–4): 228–234.
Croq, L., and D. Garrioch (2013), *La religion vécue – Les laïcs dans l'Europe modern*, Rennes: Presses universitaires de Rennes.
Certeau, M. de (1984), *The Practice of Everyday Life*, vol. 1, Berkeley: University of California Press.
Ellis Nilsson, S., W. Kolbe and T. Zachrisson, eds (2022), *Levd religion i det förmoderna Nordeuropa*, special issue in *Scandia: tidskrift för historisk forskning* 88 (2).
Enstedt, D., and J. Moberg (2023), 'Performative Animism: New Directions for a Contested Concept in Religious Studies', *Method and Theory in the Study of Religion* 35: 111–39.
Enstedt, D. (2022), 'Religious Literacy in Non-Confessional Religious Education and Religious Studies in Sweden', *Nordidactica* 12 (1): 27–48.
Enstedt, D. (2020), 'Russinet i mindfulness: Erfarenhetsbaserad utbildning och praktik i religionsvetenskap', *Högre Utbildning* 10 (1): 59–71.
Enstedt, D., and K. Plank (2021), 'Utövad och utlärd religion', *Levd religion: praktiker i vardagen och didaktiska perspektiv, Föreningen Lärare i religionskunskap, Årsbok* 11–36, Malmö: Föreningen Lärare i religionskunskap (FLR).
Enstedt, D. (2018a), 'Understanding Religious Apostasy: Disaffiliation and Islam in Contemporary Sweden', in K. van Nieuwkerk (ed.), *Moving in and out of Islam*, 67–87, Austin: University of Texas Press.
Enstedt, D. (2018b), 'Levd apostasi bland ex-muslimer i Sverige', in D. Enstedt and K. Plank (eds), *Levd religion. Det heliga i vardagen*, 326–41, Lund: Nordic Academic Press.
Enstedt, D., and K. Plank, eds (2018), *Levd religion: Det heliga i vardagen*, Lund: Nordic Academic Press.
Enstedt, D., G. Larsson and T. Mantsinen, eds (2019), *Handbook of Leaving Religion*, Leiden: Brill.

Fitzgerald, T. (2000), *The Ideology of Religious Studies*, New York: Oxford University Press.
Febvre, L. (1953), *Combats pour l'histoire*, Paris: Armand Colin.
Ganzevoort, R., and J. Roeland (2014), 'Lived Religion: The Praxis of Practical Theology', *International Journal of Practical Theology* 18 (1): 91–101.
Gasparini, V., M. Patzelt, R. Raja, A.-K.. Rieger, J. Rüpke and E. Urciuoli (2020), *Lived Religion in the Ancient Mediterranean World: Approaching Religious Transformations from Archaeology, History and Classics*, Berlin: De Gruyter.
Ginzburg, C. (1976), *Formaggio e vermi: Il mondo di un mugnaio del '500*, Torino: Einaudi.
Gregg, S., and L. Scholfield (2015), *Engaging with Living Religion*, London: Routledge.
Grimes, R. L. (2014), *The Craft of Ritual Studies*, New York: Oxford University Press.
Hall, D., ed. (1997), *Lived Religion in America: Toward a History of Practice*, Princeton: Princeton University Press.
Hall, E., and B. Liljefors Persson, eds (2021), *Levd religion: Praktiker i vardagen och didaktiska perspektiv, Föreningen Lärare i religionskunskap, Årsbok*, Malmö: Föreningen Lärare i religionskunskap (FLR).
Halvarson Britton, T. (2019), *Att möta det levda: Möjligheter och hinder för förståelse av levd religion i en studiebesöksorienterad religionskunskapsundervisning*, Stockholm: Stockholm University.
Hervieu-Léger, D. (2000), *Religion as a Chain of Memory*, Cambridge: Polity Press.
Heiding, F., and M. Nyman (2016), *Doften av rykande vekar*, Skellefteå: Artos.
Hornborg, A.-C. (2001), *A Landscape of Left-Overs: Changing Conceptions of Place and Environment among Mi'kmaq Indians of Eastern Canada*, Lund: Lund University.
Hornborg, A.-C., ed. (2010), *Den rituella människan: Flervetenskapliga perspektiv*, Linköping: Linköping University Electronic Press.
Hornborg, A.-C. (2012), *Coaching och lekmannaterapi: en modern väckelse?*, Stockholm: Dialogos.
Kardemark, W., and J. Moberg (2017), 'Att spela innebandy på ett kristet vis: Sportkultur i KRIK Göteborg student', *Prismet: Religionspedagogisk tidsskrift* 68 (1–2): 43–56.
Kittelmann Flensner, K. (2015), *Religious Education in Contemporary Pluralistic Sweden*, Göteborg: University of Gothenburg.
Knibbe, K., and H. Kupari (2020), 'Theorizing Lived Religion: Introduction', *Journal of Contemporary Religion* 35 (2): 157–76.
Kuhlin, J. (2022), *Lived Pentecostalism in India: Middle Class Women and Their Everyday Religion*, Uppsala: Uppsala University.
Keinänen, M.-L. (2003), *Creating Bodies: Childbirth Practices in Pre-Modern Karelia*, Stockholm: Stockholm University.
Larsson, G. (2018), 'Let's Talk about Apostasy! Swedish Imams, Apostasy Debates, and Police Reports on Hate Crimes and (De)conversion', in K. van Nieuwkerk (ed.), *Moving in and out of Islam*, 385–404, Austin: University of Texas Press.
Leach, E. (1985), 'Anthropology of Religion: British and French Schools', in Ninian Smart (ed.), *Nineteenth Century Religious Thought in the West*, vol. 3, 215–62, Cambridge: Cambridge University Press.
Le Roy Ladurie, E. (1975), *Montaillou, Village Occitan de 1294 à 1324*, Paris: Gallimard.
Lundgren, L., K. Plank and H. Egnell (2023), 'Nya andliga praktiker i Svenska kyrkan: Från exklusiva retreatmiljöer till kyrklig vardagspraktik', *Svensk Teologisk Kvartaltidskrift* 99 (3).
Mahmood, S. (2005), *Politics of Piety: The Islamic Revival and the Feminist Subject*, Princeton: Princeton University Press.

Mauss, M. (1935), 'Les techniques du corps', *Journal de psychologie normal et patholigique*, AnnCe XXXII: 271–93.
McCutcheon, R. T. (1995), 'The Category "Religion" in Recent Publications: A Critical Survey', *Numen* 42 (3): 284–309.
McDannell, C. (1995), *Material Christianity: Religion and Popular Culture in America*, New Haven: Yale University Press.
McGuire, M. (2008), *Lived Religion: Faith and Practice in Everyday Life*, New York: Oxford University Press.
Moberg, J. (2013), *Piety, Intimacy and Mobility: A Case Study of Charismatic Christianity in Present-day Stockholm*, Göteborg: University of Gothenburg.
Moberg, J. (2016), 'Spiritualistisk bevisföring i ny tappning: Omvändelseberättelser och redigeringstekniker i Det okända', in D. Enstedt, G. Larsson and F. Sardella (eds), *Religionens varp och trasor: En festskrift till Åke Sander*, 97–107, Göteborg: Institutionen för litteratur, idéhistoria och religion.
Moberg, J. (2018), 'Nya pentekostala ordningar: Doxa, ortodoxi och heterodoxi bland väckelsekristna i Stockholm', in D. Enstedt and K. Plank (eds), *Levd religion. Det heliga i vardagen*, 29–44, Lund: Nordic Academic Press.
Moberg, J. (2019), 'Franchising Occulture: On the Introduction and Developments of Occult Reality TV in Sweden', *Nordic Journal of Religion and Society* 32 (2): 117–31.
Moberg, J., and W. Kardemark (2022), 'It Is After All a Churchyard: Orthodox and Heterodox Spatial Embodiments at Three Cemeteries in Gothenburg, Sweden', in E. Punzi, C. Singer and C. Wächter (eds), *Negotiating Institutional Heritage and Wellbeing. Spatial Practices*, 21–46, Leiden: Brill.
Morgan, D. (2010a), 'The Material Culture of Lived Religion: Visuality and Embodiment', in Johanna Vakkari (ed.), *Mind and Matter: Selected Papers of Nordik 2009 Conference for Art Historians, Studies in Art History, No. 41*, 14–31, Helsinki: Helsingfors.
Morgan, D., ed. (2010b), *Religion and Material Culture: The Matter of Belief*, London: Routledge.
Myrvold, K. (2007), *Inside the Guru's Gate: Ritual Uses of Texts among the Sikhs in Varanasi*, Lund: Lund University.
Möller, A. (2005), *Ramadan in Java: The Joy and Jihad of Ritual Fasting*, Lund: Lund University.
Niemi, K. (2018), 'Religionsvetenskapliga tröskelbegrepp: Stötestenar och språngbrädor vid utvecklingen av ett ämnesperspektiv', *Nordidactica* 2018 (2): 1–22.
Nordin, M. (2018), 'Levd religion på sjukhus. Religionsöverskridande och utebliven religiös praktik', in D. Enstedt and K. Plank (eds), *Levd religion. Det heliga i vardagen*, 241–57, Lund: Nordic Academic Press.
Nyhagen, L. (2017), 'The Lived Religion Approach in the Sociology of Religion and Its Implications for Secular Feminist Analyses of Religion', *Social Compass* 64 (4): 495–511.
Orsi, R. (1985), *The Madonna of 115th Street: Faith and Community in Italian Harlem 1880–1950*, New Haven: Yale University Press.
Plank, K. (2011), *Insikt och närvaro: Akademiska kontemplationer kring buddhism, meditation och mindfulness*, Göteborg: Makadam.
Plank, K. (2013), 'Vessantara Jataka i Dalarna – om text, representation och materialitet i studiet av thailändsk theravadabuddhism i Sverige', *Chaos* 59: 125–64.
Plank, K. (2014a), 'När karma blev konkret: Erfarenhetsbaserad pedagogik som utmaning för lärare och studenter i högre utbildning', *Högre utbildning* 4 (2): 127–39.

Plank, K. (2014b), 'Bildanvändning i thailändsk buddhism i Sverige', in M. Fahlén (ed.), *Bildens kraft: Samtida utmaningar i religioner*, 111–42, Lund: Studentlitteratur.

Plank, K. (2015), 'Sacred Foodscapes in Thai Buddhist Temples in Sweden', *Religion and Food*, Scripta Insituti Donneriani Aboensis, 26: 201–24.

Plank, K. (2017), 'Klibbigt ris och karma', in L. Roos and L. Nordenstorm (eds), *Religion och bibel: Nathan Söderblom-sällskapets årsbok. 2012–2013: Gudomligt gott: om religion och mat*, 165–202, Uppsala: Nathan Söderblom-sällskapet.

Plank, K., E. Raddock and P. Selander (2016), 'The Temple Mount of Fredrika – Translocality and Fractured Transnationalism of a Visionary Thai Buddhist Retreat Centre', *Contemporary Buddhism* 17 (2): 405–26.

Prosén, M. (2021), *A Rhythm that Connects My Heart with God: Worship, Ritual and Pentecostal Spirituality as Theology*, Lund: Lund University.

Riis, O., and L. Woodhead (2010), *A Sociology of Religious Emotion*, Oxford: Oxford University Press.

Rüpke, J. (2016), *On Roman Religion: Lived Religion and the Individual in Ancient Rome*, Ithaca: Cornell University Press.

Skolverket (2022), *Kommentarmaterial till kursplanen i religionskunskap*, https://www.skolverket.se/getFile?file=9799 (accessed 18 April 2023).

Smith, J. Z. (2004), 'Here, There and Everywhere', in J. Z. Smith (ed.), *Relating Religion: Essays in the Study of Religion*, 323–39, Chicago: University of Chicago Press.

Sorgenfrei, S. (2013), *American Dervish: Making Mevlevism in the United States of America*, Göteborg: University of Gothenburg.

Thorsén, E. (2022), *In Search of the Self: A Study of the International Scene of Modern Advaitic Satsang in Present-day Rishikesh*, Göteborg: University of Gothenburg.

Thurfjell, D. (2013), *Faith and Revivalism in a Nordic Romani Community: Pentecostalism amongst the Kaale Roma of Sweden and Finland*, London: I. B. Tauris.

Thurfjell, D. (2006), *Living Shi'ism: Instances of Ritualisation among Islamist Men in Contemporary Iran*, Leiden: Brill.

Trulsson, Å. (2010), *Cultivating the Sacred: Ritual Creativity and Practice among Women in Contemporary Europe*, Lund: Lund University.

Wiebe, D. (1988). 'Why the Academic Study of Religion? Motive and Method in the Study of Religion', *Religious Studies* 24 (4): 403–13.

Willander, E. (2018), 'Bortom den nordiska paradoxen. Levd religion i statistiken', in D. Enstedt and K. Plank (eds), *Levd religion. Det heliga i vardagen*, 223–40, Lund: Nordic Academic Press.

Willander, E. (2020), *Unity, Division and the Religious Mainstream in Sweden*, Cham: Palgrave Macmillan.

Chapter 16

GENDER STUDIES

Manon Hedenborg White

Introduction

The academic study of gender is an interdisciplinary research domain that, broadly speaking, centres on how sex, gender and sexuality are articulated, constructed, reproduced and challenged in social life. It is important to stress that neither gender, sex nor sexuality can be pinned down to singular, stable meanings; on the contrary, these categories are continuously contested and debated among feminist scholars. The study of gender developed largely out of the so-called second wave of feminism in the 1970s and 1980s. During this period, feminist scholars sought to rectify what they perceived as blind spots in mainstream historiography and a resulting dearth of knowledge regarding women's lives, histories and contributions in fields such as culture, labour, science, philosophy, literature, politics and art. Thus emerged the intersecting fields of women's studies and women's history. Over time, such additive or corrective approaches increasingly paved the way not only for the study of women but also for critical examinations of gender – in other words, how both masculine and feminine social roles have been constructed, why and how this has developed over time in different geo-cultural locales – as well as of men and masculinities (cf. Scott 1986).

Early gender theory hinged on a nature–culture binary distinguishing between biological sex and (sociocultural) gender (e.g. de Beauvoir 1984 [1953]). This allowed feminist scholars to theorize the social and cultural meanings, roles and expectations embedded in concepts of masculinity and femininity as separate from the supposedly stable bodies they were projected onto. From the early 1990s on, postmodern and poststructuralist interventions have prompted deconstructions of the sex/gender distinction, highlighting how the assumption of two natural, stable and complementary sexes is itself a historical and cultural construct linked to specific ideological assumptions (e.g. Butler 1990; Laqueur 1990). Queer theory has problematized and challenged the stability of gendered categories, highlighting how the construction of sex and gender are linked to notions of normative and aberrant sexuality, and calling attention to the dynamics of power whereby specific gender identities and forms of desire are constructed as normative or deviant (e.g. Butler 1990; Kosofsky Sedgwick 1985; Warner 1993).

Some twenty years ago, scholar of religion Ursula King referred to the nexus of gender and religion as characterized by a sort of 'double blindness'. King observed that, while many scholars of gender have failed to engage with religion as a category, scholars of religion have similarly overlooked the ways in which gender shapes religion (King 2005: 3297; cf. Gemzöe and Keinänen 2016: 4). Scholarship on religion during the first half of the twentieth century was characterized by androcentrism; scholars largely focused on 'official' religion, situated at the level of learned texts and formal institutions. Resultingly, religious women (often marginalized in both domains) were rendered largely invisible or seen as passive recipients or victims of theological and ritual prescriptions regarding women's inherent sinfulness, uncleanliness or lack of fitness for leadership. As Linda Woodhead (2001) and Randi Warne (2000) have both drawn attention to, dominant theories within the sociology of religion, such as secularization, have also failed to account for men's and women's differing patterns of religiosity in modernity (cf. Keinänen 2010). Nonetheless, from the 1980s on, an increasing number of scholars have challenged androcentrism and brought attention to women's religious lives, as well as broader issues of gender in religions (e.g., Gross 1977, 1996; King 1995). Counterbalancing earlier scholarship, many of these studies have highlighted female agency and how women have and continue to creatively navigate, negotiate and resist even strongly patriarchal religious systems (e.g. Sered 1999). The increasing attention to women in religions has coincided with a stronger focus on practice (cf. King 2005), 'lived' (McGuire 2008) or 'everyday' religion (Ammerman 2007; Keinänen 2010) as realms in which women negotiate and sometimes resist patriarchal traditions.

This chapter aims to provide a selective overview of Swedish scholarship on gender and religion. It is the nature of an overview not to be comprehensive. Mirroring the aims and scope of this volume, this chapter will centre on the study of religions as an academic field, primarily engaging with research produced by scholars trained or working in (i.e. who regularly communicate their scholarship via publication channels related to) the study of religions. There are a few notable exceptions to this, which will become apparent below; several scholars in other fields (e.g. anthropology and history) have contributed in such a way to the study of religion and gender in Sweden that an overview of this domain would be incomplete without mention of their work.

In this chapter, I will adopt a broad definition of gender research that encompasses historical and sociological research on women and men as gendered beings, critical analyses of gender, gender expression and identity, and sexuality, as well as everything in between. I have not limited my inquiry to particular research methods or theoretical paradigms, in congruence with the diversity within the academic study of gender by and large. Contrastingly, in this chapter, I am using the term 'study of religions' in a relatively narrow sense (what I shall be referring to henceforth as the study of religions *sensu stricto*), roughly equivalent to the German *Religionswissenschaft*, which customarily denotes the critical, unbiased, non-confessional study of various religions or of religion as a phenomenon.

Following historical custom in Swedish academia, I am thus treating the study of religions as largely distinct from the fields associated with the domain of theology, such as mission studies, Bible studies, ethics, philosophy of religion and systematic theology. However, it is worth noting that the landscape of Swedish academia is changing, and the lines between the study of religions and theology are becoming increasingly blurred (Thurfjell 2015b). Further, the non-prescriptive identity of the study of religions is, in some instances, challenged by the frequently socially engaged nature of gender scholarship. While scholars of religion who study gender rarely take a normative stance regarding what constitutes the (in)correct reading of a religion or its associated traditions, feminist scholars have critiqued notions of objective detachment and are frequently motivated by notions of how to make society better and more equal (e.g. Harding 1991).

Historical Overview

Paralleling the international development, women's and gender studies emerged as an academic field in the Nordic countries (including Sweden) between 1975 and 2005. As an analytical concept, the term *genus* (the Swedish equivalent of the English term 'gender', used to denote social or cultural norms, roles and expectations linked to men and women, as distinct from physical sex) entered women's studies in the Nordic countries in the late 1980s (Hirdman 1988; cf. Dahl, Liljeström and Manns 2016). The term 'gender' is not native to any of the Nordic languages; however, its integration as an analytical concept happened largely without resistance. An important signal of the transition from women's to gender studies is the peer-reviewed journal *Kvinnovetenskaplig tidskrift* (Eng. 'Journal of Women's Studies'), central to the development of the field in Sweden, changing its name to *Tidskrift för genusvetenskap* (Eng. 'Journal of Gender Studies') in 2006. Swedish scholars of gender Ulrika Dahl, Marianne Liljeström, and Ulla Manns have suggested that Nordic scholars' readiness to accommodate the term *genus* points to the compatibility between gender as a framework of analysis and the strong emphasis on the equality of men and women in Nordic public policy during the late twentieth and early twenty-first centuries (Dahl, Liljeström and Manns 2016: 11).

King's (2005, mentioned above) remarks about the reciprocal 'double blindness' of the study of gender and religion is applicable to Swedish scholarship historically. In 1998, historian Inger Hammar (Lund University) similarly described Swedish women's history research as *religionsblind* (Eng. 'religion blind', Hammar 1998a). This sparked an important debate with fellow historian Manns (1998, then Stockholm University, now Södertörn University) in the peer-reviewed history journal *Historisk tidskrift* around the role of religion in Swedish women's struggle for emancipation. Hammar (1998b) has subsequently argued for the importance of religion in understanding women's struggle for emancipation in the late nineteenth and early twentieth centuries. Mirroring international scholarly critiques of the secularization paradigm, Hammar stressed that Swedish women's secularization did not parallel that of men, and that women operated largely within a Christian world view until the early twentieth century (1998b). Hammar's (e.g. 1998b, 1999) and Manns's (e.g. 2010, 2011) later, respective work on the early Swedish women's movement has contributed importantly to the understanding of how religion both enabled and conditioned women's emancipation. This is also true of church historian Gunilla Gunner's (2003, then Uppsala University, now Södertörn University) work on the Swedish preacher Nelly Hall, which highlighted previously overlooked connections between the women's movement and the Protestant revival movement in Sweden. Gunner's scholarship was honoured in 2020 with a *festschrift* on women's religious leadership, including contributions by more than twenty Swedish scholars of religion (Sorgenfrei and Thurfjell 2020).

Another Swedish scholar working outside of the study of religions, who nonetheless deserves mention in this context, is social anthropologist Lena Gemzöe (Stockholm University). Gemzöe's (2000) doctoral dissertation analysed Catholic women's religious beliefs, practices and agency in a Portuguese town, arguing for the importance of considering gender as a principle of social organization in anthropological research on religion. Gemzöe challenged tendencies in earlier scholarship on women in Catholicism, critiquing the idea of Catholic women as passive recipients or subjects of official theology, including theological beliefs about women's inherent sinfulness. Drawing on Susan Sered's (1999) distinction between 'woman' as symbol and women as agents, Gemzöe emphasized her Portuguese interlocutors as active creators of religious tradition, highlighting how Catholic women navigate and negotiate official doctrine, creating space for both agency and authority. In so doing, Gemzöe also problematized the distinction between 'official' and 'popular' or 'folk' religion, arguing for gender as a central category for understanding the tension between these dimensions (Gemzöe 2000: e.g. 15–16). In recent years, Gemzöe has continued to produce important work on female pilgrims (e.g. Gemzöe 2005).

Within the study of religions *sensu stricto*, historian of religion Eva Hellman (Uppsala University) has produced important work on women's roles, goddesses and gender norms in Hindu traditions (e.g. 1998). Hellman has highlighted fundamentalist women in the Hindutva movement (2007a) and in Buddhist Sri Lanka (2007b), as well as Hindu feminist theologies, stressing that the presence of goddesses within a religious world view is not in itself sufficient for ensuring egalitarian gender roles (2003). Historian of religion Marja-Liisa Keinänen (Stockholm University) has highlighted various aspects of vernacular religion and gender, with an emphasis on women's ritual agency and practice. Keinänen's (2003) doctoral dissertation considered women in Russian Orthodox Karelia, and she has subsequently spearheaded edited volumes on women and gender in religion (Keinänen 2010b), also collaborating with anthropologist Gemzöe and cultural geographer April Maddrell in this regard (Gemzöe, Keinänen and Maddrell 2016).

Key Issues and Scholars

In composing this review of the current state of research, I have utilized several sources. First, the database GENA (*GENusAvhandlingar*, Eng. 'Gender

Dissertations'), a register of Swedish doctoral dissertations in the areas of women's studies, men's studies and gender research, from 1960 to 2023. The database is managed by Kvinnsam – National Resource Library for Gender Studies, a research infrastructure at the University of Gothenburg, in cooperation with the Swedish Secretariat for Gender Research, a unit at the University of Gothenburg established in 1998. Second, I have considered funded research projects initiated by senior scholars as listed in the Swedish national research database SweCris. SweCris is administered by the Swedish Research Council on behalf of the Swedish government and correlates funded projects from eleven major Swedish governmental and private funding bodies from 2008 on. Third, I have conducted searches in *Digitala Vetenskapliga Arkivet* (DiVA, Eng. 'Digital Scientific Archive'), a search tool and institutional repository that comprises bibliographic information about research publications and student theses from fifty universities and research institutions in Sweden. Put together, these databases indicate a slow but progressive increase in doctoral dissertations within the study of religions *sensu stricto* that take gender into account, as well as a relatively steady level of research projects initiated by senior scholars since 2008 (cf. Nationella Sekretariatet för Genusforskning 2007).

Gender and Women in Islam

In recent decades, international feminist scholarship on religion has produced several influential studies of women and gender in Islam (e.g. Mahmood 2005). This tendency appears to be reflected in the Swedish study of religions, where several doctoral dissertations on women, gender or women *and* gender in Islam have been produced in recent years. This is, perhaps, unsurprising: the Muslim minority is the largest non-Christian religious group in Sweden, having grown considerably in size and visibility from the 1990s on, and the position of Islam in Swedish society has increasingly become a topic of political controversy (Willander 2019). Existing scholarship on gender and Islam comprises both textual and ethnographic approaches, though the latter are more well represented. An early example of a textually based study is historian of religions Jonas Svensson's (2000, published in English, Lund University) doctoral dissertation, which draws on discourse analysis and the sociology of knowledge to analyse texts by Muslim scholars that attempt to accommodate international human rights norms in the definition of women's rights.

On the ethnographic side, historian of religion Rannveig Jetne Haga's (2009, published in English, Uppsala University) doctoral dissertation draws on interviews and participant observation among women transnational Somali traders, analysing both how tradition and gender norms constrain the women's activities as well as how the women enact agency by acting as entrepreneurs, providers and pious women. Haga thus contributes to the debate around agency, women and Islam, challenging the victimization of Muslim women in general, and especially Somali women.

Focusing on Muslim women in Sweden and the Nordic region, sociologist of religion Madeleine Sultán Sjöqvist (2006, published in Swedish, Uppsala

University) has interviewed Swedish women who have converted to Islam. Sultán Sjöqvist draws on, among other frameworks, gender theory to analyse how gender is socially constructed in her interviewees' responses, indicating a tension between striving towards the correct form of tradition and construing religious engagement as a form of women's emancipation. Sultán Sjöqvist's interlocutors emphasize that Islam represents gender equality as well as a benevolent patriarchy where women defer to their husbands. More recently, historian of religion Nina Jakku's dissertation (2019, published in Swedish, Lund University) analyses Muslim women's experiences of Swedish society as well as media representations of Muslim women in Sweden. Sociologist of religion Vanja Mosbach's doctoral dissertation (2022, published in English, Uppsala University) draws on interviews with women who position themselves as Muslim feminists in Sweden and the Øresund region. Mosbach engages critically with the framework of religious individualization, arguing that the participants' religiosity is shaped in dynamic tension between foundational texts and the individual authority of the self as well as politicized understandings of Islam and Muslims.

Swedish research on gender and Islam has largely emphasized women and/or women's issues, with a few notable exceptions. Historian of religion David Thurfjell's doctoral dissertation (2003, published in English, Uppsala University) analyses the religiosity of male Iranian Islamists, though Thurfjell does not operationalize gender as an analytical category. Historian of religion Erica Li Lundqvist's (2013, published in English, Lund University) doctoral dissertation analyses queer men and masculinities in present-day Lebanon based on interviews and participant observation among men with same-sex desire who did not fully identify with the LGBTQ acronym. In highlighting her interlocutors' strategies for negotiating religious, societal and familial resistance, Lundqvist problematized the stability of the identity categories of being both gay and Muslim.

Women and Gender in Modern Alternative Religiosity

Recent decades have witnessed several studies on women or gender in modern alternative religiosity, including utopian movements, 'new age' spirituality, contemporary Paganisms and Western esotericism. Once again, this is perhaps unsurprising: both national (e.g. Thurfjell 2015a; Willander 2019) and international scholarship (e.g. Frisk and Åkerbäck 2015; Norris and Inglehart 2004) has highlighted Sweden as an exceptional case of the transformation of religion, with a high degree of sympathy for beliefs and practices linked to esotericism and alternative spirituality. However, several Swedish studies of gender in alternative religions focus on movements outside of Sweden. Though outside of the study of religions *sensu stricto*, it is worth mentioning intellectual historian Inga Sanner's doctoral dissertation (1995, published in Swedish, Stockholm University) on utopian movements (including Spiritualism, Unitarianism, Theosophy and anarchism) in nineteenth-century Sweden as an early instance of scholarship in this area.

Several Swedish scholars have surveyed modern Goddess spirituality in various forms. Psychologist of religion Petra Junus's (1995, published in Swedish, Uppsala

University) doctoral dissertation, analysing Swedish, Goddess-oriented feminists, is an early example both of the study of contemporary Paganism as well as religion and gender in Sweden. Junus argues that Goddess-related symbolism can have an emancipatory function for women seeking to disrupt gender norms. Historian of religion Åsa Trulsson's doctoral dissertation (2010, published in English, Lund University) draws on ethnographic research on ritual creativity among women practitioners of Goddess spirituality in Europe. Conducting participant observation at various spiritual festivals, Trulsson critiques the predominance of textual approaches in the study of religions and argues for the importance of practice and embodiment in contemporary spirituality. Religious studies scholar Magdalena Raivio's doctoral dissertation (2014, published in Swedish, Karlstad University) comprises a textual analysis of the writings of influential authors on witchcraft and Goddess spirituality, Monica Sjöö and Starhawk. Raivio analyses how these authors construct subjectivity and feminist affinities and situates them within feminist history more broadly.

In the area of women, gender and Western esotericism, historian of religion Per Faxneld's doctoral dissertation (2014, in English, Stockholm University; later published in English as Faxneld 2017) analysed the motif of the Devil as the liberator of woman in nineteenth-century culture, drawing on analysis of literature, visual arts and artefacts. Though Faxneld highlights how the motif was mainly invoked as a misogynist trope, he also shows how the idea of Lucifer as sympathetic to women's lives and struggles was adopted via a form of 'rebellious hermeneutics' by avantgarde artists, writers and esotericists. In article form, Faxneld has also analysed aspect of gender in Western esotericism and occulture, including Theosophy (e.g. Faxneld 2012).

Historian of religion Manon Hedenborg White's doctoral dissertation (2017, in English, Uppsala University; later published in English as Hedenborg White 2020) analyses constructions of femininity and feminine sexuality in modern Western esotericism, centring on interpretations of the goddess Babalon, a central deity within the British occultist and poet Aleister Crowley's religion Thelema, from the early twentieth century until today. Drawing on critical theorization on femininities including queer and femme approaches, the study is based on qualitative content analysis of published and unpublished esoteric writings from *c*. 1900 until today as well as semi-structured interviews and participant observation among present-day practitioners. In article form, Hedenborg White has continued to analyse women's roles and gender issues in esotericism (e.g. Hedenborg White 2021).

Queer Identities and Approaches

Queer theoretical approaches to the study of religions *sensu stricto* are, thus far, relatively marginal in Sweden, with some notable exceptions. In this context, it is worth mentioning as a pioneering example Lars Gårdfeldt's (2005, published in Swedish, Karlstad University) doctoral dissertation in religious studies, which drew on liberation theology to argue for the inclusion of LGBTQ persons in Christian churches. Biblical scholar Malin Ekström's (2011, published in Swedish,

Uppsala University) doctoral dissertation, comprising a queer theoretical reading of the Book of Ruth, is also relevant here. Historian of religion Paulina Partanen's doctoral dissertation (2016, published in English, Uppsala University) draws on the work of Judith Butler and J. Jack Halberstam as well as the spatial methodology of Kim Knott to analyse female immortals in Homer's *Odyssey*. Partanen demonstrates that female immortals such as Circe and Calypso demonstrate power over the mortal man Odysseus but are simultaneously bound by the gender hierarchies of the immortal realm. In so doing, Partanen questions normative assumptions about sex, gender and power in Homer's epic. Partanen's dissertation also comprises a rare example of a Swedish scholar combining gender and queer theory with traditional philological methods.

A number of scholars have applied queer theoretical perspectives to modern religiosity, including Lundqvist's (2013) above-mentioned study of queer Muslim men in Lebanon. Hedenborg White's doctoral dissertation (2017/2020), mentioned above, utilizes queer perspectives, as does sociologist of religion Oriol Poveda Guillén's doctoral dissertation (2017, published in English, Uppsala University), which analyses transgender identities and experiences in Orthodox Judaism in Israel and North America based on interviews. Poveda Guillén analyses how his interviewees negotiate gendered religious practices, and he has sought to theorize, in dialogue with the interviewees, how the Orthodox community may respond to openly transgender members. Finally, sociologist of religion Evelina Lundmark (2019, English, Uppsala University; later published in English as Lundmark 2023) draws on queer theory to analyse female atheists' performance of self online (more of which below). While possibly coincidental, it is interesting to note that Ekström, Partanen, Hedenborg White, Poveda Guillén and Lundmark all produced their doctoral dissertations at the Department of Theology at Uppsala University, suggesting this as a possible significant node in the development of queer approaches to the study of religions in Sweden.

Men and Masculinities in Religion

In general, research on men and masculinity is underdeveloped in the Nordic study of religions. Keinänen (2016) notes that it is, instead, historians who have laid the foundation for men's studies in religion in the region. This includes the work of historian Johan A. Lundin (2013), based at Malmö University, on constructions of femininity and masculinity in the Salvation Army and, perhaps especially, Lund University historian Yvonne-Maria Werner's (e.g. 2008, 2009, 2011) research on Christian masculinity. Werner has challenged the so-called feminization thesis – the notion of women's greater involvement in Western Christian churches – and highlighted converse processes of masculinization in churches in the nineteenth and twentieth centuries. Werner's scholarship has been described as 'trailblazing' (Keinänen 2016: 57) but has also incited critique from other gender scholars for overlooking gendered power imbalances and male conservative resistance to women's emancipation (e.g. Ohlander 2005; cf. Keinänen 2016). As noted above, historians of religion Thurfjell's (2003) and Lundqvist's (2013) doctoral dissertations represent important works on Muslim men and masculinities. Church and mission studies scholar Martin Nykvist's (2019, published in Swedish, Lund University) work on homosociality and masculinity in the Church of Sweden is also relevant here.

Gender, Media and Religion

A final area of research worth mentioning in this chapter is the nexus of religion, media and gender. Sociologist of religion Mia Lövheim, based at Uppsala University, is distinctively the most established and internationally recognized Swedish scholar in this area. Lövheim has especially highlighted young women's agency in digital media, such as how Swedish female top bloggers co-construct values and relations between themselves and their readers (2011, 2013, 2016). Sociologist of religion Anneli Winell's (Uppsala University) doctoral dissertation (2016, published in Swedish) analyses everyday religion in Swedish women's magazines and indicates a neoliberal self-help paradigm that feminizes well-being. In the magazines, Winell argues that care for the female reader's body is construed as an essential tool for controlling her own life and achieving social gender equality. Sociologist of religion Lundmark's doctoral dissertation (2019, 2023; see above) analyses female atheists' performance of self through digital media, and Lövheim and Lundmark (2019) have jointly analysed how women negotiate authority to speak about religion online.

Impact and International Significance

It is difficult to assess the impact and significance of Swedish research on gender and religion. The societal impact *within* Sweden is, potentially, quite substantial for the study of gender and religion on the whole, if the educational system is taken into account. As noted above, Swedish public policy in the second half of the twentieth century has strongly emphasized gender equality. This is reflected in the school curriculum, which emphasizes 'equality between women and men', non-discrimination on the basis of sex as well as gender expression and identity, along with the obligation of schools to make visible, and work to counteract, restricting gender norms and to encourage children and young people to develop their interests and abilities regardless of sex (Skolverket 2022a). The 2022 curriculum for Religion Education (RE) emphasizes this by stipulating that children and young people should learn about, for instance, religious attitudes to men's and women's roles as well as different sexual orientations, and the relationship between religious world views and gender equality (Skolverket 2022b). While a discussion about RE may appear tangential to an overview of research on gender and religion, it is relevant in this context as RE teacher students comprise a sizeable portion of Swedish university students enrolled in courses in the study of religions, and a large component of tenured scholars of religion in Sweden have some degree of involvement in teacher education (cf. Thurfjell 2015b). Research in the didactics of religion suggests that RE teachers strive to emphasize women's agency; however, gender stereotypes have also been shown to persist in Swedish schools (Berglund 2011).

In terms of international research impact, the question is more complex. Based on aggregated number of citations, the most internationally impactful researcher mentioned here is, seemingly, sociologist of religion Lövheim, who is a well-established name in the study of media and religion internationally. However, many of Lövheim's most-cited studies do not consider gender in particular. Within the study of gender and religion, anthropologist Gemzöe and historian Werner also have some degree of broader international impact. Several of the above-discussed scholars could also be said to have a relatively high degree of impact within more demarcated fields. Faxneld's (2014/2017; see above) work is an example of this, and it is frequently cited in the study of Satanism, esotericism and gender. It is also worth mentioning that several Swedish doctoral dissertations considering gender and religion published in recent years have been acquired by internationally top-ranked publishers such as Oxford University Press and Routledge (see Faxneld 2017; Hedenborg White 2020; Lundmark 2023). This is not unremarkable for such a small country as Sweden, where a sizeable number of doctoral dissertations continue to be published in Swedish.

Conclusions

The development of the study of religions and gender in Sweden largely mirrors international trends, albeit with a certain temporal delay. Congruent with the international research front, Swedish scholars of gender and religion have predominantly emphasized women and women's issues. While increased scholarship on men and masculinity is certainly desirable, this relative imbalance can also be considered as a corrective to historical androcentrism within the field (cf. Keinänen 2016). Recent doctoral dissertations (produced in the last twenty years) also suggest that the study of religions and gender in Sweden mirrors wider disciplinary developments regarding methods and approaches. Thurfjell (2015b) notes an increasing shift away from traditional History of Religions approaches (associated with historical-philological methods and specialized competence in languages) towards the broadened label *religionsvetenskap* (Religious Studies, encompassing sociological, psychological and didactical approaches), coinciding with a stronger emphasis on anthropologically or sociologically oriented scholarship on contemporary conditions in milieus that are geographically or culturally close to the researcher's home turf. By and large, as seen above, scholarship on religion and gender in Sweden has an ethnographic and sociological bias, and historical-philological scholarship on gender and religion is scarcer. As noted above, within the study of religions *sensu stricto*, Partanen's (2016) work on Homer's *Odyssey* represents an exception, as does historian of religion Therese Rodin's (2014, published in English, Uppsala University) doctoral dissertation, which analyses myths surrounding the Sumerian mother goddess. However, the general scarcity of traditional, philological research on religion taking gender into account is worrying, and it reflects a general decline of specialized language skills as well as how scholars and PhD students are increasingly pushed towards identifying 'societal issues where knowledge about religion can be helpful and to steer their research in that direction' (Thurfjell 2015b: 167). While new research on how gender shapes contemporary religious and non-religious life in Sweden and beyond is certainly important, I am hopeful that the field will increasingly encourage a variety of research methods, specializations and working languages, allowing Swedish scholars and students of religion to engage with the myriad ways in which gender and religion have intersected throughout history and space.

References

Online databases

DiVa (Digitala Vetenskapliga Arkivet): https://www.diva-portal.org
GENA Database – Gohenburg University Library: http://www2.ub.gu.se/kvinn/gena/
Swecris – search for Swedish research projects: https://www.vr.se/english/swecris.html#/

Published

Ammerman, N. T. (2007), 'Introduction: Observing Religious Modern Lives', in N. T. Ammerman (ed.), *Everyday Religion: Observing Modern Religious Lives*, 3–18, New York: Oxford University Press.
Berglund, J. (2011), 'Global Questions in the Classroom: The Formulation of Islamic Religious Education at Muslim Schools in Sweden', *Discourse: Studies in the Cultural Politics of Education* 32 (4): 497–512.
Butler, J. (1990), *Gender Trouble: Feminism and the Subversion of Identity*, New York: Routledge.
Dahl, U., M. Liljeström and U. Manns (2016), 'Introduction', in U. Dahl, M. Liljeström and U. Manns (eds), *The Geopolitics of Nordic and Russian Gender Research 1975–2005*, 9–32, Huddinge: Södertörn University.
de Beauvoir, S. (1984 [1953]), *The Second Sex*, trans. H. Parshley, Harmondsworth: Penguin Books.
Ekström, M. (2011), *Allvarsam parodi och möjlighetens melankoli: En queerteoretisk analys av Ruts bok*, Uppsala: Uppsala University.
Faxneld, P. (2012), 'Blavatsky the Satanist: Luciferianism in Theoosophy, and Its Feminine Implications', *Temenos* 48 (2): 203–30.
Faxneld, P. (2014), *Satanic Feminism: Lucifer as the Liberator of Woman in Nineteenth-Century Culture*, Stockholm: Molin & Sorgenfrei.
Faxneld, P. (2017) *Satanic Feminism: Lucifer as the Liberator of Woman in Nineteenth-Century Culture*, New York: Oxford University Press.
Frisk, L., and P. Åkerbäck (2015), *New Religiosity in Contemporary Sweden: The Dalarna Study in National and International Context*, Sheffield: Equinox.

Gårdfeldt, L. (2005), *Hatar Gud bögar? Teologiska förståelser av homo-, bi- och transpersoer. En befrielseteologisk studie*, Stockholm: Normal Förlag.
Gemzöe, L., and M.-L. Keinänen (2016), 'Contemporary Encounters in Gender and Religion: Introduction', in L. Gemzöe and M.-L. Keinänen (eds), *Contemporary Encounters in Gender and Religion: European Perspectives*, 1–28, Cham: Palgrave Macmillan.
Gemzöe, L. (2000), *Feminine Matters: Women's Religious Practices in a Portuguese Town*, Stockholm: Stockholm University.
Gemzöe, L. (2005), 'The Feminization of Healing in Pilgrimage to Fátima', in J. Dubisch and M. Winkelman (eds), *Pilgrimage and Healing*, 25–48, Tucson: University of Arizona Press.
Gemzöe, L., M.-L. Keinänen and A. Maddrell, eds (2016), *Contemporary Encounters in Gender and Religion: European Perspectives*, Cham: Palgrave Macmillan.
Gross, R. M., ed. (1977), *Beyond Androcentrism: New Essays on Women and Religion*, Missoula: Scholars Press for the American Academy of Religion.
Gross, R. M., ed. (1996), *Feminism and Religion: An Introduction*, Boston: Beacon Press.
Gunner, G. (2003), *Nelly Hall: Uppburen och ifrågasatt: Predikant och missionär i Europa och USA 1882–1901*, Uppsala: Svenska institutet för missionsforskning.
Hammar, I. (1998a), 'Några reflexioner kring "religionsblind" kvinnoforskning', *Historisk tidskrift* 1: 2–29.
Hammar, I. (1998b), 'Den svårerövrade offenligheten: Kön och religion i emancipationsprocessen', *Tidskrift för genusvetenskap* 2: 16–28.
Hammar, I. (1999), *Emancipation och religion: Den svenska kvinnorörelsens pionjärer i debatt om kvinnans kallelse ca 1860–1900*, Stockholm: Carlsson.
Harding, S. (1991), *Whose Science? Whose Knowledge? Thinking from Women's Lives*, Buckingham: Open University Press.
Hedenborg White, M. (2017), *The Eloquent Blood: The Goddess Babalon and the Construction of Femininities in Western Esotericism*, Uppsala: Uppsala University.
Hedenborg White, M. (2020), *The Eloquent Blood: The Goddess Babalon and the Construction of Femininities in Western Esotericism*, New York: Oxford University Press.
Hedenborg White, M. (2021), 'Double Toil and Gender Trouble? Performativity and Femininity in the Cauldron of Esotericism Research', in E. Asprem and J. Strube (eds), *New Approaches to the Study of Esotericism*, 182–200, Leiden: Brill.
Hellman, E. (1998), *Hinduiska gudinnor och kvinnor: En introduktion*, Nora: Nya Doxa.
Hellman, E. (2003), 'Kampen om gudinnan: Lina Guptas hinduiska feministteologi', *Kvinnovetenskaplig tidskrift* 3-4: 55–69.
Hellman, E. (2007a), 'Open Space and Double Locks: The Hindutva Appropriation of Female Gender', in A. Sharma and K. K. Young (eds), *Fundamentalism and Women in World Religions*, 29–61, New York: T&T Clark.
Hellman, E. (2007b), 'Women as Fundamental and Fundamentalist Women: The Case of Buddhist Sri Lanka', in A. Sharma and K. K. Young, *Fundamentalism and Women in World Religions*, 1–32, New York: T&T Clark.
Hirdman, Y. (1988), 'Genussystemet: Reflexoner kring kvinnors sociala underordning', *Kvinnovetenskaplig tidskrift* 9 (3): 49–63.
Jakku, N. (2019), *Muslimska kvinnors mobilitet: Möjligheter och hinder i de liberala idealens Sverige*, Lund: Luns universitet.
Jetne Haga, R. (2009), *Tradition as Resource: Transnational Somali Women Traders Facing the Realities of Civil War*, Uppsala: Uppsala University.

Junus, P. (1995), *Den levande gudinnan: Kvinnoidentitet och religiositet som förändringsprocess*, Nora: Nya Doxa.

Keinänen, M.-L. (2003), *Creating Bodies: Childbirth Practices in Pre-Modern Karelia*, Stockholm: Stockholm University.

Keinänen, M.-L., ed. (2010), *Perspectives on Women's Everyday Religion*, Stockholm: Stockholm University.

Keinänen, M.-L. (2016), 'Feminist Reflections on the Study of the Feminization and Masculinization of Religion', in L. Gemzöe, M.-L. Keinänen and A. Maddrell (eds), *Contemporary Encounters in Gender and Religion: European Perspectives*, 55–76, Cham: Palgrave Macmillan.

King, U. (1995), *Religion and Gender*, Oxford: Blackwell.

King, U. (2005), 'Gender and Religion: An Overview', in L. Jones (ed.), *Encyclopedia of Religion*, vol. 5, 2nd edn, 2396–3310, Detroit: Macmillan Reference.

Kosofsky Sedgwick, E. (1985), *Between Men: English Literature and Male Homosocial Desire*, New York: Columbia University Press.

Laqueur, T. (1990), *Making Sex: Body and Gender from the Greeks to Freud*, Cambridge, MA: Harvard University Press.

Lövheim, M. (2011), 'Young Women's Blogs as Ethical Spaces', *Information, Communication & Society* 14 (3): 338–54.

Lövheim, M., ed. (2013), *Media, Religion and Gender: Key Issues and New Challenges*, Abingdon: Routledge.

Lövheim, M. (2016), 'Mediatization: Analyzing Transformations of Religion from a Gender Perspective', *Media, Culture & Society* 38 (1): 18–27.

Lövheim, M., and E. Lundmark (2019), 'Gender, Religion and Authority in Digital Media', *Journal for Communication Studies* 12 (2:24): 23–38.

Lundin, J.A. (2013), *Predikande kvinnor och gråtande män: Frälsningsarmén i Sverige 1882-1921*, Malmö: Kira.

Lundmark, E. (2019), *'This Is the Face of an Atheist': Performing Private Truths in Precarious Publics*, Uppsala: Uppsala University.

Lundmark, E. (2023), *Performing Atheist Selves in Digital Publics: U.S. Women and Non-Religious Identity Online*, Abingdon: Routledge.

Lundqvist, E. L. (2013), *Gayted Communities: Marginalized Sexualities in Lebanon*, Lund: Lund University.

Mahmood, S. (2005), *Politics of Piety: The Islamic Revival and the Feminist Subject*, Princeton: Princeton University Press.

Manns, U. (1998), 'Den religionsblinda kvinnorörelseforskningen – en kommentar till Inger Hammars kritik', *Historisk tidskrift* (2): 197–8.

Manns, U. (2010), 'Fredrika Bremer: A Preacher on the Borders of Religion', in M.-L. Keinänen (ed.), *Perspectives on Women's Everyday Religion*, 41–50, Stockholm: Acta Universitatis Stockholmiensis.

Manns, U. (2011), 'Identity and Collective Memory in the Making of Nineteenth-Century Feminism', in H. Ruin and A. Ers (eds), *Rethinking Time: Essays on History, Memory, and Representation*, 291–300, Huddinge: Södertörn University.

McGuire, M. (2008), *Lived Religion: Faith and Practice in Everyday Life*, New York: Oxford University Press.

Mosbach, V. (2022), *Voices of Muslim Feminists: Navigating Tradition, Authority, and the Debate about Islam*, Uppsala: Uppsala University.

Nationella Sekretariatet för Genusforskning (Swedish Secretariat for Gender Research) (2007), *Genusforskning pågår: En kartläggning av i vilka institutionella miljöer forskning inom genusfältet bedrivs i Sverige*, Gothenburg: University of Gothenburg, http://www.genus.se/wp-content/uploads/Genusforskning-pagar.pdf (accessed 15 March 2023).

Norris, P., and R. Inglehart (2004), *Sacred and Secular: Religion and Politics Worldwide*, Cambridge: Cambridge University Press.

Nykvist, M. (2019), *Alla mäns prästadöme: Homosocialitet, maskulinitet och religion hos Kyrkobröderna, Svenska kyrkans lekmannaförbund 1918–1978*, Lund: Nordic Academic Press.

Ohlander, A.-S. (2005), 'Okunskap eller medveten negligering?', *Genus: Aktuellt magasin från Nationella sekretariatet för genusforskning* 1.

Partanen, P. (2016), *Navigating Female Power: (De-)Constructing the Space of the Immortal Threat in Homer's Odyssey*, Uppsala: Uppsala University.

Poveda Guillén, O. (2017), *According to Whose Will: The Entanglements of Gender & Religion in the Lives of Transgender Jews with an Orthodox Background*, Uppsala: Uppsala University.

Raivio, M. (2014), *Gudinnefeminister: Monica Sjöös och Starhawks berättande – subjektskonstruktion, idéinnehåll och feministiska affiniteter*, Karlstad: Kalstad University.

Rodin, T. (2014), *The World of the Sumerian Mother Goddess: An Interpretation of Her Myths*, Uppsala: Uppsala University.

Sanner, I. (1995), *Att älska sin nästa såsom sig själv: Om moraliska utopier under 1800-talet*, Stockholm: Carlsson.

Scott, J. W. (1986), 'Gender: A Useful Category of Historical Analysis', *Historical Review* 91 (5): 1053–75.

Sered, S. (1999), '"Woman" as Symbol and Women as Agents: Gendered Religious Discourses and Practices', in M. M. Ferree, J. Lorber and B. B. Hess (eds), *Revisioning Gender*, 193–222, Thousand Oaks: Sage.

Skolverket (2022a), 'Läroplan för grundskolan samt för förskoleklassen och fritidshemmet', https://www.skolverket.se/undervisning/grundskolan/laroplan-och-kursplaner-for-grundskolan/laroplan-lgr22-for-grundskolan-samt-for-forskoleklassen-och-fritidshemmet (accessed 15 March 2023).

Skolverket (2022b), 'Lgr 2022, Kursplan – Religionskunskap', https://www.skolverket.se/undervisning/grundskolan/laroplan-och-kursplaner-for-grundskolan/laroplan-lgr22-for-grundskolan-samt-for-forskoleklassen-och-fritidshemmet?url=-996270488%2Fcompulsorycw%2Fjsp%2Fsubject.htm%3FsubjectCode%3DGRGRRE L01%26tos%3Dgr&sv.url=12.5dfee44715d35a5cdfa219f (accessed 15 March 2023).

Sorgenfrei, S., and D. Thurfjell, eds (2020), *Kvinnligt religiöst ledarskap: En vänbok till Gunilla Gunner*, Huddinge: Södertörn University.

Sultán Sjöqvist, M. (2006), *'Vi blev muslimer': Svenska kvinnor berättar: en religionssociologisk studie av konversionsberättelser*, Uppsaa: Acta Universitatis Uppsaliensis.

Svensson, J. (2000), *Women's Human Rights and Islam: A Study of Three Attempts at Accommodation*, Stockholm: Almqvist & Wiksell International.

Thurfjell, D. (2003), *Living Shi'ism: Instances of Ritualisation among Islamist Men in Contemporary Iran*, Uppsala: Uppsala University.

Thurfjell, D. (2015a), *Det gudlösa folket: De postkristna svenskarna och religionen*, Stockholm: Molin & Sorgenfrei.

Thurfjell, D. (2015b), 'The Dissolution of the History of Religions: Contemporary Challenges of a Humanities Discipline in Sweden', *Temenos* 51 (2): 161–75.

Trulsson, Å. (2010), *Cultivating the Sacred: Ritual Creativity and Practice among Women in Contemporary Europe*, Lund: Lund University.

Warne, R. (2000), 'Gender', in W. Braun and R. T. McCutcheon (eds), *Guide tot he Study of Religion*, 140–54, London: Cassell.

Warner, M., ed. (1993), *Fear of a Queer Planet: Queer Politics and Social Theory*, Minneapolis: University of Minnesota Press.

Werner, Y.-M. (2008), 'Kristen manlighet i teori och praxis', in Y.-M. Werner (ed.), *Kristen manlighet: Ideal och verklighet 1830–1940*, 9–21, Lund: Nordic Academic Press.

Werner, Y.-M. (2009), 'Religious Feminisation, Confessionalism and Re-Masculinisation in Western European Society 1800–1960)', in L. Sjørup and H. R. Christensen (eds), *Pieties and Gender*, 141–66, Leiden: Brill.

Werner, Y.-M. (2011), 'Studying Christian Masculinity: An Introduction', in Y.-M. Werner (ed.), *Christian Masculinity: Men and Religion in Northern Europe in the 19th and 20th Centuries*, 7–17, Leuven: Leuven University Press.

Willander, E. (2019), 'Sveriges religiösa landskap: samhörighet, tillhörighet och mångfald under 2000-talet', *Swedish Agency for Support to Faith Communities*, https://www.myn dighetensst.se/download/18.3907b1d0169055cec1fa7a49/1554715170878/Nr%20 8,%20sverigesreligiosalandskap_utskrift.pdf (accessed 15 March 2023).

Winell, A. (2016), *'Godis för kropp och själ': Välbefinnande och vardagsandlighet i tre svenska kvinnotidningar*, Uppsala: Acta Universitatis Uppsaliensis.

Woodhead, L. (2001), 'Feminism and the Sociology of Religion: From Gender-Blindness to Gendered Difference', in R. K. Fenn (ed.), *The Blackwell Companion to Sociology of Religion*, 67–84, Oxford: Blackwell.

Chapter 17

VIOLENCE

Tomas Lindgren, Göran Larsson and Isak Svensson

Following growth over the past decades in publications that address the potential nexus between religion and violence, it is easy to get the impression that this is a recent research topic within the academic study of religions. Even though it is most likely true that the number of publications that deal with religion and violence have grown rapidly since the 9/11 attacks, and even more so with the rise of terrorist organizations like the Islamic State (IS), studies that focus on religion and violence are far from novel (e.g. Wellman 2007). Several classical theoreticians within the study of religions (e.g. James G. Frazer, Sigmund Freud, René Girard, Walter Burkert and Jan Assmann) have all paid close attention to the role and function of violence in myths, rituals and social dynamics. Most of them claim that violence is intrinsic to religion, and some also see it as 'unavoidable and, in fact, as socially productive' (Kippenberg 2011: 7).

Building on classical and contemporary studies, Swedish scholars from various disciplines, such as the History of Religions (e.g. Göndör 2018; Larsson 2022; Peste 2003), biblical studies (e.g. Nord 2022), the sociology of religion (e.g. Dahlgren 2011; Lundgren 2008; Nilsson 2018, 2020; Poljarevic 2021), psychology of religion (e.g. Cetrez 2012; Hermanson 2011; Lindgren 2023) and political science (e.g. Ranstorp 1996), have grappled – at least to a certain extent – with the issue of how to define religion and violence, on the one hand, and how to understand the nexus between religious beliefs and violence, on the other. In this short overview, we will provide some examples that show how Swedish scholars have understood and studied the relationship between religion and violence and how Swedish researchers have been engaged with and contributed to international research. Contrary to academic subjects like international relations or peace and development studies, which have built centres or institutions or developed academic programmes for the study of violence, no Swedish department of religious studies (or theology for that matter) has made religion and its potential nexus with violence its profile. That said, the topic of religion and violence has been of great interest to many Swedish academics and some institutions, both at the university and governmental levels, as will be discussed in the present chapter.

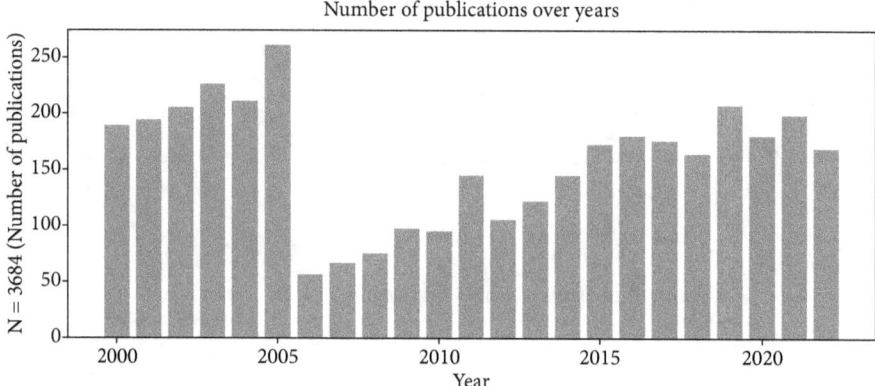

Figure 17.1 The graph builds on data published by scholars associated with Swedish universities (here defined as Swedish researchers) retrieved from four Swedish databases of academic publications (Swepub, DIVA, LUB and GUP) between 2000 and 2022. The following keywords were used: Religion, Violence, Conflict, Terrorism, Islam, Christianity, Judaism, Hinduism, Buddhism and 'other religions'.

Nonetheless, before we discuss briefly about how Swedish scholars have defined and studied religion and violence, Figure 17.1 illustrates that publications addressing these topics are quite common among Swedish scholars.[1]

The Study of Religion and Violence

Much like religion, violence is notoriously difficult to pin down as a single, determinate concept. In a couple of seminal articles, the Norwegian peace researcher Johan Galtung, who defines violence as 'that which increases the distance between the potential and the actual, and that which impedes the decrease of this distance' (Galtung 1969: 168), distinguishes between three different types of violence: direct, structural and cultural (for a similar distinction, see Žižek 2009). Using these concepts, Galtung draws our attention to the different expressions of violence and their varying degrees of visibility. Direct violence involves actions perpetrated by individuals (interpersonal violence) or groups (collective violence) that inflict, threaten or cause physical and/or psychological injury. Structural violence, in contrast, is more indirect and refers to the preventable harm that is built into social, economic and/or political structures (Galtung 1996). Recognizing that the concept of structural violence is very broad and elusive, to the extent that finding generally acceptable empirical measurements for it has so far defeated the scholarly community, we still think that the concept itself is valid. Cultural violence, finally, are those aspects of a culture 'that can be used to justify or legitimize direct and structural violence' (Galtung 1990: 291; for criticism of this distinction, see Keane 1996).

The study of religions in Sweden has related to each of these three types of violence, for instance, Eva Lundgren's (1987, 1992) interview studies of religiously motivated violence against women, Åsa Eldén's (2003) qualitative study of religious meaning-making in relation to honour-related violence, Mattias Gardell's studies of islamophobia (2010), torture (2008) and racism (2003) – which include studies of violence carried out both by and against religious actors – and Per-Erik Nilsson's (2019) study of the intersections of secularism, far-right populism and nationhood in contemporary France.

In this chapter, we will concentrate on studies of the relationship between religion and direct collective violence, which includes studies of the connection between new religious movements and violence, such as Henrik Bogdan's (2011) analysis of murder and suicides in the Order of the Solar Temple in the 1990s and Eva Lundgren's (2008) and Jonathan Peste's (2011) studies of violence in the Knutby Filadelfia community in Sweden at the beginning of this century. On religious conflicts, there are Isak Svensson and his colleagues' quantitative studies of inter- and intra-religious conflicts (e.g. Finnbogason, Larsson and Svensson 2019; Svensson 2007, 2012, 2013, 2016; Svensson and Harding 2011; Svensson and Nilsson 2018) and Tomas Lindgren's qualitative studies of religious conflicts in Southeast Asia and beyond (Lindgren 2012, 2014, 2018; Lindgren and Sonnenschein 2021). On religious terrorism, there are Magnus Ranstorp's study of religiously motivated terrorism from a political science perspective (e.g. Ranstorp 1996), Peste's interdisciplinary study of the relationship between religion and terrorism (Peste 2003), Göran Larsson's in-depth analysis of Western anti-IS fighter's autobiographical accounts (Larsson 2022), Marco Nilsson's studies of radicalization processes amongst jihadist individuals (e.g. Nilsson 2015, 2021), Gardell's studies of so-called lone-wolf terrorism (e.g. Gardell 2015, 2017), Mimmi Söderberg Kovacs's work on the conditions under which Islamist armed groups turn into political parties or movements (Krause and Söderberg Kovacs 2022) and Lindgren and his colleagues' psychological and critical studies of terrorism, radicalism and radicalization (Lindgren 2016, 2023; Lindgren, Sonnenschein and Eriksson 2022; Sonnenschein and Lindgren 2020; see also Poljarevic 2012).

A review of the literature reveals that, with some notable exceptions (e.g. Lindgren and Sonnenschein 2021), most scholars in the field of religion and violence simply use the term 'religion' without ever defining it, as if its meaning were self-evident (e.g. Göndör 2018; Ranstorp 1996). Here they often cite established, typically substantivist definitions of religion (e.g. Svensson 2012) or, more rarely, make up their own, again typically substantivist definitions, which are usually influenced by established definitions in the field of religious studies (e.g. Lindgren 2023). Functionalist definitions of religion are virtually non-existent in the literature, which is not particularly surprising, since it would make the category of religion so all-encompassing and inclusive as to be of little analytical value in this context. Most scholars thus assume that religion is a relatively stable phenomenon in the world – a genus of which there are several species, such as Hinduism, Islam and Christianity – which influences behaviour and promotes violence (Lindgren 2018). Religion, a religion and/or religions in the plural are, in other words, seen by many as facts, usually not as brute facts, but as social facts (which 'are nevertheless real facts – if only for the community that recognizes them as such', as Craig Martin succinctly puts it (2017: 48)).

The meaning of the term 'violence' is, with some notable exceptions (e.g. Lindgren 2023), assumed rather than defined, but associated terms, like conflict and terrorism, are usually coherently defined or problematized (or deconstructed) in the literature (e.g. Lindgren 2023; Peste 2003; Svensson 2012). Terms like 'religious violence', 'religious conflict' and 'religious terrorism' are typically used as shorthand descriptors for what are thought of as distinct categories of violence, conflict or terrorism. This entails the assumption that they are different from their secular counterparts in whole or in part. It is the concern with categories such as the 'religious sphere' (Svensson 2013) or 'superhuman powers' (Lindgren 2023) that distinguishes religious from secular violence. However, this does not necessarily imply that religious violence, religious conflict or religious terrorism are understood as unitary phenomena. 'Religious conflicts are not one unitary group of conflict,' Svensson rightly points out; 'they are diverse in many ways but similar in the sense that they [all] have religious dimensions' (Svensson 2012: 48).

Much of the literature on religion and violence argues that religious violence is the result of a complex interaction of endogenous factors, such as certain religious beliefs, charismatic leadership, social encapsulation and totalistic groups, and exogenous social, economic and political factors. Peste, for instance, concludes that it is

> highly unlikely that religion is the only factor to take into account when explaining the origins of violence in religious communities. Particularly in small, close-knit groups that set themselves in opposition to the surrounding society for ideological or political reasons, many important factors come into play – including ideology-theology, group dynamics and behavior, personal background of the followers and leaders, as well as relationships with nonmembers and the larger society. (Peste 2011: 225; see also Peste 2003)

Svensson similarly argues that religion is neither the main problem nor the original cause of 'most, if not all, of the armed conflicts around the world' (2012: XII; see also Lindgren 2018). Although most such scholars recognize that religious violence is a multidetermined and multifactorial phenomenon, they tend to emphasize the crucial importance of religious identities or religious beliefs (or ideologies) that is reflected in the distinction between identity-based and issue-based religious conflicts. However, very few argue that religions – at least liberal interpretations of religion – are more prone to violence than secular phenomena. Still, whether certain religious dimensions are associated with a higher risk of violence is an empirical question, some evidence providing indications in that direction, a point we will return to below.

The concept of religious violence implies a link between religion and violence, and many scholars appear to think that violence somehow emerges from (certain) religious identities or religious beliefs. This can be seen, for instance, in the emphasis on mapping, describing or analysing the beliefs or ideologies of religious actors who have been – or are suspected of having been – involved in violence (e.g. Gardell 2003; Göndör 2018). The importance placed on (certain) identities or beliefs (or ideologies) suggests a correspondence bias, that is, a well-documented human tendency to think that other people's behaviour reflects the underlying internal traits.

Ending Religious Wars

Leaving the problem of finding an overarching definition of religion, some research has instead proceeded on the basis that subjective self-definitions can still work as a basis for studying the phenomena under interest. For example, armed groups can be considered religious if they describe their aspirations in religious terms, such as demands for a particular role for their religion in their state. Religious actors in armed conflicts – governments and rebel groups – can thus be defined as such if they make explicit demands anchored in a religious claim. While this approach does not necessarily solve the problem of how to define religion, it does lend itself to studying its consequences on violence empirically.

Using conflict parties' self-description obviously comes with the inherent problems in that parties may be misrepresenting their true motives because of the lack of a deeper understanding of their own motives, or for strategic reasons. As for the latter, religious actors may hide their true preferences behind secular language, or, conversely, actors with worldly concerns may dress up their true aspirations in religious rhetoric. How to understand religious actors' self-descriptions, how these are situated within larger religious ideological trajectories and the extent to which religious actors may be considered 'authentic' representatives of their traditions have therefore been of central concern for research, including for Swedish scholars of religions and political science such as Fazlhashemi (2016), Hjärpe (2003), Nilsson (2020) and Poljarevic (2021).

An important insight that has emerged from these and other studies is that the role of religious dimensions may be different at different stages of a conflict. Even if a conflict was not triggered by religious factors at the start, its religious framing may affect its dynamics once it has started, and religious factors may also play a role in shaping the likelihood and form of a conflict's termination. An emphasis on *conflict phases* is central to conflict studies, being an aspect that this field of research has brought into the study of religion and violence. Whether religious groups act, organize, mobilize, negotiate or are treated in a different manner in relation to other groups once a conflict has been initiated are empirical questions. While the existing literature is not closed on this matter, some evidence does indicate that there is a discernible difference between religious (or some types of religious) groups compared to other types of groups. Several findings have emerged in support of the position that there is a connection between religion and violence in later phases of conflicts. Religiously framed (intrastate) conflicts are less likely to end through peace agreements (Svensson 2007, 2012), and religious factors may also increase the duration of (interstate) conflicts (Nilsson 2018). As for the sub-category of Islamist intrastate conflicts, they are associated with lower chances for negotiations (Nilsson and Svensson 2020) and are less likely to be subject to mediation (Lundgren and Svensson 2020), reducing the chances of their termination and increasing the risk of a return to the battlefield once a conflict has supposedly been terminated (Nilsson and Svensson 2021). Thus, empirically there is evidence indicating that there is a difference in conflict-resolution processes between those armed conflicts that are framed in religious terms and those that are not.

Why religiously motivated conflicts are more difficult to end is disputed, and explanations for it vary. Some scholars point to the role of religious beliefs in affecting conflict actors' decision-making processes in war (Nilsson 2018). Other scholars point out that the explanation behind the intractability associated with religious conflicts (or some of them) may lie less in their ideational structures per se and more in how these ideas are expressed and enable organizational and mobilizational processes. For example, the particular transnational dimension of Islamist armed conflicts, which are structured in different ways compared to other conflicts, can be an important part of the explanation for why these conflicts tend to be particularly intractable (Nilsson and Svensson 2021). It may also be more difficult for Islamist armed conflicts to identify a 'valid spokesperson', a condition which conflict theory has pointed out as important precursor for conflict-resolution processes to be initiated (Engvall and Svensson 2020). Yet other scholars point out that the causal factors may be found more on the side of the secular-leaning actor than the religious radicals. For example, summarizing one of the findings from a series of case studies on conflict-resolution processes in Islamist armed conflicts, Mimmi Söderberg Kovacs notes that 'the most reluctant or obstinate parties at the negotiation table … have [sic] been the governments fighting these non-state Islamist armed groups' (2020: 378). She also points to the use of armed actors as terrorist groups, which has increasingly been associated with Islamist armed conflicts, as it can also serve as an obstacle to the peaceful settlement of these types of conflict. To draw this debate together, the intractability of religious (or, for those particularly concerned with one sub-type, Islamist) armed conflicts can thus be explained in two different ways: (1) that religious groups and actors are different from other actors, for instance, in their capacity to absorb and tolerate costs and suffering from conflicts, or through other types of organizational networks that may cut across state and other boundaries in a way that other ideologies do not; and (2) that the other side *perceive* religious actors in a particular light and treat them exceptionally, influenced by perceptions that such actors are intransigent and impossible to make rational compromises with. These two lines of explanation are not mutually exclusive, and research on these matters conducted in Sweden has pursued explanations in both of these senses.

Our focus in this chapter is specifically on Swedish researchers who have studied the relationship between religion and violence, but any analysis of that theme would be incomplete without also taking the efforts to counter violence into account. Religious actors, institutions and ideational structures have played important roles in preventing violence, managing conflicts and building peace. The study of the religious dynamics of this sort of peacemaking is an important piece of the puzzle that provides a more comprehensive picture of religion and violence. Scholars such as Maria Småberg at Lund University (2005, 2009) have contributed to this by providing the historical accounts of faith-based peacemaking and humanitarian actions in contested areas such as Israel and Turkey. Sarah Gehlin (2020) at University College Stockholm has explored the theological underpinnings of ecumenical religious peacemaking. Dino Krause, Svensson and Larsson (2019) explore the puzzling lack of intra-Muslim dialogue and institutional peacemaking along sectarian lines. Linking to another theme in the literature on how to counter violence – the role of non-violent civil resistance to counter violence and oppression – Svensson and co-authors (Bamber and Svensson 2023; Svensson and Finnbogason 2021; Svensson et al. 2022) have explored civil resistance to jihadist groups. This theme is also central to several institutions and governmental bodies, for instance, the Segerstedt Institute at the University of Gothenburg and the Swedish Center for Preventing Violent Extremism (CVE).

Acknowledging that religions can be associated with both violence and peace, Kjell-Åke Nordquist (2013) at University College Stockholm seeks to explain this variation by identifying conditions within religious traditions themselves. In this argument, religious traditions are more likely to be associated with violence when its followers believe they need to impose their beliefs on others (imposition, as contrast to exposition), without needing to adapt their own theology to the surrounding society (fanaticism, as contrast to contextualism). While this argument has opened up a broader debate on how to explain the 'ambivalence of the sacred' (Appleby 2000), which is beyond the scope of this chapter, it does points to an important duality we can end our analysis with: religion can be associated with violence as much as with peace.

Conclusions

This chapter has shown that several scholars in Sweden have been engaged with research that deals with religion and violence. Research conducted in Sweden is closely aligned with international research, and Swedish academics have paid attention to theoretical, methodological and empirical questions, not least when it comes to studying how religious conflicts end.

Despite a rather strong interest in the study of religion and violence, no department of religious studies or theology has started a centre for the study of this topic. However, the Department of Theology at Uppsala University has launched a master's degree in religion in peace and conflict. But there are other academic milieus that have a specific focus on violence and religion, such as the Segerstedt Institute at the University of Gothenburg, while other examples are the Defence University of Sweden and the Swedish Center for Preventing Violent Extremism (CVE).

Note

1 We would like to take the opportunity to express our gratitude to both Katarina Michnik and Johan Karlsson at the University Library of the University of Gothenburg for helping us with a systematic literature review and to Aram Karimi at the Center for Digital Humanities at the same university for helping us with the layout of the graph.

References

Appleby, R. S. (2000), *The Ambivalence of the Sacred: Religion, Violence, and Reconciliation*, New York: Rowman & Littlefield.

Bamber, M., and I. Svensson (2023), 'Resisting Radical Rebels: Variations in Islamist Rebel Governance and Occurrence of Civil Resistance', *Terrorism and Political Violence* 35 (5): 1126–46.

Bogdan, H. (2011), 'Explaining the Murder-Suicides of the Order of the Solar Temple: A Survey of Hypotheses', in J. R. Lewis (ed.), *Violence and New Religious Movements*, 133–45, Oxford: Oxford University Press.

Cetrez, Ö. (2012), 'Att möta oss själva i bilden av den andre', in V. de Marinis Ö. Cetrez and O. Wikström (eds), *Inspiration till religionspsykologin – kultur, hälsa och mening*, 143–52, Stockholm: Natur och Kultur.

Dahlgren, C. (2011), 'Is Religion the Cause of Political Conflicts?', in E. Eynikel and Z. Angeliki (eds), *Religion and Conflict: Essays on the Origins of Religious Conflicts and Resolution Approache*, 200–13, London: Harptree.

Eldén, Å. (2023). *Heder på liv och död: Våldsamma berättelser om rykten, oskuld och heder*, Uppsala: Acta Universitatis Upsaliensis.

Engvall, A., and I. Svensson (2020), 'Peace Talks and Valid Spokespersons: Explaining the Onset of Negotiations in Southern Thailand', *International Negotiation* 25 (3): 495–518.

Fazlhashemi, M. (2016), 'Den våldsbejakande islamismens teologiska rötter', in C. Edling and A. Rostami (eds), *Våldets sociala dimensioner: Individ, relation, organisation*, 81–104, Lund: Studentlitteratur.

Finnbogason, D., G. Larsson and I. Svensson (2019), 'Is Shia–Sunni Violence on the Rise? Exploring New Data on Intra-Muslim Organised Violence 1989–2017', *Civil Wars* 21: 25–53.

Galtung, J. (1969), 'Violence, Peace and Peace Research', *Journal of Peace Research*, 3: 167–191.

Galtung, J. (1990), 'Cultural Violence', *Journal of Peace Research* 3: 291–305.

Galtung, J. (1996), *Peace by Peaceful Means: Peace and Conflict, Development and Civilization*, London: Sage.

Gardell, M. (2003), *Goods of the Blood: The Pagan Revival and White Separatism*, Durham, NC: Duke University Press.

Gardell, M. (2008), *Tortyrens återkomst*, Stockholm: Leopard förlag.

Gardell, M. (2010), *Islamofobi*, Stockholm: Leopard förlag.

Gardell, M. (2015), *Raskrigaren: Seriemördaren Peter Mangs*, Stockholm: Leopard förlag.

Gardell, M. (2017), 'Lone wolves – hotet från ensamagerande politiska våldsbrottslingar', in M. Gardell, H. Lööw and M. Dahlberg-Grundberg (eds), *Den ensamme terroristen? Om Lone Wolves, näthat och brinnande flyktingförläggningar*, Stockholm: Ordfront.

Gehlin, S. (2020), *Pathways for Theology in Peacebuilding: Ecumenical Approaches to Just Peace*, Leiden: Brill.

Göndör, E. (2018), *I guds namn: Om våld och politik i islam*, Stockholm, Fri Tanke.

Hermanson, J. (2011), 'Religion and Prejudice: Some Aspects from the Perspective of Psychology', in E. Eynikel and Z. Angeliki (eds), *Religion and Conflict: Essays on the Origins of Religious Conflicts and Resolution Approaches*, 214–29, London: Harptree.

Hjärpe, J. (2003), 'Diskussionen om självmordsattentatens religiösa legitimitet', in D. Amnéus and G. Gunner (eds), *Mänskliga rättigheter. Från forskningens frontlinjer*, Uppsala: Iiustus.

Keane, J. (1996), *Reflections on Violence*, London: Verso.

Kippenberg, H. G. (2011), *Violence as Worship: Religious Wars in the Age of Globalization*, Stanford: Stanford University Press.

Krause, D., I. Svensson and G. Larsson (2019), 'Why Is There So Little Shia–Sunni Dialogue? Understanding the Deficit of Intra-Muslim Dialogue and Interreligious Peacemaking', *Religions* 10 (10), https://doi.org/10.3390/rel10100567.

Krause, D., and M. Söderberg Kovacs (2022), 'The Political Integration of Islamist Armed Groups', in J. Ishiyama and G. M. Sindre (eds), *The Effects of Rebel Parties on Governance, Democracy and Stability after Civil Wars: From Guns to Governing*, 122–39, London: Routledge.

Larsson, G. (2017), 'Apostasy and Counter-narratives—Two Sides of the Same Coin: The Example of the Islamic State'. *The Review of Faith & International Affairs* 15(2):45–54.

Larsson, G. (2022), 'Those Who Choose to Fight the Islamic State: Autobiographical Accounts of Western Volunteers', *Terrorism and Political Violence* 34 (8): 1758–73.

Lindgren, T. (2012), 'Religion och våld – exemplet Indonesien', in V. de Marinis Ö Cetrez and O Wikström (eds), *Inspiration till religionspsykologin – kultur, hälsa och menin*, 133–42, Stockholm: Natur och Kultur.

Lindgren, T. (2014), *Religion och konflikt: Komplexa samband, komplexa orsaker*, Skellefteå: Artos.

Lindgren, T. (2016), 'The Psychological Study of Religious Violence: A Theoretical and Methodological Study', *Al-Albab* 5: 155–74.

Lindgren, T. (2018), 'Religious Conflicts: Opportunity Structures, Group Dynamics, and Framing', *Al Albab* 7: 17–32.

Lindgren, T. (2023), *Fundamentalism och helig terror: Religionspsykologi för vår tid*, Lund: Studentlitteratur.

Lindgren, T., and H. Sonnenschein (2021), 'Bloody, Intense, and Durable: The Politics of "Religious Conflict"', *Temenos* 5: 59–80.

Lindgren, T., H. Sonnenschein and J. Eriksson (2022), 'Moderate and Radical Muslims, but for Whom and for What Purpose?', in R. Hood Jr. and S. Cheruvallil-Contractor (eds), *Research in the Social Scientific Study of Religion*, 78–100, Leiden: Brill.

Lundgren, E. (1987), *Prester i lyst og last: Om kjønn, makt og erotikk i den norske kirkens sjelesorg*, Oslo: J. W. Cappelens Forlag.

Lundgren, E. (1992), *Gud och alla andra karlar: En bok om kvinnomisshandlare*, Stockholm: Natur och kultur.

Lundgren, E. (2008), *Knutbykoden*, Stockholm: Modernista.

Lundgren, M., and I. Svensson (2020), 'The Surprising Decline of International Mediation in Armed Conflicts', *Research & Politics* 7 (2): 1–7.

Martin, C. (2017), *A Critical Introduction to the Study of Religion*, London: Routledge.

Nilsson, D., and I. Svensson (2020), 'Resisting Resolution: Islamist Claims and Negotiations in Intrastate Armed Conflicts', *International Negotiation* 25 (3): 389–412.

Nilsson, D., and I. Svensson (2021), 'The Intractability of Islamist Insurgencies: Islamist Rebels and the Recurrence of Civil War', *International Studies Quarterly* 65 (3): 620–32.

Nilsson, M. (2015), 'Foreign Fighters and the Radicalization of Local Jihad: Interview Evidence from Swedish Jihadists', *Studies in Conflict & Terrorism* 38 (5): 343–58.

Nilsson, M. (2018), 'Causal Beliefs and War Termination: Religion and Rational Choice in the Iran–Iraq War', *Journal of Peace Research* 55 (1): 94–106.

Nilsson, M. (2020), 'Hezbollah and the Framing of Resistance', *Third World Quarterly* 41 (9): 1595–1614.

Nilsson, M. (2021), 'Jihadiship: From Radical Behavior to Radical Beliefs', *Studies in Conflict & Terrorism* 44 (3):181–97.

Nilsson, P.-E. (2018), *Open Source Jihad: Problematizing the Academic Discourse on Islamic Terrorism in Contemporary Europe*, Cambridge: Cambridge University Press.

Nilsson, P.-E. (2019), *French Populism and Discourses on Secularism*, London: Bloomsbury.

Nilsson, P.-E. (2020), 'The Crocodile and the Gardener: Swedish Radical Nationalism and Critique of Religion', in M. Lövheim and M. Stenmark (eds), *A Constructive Critique of Religion: Encounters Between Christianity, Islam, and Non-Religion in Secular Societies*, 124–34, London: Bloomsbury.

Nord, E. (2022), *Vindicating Vengeance and Violence? Exegetical Approaches to Imrecatory Psalms and Their Relevance for Liturgy*, Lund: Lunds Universitet.

Nordquist, K.-Å. (2013), 'Linking Religion and War: Some Observations', in K.-Å. Nordquist (ed.), *Gods and Arms: On Religion and Armed Conflict*, 142–63, Eugene, OR: Pickwick.

Peste, J. (2003), *Religion och terrorism: Mellan samvaro och radikalism*, Studentlitteratur, Lund.

Peste, J. (2011), 'Murder in Knutby: Charisma, Eroticism, and Violence in a Swedish Pentecostal Community', in J. R. Lewis (ed.), *Violence and New Religious Movements*, 217–31, Oxford: Oxford University Press.

Poljarevic, E. (2012), 'In Pursuit of Authenticity: Becoming a Salafi', *Comparative Islamic Studies* 1–2: 139–64.

Poljarevic, E. (2021), 'Theology of Violence-oriented Takfirism as a Political Theory: The Case of the Islamic State in Iraq and Syria (ISIS)', in M. A. Upal and C. M. Cusack (eds), *Handbook of Islamic Sects and Movements*, 485–512, Leiden: Brill.

Ranstorp, M. (1996), 'Terrorism in the Name of Religion', *Journal of International Affairs* 1: 41–62.

Söderberg Kovacs, M. (2020), 'Negotiating Sacred Grounds? Resolving Islamist Armed Conflicts', *International Negotiation* 25 (3): 375–88.

Sonnenschein, H., and T. Lindgren (2020), 'The Shapeshifting Self: Narrative Pathways into Political Violence', *Religions* 11 (9): 464, https://doi.org/10.3390/rel11090464.

Småberg, M. (2005), *Ambivalent Friendship: Anglican Conflict Handling and Education for Peace in Jerusalem 1920–1948*, Lund: Lund University.

Småberg, M. (2009), 'Witnessing the Unbearable: Alma Johansson and the Massacres of the Armenians 1915', in K. Aggestam and A. Björkdahl (eds), *War and Peace in Transition: Changing Roles of External Actors*, 107–27, Lund: Nordic Academic Press.

Svensson, I. (2007), 'Fighting with Faith: Religion and Conflict Resolution in Civil Wars', *Journal of Conflict Resolution* 51: 930–49.

Svensson, I. (2012), *Ending Holy Wars: Religion and Conflict Resolution in Civil Wars*, St Lucia, New Zeeland: University of Queensland Press.

Svensson, I. (2013), 'One God, Many Wars: Religious Dimensions of Armed Conflict in the Middle East and North Africa', *Civil Wars* 15: 411–30.

Svensson, I. (2016), 'Conceptualizing the Religious Dimensions of Armed Conflicts: A Response to "Shrouded: Islam, War, and Holy War in Southeast Asia"', *Journal for the Scientific Study of Religion* 55: 185–9.

Svensson, I., and D. Finnbogason (2021), 'Confronting the Caliphate? Explaining Civil Resistance in Jihadist Proto-States', *European Journal of International Relations* 27 (2): 572–95.

Svensson, I., and D. Nilsson (2018), 'Disputes over the Divine: Introducing the Religion and Armed Conflict (RELAC) Data, 1975 to 2015', *Journal of Conflict Resolution* 62: 1127–48.

Svensson, I., and E. Harding (2011), 'How Holy Wars End: Exploring the Termination Patterns of Conflicts with Religious Dimensions in Asia', *Terrorism and Political Violence* 23: 133–49.

Svensson, I., D. Finnbogason, D. Krause, L. M. Lorenzo and N. Hawach (2022), *Confronting the Caliphate: Civil Resistance in Jihadist Proto-States*, Oxford: Oxford University Press.

Wellman, J. K. (2007), *Belief and Bloodshed: Religion and Violence Across Time and Tradition*, Lanham: Rowman & Littlefield.

Žižek, S. (2009), *Violence: Six Sideways Reflections*, London: Profile Books.

AFTERWORD: REFLECTIONS ON THE STUDY OF RELIGION IN SWEDEN THROUGH THE LENS OF IAHR AND EASR

Jenny Berglund and Tim Jensen

The Study of Religion in Sweden: Past, Present and Future provides a comprehensive exploration of the field and sheds light on the history as well as on the current state of the non-confessional study of religions in Sweden. The various chapters demonstrate the past and present diversity of the field, and a vast number of scholars, past and present, are mentioned.

Some of the scholars mentioned have been or still are internationally renowned scholars, and some have been or still are actively engaged in organized and institutionalized international and European collaboration, as mentioned by the two editors in their introduction. Geo Widengren may have been, with his engagement in the beginnings of the International Association for the History of Religions (IAHR) and his ten years (1960–70) as IAHR president, the most famous or conspicuous of those scholars.[1] It is, however, our contention that the current flourishing of the study of religions in Sweden has been inspired by collaboration with and support from the IAHR and the European Association for the Study of Religions (EASR).[2] Furthermore, Swedish as well as non-Swedish individual scholars – 'religious studies diplomats' as T. Bubík and D. Václavík (2021) call them[3] – linked to the IAHR and EASR have played important roles when it comes to encouraging the collaboration and also what may be termed the 'boosting' of Swedish scholarship on religion. That this institutionalized collaboration as well as the inspiration from 'religious studies diplomats' is not unique to Sweden, has, we think, been convincingly shown by Bubík and Václavik. In the same way that a 2008 EASR annual and IAHR special conference in Brno, according to Bubík and Václavik, served as the then culmination of decades of increasing collaboration of Czech scholars and the Czech Association for the Study of Religions (CASR) with IAHR and EASR, we argue that the 2007 and 2012 IAHR and EASR conferences held in Södertörn proved to be crucial to supporting and boosting a young generation of Swedish scholars. Those two conferences, thus, somehow can be seen as linked also to the 1970 Stockholm IAHR World Congress. We also contend that though Widengren may well be the most famous Swedish scholar directly engaged in the IAHR, several other Swedish scholars have played and still play key roles in the institutionalized study of religions, internationally and in Europe. Last, but not least, we shall mention the importance of the link between Swedish academic studies of religions departments to the long and unique non-confessional religion education in Swedish public schools as another highly important reason for the past and present well-being of the study of religions in Sweden.

The Creation of a National Community of Scholars on the International Scene

Henrik Bogdan and Göran Larsson, in their introductory chapter, point out that Widengren was one of the founding fathers of the IAHR.[4] Larsson (2022b) has, however, using the example of Widengren, problematized the idea of the influence of a single enlightened genius and showed that there were, already in the time of Widengren, many more fellow scholars involved. Looking at the opening address given by the very same 'enlightened genius' Widengren, the then outgoing IAHR president, at the 1970 IAHR World Congress in Stockholm, it is, we think, fair to say that Widengren himself seemed very well aware of the importance of less famous and younger scholars. Having deplored the absence at the congress of certain internationally famous and important scholars, an absence due to, inter alia, the 'compartmentalization of scholarship in our day' (Widengren 1975: 21), Widengren writes,

> For the reasons indicated, fewer big guns are to be fired at this congress as at earlier ones. Though I feel the absence of some outstanding scholars is regrettable …, their absence has led to a pleasant feature of this congress: here we meet more young scholars than before. In this regard, the difference between 1970 and 1900 [the year of the first history of religions world congress held in Paris] is simply fantastic. I am indeed glad to see this week so many younger workers in the field. I have tried to encourage this trend as much as possible. Their presence here is a symptom of the progress of our studies. After all, a new generation of scholars enters the stage.

Bypassing, in all haste, Widengren's additional remark (1975: 21) that the 'big guns' are 'sometimes loaded with blank ammunition', we want to make a giant leap to the EASR and IAHR conferences in 2007 and 2012, respectively, in Stockholm. Both of them marked a significant change in terms of international activity by Swedish scholars who, for reasons mentioned by Bogdan and Larsson in the introduction to this volume, had become less and less connected with the international research field during the 1960s and 1970s.

With regard to the EASR, only a few words can be mentioned here:[5] the EASR was founded in Krakow in 2000, with a series of famous international scholars as the founders (and Tim Jensen serving as the first general secretary). During the early years of the EASR, few Swedish scholars engaged in the annual

EASR conferences. When, however, David Thurfjell in 2005 visited the national conference of the *Deutsche Vereinigung für Religionswissenschaft* (DVRW), one of the biggest IAHR and EASR member associations, something new took its beginning. The conference, Thurfjell recalls, was quite different to what he had experienced in Sweden, where – despite what Widengren may have wished for – the meetings of the Swedish IAHR member society, the SSRF, mainly consisted of (senior) professors talking to each other. At the DVRW conference, Thurfjell also talked to Michael Pye, not only such a 'senior professor' but also former secretary general and president of the IAHR (and key player in the founding of the EASR) about the possibility of arranging a conference in Sweden. Upon Thurfjell's return and following discussions with some colleagues in Sweden, plans for a large-scale international conference began to take shape; Jensen, then IAHR secretary general, remembers talks in Södertörn, Stockholm, with a team of 'junior scholars' who had a dream (their own words) of revitalizing the study of religion in Sweden. Consequently, an EASR and IAHR special conference titled 'Religion on the Borders: New Challenges in the Academic Study of Religion' took place in April 2007 hosted by Södertörn University and arranged by some members of the SSRF.[6] The conference proved to become the largest study-of-religions conference that had ever taken place in Sweden. It created a strong sense of community among Swedish scholars, and more and more Swedish scholars started to conceive of EASR and IAHR meetings as an important and natural part of their scholarly work. The conference thus helped boost or revitalize Swedish scholarship, and it served, not least, to support emerging groups of younger Swedish scholars working at a growing number of departments for the study of religion. It, therefore, came as no surprise that Swedish scholars were recognized by the IAHR and the EASR to be more than capable of hosting, in Södertörn in 2012, an official EASR annual conference, titled 'Ends and Beginnings', a conference that also served as an IAHR special conference. This conference gathered even more scholars than the conference five years earlier.[7]

Jensen, in 2007 as well as in 2012, serving as the IAHR general secretary, in his opening talk said, inter alia:

> In 2007 the IAHR Special Conference on 'Religion on the Borders: New Challenges in the Academic Study of Religion' was organized by a group of people calling themselves 'junior scholars'. Some of these are also in the 2012 organizing committee, though now they carry titles of senior lecturers. However, to me, they are still young and upcoming. But what matters is that they have done great work. Without such younger colleagues ready to link up with the work of the IAHR and EASR, sharing at least some of the visions and aims with such associations, neither the IAHR nor the EASR could function as well as they actually do. Without their energy and drive, the time-honoured institutions might petrify. Even if the so-called senior scholars (as for instance in Södertörn professor David Westerlund, in 2007 as well as in 2012) actually quite often have taken the lead in the renewal and birth of up-to-date studies of religion and associations. (Jensen's unpublished notes for the talk)

Meeting at these international conferences, thus, not only meant creating international contacts. It also fostered, as mentioned above, a strong sense of community among Swedish scholars and a sense of being part of a larger international scene and community as well. On top of this, it helped shape the contents of the study of religions in Sweden. Something that is reflected in this volume. Today the study of religions in Sweden is, we contend, made up of a strong collective of scholars who not only know each other's research well but also know each other very well. In addition to the successful organization of international conferences, there are a number of other positive outcomes of this strong research community. One example is the establishment of a new type of national conference, *Religionsvetarmötet*, while other examples are the collective pulling in of research grants – often in collaboration with international scholars.

Thus, in 2023, a group of Swedish Islamic studies scholars pulled in a grant for the largest graduate school in the humanities in Sweden. The grant, beginning in 2023, will fund twelve new PhD positions in the study of religion.[8] Moreover, mention has already been made of yet another EASR and IAHR conference to be hosted by Swedish scholars, namely the one to take place in 2024 in Gothenburg. An event during which this book and the Swedish history of the study of religions will be presented to 'the world at large'.

Another Kind of Institutional Development

Apart from the importance of collaboration with the IAHR and the EASR, the impetus of senior Swedish and international scholars, and the initiatives taken by, not least, the Södertörn-based 'junior scholars', other developments leading to a growth of locations for Swedish scholars to be employed and to work must also be mentioned. Jensen and Geertz (2015), describe and underline the importance of Danish university departments for the history/study of religions having responsibility for the university education of the religion education teachers for the non-confessional 'mini' study-of-religions school subject in the Danish Gymnasium (Upper Secondary School). In terms of institutional developments, the importance of the non-confessional study of the religion-based school subject *Religionskunskap* (in Sweden, in place since 1969 in both elementary, secondary and upper-secondary schools) for the development of the study of religions in Sweden must be stressed even more than what is the case in Denmark.[9] One of the reasons for this development is linked to the same social engineering strategy accused of marginalizing interest in classical studies in the 1960s and 1970s (see the introduction of this volume): in line with seeing higher education as a school for civil servants, its role in teacher education became clear. Since Sweden had made non-confessional religion education a mandatory school subject, school teachers trained in the study of religions were required (see Chapter 12 in this volume). Today, education for religion education is organized very differently at different universities. Students, pursuing a qualification in secondary and upper-secondary religion education, study at study-of-religions departments. Some universities organize courses specifically for teacher education students, but at others, teacher education students study the same courses as any other student in the study of religions. Courses on different religions from a history-of-religions perspective are, however, always part of teacher training. The number of semesters and credits required are determined by the future level of teaching (2–4 semesters i.e. 45–90 ECTS). Primary school teachers are educated to teach a range of school subjects. For them, religion education is often combined with history, civics and geography. At most universities, the students for these 'social study subjects' study interdisciplinary courses taught by scholars from the fields of history, study of religion, geography, political science and education. Since religion education is an obligatory, non-confessional school subject taught at all levels of the school system, *many* teachers need to be trained. Departments of study of religions have the responsibility for the contents and are involved in the training to varying degrees (depending on the level in the school system). One result of this is that there are study-of-religions departments at more than fifteen universities or university colleges in Sweden. Considering the size of the country's population, this is a significant number compared to many other European countries.

*

Looking back and ahead, we can thus conclude that the IAHR and the EASR, as well the SSFR, have played considerable roles in promoting and stimulating the study of religions in Sweden – and especially in supporting, engaging and encouraging younger scholars of religion. The national, regional and international structure and interconnection of the 'learned societies' built and upheld by past generations of scholars (not just the 'big guns') have proved their vitality and value also with regard to the field and discipline of the study of religions in Sweden. Widengren, we guess, would have been proud and happy to see that, long after his time, 'many younger workers in the field' have been assisted by the IAHR (and the IAHR regional member association, the EASR) and that the same younger scholars of religion likewise have impacted the IAHR, the EASR and not least the study of religions in Sweden. The developments, including the above-mentioned two past EASR and IAHR conferences and the forthcoming conference in 2024 in Gothenburg, beyond a doubt prove the importance of the active engagement of Swedish scholars, past and present, big guns and smaller guns, in the work and activities of the associations. Individual Swedish scholars (senior as well as junior) have served, and today serve, in the executive committees of the IAHR and the EASR. Apart from those individuals, though, it is the above-mentioned strong collective of scholars who know not just each other's research but also each other (very well, indeed), which to us seem most important for the strength, well-being and dynamics of the Swedish scene. It is a fact that this group of scholars can arrange international conferences, present papers and produce books that are internationally recognized. Their skills as regard socializing with each other, which are obvious from observations of their gatherings at restaurants and bars during conferences, are equally remarkable and important.

Notes

1. See Larsson 2022a and Jensen and Fujiwara 2022.
2. We think that this volume, as well as the EASR and IAHR conference to be held in Gothenburg in 2024, indicates that 'flourishing' is a correct characterization of current Swedish scholarship on religion, including what is linked to the *Svenska Samfundet för Religionshistorisk Forskning* (SSRF, Swedish Association for Research in Comparative Religion).
3. T. Bubík and D. Václavík (general secretary of the EASR, 2011–13) argue – convincingly, we think – in their 2021 article in *Studi e Materiali di Storia delle Religioni* (SMSR) that various kinds of cooperation with the IAHR, and later with the EASR, cannot be underestimated as regards the development and disciplinary identity of the academic, institutionalized Czech study of religion (History of Religions/*Religionswissenschaft*), not least from 1989 onwards.
4. See Jensen and Geertz (2015) for a detailed and variegated introduction to the IAHR, past and present.
5. See Pye (2015) for an introduction to the founding of the EASR and Jensen (2015) for an introduction to the founding of the EASR within the world scenario of the IAHR.
6. The organizing committee consisted of Jenny Berglund, Peter Jackson, Marja-Liisa Keinänen, Lena Roos and David Thurfjell.
7. The organizing committee consisted of Jenny Berglund, Susanne Olsson, David Thurfjell and David Westerlund.
8. See https://lnu.se/en/research/PhD-studies/religion/graduate-school-in-islamic-studies/.
9. For a discussion on Swedish religion education, see, for example, Berglund (2023).

References

Berglund, J. (2023), 'Swedish Religion Education in Public Schools – Objective and Neutral or a Marination into Lutheran Protestantism?', *Oxford Journal of Law and Religion* 11 (1): 109–21.

Bubík, T., and D. Václavik (2021), 'The Czech Study of Religions and Western Scholarship', *Studi e Materiali di Storia delle Religioni* (SMSR) 87 (2): 554–79.

Jensen, T. (2015), 'The EASR within (the World Scenario of) the IAHR: Observations and Reflections', in T. Jensen and A. W. Geertz (eds), *NVMEN, the Academic Study of Religion, and the IAHR: Past, Present, and Prospects*, 163–217, Leiden: Brill.

Jensen, T., and S. Fujiwara (2022), 'Professor Geo Widengren, IAHR Vice-Preseident 1950–1960, IAHR President 1960–1970, IAHR Honorary Life Member 1996', in G. Larsson (ed.), *The Legacy, Life and Work of Geo Widengren and the Study of the History of Religions after World War II*, 50–70, Leiden: Brill.

Jensen, T., and A. W. Geertz (2014), 'From the History of Religions to the Study of Religion in Denmark: An Essay on the Subject, Organizational History and Research Themes', *Temenos* 50 (1): 79–113.

Jensen, T., and A. W. Geertz, eds (2015), *NVMEN, the Academic Study of Religion, and the IAHR: Past, Present, and Prospects*, Leiden: Brill.

Larsson, G., ed. (2022a), *The Legacy, Life and Work of Geo Widengren and the Study of the History of Religions after World War II*, Leiden: Brill.

Larsson, G. (2022b), 'Pondering the Legacy of Geo Widengren: Isolated Genius, or Uncritical Supporter of a Band of Brothers?', *Method & Theory in the Study of Religion*, 35(4): 281–92. doi.org/10.1163/15700682-bja10093.

Pye, M. (2015), 'IAHR Landmarks and Connections', in T. Jensen and A. W. Geertz (eds), *NVMEN, the Academic Study of Religion, and the IAHR: Past, Present, and Prospects*, 221–43, Leiden: Brill.

Widengren, G. (1975), 'The Opening Address', in C. J. Bleeker, G. Widengren and E. J. Sharpe (eds), *Proceedings of the XIIth International Congress of the International Association for the History of Religions, Stockholm 1970*, 14–22, Leiden: Brill.

INDEX OF NAMES

Åberg, Johan 70, 75
Ackfeldt, Anders 89
Adam of Bremen 39
Aggestam, Karin 75
Ahlin, Lars 130, 135, 136
Ahmadi, Fereshteh 150
Åkerbäck, Peter 132, 133, 136, 137
Åkerberg, Hans 143, 148, 149
Åkesson, Lynn 219
Allport, Gordon W. 149
Allwood, Carl Martin 219
Alm, Ivar 145
Almbladh, Karin 74
Almén, Edgar 196
Almgren, Oscar 42
Almqvist, Bo 43
Almqvist, Carl Johan Love 40
Alvarsson, Jan-Åke 63
Alvstad, Erik 74, 75
Alwall, Jonas 88, 133
Ammerman, Nancy T. 230, 231, 234
Andersson, Daniel 10, 61
Andersson, Jakob 24
Andersson, Lars M. 69
Andersson, Tobias 89
Andersson, Thorsten 44
Andræ, Tor 2, 4–7, 83, 84, 116–18, 144–6, 207
Andrén, Anders 44, 47
Aneer, Gudmar 87
Annerstedt, Claes 115
Arbman, Ernst 5, 6, 99, 145, 207–10
Arendt, Hannah 74
Århem, Kaj 62, 63
Arvidsson, Stefan 180
Asprem, Egil 10, 114, 121, 124, 180, 182
Assmann, Jan 257
Atran, Scott 178, 181, 183
Atterbom, Per Daniel Amadeus 40
Axelsson, Stohlander 5, 14
Ayim-Aboagye, Desmond 147

Baetke, Walter 42
Bang, Jacob Peter 144
Barker, Eileen 131
Bauman, Zygmunt 135
Belfrage, Lennart 150
Bell, Catherine 219
Bender, Courtney 231
Benz, Ernst 129
Bergenhorn, Mats 89
Berggren, Åsa 219
Berglie, Per-Arne 99, 210, 214, 232
Bergling, Kurt 148, 193, 196
Berglund, Axel-Ivar 59
Berglund, Jenny 11, 89, 196, 273
Bergman, Jan 22, 25
Bergson, Henri 146
Bergstedt, Carl Fredrik 96
Berndtsson, Tim 123
Bernström, Mohammed Knut 151
Biezais, Haralds 43
Billing, Nils 25
Bjerre, Poul 145
Björk, Ulrika 74
Björkhem, John 126, 145
Bleeker, Claas Jouco 11
Blomqvist, Håkan 75
Bogdan, Henrik 11, 119, 120, 124, 125, 134, 136, 223, 259, 269
Bopp, Franz 40
Borgehammar, Stephan 219
Bourignon, Antoinette 145
Boyer, Pascal 178, 181, 183
Brach, Jean-Pierre 113
Braidotti, Rosi 123
Briem, Efraim 5, 23, 24, 26, 29, 116–18, 125, 126, 144
Brink, Stefan 44
Brissman, Ive 225
Brodin, Jenny-Ann 133, 135
Brusi, Frederic 233

Bubík, Tomáš 268, 273
Bugge, Sophus 42
Burén, Ann af 233, 237
Bureus, Johannes 39, 122, 128
Burkert, Walter 257
Butler, Judith 28, 249
Bäckman, Louise 58, 210, 214
Bäckström, Anders 165, 167

Callewaert, Inger 60
Campbell, Heidi 236
Carlesson Magalhães, Jens 76
Carlsson, Carl-Gustav 119, 132
Carlsson, Carl Henrik 73
Cato, Johan 88
Cejvan, Olivia 119, 120, 124, 225
Celander, Hilding 42
Cetrez, Önver 150
Charles XIII, King 116
Charpentier, Jarl 97
Ciurtin, Eugen 22
Crowley, Aleister 120, 123, 124
Csordas, Thomas 221
Cumont, Franz 23
Cöllen, Sebastian 46
Cöster, Henry 194

Dahl, Ulrika 224
Dahlgren, Curt 161
Dalin, Olof von 39
Dalström, Kata 2
Darwin, Charles 4
Daryaee, Touraj 23
Davidovich, Tal 75
Deißmann, Adolf 7
DeMarinis, Valerie 149, 150
Dencik, Lars 75
Diehl, Carl Gustav 100
Djurdjevic, Gordan 120
Dostoyevsky, Fyodor 149
Douglas, Mary 135
Drobin, Ulf 43, 46, 212, 213
Dudas, Victor 150
Dumézil, George 6, 8, 40, 41, 43, 211–13
Durkheim, Émile 5
Düwel, Klaus 42
Dyrendal, Asbjørn 122
Dziaczkowska, Magdalena 73

Edenborg, Carl-Michael 122
Edenius, Jordan 69
Edgren, Hjalmar 96
Edholm, Erik af 99, 214
Edholm, Klas Wikström af 47
Edman, Gunnar 149
Edsman, Carl-Martin 7, 26, 27, 29, 58, 208, 209, 212, 214
Eek, Jonas 148
Ehnmark, Erland 7, 26–9, 59
Eidevall, Göran 22
Ekedahl, Marianne 150
Ekenstam, Fabian Wilhelm af 96
Eklund, Pehr 14
Ekström, Hjalmar 149
Ekström, Malin 249
Eldén, Åsa 259
Eliade, Mircea 6, 9, 44, 211–13
Elmevik, Lennart 44
Emanuelson, Ingrid 194
Eneborg, Yusuf Muslim 120
Engelhart, Monica 64
Englund, Martin 74
Enstedt, Daniel 233–6
Erdmann, Axel 96
Ergardt, Jan 100
Eriksson, King Gustav Vasa 37
Essén, Charlotte 136
Evers Rosander, Eva 87

Faivre, Antoine 113, 114, 120
Farrakhan, Louis 89
Faxneld, Per 121, 122, 124, 125, 248, 251
Fazlhashemi, Mohammad 87, 261
Fensham, Peter 197, 198
Fernandes, Silvia 234
Fitger, Malin 122, 138, 185
Flensburg, Nils 97
Fogelklou, Emilia 143–5
Fossmo, Helge 137, 138
Frazer, James G. 257
Freud, Sigmund 144, 145, 257
Frisk, Liselotte 104, 119, 131–4, 136, 137
Frisk, Sylva 87

Galtung, Johan 258
Gardell, Mattias 89, 259
Gardie, Magnus Gabriel De la 38

Geels, Anton 10, 104, 148, 149
Geertz, Armin 178, 271, 273
Gehlin, Sarah 263
Geijer, Erik Gustaf 40
Gemzöe, Lena 245, 251
Gennep, Arnold van 222
Gestermann, Louise 25
Geverts, Kvist 72
Geyer, Karl 147
Giddens, Anthony 135
Giertz, Bo 149
Gilhus, Ingvild 30
Girard, René 257
Giudice, Christian 120, 125
Goethe, Johann Wolfgang 40, 47
Goldziher, Ignaz 7
Goodrick-Clarke, Nicholas 114
Granholm, Kennet 122
Granqvist, Karin 59
Granqvist, Pehr 151, 184
Grant, Kenneth 123
Gregorius, Fredrik 119, 135
Gren, Nina 77
Gren-Ekholm, Gunilla 97
Grimes, Ronald 218
Grimm, Jacob 40
Gruffman, Paulina 124
Gruneau Brulin, Joel 151
Gräslund, Bo 44, 46
Gräslund, Anne-Sofie 44
Gröndahl, Run 105
Grözinger, Karl-Erich 70
Grønbech, Vilhelm 144, 148
Guggenmos, Esther-Maria 101
Gunner, Gunilla 245
Gustafsson, Berndt 160, 161, 168
Gustafsson, Gabriella (Beer) 27
Gustafsson, Göran 10, 161, 163, 167, 168
Gustafsson, Ingmar 130
Gustav III, King 69, 116
Guthrie, Stewart 178
Gårdfeldt, Lars 248
Göndör, Eli 88
Götze, Albrecht 209

Habermas, Jürgen 213
Halberstam, Jack J. 28, 249
Hall, David 230
Hall, Nelly 245
Halldén, Philip 88
Hallgren, Roland 60
Hanafi, Hasan 88
Hanegraaff, Wouter J. 114
Hamberg, Eva 161, 162, 164
Hammar, Inger 244
Hammer, Olav 119, 120, 124, 132, 180
Harnack, Adolf von 4
Hartman, Sven S. 8, 23, 190–4, 207
Hedenborg White, Manon 114, 123–5, 248, 249
Hedenius, Ingemar 2
Hedin, Christer 4, 87
Heike, Peter 24
Hellberg, Lars 44
Hellman, Eva 99, 245
Hellman, Jörgen 87
Hellner Taylor, Kristina 64
Hermansson, Jan 149
Herschend, Frands 44
Hessler, Heinz Werner 98
Hidal, Sten 24
Hirsig, Leah 124
Hjärpe, Jan 4, 84–8, 90
Hofstee, Willem 12
Holm, Nils G. 147
Holmberg, Per 46
Hornborg, Alf 63
Hornborg, Anne-Christine 61, 100, 222, 232, 233
Hout, Theo van den 24
Hubert, Henri 5
Hultgård, Anders 4, 23, 29, 43, 46, 47, 213
Hultkrantz, Åke 5, 6, 8, 10, 56–8, 60, 99, 145, 209, 210–14, 217
Hultman, Maja 75, 77
Hylén, Torsten 89
Härenstam, Kjell 87, 105, 194
Höfler, Otto 23, 41, 208

Illman, Ruth 71
Inden, Ronald 102
Inglehart, Ronald 162, 167
Irigaray, Luce 23

Jackson Rova, Peter 28, 46, 47, 99, 273
Jakku, Nina 88, 247

James, William 148, 179
Jansson, Eva-Maria 70
Jansson, Hedda 122
Janson, Torsten 89
Jensen, Tim 13, 269–71
Jetne Haga, Rannveig 246
Johansson, Karl Ferdinand 97
Johansson, Peter 59
Johansson, Rune E. A. 98
Johansson Dahre, Ulf 64
Johnson, Bo 70
Jones, William 96, 106
Jung, Carl Gustav 145
Junus, Petra 149, 248

Kahle, Sigrid 22
Kaliff, Anders 44
Kardemark, Wilhelm 233
Karlsson, Bengt G. 64
Karlsson, Johan 264
Karlsson, Thomas 122
Karsten, Rafael 57
Katz, Marc 105
Keim, Katharina 71, 73
Keinänen, Marja-Liisa 233, 245, 249, 273
Kella, Elizabeth 75
Kerényi, Karl 27
Key, Ellen 2, 122
Khan, Inayat 117
Khan, Wahiduddin 88, 151
King, Ursula 243
Kittelmann Flensner, Karin 196
Klingenberg, Maria 162
Knibbe, Kim 234
Knutson Bråkenhielm, Lotta 181, 182
Koblik, Steven 72
Kohlberg, Lawrence 193
Kolmodin, Johannes 8
Koskinen-Hagman, Marcus 148
Kraus, Dino 263
Kuhlin, Julia 233
Kupari, Helena 234
Kurkiala, Mikael 61
Kuusela, Tommy 47
Källstad, Thorvald 148

Lamm, Martin 115, 116
Lang, Andrew 209
Larsen, Lars Steen 119

Larsson, Göran 23, 73, 89, 180, 233, 259, 263, 269
Larsson, Rune 193
Lawrence, Nicolas 74
Lawson, Thomas E. 178
Ledman, Anna-Lill 59
Leeuw, Gerardus van der 6
Lehman, Edvard 5
Lejon, Håkan 122
Lengborn, Torbjörn 149
Lerjeryd, Per 27, 28
Lévi-Strauss, Claude 8, 59, 100
Leviathan, Daniel 75
Lewis, James R. 120, 134, 136
Lidén, Evald 97
Lidman, Sven 149
Liebert, Gösta 97
Lienhard, Siegfried 98
Liljas Ståhlhandske, Maria 150, 222
Liljefors Persson, Bodil 61
Lincoln, Bruce 45, 96, 212, 214
Lindberg, Christer 60
Lindberg, Hans 72
Lindenfors, Patrik 184
Lindeskog, Gösta 69
Lindgren, Tomas 68, 124, 151, 183, 184, 259
Lindholm Schulz, Helena 75
Lindmark, Daniel 58
Lindquist, Galina 135
Lindquist, Karl Sigurd 145
Lindquist, Sune 42
Lindquist, Torkel 75
Lindroth, Sten 116
Ling, Pehr Henrik 40
Linton, Ralph 147
Ljungberg, Helge 43
Lloyd, Christina 150
Loman, Rikard 219
Lund, Martin 70, 75
Lundberg, Magnus 62
Lundin, Johan A. 249
Lundius, Jan 61
Lundgren, Eva 137, 138, 259
Lundgren, Svante 71
Lundmark, Evelina 249, 250
Lundmark, Mikael 150
Lundqvist, Erica Li 88, 247, 249
Lundqvist, Pia 74

Index of Names

Lönnroth, Lars 42, 43, 46
Lövheim, Mia 10, 161, 162, 250, 251
Löwén, Åsa 150

Maddrell, April 245
Magnus, Johannes 37, 38
Magnus, Olaus 37, 38
Magnusson, Jörgen 28
Maimon, Salomon 74
Makeef, Tao Thykier 224
Malm Lindberg, Ingrid 185
Malmberg, Håkan 83
Manns, Ulla 244, 245
Markussen, Hege Irene 88
Marton, Ference 194
Maslow, Abraham 222
Mauss, Marcel 5, 231
Martin, Craig 260
Martin, Luther H. 178
McCauley, Robert 178
McGuire, Meredith B. 229, 231
Mead, George Herbert 147
Meillet, Antoine 7
Melder, Cecilia 150
Meurling, Per 212
Meyer-Dietrich, Erika 25, 29
Miaji, Abdel Baten 88
Moberg, Jessica 224, 233
Modéus, Martin 223
Morello, Gustavo 234
Morgenstierne, Georg von Munthe af 97
Mosbach, Vanja 88, 247
Moulton, James 21
Myrvold, Kristina 100, 223, 232
Müller, Friedrich Max 2, 4, 13, 40, 206, 209, 211
Månsson, Anna 89
Mårtensson, Ulrika 89
Möller, André 87, 223, 232

Nahlbom, Yukako 151
Nerman, Birger 42
Newcomb, Theodore 147
Niemi, Kristian 234
Nietzsche, Friedrich 21
Nilsson, Johan 119, 120, 124
Nilsson, Marco 259
Nilsson, Martin P. 7, 8, 26, 56, 59, 209, 210, 214

Nilsson, Per-Erik 259
Nilsson, Sanja 137, 138
Nilsson Stutz, Liv 219
Nordberg, Andreas 46
Nordenskiöld, Erland 61, 62
Nordin, Andreas 180, 184
Nordin, Magdalena 10
Nordquist, Kjell-Åke 263
Nordquist, Ted 131
Nyberg, Henrik Samuel 8, 22, 23, 29, 41, 207, 208, 211
Nycander, Svante 130
Nyhlén, Erik 129
Nykvist, Martin 250
Nyord, Rune 25
Nyström, Jennifer 70
Näsström, Britt-Mari 27, 29, 43, 46, 217, 218

Oetke, Claus 98
Ohlmarks, Åke 43
Ohlsson, Henrik 224
Ojala, Carl-Gösta 59
Oksanen, Antti 148
Olerud, Anders 208, 209, 214
Olofsson, Ebba 59
Olsen, Olaf 42
Olsson, Lennart 29
Olsson, Susanne 88, 273
Olsson, Tord 7–9, 59, 218, 219, 232
Orest, Febe 149
Orsi, Robert 231
Otterbeck, Jonas 10, 88, 90
Otto, Rudoph 5

Page, Sophie 125
Palmer, Susan 137
Panoussis, Zenon 134
Paracelsus, Theophrastus von Hohenheim 116
Parsons, John W. 123
Partanen, Paulina 27, 28, 249, 251
Partridge, Christopher 132
Pasi, Marco 122
Pehrsson-Bramstorp, Axel 117
Pering, Birger 43
Permanto, Stefan 62
Persson, Anders 75
Persson, Bertil 129
Persson, Christer 59

Persson, Göran 71
Peste, Jonathan 120, 259, 260
Petersen, Jesper 88
Petersson Bouin, Yvonne 148
Petri, Olaus 29
Pettazzoni, Raffaele 7
Pettersson, Olof 8, 59
Pettersson, Thorleif 161, 162, 167, 168
Pfeiffer, Robert 24
Piaget, Jean 193
Piraino, Francesco 122
Plank, Katarina 10, 100, 104, 232–6
Plato 39
Ploeg, Johannes van der 24
Poveda Guillén, Oriol 249
Price, Neil 44
Principe, Lawrence 125
Prosén, Martina 224, 237
Pruyser, Paul 149
Pye, Michael 270
Pyysiäinen, Ilkka 179

Qvarnström, Olle 100

Raivio, Magdalena 248
Ranstorp, Magnus 259
Rappaport, Roy 222
Rask, Rasmus Kristian 40
Raudvere, Catharina 46
Reitzenstein, Richard 209
Resen, Peder 38
Reuterskiöld, Edgar 4, 57, 144
Ringgren, Helmer 10, 24, 29, 211
Rizzuto, Ana-Maria 149
Roald, Anne Sofie 88
Robbins, Anthony 220
Rodhe, Sten 99
Rodin, Therese 24, 25, 29, 251
Roitto, Rikard 181
Roos, Lena 73, 273
Rosengren, Dan 63
Ross Solberg, Anne 88
Rothstein, Mikael 119
Rubensson, Lisbeth 149
Rudbeck, Olaus 39
Ruong, Israel 53
Rüpke, Jörg 27, 231
Rushdie, Salman 89
Ryd, Lilian 59

Rydberg, Viktor 29, 40
Rydving, Håkan 25, 58, 179, 213
Rönnow, Kasten 207–209
Rudolfsson, Lisa 150
Runestam, Arvid 145

Sahlgren, Jöran 41, 42, 44
Sahlin, Björn 130
Salomonsson, Karin 219
Sander, Åke 10, 87, 101
Sanner, Inga 247
Sarasvati, Bhaktisiddhanta 102
Sarbin, Theodore R. 147
Sardella, Ferdinando 99
Saussaye, Daniel Chatepie de la 6
Schalk, Peter 99, 101
Schefferus, Johannes 38, 39
Schierenbeck, Isabell 75
Schippers, Mimi 123
Schleiermacher, Friedrich 4, 5
Schmidt, Garbi 89
Schmidt, Wilhelm 7
Schulz, Michael 75
Schumann, Åsa 150
Schwarz, Jan 70, 74
Seckler, Phyllis 124
Secret, François 113
Segerstedt, Torgny 5, 8, 26, 29, 84, 209, 263
Sered, Susan 245
Sharp, Eric J. 99, 144
Sigfússon, Sæmundr 38
Silberstein, Margit 75
Simma, Birgitta 59
Simonsson, Nils 97
Singer, Isaac Bashevis 70, 77
Sjöberg, Katarina 63, 64
Sjöborg, Anders 162
Sjöö, Monica 248
Skarström Hinojosa, Kamilla 74
Skog, Margareta 132
Skogar, Björn 194
Skott, Fredrik 135
Smith, Helmer 97
Smith, William 98
Småberg, Maria 263
Snoek, Jan A. M. 120
Sorgenfrei, Simon 14, 73, 120, 121, 224, 233, 237
Spencer, Herbert 209

Sperber, Dan 178
Sporre, Karin 196
Starr, Martin P. 120
Stausberg, Michael 12, 14, 22
Stephanius, Stephanus Johannis 38
Stenberg, Leif 88
Strindberg, August 2, 115
Strube, Julian 114, 122
Ström, Folke V. 10, 43, 46
Ström, Åke V. 29, 41, 43, 46, 211
Strömbom, Lisa 75
Strömbäck, Dag 42, 43, 46
Stuckrad, Kocku von 114, 119
Ståhl, Bo R. 129
Ståhlberg, Gustaf 150
Ståhle, Göran 105
Suneson, Carl 98
Stendahl, Krister 73
Sturluson, Snorri 38
Sultán Sjöqvist, Madelene 89, 246, 247
Sundén, Hjalmar 10, 86, 104, 146–9, 151, 152, 180
Sundqvist, Olof 10, 46
Sundström, Erland 130
Sundström, Olle 59
Svanberg, Ingvar 87, 132
Svartvik, Jesper 70
Sveinsson, Brynjólfur 38
Svensson, Isak 259, 260, 263
Svensson, Jonas 88, 180, 182, 246
Swedenborg, Emanuel 115, 132
Sydow, Carl Wilhelm von 41
Säve-Söderbergh, Torgny 25, 30
Söderberg Kovacs, Mimmi 259, 262
Söderblom, Nathan 2–7, 21, 22, 26, 28, 83, 84, 97, 117, 143, 144, 146, 148, 149, 152, 206, 207, 209, 213, 214
Södergård, Peter J. 181
Sørensen, Jesper 180

Tagore, Rabindranath 117
Taves, Ann 147, 180, 182
Tegnér, Essias 40
Tengberg, Violet 149
Tessmann, Anna 120
Thor Tureby, Malin 74
Thouless, Roberg H. 144
Thurfjell, David 88, 121, 162, 223, 233, 247, 249, 251, 270, 273

Tiele, Cornelius Petrus 206
Tilander, Åke 149
Timuş, Mihaela 23
Todd, Sharon 196
Toll, Christopher 83
Trautner-Kromann, Hanne 70
Trulsson, Åsa 224, 232, 248
Tullberg, Otto Fredrik 95, 96
Turner, Victor 60, 222
Tylor, Edward Burnett 209
Törngren, Anna 24, 27, 28

Umma, Lotta 59

Václavík, David 268, 273
Valentin, Hugo 69, 73
Valley, Eli 75
Verelius, Olaus 38, 39
Vikstrand, Per 44
Vincent, Alana 74
Virdi Kroik, Åsa 59
Visuri, Ingela 181, 183, 184

Waldau, Åsa 137
Waldby, Catherine 123
Walldén, Ruth 97
Wallenstein, Frederik 46, 47
Wassén, Cecilia 69
Wassén, Henry 62
Weber, Max 122
Werner, Yvonne-Maria 249, 251
Westerlund, David 60, 87, 132, 270, 273
Westin, Gunnar 129
Westman, Knut B. 143
Whitehouse, Harvey 178
Widengren, Geo 5–7, 8, 10, 11, 22, 23, 25, 29, 41, 84, 85, 87, 143, 146, 207, 209–214, 268–70, 272
Wikander, Stig 8, 23, 41, 207–9, 211, 212
Wikström, Lester 130
Wikström, Ove 10, 118, 148–50
Willander, Erika 162, 234, 235
Williams, Henrik 46
Winell, Anneli 250
Witt, R. E. 25
Wolf, Pavel 64
Wolfe, Jane 124
Woodhead, Linda 125, 243

Worm, Ole 38
Wulff, David M. 148
Wüst, Walter 208

Yahya, Harun 88

Zachrisson, Torun 44
Zetterholm, Karin Hedner 70, 71, 74
Zetterholm, Magnus 74
Zettersteén, Karl Vilhelm 83
Zorya, Kateryna 121

www.ingramcontent.com/pod-product-compliance
Lightning Source LLC
Chambersburg PA
CBHW071808300426
44116CB00009B/1234